ADANI
and the
WAR
OVER
COAL

QUENTIN BERESFORD has had a diverse career in teaching, the public service and journalism. He is the author of several books including *Rites of Passage: Aboriginal Youth Crime and Justice* (1996); *Our State of Mind: Racial Planning and the Stolen Generations* (1998), which won the Western Australian Premier's non-fiction prize; the multi-award winning biography, *Rob Riley: An Aboriginal Leader's Quest for Justice* (2006); *The Godfather: The Life of Brian Burke* (2008) and *The Rise and Fall of Gunns Ltd* (2015), which won the Tasmanian Premier's Literary Prize. He is professor of politics at Edith Cowan University in Perth, Western Australia.

To Marilyn and to our grandchildren

ADANI
and the
WAR
OVER
COAL

QUENTIN BERESFORD

NEWSOUTH

A NewSouth book

Published by
NewSouth Publishing
University of New South Wales Press Ltd
University of New South Wales
Sydney NSW 2052
AUSTRALIA
newsouthpublishing.com

© Quentin Beresford 2018
First published 2018

10 9 8 7 6 5 4 3 2 1

 A catalogue record for this book is available from the National Library of Australia

ISBN   9781742235936 (paperback)
          9781742244228 (ebook)
          9781742248646 (ePDF)

Design Josephine Pajor-Markus
Cover design Luke Causby, Blue Cork
Map Josephine Pajor-Markus
Printer Griffin Press

All reasonable efforts were taken to obtain permission to use copyright material reproduced in this book, but in some cases copyright could not be traced. The author welcomes information in this regard.

This book is printed on paper using fibre supplied from plantation or sustainably managed forests.

Contents

GALILEE
BASIN

☐ CHINA STONE

CARMICHAEL ◉

☐ DEGULLA

☐ ALPHA NORTH

☐ KEVIN'S CORNER

ALPHA WEST ☐

☐ ALPHA COAL

☐ CHINA FIRST

☐ SOUTH GALILEE
COAL PROJECT

Cairns

GREAT BARRIER REEF WORLD HERITAGE AREA

Townsville

Abbot Point • Bowen

GALILEE
BASIN

— Proposed
rail line

Mackay
Hay Point

Carmichael Mine
Doongmabulla
Springs

Rockhampton

Gladstone

Great Artesian Basin

QUEENSLAND

0   200

km

BRISBANE

☐ Great Artesian Basin   ◉ Exisitng Mines

Introduction

On 9 February 2017, federal Liberal Treasurer Scott Morrison rose from his parliamentary front-bench seat and delivered one of the most colourful but disturbing political stunts in recent federal Parliamentary history. Clutching a lump of black coal, the burly, sports-loving and pugnacious minister ridiculed the Labor Opposition's recent call for a higher renewable energy target, amid new record summer temperatures.

The coal had been supplied by the Minerals Council of Australia, a key backer of the conservative side of politics, and it had been conveniently coated with lacquer so as not to blacken the minister's hand.[1] In a performance that went beyond mocking the fear of climate change into a defiance of nature itself, Morrison, amid guffaws of laughter from his colleagues, teased the Labor Party: 'Don't be afraid, don't be scared, it won't hurt you, it's coal'. He accused the Opposition of 'coal-o-phobia'. Morrison then handed the non-blackening coal around members of the front bench as if they were all in on the stunt. Photographs of Morrison holding aloft his lump of coal show fellow Liberal minister Christopher Pyne smirking and a cartoonish laugh breaking across the face of National party leader, Barnaby Joyce.

In addition to trying to wedge Labor over its traditional links with the mining workers union, the Construction, Forestry, Mining and Energy Union, the artefact from the fossil fuel age was intended to resonate with the federal Coalition's base, where denial of climate change and opposition to renewable energy have deep roots. Morrison, with his strong evangelical Christian background, plays well with this constituency. Although ensconced in the bunker of the Treasury portfolio, Morrison's reputation as a polarising politician was well established. He had doggedly pursued the Coalition's 'Stop the Boats' policy towards the unauthorised arrivals of refugee claimants when in the Abbott government. 'He hasn't been afraid to pitch to the right of the party', wrote Deborah Snow in a profile piece for the *Sydney Morning Herald*.[2]

Afterwards, Morrison appeared on radio 'shock-jock' Ray Hadley's 2GB program. Hadley, a prominent climate change denier, shared a joke with his guest about the stunt. Amid the mutual jocularity, Morrison had a point to make: 'We have no more a fear of coal than we have a fear of wind, or solar, or wave energy, or pump-hydro, or whatever the option is'.[3]

Played across the various media outlets, Morrison's coal antics sent yet another message that the federal Liberal Party and its Coalition partner, the Nationals, were avowedly pro-coal.

Morrison's performance drew some harsh criticism from the mainstream press. The *Canberra Times* commented:

> Hailing coal – arguably the single-largest contributor to man-
> made climate change – as the solution to our hot-weather
> energy needs was so counter-intuitive that commentators
> and social media could not help drawing parallels with the
> 'alternative facts' debate across the Pacific [that is, the United
> States under Donald Trump].[4]

Respected business journalist Alan Kohler was even more scathing. Widely known and admired for his informative finance report on ABC TV news, Kohler describes being 'infuriated and dismayed by that stunt'.[5] The following day he wrote a blistering critique in the *Australian* titled 'The Great Coal Hoax', in which he argued that the energy crisis engulfing the country was entirely the Liberal Party's fault. The problem, as he saw it, was straightforward. Since cutting down Malcolm Turnbull as leader in 2009 and replacing him with Tony Abbott, the Liberal Party had been transformed into 'fervently pro-coal activists'. Kohler crisply recapped these historic events as the shift from bipartisanship on an emissions trading scheme (ETS) to Abbott's hyper partisan opposition to the policy.

After the 2007 federal election, both the new Labor government under Kevin Rudd and the Liberal Opposition under Malcolm Turnbull supported an ETS.[6] The ascension of Abbott to the leadership in 2009 wrecked this consensus: 'from agreeing that climate change was a problem that needed a price to be put on carbon, to denying that it was much of a problem at all, and calling the proposed emissions trading scheme a great big tax on everything'.[7]

Morrison's antics revived the coal wars that had been simmering for years. Wrapped up in the complex, often bitter debates about climate change and about energy policy, coal is in many ways the political, economic and cultural totem for these broader questions: what to do about Australia's vast reserves of coal, and the powerful corporations that mine the resource in an age of global warming? As astute commentators noted, the Liberal Party had unapologetically taken up one side of this conflict and it had been cheered on by some powerful forces, including the nation's shock-jock media.

In his article, Kohler was right to question how Australia had gotten itself into this mess. Australia sits on a mother lode of coal but the industry's contribution to the national economy is relatively small, despite the best efforts of the Minerals Council of Australia to bolster the figures. From a peak in 2012, when coal represented 4.5 per cent of GDP, by 2016 this had shrunk to 2 per cent and comprised less than 1 per cent of total employment and federal taxes.[8]

Yet it is not surprising that coal looms large in the national imagination. We have become a coal nation. Approximately 70 per cent of Australia's electricity is generated by coal and we are the world's leading exporter of coal in an industry that still produces around 40 per cent of global electricity. Exports of coal constitute 30 per cent of export income which, together with iron ore, fuel the national narrative – propelled by the mining lobby – that mining is the engine of Australian economic growth and prosperity. The export coal industry has been on an inexorable growth path since the first exports in the late 1950s to the emerging economies of East Asia.

However, the commanding position of coal in the national narrative has left Australia with a deep conundrum. The industry has been put on notice by the international agreements to deal with climate change and by the corresponding rise of the renewable energy industry.

Given these developments, Australia has needed a rational debate on transiting out of coal. Yet the Adani Carmichael mine, and the promise of opening up the Galilee Basin, has helped lock Australian politics into the fossil fuel age. There has been bipartisan support for expanding Australia's coal industry and opening up the Galilee Basin. The question here is how did this happen?

This book unpacks the war over coal and the pivotal role of Adani's Carmichael mine in this conflict. In Australia, there are few bigger political fights to take on. As a consultant to activist group GetUp! observed:

What oil is to Texas and Tar Sands is to Canada, coal is to Australia. This campaign [against Adani] had to not only stop a new multi-billion mine (that would crack open a valley with another half a dozen mega-mines behind it) it had to break an old industrial addiction that's enriched elites for generations, and is embedded in the country's founding story and mythology. Not so easy a task.[9]

By the time Adani began developing its proposal for the Carmichael mine in 2010, the competing forces around coal had taken root. Firstly, a bipartisan commitment existed to expand Australia's fossil fuel industry, with a key role for coal. Labor and the Coalition differed in how they constructed and articulated this goal, but each backed the ambitions of the industry. Secondly, by 2010, the environmental forces opposed to this expansion had begun to organise at the grassroots. The coal wars had begun.

This book examines the struggle between these two forces and their intense clash over Adani's Carmichael mine. It sets this struggle against the creation of a fossil fuel power network linking mining companies, the big four Australian banks, right-wing think tanks, lobby groups and the conservative media. In addition, the geo-political forces propelling the demand for coal in the midst of growing concern over climate change is an important theme. The rise and development of a social movement promoting action on climate change is crucial in understanding why there was such vigorous opposition to the Carmichael mine. Indeed, this movement succeeded in making Adani a totemic issue in the fight against climate change.

And then there is Adani as a company. By any measure, Adani Enterprises is a rogue corporation. This is not to suggest that the company has broken any laws in Australia; rather, that it has a track record in India of poor corporate and environmental ethics. Why did both the major Australian parties embrace such an operator? In particular, what does this say about Australia's compliance with the democratic norms of good governance? The fact that the federal government saw no problem with embracing Adani's operations in Australia reveals that crony capitalism is remarkably similiar in Australia and India.

I started work on this project soon after my book *The Rise and Fall of Gunns Ltd* was published in 2015. That book explored similar themes in the disturbing story of how Australia's largest timber company grew topsy-like out of favourable deals with successive Tasmanian and federal governments, with its ambitious CEO seeking to build one of the world's largest pulp mills in the pristine Tamar Valley north of Launceston. Gunns was eventually brought down by a combination of its own overreach and a relentless campaign waged by state and national environmental groups.

Adani's Carmichael coal mine has followed a similar trajectory, only larger and more complex in its dynamics because of its links to the geopolitics of coal, climate change and the war over coal and energy policy in Australia. It is a giant, octopus-like story with tentacles in many contentious contemporary issues. Can the world navigate climate change while powerful vested interests continue to push such mega fossil fuel projects? The fact that Adani gained quick approval from both the Queensland and federal governments, and involving both Labor and Coalition governments, suggest deep flaws in our political system.

When I began work on the book, the outcome was unclear. Was this going to be an account of the success of Adani's model of insider politics and the power wielded by the fossil fuel lobby, or another in a string of examples where environmental groups have succeeded in turning the development project into a successful people's movement? This was the case with Gunns and, likewise, the opposition to Adani became a lightning rod for public concern about climate change, the fate of the Great Barrier Reef, the rights of Indigenous people and the corrupted nature of our political system. But only in the latter stages of the project did it appear that the activist movement opposing the mine had brought the project to an apparent standstill, uncertain that it would ever proceed.

There are, therefore, two parts to this saga. The first examines why the mine was promoted both in India and Australia, the forces that continue to drive coal production in an age of global warming, and the rapid development of renewable energy. How did the network of power that has coalesced around fossil fuels operate to

6

secure quick approval for the mine? And what does this say about Australian governments' lack of commitment to environmentalist principles?

The second part of the story examines the ways in which a range of disparate environmental and activist groups opposed the mine. Given that the options for commencing the mine now look bleak, what assessment can be made of the power of progressive, activist politics in Australia? Have we now reached a stage where a new dynamic is making its presence felt and is capable of seriously challenging the influence of corporate power on our democracy?

As a social scientist, I believe the evidence does not support a rational case for building the world's second biggest coal mine given that global warming is a reality. The key question, therefore, is why this was allowed to happen. It has been one of the biggest battles of development versus the environment in Australian history.

CHAPTER ONE

The great coal rush

In the battle over climate change, the years 2000–2012 will hold a special place. As if to mock the inability of world leaders to grapple with the seriousness of the problem, the world went on a binge of constructing coal-fired power stations, increasing the generating capacity three-fold.[1] China drove most of the demand, as coal underpinned its double-digit growth rates. But India and Japan were close on China's heels. Indian governments had emulated the Chinese model and rapidly expanded India's coal-fired power capacity while Japan turned to coal to fill the gap after closing down its nuclear plants following the 2011 Fukushima accident.

Australia was a major player in servicing this binge, with exports nearly doubling from 80 to 160 million tonnes between 2000 and 2012. Dominated by the big four companies – BHP, Rio Tinto, Xstrata and Anglo American – Australia quickly emerged as the world's second largest exporter of coal and, in the process, fuelled a fierce debate on Australia's coal industry at a time of growing concern about climate change. Allowing the rapid expansion of the industry, successive state and federal governments have, according to some commentators, created a situation where Australia 'is teetering on the greatest strategic blunder in its history' by equipping the nation for a carbon future that will have a limited life span.[2] Financed by some of the world's largest banks, the coal binge threatened to put any realistic climate agreement beyond reach. But that didn't stop a geo-political competition for new fields to mine. The Galilee Basin with its untapped mega-reserves became 'the new frontier' in this 'great coal rush', a term coined by the Indian media.[3] 'The prize here', wrote a journalist for *Forbes Asia*, 'is millions of tonnes of quality thermal coal, and a bunch of aggressive miners from India and China are staking multi-billion dollar bets to snag it'.[4] Thus was born a critical phase in the war over coal.

The pressure to meet what those in the coal industry perceived as a long-term rising demand brought forward entrepreneurs willing to take the risk in the Galilee Basin, a region mining companies had long sought. But the daunting logistic problem of the region's remoteness and lack of infrastructure had so far deterred investment. Now the equation had changed. The opportunity to extract billions of tonnes of coal at historically high prices produced what Royal Dutch Shell termed the 'Scramble' in 2008 – a frenzied search for the last large-scale fossil fuel supplies, driven by short-term commercial self-interest.[5]

The dreams propelling this frenzy could also be seen as fantasies and not just because they were disconnected from the reality of rising global greenhouse gas emissions. The entrepreneurs bidding for the riches of the Galilee were all self-made tycoons, three of whose companies carried significant risk profiles. The Galilee was a gamble for the four mining magnates driving Australia's version of the coal rush: Indian billionaire Gunupati Venkata Krishna (GVK) Reddy, whose partner was Australia's own Gina Rinehart; Australia's brash and colourful business tycoon Clive Palmer, who planned to sell coal into China; and Gautam Adani, India's own version of a rags to riches billionaire.

Although strategic rivals, the four shared much in common. Each assumed that coal had a long-term viable future as a power source; each was a billionaire insider political operator used to securing deals from government; each was an active climate change denier; each couched their involvement in coal mining in the Galilee as a moral cause to help the world's poor; and each tended to underestimate the formidable array of opponents concerned about climate change, the Great Barrier Reef, the Great Artesian Basin water supply and native title rights. These were seen as merely obstacles to get around.

Internationally, the coal rush came at a strategically opportune time. The 2009 UN-sponsored Copenhagen climate talks had failed to produce a binding agreement, leaving a hiatus in global cooperation to limit global warming. In the United States, the fossil fuel lobby had been waging 'an all-out war' to prevent Congress from tackling carbon pollution, leaving little room for the Obama administration to advance American leadership on the issue. Into this vacuum came China and India, seeking to secure their long-term supplies of coal. As Adani's Australian chief executive, Jeyakumar Janakaraj, explained: 'It's not about a two-year scenario or a five-year scenario, it is about a 30-, 40-, 50-year scenario that we have thought about and planned'.[6]

In neither China nor India did the impact of the Global Financial Crisis (GFC) dent these long-term strategic interests. Although the manufacturing sector in China was severely hit, the Chinese government implemented an aggressive economic stimulus plan that returned growth rates to their normally buoyant levels of above 9 per cent annual growth by 2008.[7] The Indian economy relied less on consumer exports, and the dynamic forces of privatisation and de-regulation of the state-controlled economy that had already been unleashed quickly reversed the dip in growth rates. In addition to Adani Enterprises and GVK, other big Indian private power companies were on a global search for coal mines.

Many of the same factors drove the feverish demand from both India and China. Thermal coal plants constituted most of the power generated in both countries. In the years immediately after the GFC, analysts forecast a 'massive' mismatch of demand over supply in the years ahead.[8] India's demand for increasing coal supplies was even higher than China's. To fuel its growing economy, India was adding massive amounts of coal-fired power every year. In 2010, total coal imports stood at 73 million tonnes, up from 60 million just the year before. Analysts didn't see much choice for India at the time. If it wanted to emulate China's growth rates, so the argument went, it desperately needed thermal coal generation. Although India is a significant producer of coal, its domestic supply couldn't keep pace with demand because its coal production was state controlled and inefficient. Corruption and environmental disputes further hampered supply. Opening up power generation to the private sector meant key companies – Adani among them – were keen to secure long-term coal imports. Hence, Indian companies were racing to secure coal assets across the globe.[9] As the *Times of India* wrote in 2009: 'imported coal supply is a life-and-death-matter for giant power plants. If they don't want to be held to ransom by coal traders, they need mines'.[10] Consequently, Indian companies were prepared to pay a premium for assets.

Guaranteed supply

The sheer size of the deposits in the Galilee excited Indian, Australian and Chinese companies. The concentration of coal deposits was equivalent in size to the United Kingdom. But securing the development of the mines was a gamble for all four main proponents. Not only did their plans open up one of the fiercest battles with environment groups in Australian history, the plans threatened to derail global attempts to deal with climate change.

Adding to the gamble in the Galilee, the strategic rivalry between the players worked against the co-operation necessary to get the railway infrastructure and port development built. However, as events unfolded, the risks associated with opening up the Galilee Basin also lay within the operations and structures of each of the companies involved. All the four corporate players were self-made tycoons whose drive and ambition shaped their company's fortunes.

Reddy and Adani were part of a dynamic class of risk-taking billionaires and many saw their rapid rise to power as a symbol of modern India. The two Australian proponents – Rinehart and

Palmer – were part of a powerful class of mining tycoons enjoying the riches of the country's mining boom. <u>International observers noted the roguish manner in which Australia's mining magnates operated.</u> Their unabashed notoriety, one observer wrote, has attracted attention 'for their excesses, squabbles and political meddling'. Dubbed the 'feral billionaires' for their 'wild and unbecoming public behaviour', the Australian mining magnates have been likened to Russia's oligarchs.[11] While not a direct comparision, Australia, like Russia, has created its own version of mega-rich and self-interested oligarchs who use the political system to pursue their commercial interests.[12]

Clive Palmer's China First

On the first weekend in February 2010, Queensland's *Sunday Mail* newspaper carried a front page image of Clive Palmer dressed as Superman. The paper reported 'Mining billionaire Clive Palmer became an economic superhero … signing the biggest ever export deal in Australia's history and securing Queensland's financial future'.[13] Standing beside him was the premier Anna Bligh. Her presence was curious, to say the least, because at the time Palmer was in the process of suing her. But Bligh talked up the project's benefits as much as Palmer did. What enticed the premier to share a platform with Palmer – who was not only taking legal action against her, but had no record as a developer of big mining projects – says everything about the pro-coal mentality in Queensland. Bligh wanted the Galilee opened up. Her government was working on *Coal Plan 2030*, a policy framework for the continued expansion of the State's coal industry. Its basis was the premier's view that there was no such thing as a bad coal mine for Queensland. As she stated publicly: 'Proposals not to approve any further coalmines [are] … just simply preposterous, they would spell economic and social catastrophe for Queensland and the national economy'.[14]

The plan predicted continued bullish demand from countries outside the Organisation for Economic Co-operation and Development (OECD) attracted by cheaper fossil fuels. Further rail and port developments, including at Abbot Point, were needed to feed this continued demand. Coal from the Galilee Basin was expected to play a role in this boom, and the government assessed that the first shipments from the region could come as early as 2013.[15] The only note of uncertainty in the plan was the future direction of greenhouse gas mitigation. But it confidently predicted that coal would continue to outstrip green technologies. In sum, the policy framework sought to lock Queensland into a coal future.

Palmer's bid for the Galilee envisaged a deal which was to supply $60 billion worth of coal over a 20-year period to China Power International Development Ltd, the State-owned electricity generator. For reasons that weren't entirely clear, Swiss company Vitol became a partner in the venture, agreeing to buy half the volume of coal. In 2009, Palmer had used his own company, Waratah Coal, to announce the discovery of 4.4 billion tonnes in the Galilee, and another of his companies, ResourceHouse, negotiated the deal which Palmer called the China First coal mine project. Palmer was typically upbeat; the deal would provide up to 60000 direct and indirect jobs and would restore the State's AAA credit rating. According to Palmer, the Export Import Bank of China was 'locked in' to finance the deal.[16]

But a few days later it didn't seem such a 'done deal' after all. The ABC's reporter in China, Stephen McDonell, found a different version of the project:

> By last night it seemed unclear if there had even been a real
> contract signed. The confusion started when the Hong Kong
> Stock Exchange received an announcement from China Power
> International Development, the company said to be buying
> all this coal. The company's statement said that it didn't have

an agreement with [Palmer's] ResourceHouse and it warned shareholders and potential investors to exercise caution when dealing with the Australian company.[17]

China Power International Development Ltd told McDonell that it was 'a framework agreement only which does not involve any specific price. The Sales and Purchase of Coal Agreement shall be the subject of further negotiations between the parties'.

Premier Anna Bligh was, understandably, caught on the back foot. She'd seen documents attesting to the deal, she was forced to explain.[18] Palmer was adamant that the project would go ahead. The competing accounts of the announcement of China First, the first project signed to mine the Galilee, revealed much about Palmer's operating style: big on promotion and often short on actual achievement.

Of all the players seeking to mine the Galilee Basin, Clive Palmer was the most mercurial. At the time of the China First announcement, he was little known outside his native Queensland. Within a few years he had become a household name as the founder of the populist Palmer United Party, which flamed and fizzed across the political landscape between 2013 and 2016. Palmer's declining fortunes, which coincided with the end of his parliamentary career, have also played out in public. The descent into bankruptcy in 2016 of his Yabulu nickel plant in Townsville amid claims of mismanagement and breaches of company law forced the normally media-hungry businessman into an ignoble retreat from public life, although his fortunes have recently turned around with his recent court victory in a royalty dispute with Chinese-owned Citi Pacific. However, Palmer's carefully crafted image as a champion of ordinary people has been severely damaged. Amid these dramatic events, his involvement in the Galilee Basin had helped shape not just the politics of the coal mining industry, but of Australian politics more widely. Palmer had played an historic role, just not the one he had imagined.

Palmer's urge to become a mining magnate came later in his life. He was the son of unconventional parents who offered him unique adventures for a young man in the 1960s, including visits to China at the height of the Cold War and to the United States during the Kennedy era. Palmer found his niche as a real estate salesman after a period of aimless wandering during his young adulthood. His gift for selling property on Queensland's burgeoning Gold Coast soon made him a powerhouse in the industry and earned him a fortune. By the mid-80s he had retired, but he decided a retirees' cruise-ship life wasn't for him.[19] His true interests lay in mixing business with politics; spruiking big deals, negotiating in the corridors of power and selling his projects to the public as vital to securing Queensland's future.

Palmer's sunny, optimistic public persona, manifest in his broad smile and jokey manner, masked a more complex character. He was driven by grandiosity. After abandoning retirement, he resolved to use his wealth to create a resources empire. His instincts were rewarded. In his first foray into the industry he managed to pull off a big win. Finding out by chance that an American mining company hadn't made its lease rent payments on its iron ore tenement in the ore-rich Pilbara, Palmer swooped, gaining the lease for himself through his newly formed private company, Mineralogy, in circumstances that remain clouded. Years later, he sold the rights to the rich deposit to Citi Pacific for hundreds of millions of dollars. Palmer the mining tycoon was born.[20] More accurately, the image-conscious Palmer fashioned the legend of his success as a mining tycoon. Over the years, it became increasingly hard to separate his claims about the success of Mineralogy and its offshoot Waratah Coal, and his performance. Palmer liked to keep his business structure opaque. Even his personal worth was hard for financers to assess, estimated variously between $750 million and $1.3 billion.

Known for promoting some wacky conspiracy theories, notably that the CIA was funding green groups to destroy the coal industry,

Palmer was also part of the climate change denying conservative class. 'Historically, the climate on earth has always changed', he once explained to the media.[21] Yet, while he denigrated the work of climate scientists, he valued those who worked for a company he started to try to commercialise scientific research and developments – 'we have a lot of faith in these scientists'.[22]

With his Rolls Royce and private jet, Palmer lived the lifestyle of the billionaire class. But critics claimed that behind the tinsel and toys, Palmer had a dubious record as a businessman. While he had a good eye for assets, he had a chaotic management style and little in the way of a coherent strategy behind his tendency to hyper invest in, and over-promote, his activities. To some, he was a 'chancer'.[23] Those who respected him more as a business figure saw his skills as those of an asset investor rather than a mining entrepreneur.[24]

Not long after Palmer announced his China First deal, business academic Jason West made a prescient observation about the likely success of the deal:

> The float was a thinly veiled pitch to the sentiments of Chinese investors seeking an easy entry to the global resources sector. The trouble with it is that the average Chinese investor is a shrewd judge of value … For an investment of this magnitude they would want an experienced miner at the helm.[25]

West saw in Palmer's pitch for Galilee Basin coal 'his one great hope of reaching true billionaire status'. Writer and political commentator Guy Rundle, who had studied Palmer closely, saw a contradictory character driven by self-belief:

> Who is Clive Palmer? He's a man so utterly a creation of the Gold Coast that you can smell the coconut oil and sand on him, but he's also an observant Catholic whose public statements have the timbre of religious tradition about them.

He's a man who wanted to be a lawyer and a stable man of the establishment, but found that his truer nature as a natural-born salesman and wheeler-dealer would win out in the end.[26]

But as the politics of the Galilee unfolded, such self-belief would prove to be shaky ground for securing a mine in the Galilee.

GVK-Hancock

On 11 June 2011, Gina Rinehart (nee Hancock) attended the 'power wedding' of the granddaughter of her friend and business partner, GVK Reddy, known as India's 'infrastructure czar' and one of the nation's wealthiest businessmen. Thousands of guests joined the family at the extravagant wedding, estimated to have cost US$20 million, including many of India's A-list elites. Accompanying Rinehart were three senior federal Coalition politicians: Barnaby Joyce, Julie Bishop and Theresa Gambino. Rinehart had flown the three Opposition politicians to the event in a private jet. At the time, she was negotiating a A$1 billion deal with GVK for the sale of her Galilee Basin coal leases, one of which she had purchased in the 1990s and the other which she had inherited from her father, the legendary miner Lang Hancock. According to Gambino, the flight over wasn't much fun: "'I haven't met anyone else who can talk coal for nine hours." All the way to India? "Pretty much"'.[27]

The three Coalition politicians, who were in the country for little more than a day, were on hand to 'lend cachet' to Rinehart in a culture where political connections are essential to doing business.[28] The three obliging politicians used their parliamentary expenses allowance for the return flight to Australia, intensifying a long-running debate about politicians' abuse of the expenses scheme. In his obligatory report to federal parliament, Joyce offered the lame excuse that he had spent a day in Malaysia on his return which was 'of great assistance' in helping familiarise him with the country.[29]

A few months later, the deal was sealed; Rinehart demonstrated her business savvy by selling at the top of the market. The deal thrust her into the status of the richest woman in the world. She retained a 21 per cent stake in what became known as the Alpha Coal and Alpha West mines while Reddy bought 100 per cent of the mine site called Kevin's Corner. Rinehart lent her powerful brand name to the partnership in all three mines: GVK-Hancock. She was upbeat about GVK's acquisition, saying that it would lead to 'on-going operations over decades. We are very pleased with this strategic alliance with a country, via GVK, that needs our coal'.[30] Rinehart was enthusiastic for another reason: the billion dollars could be put towards the development of her second major Pilbara iron-ore project at Roy Hill, helping, she hoped, to cement her legacy as a true mining entrepreneur and not just an heiress – a term she loathes.

Insiders in the mining industry thought that GVK was lucky to have 'one of the toughest Aussie voices on its side'.[31] According to her biographer, Gina Rinehart had 'learnt from an early age to confront anything and anybody that stood in her way'.[32]

The Hancock name needs little introduction to most Australians. Even though the normally media-shy billionaire daughter of mining pioneer Lang Hancock keeps a low profile, her story is a modern-day family saga of extreme wealth and privilege, bitter family feuds and regular resort to litigation. It's a story worthy of a television series, which indeed it became in 2017 with Channel's Nine's *The House of Hancock*. Rinehart's family story has the flavour of a soap opera, involving bitter disputes with her first husband, her father, her father's second wife, her father's business partner and then three of her four children. Combative by nature, Hancock is renowned for churning through lawyers in courtroom battles against former friends and family members.

The family's wealth was founded in her father Lang's discovery of rich iron ore deposits in the remote Pilbara region of Western

Australia in the 1960s. The telling and re-telling of how Lang was supposed to have made the discoveries almost by chance, flying in a small plane buffeted by stormy weather, is now threaded into the family's, and the country's, history. Rinehart, in particular, is said to embrace the legend that the family's contribution to the nation's prosperity deserves more recognition. Others take a more sanguine view: Hancock was granted favourable 'rivers of gold', royalties to dig up the people's resource.[33]

Part of her drive for influence is her grievance that 'Australia's traditional east coast elites have not recognised her family's contribution to the country's development, nor the local media'.[34] Even though she has built impressively upon her father's pioneering efforts and cleaned up the financial mess he left, the family's wealth grew from the favourable royalties Lang negotiated with Rio Tinto to develop his discoveries. The 2000s mining boom, which inflated the price of iron ore, has propelled her net worth to A$21.5 billion by 2017, placing her in the top 100 wealthiest people in the world.[35]

Notoriously private, Rinehart's tumultuous personal life and polarising public persona have been well covered and don't need re-telling here.[36] However, her reputation for hard-baked right-wing political views go hand in hand with her steely determination and often hectoring, autocratic manner. According to observations from people close to her, Rinehart's years of living in the shadow of her father's towering figure have left her uncomfortable in her own skin.[37]

Lang Hancock was once described by a journalist as 'a swash-buckling right-winger who believed people and governments should bow to his will'. Gina inherited both his extreme political views and his tenacity. His world became hers. Consequently, she has spent a lifetime fulfilling his dream of developing mines in the Pilbara and espousing his libertarian views: unregulated free enterprise, low regulation and cuts to wages. Rinehart also espouses the traditional stable of far-right fetishes – a war on welfare, climate change denialism and a strong dislike of the ABC. She has railed at what she sees as Australia's excessive costs in getting mines up and running. Her call to introduce cheap Asian labour allowed her critics to caricature her as a modern-day Marie Antoinette.

Averse to giving media interviews, Rinehart had been quietly cultivating her influence inside the Liberal Party since she was a young woman, firstly under the tutelage of her father and then, from her early twenties, in her own right. As her influence grew, Gina started to prime a younger generation of conservative politicians. Her targets were 'a cabal of young Liberal students who had distinguished themselves in the eyes of the Hancocks by vanquishing the hard-left activists then trying to seize control of the Australian Union of Students'.[38] As journalist Nick Bryant has written: 'In her career-long quest for access and influence in the vital centres of Australian power, these trips were one of Gina's more astute long-term investments'.[39]

Just before striking the deal with GVK Reddy, Reinhart's political profile rose dramatically. Shedding her normally private persona, she joined forces during 2010 with other mining identities to fight the Rudd Labor government's introduction of the super profits mining tax, which sought to redistribute the nation's mineral resources more widely. In June 2010, she addressed a rally on the Perth riverfront just in front of the gleaming towers of the CBD. By any measure, it was an unusual rally. The wealthy of Perth were among those who stood to lose the most from the introduction of the 'super tax'. They gathered in their suits and ties, waving placards – handed out by the mining industry – to hear two billionaires, Andrew (Twiggy) Forrest and Gina Rinehart, deliver impassioned speeches from the back of a flatbed truck. Wearing a string of large pearls that glistened in the sunshine, Rinehart grabbed the loudhailer and denounced the tax to the boisterous, 1200-strong crowd until she went hoarse.[40]

As I discuss in Chapter 4, the success of the campaign against the mining tax demonstrated the raw power of the mining industry. A fortnight after the rally, Julia Gillard deposed Rudd in a political coup and then declared a compromise, in what amounted to a massive victory for the mining industry. It was a decisive moment for Rinehart, as one journalist observed:

> [S]ince grabbing the loudhailer, Rinehart has not let go, rising in power and profile to become one of Australia's most talked about and polarising figures: an 'Iron Lady' who is a source of intrigue and consternation to the media she increasingly owns, and the political classes she seeks to influence.[41]

From 2010 onwards, Rinehart's 'billionaire activism' helped her to promote her agenda: the development of iron-ore and coal mining, opening up the Galilee Basin and promoting the climate change denialism associated with Australia's massive coal mining industry. As journalist Samiha Shafy wrote not long after Rinehart signed the deal with GVK Reddy:

> Her vision is a radical one: She wants an Australia in which the interests of the extractive industry are paramount, a place with little regulation, no taxes on natural resources or CO_2, but massive numbers of low-wage guest workers from Asia, so that planned mega-projects can be implemented as quickly as possible. Rinehart uses her money and influence to make the voices of climate change deniers heard, and she has developed a following of like-minded billionaires and politicians.[42]

Inside the Liberal Party, she wields her power like a queen with her courtiers although, as the following report from the *Sydney Morning Herald* suggests, the secrecy surrounding her meetings with party members makes it hard to gauge just how much influence she has:

> Australia's richest woman, Gina Rinehart, invited a small group of Coalition friends for drinks in her private hotel suite, after

21

planning a secret flight to Canberra to visit the Agriculture
Minister Barnaby Joyce. Some of Mrs Rinehart's closest political
friends, the Speaker Bronwyn Bishop and Liberal Party senators
Cory Bernardi and Michaelia Cash, were invited to join the
billionaire for the intimate gathering on Wednesday night. The
iron ore magnate, who has vigorously supported Prime Minister
Tony Abbott's plans to abolish the carbon and mining taxes,
suggested the politicians meet for drinks in her Canberra hotel
room to avoid media attention.[43]

This is Rinehart's preferred style of operating. As one of her biog-
raphers confirms: 'like the rest of corporate Australia she is increasingly turning to more behind-the-scenes methods to wield influence
in politics – most of which the public will never see'.[44]

Rinehart's influence extends to the top of conservative politics.
Opposition leader turned prime minister Tony Abbott claims to be
a close friend[45] while deputy leader and later leader of the National
Party Barnaby Joyce is happy to be cast as one of her cheerleaders.
Joyce had built a name for himself 'by talking in one long string of
hyperboles after another against the evils of environmental protection policies'.[46] In 2013, Joyce declared that 'Gina is a great friend
and I'm a good mate of Gina's and she's got an Australian company
which employs Australian people which pays tax in this nation and
I'm so proud. ... We need lots of Gina Rineharts, not one, [because]
when we have a nation of lots of them we're going to be a stronger
nation'.[47]

Joyce supports Rinehart's efforts to develop northern Australia.
Rinehart wanted to create a special economic zone in the whole of
northern Australia which would be granted tax cuts and regulatory
exemptions for large infrastructure projects. The idea was promoted
through the Institute of Public Affairs, of which Rinehart was a
member. The policies of the federal Labor government, she argued,
were killing the mining sector. Critics labelled her proposal Rinehart's

'northern libertarian paradise'.[48] Undeterred, Rinehart established the lobby group Australians for Northern Development and Economic Vision to press her case. The enormous profits her company and the other big miners continued to reap from the mining boom sat oddly with her call for more subsidies for the industry. Hence, critics saw her proposal as 'a stalking horse for her real desires', which one commentator summarised as the following:

> Australians don't want to live in sweltering Northern Australia where all the goodies are buried, so we need to regulate them less, tax them less and cut payroll and company tax, stamp duty and the like to make it more economically attractive to relocate. Failing that, we should '… consider the terrible plight of very poor people in our neighbouring countries in Asia. We should, on humanitarian grounds, give more of these people the opportunity of guest labour work in Australia'.[49]

Rinehart has actively supported the conservative push to promote climate change denialism both in the broader community and in the conservative parties. Rejecting the sceptical position popular among some conservatives, she is an unashamed denier.

Rinehart has been a key link in the corporate-funded network that has fostered climate change denialism in Australia. Wherever climate policy has been hijacked, her influence is apparent. In her links with the Institute of Public Affairs, the various mining industry's peak bodies and their publicity outlets, and the media, she has made her unapologetic opposition to climate science a key platform in her public career. Her contribution to denialism has had a major impact not only on Australia's debilitating paralysis on climate policy but on the debate about the Galilee Basin. It has helped to promote the parallel denialism: that the coal industry has nothing to do with either global warming or, by extension, the slow destruction of the Great Barrier Reef.

Rinehart's promotion of Andrew Bolt into television is said to have occurred after she joined the board of Channel 10. Bolt and Rinehart had both shared long-held ambitions to develop a Fox News model in Australia.

Rinehart also sponsored two visits to Australia by Christopher Monckton, who from 2007 onwards became one of the most extreme climate change denialists working the speaking circuit and 'the great white hope' of the conservative denialist movement.

Asked by a journalist in 2007 to explain his critique of the scientific consensus, Monckton offered the following:

> 'Well', he says, breezily, 'for a few years, the temperature will continue to rise, but nowhere near as fast as the alarmists would wish it to rise. Then solar physicists suggest that in the next solar cycle but one, and a solar cycle is about 10.6 years, there will be a considerable cooling of the Sun. And the panic will disappear'. Hey presto.[50]

Monckton's rise to climate change expert owed a great deal to the support he received from a range of right-wing American think tanks that deny global warming is occurring, including the Science and Public Policy Institute and the Heartland Institute. The latter organisation, in particular, has routinely spread misinformation about climate science, including deliberate attacks on climate scientists.[51] In each of his Australian tours, sponsored by Rinehart, the media gave Monckton plenty of space to air his views.

Adding to Rinehart's gravitas in right-wing climate denying circles was the support she gave to Professor Ian Plimer, who was seen as the most 'intellectual' of the climate change deniers because of his position as Professor of Geology at Adelaide University. His association with both academia and the scientific discipline of geology gave him more cachet than Monckton had. But the link between the discipline of geology and climate change scepticism is not a strong one.

The broader community of geologists seem to be convinced by the evidence that humans are causing global warming. The European Federation of Geologists, the Geological Society of America and the Geological Society of London all accept the science and risks associated with global warming.[52] Nevertheless, some geologists oppose the science and are among the lone voices in the scientific community to disagree with the scientific consensus on the issue.

At the time he and Rinehart formed a close association, Plimer was, in addition to his academic position, a director of multiple exploration and mining companies which were said to have earned him more than $400 000 between 2008–2010 – and mining shares and options worth hundreds of thousands of dollars more.[53] He is the author of the sceptical tome *Heaven and Earth* which, by 2010, had sold 40 000 copies here and more overseas and catapulted Plimer onto the world stage, although the book was strongly criticised in the scientific community. Reviewing it, Michael Ashley, Professor of Astrophysics at the University of New South Wales, pulled no punches: 'The arguments that Plimer advances in the 503 pages and 2311 footnotes in *Heaven and Earth* are nonsense. The book is largely a collection of contrarian ideas and conspiracy theories that are rife in the blogosphere. The writing is rambling and repetitive; the arguments flawed and illogical'.[54] Ashley notes that Plimer had not published any peer-reviewed work in the area of climate science.

John Singleton, the colourful, blunt-speaking legend of Sydney advertising, is an old family friend of Rinehart's and a fellow global warming denialist and opponent of the mining tax. At the time, he also owned Sydney radio station 2GB, which employed Andrew Bolt, Alan Jones and Ray Hadley, who together dominated the airwaves denigrating climate science and scientists. Singleton once boasted to journalist Jane Cadzow that he and Rinehart were acting in tandem on these issues: 'We have been able to overtly and covertly attack governments … Because we have people employed by us like

Andrew Bolt and Alan Jones and Ray Hadley who agree with her thinking about the development of our resources, we act in concert in that way'.[55]

Thus Rinehart directly shaped public opinion on the most vexed and important public policy issues facing the nation. Nothing suggests that she was insincere in her beliefs about climate change. Yet her views neatly dovetailed with her commercial interests and she has the power and the money to link them together in the public debate.

Given the range of her political involvements between 2010 and 2013, it is not surprising that Rinehart and Reddy's Alpha coal project was both the one chosen to kick-start the opening up of the Galilee Basin and the first to win the approval of the Queensland and federal governments. But, despite her wealth and influence, GVK Reddy proved to be a troublesome partner.

GVK Reddy's overstretched empire

When he signed the deal to buy Rinehart's Galilee leases, GVK Reddy was a household name in India; part of the same new billionaire class as his competitor Adani. His company, though, had a longer history than did Adani's. Founded in the southern Indian city of Hyderabad in the late 1950s, GVK Power and Infrastructure had transformed into a conglomerate empire of coal-fired power plants, airports and toll roads. Reddy's son Sanjay was vice-chairman of the company. But by the time the company decided to buy into Galilee coal, it was heavily leveraged. The Indian media dubbed GVK's purchase as 'GVK's big Australian bet'.[56] Gamble or not, some thought the company had little choice: 'The GVK group had to go for it. For coal shortage is increasingly impeding Indian power companies from forging ahead with their ambitious plans'.[57] And Reddy had the entrepreneurial appetite for risk. He announced that he would raise $10 billion to fund the entire project, but the clock was already ticking on finding the initial $1 billion loan to purchase the mine.[58]

Sanjay was sent out to Australia to oversee the company's new operation. The first challenge was to try to beat its rival Adani to build a railway to Abbot Point. Adani had teamed up with Korean construction group Posco to build the 388-kilometre North Galilee Basin Rail link. Meanwhile, GVK joined forces with Aurizon to build its own rail link.

Sanjay was surprisingly candid about the challenge of making the mine profitable. The key to the project, he explained to the media, was in taking advantage of the scale of the operation and the opportunity to vertically integrate the mine into the company's power generation business. However, Sanjay explained that the biggest challenge would be overhauling the 'bloated cost structure' of Australian mining operations. They would need to reduce the cost structure from the prevailing price of $70 per tonne to $50.

Sanjay hired consultancy firm McKinsey to help bring in best practices from around the world and planned an approach in which contractors would bear increased risks around fixed timelines and costs. Introducing new, more efficient equipment was also part of the plan. He intended to use huge excavators costing $50 million to $100 million each instead of smaller bucket-wheel and other extractors. 'Bringing the Australians around to GVK's way of working was a gradual process', explained Reddy.[59]

Adani's Carmichael mine

In seeking approval for his Galilee mine, Gautam Adani, like GVK Reddy, was making the single biggest bet of his career, and operating on very similar assumptions to Reddy's: securing his own long-term supply of coal for his private power plants; expressing faith in the long-term predictions for coal, not just in India but in Asia as well; responding to a scaling back of his Indonesian coal mining imports;

and developing a vertically integrated business model that Adani called his company's 'pit-to-plug' strategy, which he believed would help to reap efficiencies, thus circumventing fluctuations in the price of coal. Adani intended to mine the coal in the Galilee Basin, transport it on his own railway line to a port in Abbot Point that he had already purchased in 2011, and then ship it to his own Indian port from where it would be taken to his power plants.[60]

How Adani planned to utilise all of his coal imports from the Galilee has been the subject of speculation. However, it is thought that about 70 per cent would be earmarked to fuel new and existing coal-fired power stations throughout India, owned or operated by Adani, as part of the growing electrification of the developing country. The remainder would be sold into the growing South East-Asian market.

Adani would emerge as the only serious contender for the Galilee. The very name 'Adani' came to symbolise and intensify the war over coal. So who is Gautam Adani and how did he develop and operate his business empire?

CHAPTER TWO
India's coal baron

For the past seven years Adani's name has rarely been out of the Australian news. The family-named company has been criticised for its poor environmental and business practices in India. Indians themselves hold contradictory views of the company. On the one hand, it is seen as one among the new breed of brash entrepreneurial companies projecting India's newly modernised image to the world. Yet the company is connected to the darker side of this modernisation – the links between big business and government.

Megha Bahree, a contributor to the business magazine *Forbes Asia*, offered a window into Gautam Adani's rarefied world. She noted that when his son was married in the coastal state of Goa in 2013, the Indian billionaire's guest list included the richest man in the country as well as numerous chief executives, top bankers and bureaucrats. Most of these A-list guests, she wrote, 'just stopped by the night before to bless the happy couple and skipped the actual wedding'. But one prominent invitee 'stayed through all the ceremonies over a couple of days, genial and relaxed like a favourite uncle'. That guest was Narendra Modi, chief minister of Adani's home state of Gujarat. The following year, Modi was elected prime minister of India.[1]

Adani has been coy about his relationship with Modi. Asked by a journalist from Reuters newsagency to explain his friendship with the prominent politician, Adani refused several times to answer directly but then attempted to dismiss the question: 'What does it mean – personal friends?' adding that he has friends across the political spectrum, but avoids politics.[2] Such high-level access to power is a far cry from Adani's humble beginnings.

Gujarat state is India's most westerly province. Its coastline sits on the Arabian Sea and it has welcomed traders from Europe and the Middle East since at least the 12th century. Old-timers still remember Gautam Adani riding around Gujarat's main city, Ahmedabad, in the early 1980s on his motor scooter making the rounds of government offices, 'looking for a breakthrough to make it big in life'. Adani, a college dropout, had discovered his 'sharp trading instincts' and, in 1988, established his own commodities trading firm after several years working with his brother in his Mumbai plastics business. Otherwise, the unassuming son of a modest textile trading family was a novice in the labyrinthine world of Indian business. His English was sketchy and he 'felt inhibited conversing with government officials'.[3]

In the decade leading up to 2010, Adani's business had grown 16-fold, his ascent ranked as 'amongst the most startling in recent Indian business history'.[4] Although often promoted as a 'rags-to-riches' story, Adani's stunning rise reveals a complex interplay of personal and political factors. Personal drive fuelled the growth of his company. Adani 'thought big. He was always ambitious. He wanted to create the largest trading house possible'.[5] Adani credits his success with an ability to assess risk in pursuing new business ventures. Like other self-made tycoons, he has followed a pattern of borrowing heavily; earnings from one business are then leveraged against more borrowings to finance expansion into new ventures.[6]

Adani has a 'knack for making useful friends'.[7] His round, jowly face and bristling black moustache convey a no-nonsense demeanour, yet he can also be extremely charming. Media photographs typically reveal a friendly expression and beaming smile. He is an adept networker. Yet he has the capacity to strike out in a decisive fashion and back his own judgment. He is a risk-taker with a reputation as something of a buccaneer.[8] He operates his increasingly sprawling empire as 'a one man band'.[9] Yet, he is the opposite of the stereotypically outsized, bombastic tycoon. By his own admission, he is an introvert, priding himself on being a very calm person, never ruffled by adversity, a quality he has called upon on two occasions when his life was in danger.

In 1997 Adani was kidnapped for ransom by two of India's most feared underworld figures acting on behalf of a Dubai-based gangster, Irfan Goga. He was released after a few hours, and only after payment of a substantial sum. Adani has been reluctant to talk about the incident, which is understandable given that he, like other wealthy Indians, remains vulnerable to such threats.

Another distressing incident occurred on 26 November 2008 while Adani was staying at the Taj Hotel in Mumbai. At 9.50 am he was relaxing in one of the complex's swish restaurants when he was shaken by the sound of automatic gunfire ringing through the building in what became India's worst terrorist attack. From five metres away, Adani witnessed the opening barrage of bullets and the mayhem of people running and screaming in all directions. Hiding himself firstly in the kitchen, then in the basement, he hunkered down throughout the night with a group of other people traumatised by the savagery of the attack.

During the night, heavily armed militants had roamed the corridors shooting and killing people, setting the building alight and exchanging fire with commandos.[10] Adani didn't safely emerge until the next morning. 'Everybody was praying for their life', Adani later explained. He tried to lift people's spirits by reminding them to have faith in God while also talking on his phone to his distressed family.[11] He later told the media that he 'can never forget the panic witnessed on people's faces that day'.

How such near-death experiences shaped his life and approach to business is not clear; perhaps they gave him a determination to leave a legacy, alongside his ability to stay calm in the face of adversity. In any event, nothing dented his drive to grow his company. He had a business instinct for risk-taking but also knew how to play the system of Indian politics – making friends in high places and using political connections to brush aside corporate ethics.

In spite of high debts, returns started flowing. Yet Adani claims not to be solely motivated by money. 'I like challenges where you feel you are part of nation-building', he told one interviewer.[12] However, this appeal to national pride fails to explain why his company has been dogged by allegations of poor business and environmental practices.

Unravelling these contradictions is difficult, especially because Adani avoids extended interviews with the press. He is both an authentic entrepreneur, driven by a big vision and a willingness to take risks, and an insider wheeler-dealer dogged by scandals. In this sense, he follows a path many self-made tycoons have trodden. But his one true gift, close associates say, is his ability to win people over, political or otherwise.

India Inc.

Adani's spectacular rise in Indian business is inseparable from the traditional crony model of Indian business-government relations, which has intensified in recent decades. Close relationships between government and big business have a long lineage in India, where they have been depicted as a natural Indian way of doing business. Before the Indian economy was opened up to greater private investment in the early 1990s, Indian business had a parallel tradition stressing corporate responsibility. Influenced by Ghandian philosophy, Indians 'saw their business empires as a trust held in the interests of the community at large'.[13] However, several decades of pro-free market policies have changed the character of Indian business. Accompanying India's entry into the world of global capitalism, fantastic wealth now sits alongside weak governance, trampled regulations and a widening gap between rich and poor. And, as corporate social responsibility scholars Bimal Arora and Ravi Puranik have written, big corporations in India have increasingly redefined their social responsibilities 'in their own limited ways and contexts'.[14]

Wealth inequality in India is stark: in the past 15 years, the top 1 per cent of Indians have increased their share of the country's wealth from approximately 37 per cent to 53 per cent, with the top 10 per cent owning more than 76 per cent of the nation's wealth.[15] As Trilochan Sastry, chairman of the Indian-based Association for Democratic Reforms has written, wealth inequality in India poses 'an existential threat to democracy'.[16]

Indeed, India's wealthy elite wields enormous power in the economy.[17] Deals involving natural resources including land, water, forests or minerals are made available to tycoons at bargain prices or with tax concessions in one form or another. Siddharth Varadarajan, formerly editor of the *Hindu*, who is a senior fellow at the Centre for Public Affairs and Critical Theory, New Delhi, agrees: 'Cronyism and rent-seeking have become an integral part of the way our biggest companies do business – a sort of "capitalism with Indian characteristics"'.[18] Some regard India's drift towards oligarchy as inevitable. Arvind Subramanian, an economic advisor to the Indian government, explains that, in India, 'these are also the guys who are performing. In some cases, they may be gaming the system, but they are also performing despite how bad the system is'.[19]

Patronage is integral to this system. As one prominent Indian businessman admitted: 'Nobody in India has become big without political patronage and support ... otherwise it is difficult in the present circumstances as the system is so cumbersome'.[20]

Unregulated political donations help cement business-government relationships. As the *Economist* has pointed out, money drives Indian politics to an extraordinary degree. Elections have been described as 'a dark sea of liquid assets' as nearly US$5 billion

(2012 estimates) is sloshed around the major parties, mostly as undocumented cash.[21]

As it does elsewhere, lobbying facilitates the contacts between big business and government in India. However, lobbying has remained unregulated. The veil usually drawn around the practice was suddenly lifted in 2007 when officers from the Income Tax Department taped the phone conversations of an individual lobbyist revealing 'an unholy nexus' between politicians, wealthy business-men and journalists.[22]

Not surprisingly, business scandals have been a regular occur-rence. As one newspaper reported in 2010, 'a corruption scandal erupts almost every month in India'.[23] The Adani Group has been at the centre of a number of these scandals.

In this symbiotic relationship between business and govern-ment, the environment has often been a casualty, because Indian companies can avoid violating environmental regulations by making donations and using the court system to their advantage. Ultimately projects are often assessed as just too big to fail.[24]

These practices were nowhere better established than in Adani's home state of Gujarat.

Friends in high places

From the late 1990s, Adani gained a reputation for his ability to win over people in power. Central to this reputation is the relationship he forged with Narendra Modi, one of the most powerful Indian politicians of his generation. Narendra Modi served as chief minister of Gujarat State between 2001 and 2014, the years during which the Adani Group experienced its most spectacular growth. From a market capitalisation of US$73 million in 2002, the Adani Group was worth US$7.8 billion in 2014. The most spectacular growth in the company's net worth occurred in the first eight months after Modi became chief minister; in that short time net worth tripled.[25]

The Modi–Adani relationship is central to the rapid rise of the Adani Group and its grand plans to develop a major private power-generating company based on imported coal. Unravelling this relationship is therefore crucial.

Modi has been a polarising figure throughout his long career. When he won the prime ministership in May 2014 as head of the Bharatiya Janata Party (BJP), he was widely greeted as ushering in a new era of modernisation in India. Indians, it seemed, had forgiven 'a man with a troubled past'. That past centred around Modi's rise to prominence through his involvement with the muscular Hindu nationalist organisation, the Rashtriya Swayamsevak Sangh (RSS), which sought to challenge both Islam and the West more aggressively; and particularly to overturn the Ghandian tradition of non-violent and tolerant Hinduism.[26] To a young man with little formal education and few family connections, the cultish RSS offered Modi a way to channel his ambition. He became a full-time organiser and, as he rose through the ranks, forged closer connections with the BJP, the major party of right-wing Hindu politics.

The BJP began to wield more political influence during the 1980s and 90s under their slogan 'Say with pride that we're Hindus', and especially in Gujarat, which had witnessed several serious outbreaks of communal violence between Muslims and Hindus. Modi rose on the wave of right-wing sectarian politics. Recruited as national secretary of the BJP, he was appointed chief minister of Gujarat, a position the BJP in Delhi granted him in 2001. With the RSS acting as 'the shadowy soul' of the BJP, it was the first time the ultra-Hindu nationalist organisation had reached the office of chief executive of an Indian state.

Adani's friendship with Modi was forged in unique circumstances, in the wake of the biggest scandal to have engulfed the political leader: the Gujarat riots.

On 27 February 2002, a train carrying Hindu pilgrims caught fire, burning 59 people alive. Subsequent official inquiries produced conflicting findings on the causes of the fire but initial reports suggested a group of Muslims had executed a pre-arranged attack on the train.[27] Retaliation was swift. For the next three days, Hindu mobs rampaged through Gujarat Muslim communities in an orgy of horrifying violence, killing over 1000 Muslims, raping numerous women and leaving 20 000 people homeless; the carnage played out live across Indian television. It was the worst sectarian conflict since Independence in 1947.[28]

Modi's involvement in the riots has also been subjected to varying interpretations of complicity. However, he came under immediate criticism for having allegedly turned a blind eye to the bloodshed amid claims that he instructed police officers not to intervene. Although Modi has denied any wrongdoing and has never been charged over the riots, the outbreak of such destructive violence under his administration meant his image was tarnished internationally and the United States and the European Union blacklisted him for a decade. In these difficult times, Adani was one of the few who offered Modi support.

On 6 February 2003, Modi was in Delhi attending a conference organised by the Confederation of Indian Industry (CII). The audience was shown a half-hour documentary titled *Gujarat: The Sunshine State*. Its pitch was 'the state that runs like a company'. Yet powerful figures in the CII sat stony faced during Modi's address; others openly criticised the chief minister's handling of the Gujarat riots, complaining that the whole of India would be affected. Modi reacted angrily to the jibes, telling the audience, 'You and your pseudo-secular friends can come to Gujarat if you want an answer'.[29]

After the Delhi meeting, a group of Gujarat businessmen led by Gautam Adani and Karsanbhai Patel of the Nirma Group threatened to break away from CII and form what they called the Resurgent Group of Gujarat. Adani played a key role in forming the group. Realising that this was going to significantly weaken the CII, its director-general, Tarun Das, apologised to Modi in what amounted to a humiliating backdown. In short, Gautam Adani saved the day for Modi, who never forgot the people who stood by his side when it mattered most.[30] But, as one observer has also noted, Adani had been consciously seeking out opportunities to develop ties with Modi as soon as he was appointed chief minister.[31] Nevertheless, Adani and Modi found they had much in common as outsiders with limited education but with plenty of drive and ambition.

Modi's pro-business policies produced record growth rates in Gujarat, a program he flaunted to the media as the 'Gujarat Model'. The model's key components have been identified as: extensive resource extraction, access to state resources at 'throwaway' prices to selected business figures, and a lax regulatory environment wrapped up in a brand of authority-driven personality politics.[32] The similarities with Queensland's political system are easy to recognise.

Adani's business plan was an ideal fit for the Gujarat model. It was to bypass the creaky infrastructure of the Indian state as much as possible by developing an integrated corporation built around a privately owned port facility which would land massive amounts of imported coal that, in turn, would be fed into Adani's own power plants. Adani's plan to pursue private power generation was fostered by the policy of economic liberalisation; private investment was seen as the only way to meet the needs of the economy as it continued to industrialise. The policy was further bolstered by the Indian government's visionary scheme, proclaimed in 2005, to electrify all of India's widely scattered 640 000 villages. Before the scheme, electrification was occurring at a snail's pace. For years, the large number of unlit Indian villages served as a reminder of the nation's lack of development:

> As the twilight fades over the tiny village, the kerosene lamps
> are lit and mosquito nets are hung over beds in the open air.
> The 55 villagers on the islet of Vali Tapu – which sits in the
> middle of the lily-covered waters of Kanewal Lake – might be

just 100km from India's industrial powerhouse of Ahmedabad, but they still live in the dark age.[33]

In fact, Modi says that when he first became chief minister ordinary people expected little more of him than electrification so that they didn't have to eat in the dark.[34]

Gautam Adani seized the opportunity. It appealed to both his entrepreneurial and nation-building instincts. With rights over coal mines in Indonesia to feed his hungry power plants and keep his private port bustling with activity, Adani had built something unique in the modern, global economy: a vertically integrated global supply chain reminiscent of the days when Henry Ford owned rubber plantations in Brazil to supply his car factories in the United States. A redundant model elsewhere in modern economies, it fitted India's 'dysfunctional state'.[35]

Adani thrived in this new environment of rapid development. He had not only found a close and powerful friend, but discovered a skill in networking within government. Over the years, the company recruited state politicians and bureaucrats into its operations and also obtained a controlling influence over the legal system by retaining almost every senior advocate on the Ahmedabad High Court: 'Over 20 lawyers who fought cases against the Adani Group are now on its retainership. There are just three or four lawyers who take up cases against him'.[36]

The need for massive coal imports to build his empire reflected Adani's understanding of how the environment and development collide in India. Even though India possesses the world's fifth largest coal deposits, and relies upon coal-fired power generation, many of these deposits lie beneath forests that are protected and/or populated by tribal groups. Projects commonly become embroiled in 'protests, controversy or violence'.[37]

With tentacles reaching into the power structures of the state, Adani could unleash his ambitions on Gujarat, which was in desperate need of a rescue plan. The remote region had long been known as a backwater, without the advantages of multiple large cities, a large-scale tourism industry or a life-giving river system. Moreover, the rains often failed, giving rise to dust storms that choked the atmosphere. Not surprisingly, enterprising people often moved away.

However, behind the Modi government's PR spin about the 'Gujarat miracle', the reality was more complex. The fast-paced industrial development brought benefits in the form of improved infrastructure, power generation and global trade. But there is a downside and a dark side as well. Persistent claims indicate that influential business figures, including Adani, greased the wheels that powered the model. Some allege that Adani symbolises everything that is problematic about the Gujarat model: 'Adani is blessed because he gets more permissions, and the things he does with those permissions are not taken note of'.[38] Adani, critics complain, leveraged the system of crony Indian politics.

Not surprisingly, Adani has rejected any suggestion that his dealings with Modi's government have been untoward. Responding to criticism, he explained: 'Crony capitalism should not be there. I definitely agree with that. But how you define crony capitalism is another issue ... If you are, basically, working closely with the government, that doesn't mean it's crony capitalism'.[39]

The dark side of the Gujarat Model

Adani, of course, has a point. It is perfectly legitimate for governments to work with business and, as journalist Megha Bahree has noted, it has been common practice for Indian governments to offer benefits to powerful private interests to attract investment.[40] However, allegations of cronyism are inevitable because such largesse exists outside a transparently competitive process and within a system of unregulated corporate donations to political parties.

Adani was one of the biggest donors to the BJP. He gave roughly A$721 000 to the BJP and about A$417 000 to Congress between April 2004 and March 2012, according to an analysis by the National Election Watch and the Association for Democratic Reforms. The Adani Group was not the largest donor to the Modi government. Another Gujarat company unrelated to Adani, Torrent Power Ltd (also a close supporter of Modi), gave A$2.17 million to the BJP and nearly as much to Congress.[41] But as most political donations in India are undeclared, any published figures may well understate the real amount. As the *Economist* commented, the rules that governed contributions have been flimsy 'and ultimately more dangerous. They make it a mystery who pays India's politicians'.[42]

Adani's insider deals

How critical Adani's donations were to the lucrative deals that came his way is, of course, concealed by the lack of transparency in Modi's government and because his policy was, in any event, designed to facilitate development at all costs. Nevertheless, Adani's business empire was kick started by an extraordinarily beneficial land deal courtesy of Modi.

In what amounted to a 'land grab from farmers', laws were introduced to enable the private ownership of pastoral land which, up until then, had been part of the village commons which 'every villager could access and use but none else could own'. Additional legislation diverted access to water from farmers to industry and allowed favoured companies to bypass tender procedures.[43] Modi was 'infamous for bypassing the legislature and showcasing the executive's authoritarian power'.[44]

The scale of the deals is clear enough. The Adani Group was transformed into a powerhouse from the land deals granted by the Modi government comprising leasehold of 7350 acres of land at Mundra in the Gulf of Kutch at very low prices, estimated at A$540 an acre. Adani claims that the land deals at Mundra began under previous Gujarat administrations but independent analysis shows that most of the land was granted from 2005 onwards.[45]

The Mundra port stretches along the coastline for 40 kilometres. On this vast expanse of land, Adani built his cash cows – India's largest private port and a 4620-kilowatt coal-fired power plant, India's largest private plant. Adani's business model had transformed the remote Mundra port region. It has become a hub for Adani's operation of coal-fired power stations around India. Thousands of people are employed on the site, far from any major city, drawn to working for a dynamic company. Housing developments for the employees have replaced the fishermen's shanties. Constructed as gated communities, they include a private school, hospital, health clinic and airport.

Additionally, Adani was granted a Special Economic Zone (SEZ) within the leasehold surrounding his port project to attract export-focused companies, comprising 45 000 acres. Adani was able to sublet some of his leasehold for up to A$54 000 an acre.[46] The SEZ cleared a wide area of land, displacing 56 fishing villages and 126 settlements. At the time of its development, the Gujarat government did not respond to the protests of the local people and maintained that the land given to the Adani group was waste land.[47]

Ahmedabad-based lawyer Anand Yagnik has been fighting cases in the Gujarat High Court and the Supreme Court against the Modi government's allocation of land to the Adani group. According to Yagnik, 'all clearances to Adani were made at a swift pace'.[48]

Adani had to fend off opponents, but these were not the only early threat to the company's plans for an empire based on coal-fired power. Concern about global warming was on the rise in India. In 2009, and in the midst of industrialising the country at breakneck speed, Modi rang Dr Rajendra Pachauri, head of the Energy and Resources Institute in New Delhi and former head of the UN's Intergovernmental Panel on Climate Change, to request a briefing on climate change. Pachauri was suspicious of Modi's motives but nonetheless agreed to hold a two-day seminar for the chief minister and his key advisors. Modi professed to be a changed leader as a result of the briefing. Echoing former Australian prime minister Kevin Rudd's 2007 declaration that climate change was the 'greatest moral challenge of the 21st century', Modi said that 'For me this is a moral issue. We don't have the right to exploit what belongs to future generations. We're only allowed to milk the earth, not kill it'.[49] In fact, Modi promised to transform hot, dry Gujarat into a model of sustainable development. But like Kevin Rudd, Modi would find it difficult to live up to his high-minded rhetoric. Modi's career resonated with Rudd's in other, related ways. Charismatic figures from humble backgrounds, they embodied a pragmatic approach to political problems.

Scandals erupt

It wasn't long before the Mundra port and SEZ projects were engulfed in controversy. In October 2010, and in response to a public interest petition from Mundra's fishermen, who had worked this part of the Gujarat coast for generations, the Gujarat High Court held a public hearing about the environmental destruction that had resulted from construction work. At the hearing, affected villagers exchanged angry words with district officials, accusing them of favouring Adani.[50] In their petition, the 1500 fisher families from the village of Navinal, near Mundra, complained that their daily catch had been affected by the construction activity. In February 2011, the Gujarat High Court called a halt to work at the site because it found that Adani had commenced without environmental clearances from the Ministry of Environment and Forests (MoEF). Hearing the case, the chief justice of the High Court asked, with more than a hint of amazement: 'When the SEZ's environment clearance is still pending, how did they start construction?'[52]

The destruction was widespread. One thousand hectares of mangroves had been removed in contravention of conditions stipulated by the MoEF. The Adani group was accused of 'rampant destruction' of the mangroves, which, as well as being critical to the local fishing industry, were also essential to mitigating the effects of tsunamis, given that the area is situated in a high-risk zone for earthquakes.[53]

A subsequent report conducted by MoEF found that Adani, in addition to contravening a range of environmental regulations, had a cavalier attitude to its responsibilities. Not only were local villagers concerned about the destruction of the mangroves, they complained about contamination from fly ash generated by the coal-fired power plant. The MoEF investigation found that the company was disposing of the ash using open dumpsters and other heavy vehicles on site, without any attempt to curb the generation of dust.[54] The company took a similarly lax approach to monitoring the quality of groundwater. Indeed, 'little attention had been given to their [poor villagers'] living conditions and welfare'.

It must have been a relief to the Adani Group when the MoEF report acknowledged that too much development had already taken place to call a halt to the project. Instead, it called for the establishment of an Environmental Restoration Fund, into which Adani would contribute 1 per cent of the project cost. But the ministry warned that 'the current regulatory system is not able to handle the complexity and size of projects of this nature'. As Megha Bahree wrote: 'With hundreds of millions of dollars already invested ... the question at the time was if Adani's effort had become too big to shut down'.[55]

Compounding its poor image, a state anti-corruption watchdog savagely criticised the Adani Group for what became known as the 'Belekeri port scam'. For much of 2010, suspicious-looking convoys of trucks had been thundering across India to the dusty port called Belekeri, in the state of Karnataka, on India's west coast. Surrounded by hills and known for its beautiful sunsets, Belekeri operated as a private port and was used for Indian exports to China, especially the export of iron ore. Forestry officials had been observing these movements with concern, because many of the mines from which the ore was extracted and exported came from forested areas. In the early hours of 20 February 2010, undercover forestry officer Uday Vir Singh bluffed his way past security guards to discover a substantial amount of iron ore lying around the port without the requisite export permits.

Mr Singh, perhaps, had not reckoned upon stumbling onto one of the biggest corruption scandals in recent Indian history: hundreds of Karnataka officials and politicians were in the pockets of an illegal mining mafia that, over five years, had made profits of US$2 billion or more shipping illegal iron ore to China.[56]

When officials realised that Adani was one of several high-profile companies involved in the scam, police raided the company's offices and took away computers and other documents. In the subsequent inquiry established by the Karnataka anti-corruption office (known as Lokayukta), Justice Santosh Hegde produced a damning report on the scam and on the Adani Group, which was exporting ore from the Belekeri port without a permit. Justice Hegde wrote:

> The Adani Enterprises has paid bribes for getting undue favour for illegal exports. Action should be initiated against the company to cancel the lease granted at Belekeri port. The company should be blacklisted and barred from participating in any future contract, grant or lease, etc by the Government.[57]

Despite the adverse finding, no effective action was taken against the company. Indeed, in 2011, the Adani group entered into a joint venture with the Rajasthan state government's electricity corporation to help meet its growing demands for power. Adani was given a controlling 74 per cent stake in the project. The plant was to draw on the extensive coal fields near the Hasdeo-Arand forest, one of the largest intact forest areas of central India, rich in biodiversity and home to local Indigenous peoples. It also contained an important elephant population which, over the years, had caused friction between locals and the increasingly endangered giants. An elephant corridor was established to enable the two communities to live harmoniously, and the MoEF declared the region off-limits to mining.

The State government overruled the MoEF's recommendation and granted Adani, along with several other companies, permission to clear several blocks of the forest in preparation for mining in a process locals thought lacked transparency. In a report, they claimed that all the coal blocks in the Hasdeo-Arand forest 'were arbitrary and illegal and reeked of rampant corruption'. In fact, the people of the region complained bitterly of their 'horrific' experiences with the mining companies – unkept promises, forcible acquisitions, suppression of opposition and denial of the adverse environmental consequences.[58]

Nonetheless, local residents were sufficiently concerned about the process to petition the state governor, calling for Adani to cancel work on its blocks, only to encounter harassment from local police and 'grossly misrepresented' minutes from meetings that were arranged to hear their complaints. As work progressed on the blocks, residents became alarmed because dirty water from the mine was contaminating water supplies for humans as well as domesticated animals, in direct contravention of environmental regulations.

Eventually, a local activist and lawyer petitioned the National Green Tribunal to halt Adani's forest clearing on the basis that 'the presence of an elephant corridor in the region should have meant that the coal mine should never have been established there'.[59] The Tribunal ultimately upheld the petition calling for a fresh appraisal. Adani appealed the judgment in the Supreme Court and won on the basis that his company's operations could continue while a new hearing date was granted.

Several years elapsed with no new hearing date established. In 2015, the local activist responsible for the original petition lamented that, since Modi had come to power, the Tribunal hadn't been sitting regularly; he reflected that 'companies like Adani who have influence over government, get away with anything'.[60]

As his port and power plant facilities came on stream, Adani became the largest coal importer in India with shipments largely sourced from Indonesia which, through a combination of extensive deposits, cheap prices and lax regulations, had quickly become a major exporter of low-quality thermal coal. But importers like Adani had to turn a blind eye to the rogue nature of Indonesia's coal mining operations, which included large-scale deforestation, water pollution, conflict with local and Indigenous communities and health costs from coal dust. In less than a decade, the largely unregulated industry had become a threat to the national and global environment. However, in 2011 the Indonesian government moved to clean up the industry – introducing international pricing for existing as well as new contracts and enforcing higher environmental standards. Adani was said to be 'severely affected' by the changes.[61]

Adani's Indonesian operations worsened the company's environmental reputation. When one of Adani's chartered ships with a cargo of Indonesian coal sank off the coast of Mumbai in August 2011, the incident revealed the company's lack of oversight of its environmental operations. Little more than a leaky tub, the ship foundered due to leaks in the hull. A disaster unfolded as a large, toxic oil spill drifted towards the mangroves off Mumbai, eventually destroying their ecosystem. But this was just the start of the damage. The ship was carting 60 000 tonnes of coal which now lay on the seabed, creating a continuous source of pollution.[62] Adani did nothing to clean up the mess. As a consequence, five years later the company was back in the National Green Tribunal facing court action and another fine. By 2011, Adani's reputation in India had taken a hammering. According to a journalist with the *Times of India*, Adani was little more than 'a scrappy entrepreneur from Gujarat' with a penchant for cutting corners.[63]

In a short time, Adani had his eyes on the Galilee Basin and the construction of the $16 billion Carmichael mine in central Queensland. It was to replace the poorer quality Indonesian coal, and the increased price Indonesia demanded for the resource. As one commentator has written, Adani 'sees Australia as the true fossil fuel frontier rich with goods'.[64]

An image makeover

As the scandals mounted, the normally reclusive Adani decided he could no longer afford to ignore the public perception of him and the group. So, in July 2011, he employed Wolff Olins, an upmarket consulting firm, to make over the company's image. Charles Wright, a member of the leadership team working on the project, explained to an Indian journalist that Olins was always careful before undertaking corporate brand building exercises 'as we have to be sure that the management is serious as opposed to just wanting lipstick'.[65] Stretching over more than six months, the Olins team conducted more than 60 interviews with the firm's employees, including with Adani himself, before 'getting down to crafting a vision of what the Adani Group should represent'. Wright offered a glimpse into his thinking: 'Gautam Adani may not be the most eloquent of our clients. But he is a rare visionary'.

In February 2012, Wright's handiwork was launched to great fanfare in full-page newspaper advertisements which screamed 'Adani', 'India' and 'Global' to create the image of a company transformed into an Indian multinational with a global reach. The refurbished identity came with a new logo boasting three colours – green, blue and orange – representing its three main businesses – resources, logistics and energy – that morphed into purple, the new company colour. Expert opinion was sceptical about the likely success of the rebranding. Some experts interviewed about the strategy believe that the image overhaul should have actually followed a re-engineering exercise within the group. 'A makeover without credible action is merely cosmetic', claimed Nabankur Gupta, former group president of Raymond Ltd, who is now founding CEO of Nobby Brand Architects. 'The logo change [to Adani Enterprises] should have followed an internal restructuring first. That would have driven home the point better that the group is indeed looking to make a new start.'[66] But Adani wasn't interested in changing his approach, which had helped him forge his way to the top of Indian business circles and so Gupta's point was prescient: the scandals kept coming at regular intervals.

In 2013, local fishermen challenged Adani over another of his ambitious port developments, this time at Hazira, a coal and bulk cargo port also located in Gujarat. The village of Hazira, which contained 80 fishing families – some 300 people – was surrounded by extensive mangroves and was home to critically endangered bird species. Adani obtained environmental clearances to construct the port facilities from MoEF in 2013. Subsequently, the union of local fishermen complained that the Adani development had caused massive destruction of the mangroves and that the port had expanded beyond its original plans. In a case that came before the National Green Tribunal in 2016, the Adani Group was again found to have flouted environmental regulations because it had continued expansion at the port without updated environmental clearances. The Tribunal was scathing in its assessment of Adani; it had proceeded 'undaunted' by the absence of relevant environmental clearances and 'did not care for any adverse order or adverse impact on environment'. Such an 'irresponsible' attitude on the company's part 'must be deprecated'.[67] Adani was given a Rs25 Crore fine (approximately A$500 000).

The Adani Group was dragged back into public hearings over another development at its Mundra site. In August 2013, local villagers complained about the company's ship-breaking facility. Such a facility was potentially environmentally sustainable because the useful materials in the ships were recycled, but the Adani Group approached the project with its, by now, customary disregard for environmental standards. A representative of an environmental NGO attended the hearing and explained that Adani and its consultants were desperately trying to portray their ship recycling business as a zero-waste producing facility, but this was not the case. Effluents and asbestos are an inevitable part of such a facility. The NGO representative questioned the consultants and the company about the different kind of asbestos the project would generate and how they would handle it: 'They had no answer and the surprising part was even the company officials and consultants had no knowledge of the existence of different kinds of asbestos'.[68]

At the conclusion of the hearing, most of the villagers were disappointed with the company's answers.

The pattern of disregard Adani showed towards the needs and interests of local villagers was extended to the Indian labourers who worked on some of the company's projects. A Fairfax Media investigation in 2014 into the working conditions of 6000 construction labourers at a luxury housing project in Gujarat, owned by the Adani family, uncovered lax safety standards, underage workers and regular cholera outbreaks.[69]

Located on 260 hectares on the outskirts of Ahmedabad, the Shantigram luxury estate is marketed with the tagline 'The Good Life'. But many of the workers suffered a shocking life. All were paid well below the minimum wage of $4 a day, but some were not paid at all: 'they are effectively being held in a form of bonded labour'. Widely regarded as a modern form of slave labour, bonded labour is common in parts of India:

'We have not been paid since we started work at the beginning of May', said 32-year-old tiler Bhavesh Meena, who works

10- to 12-hour days, six days a week. 'All we have been given is food expenses of 500 rupees a week [about A$9].'

'Because I have not been paid, I cannot leave until I am paid, I am trapped here', said Mr Meena, who represents a group of 45 workers in the same situation. 'We are arguing and fighting to be paid, but they keep saying they dispute what they owe us, and they never pay us except to buy food.'

One 12-year-old boy from the state of Bihar, who did not want to give his name, said he was paid 150 rupees a day, about A$2.60, to carry drinking water to the workers. He said he worked 12 hours a day, and had only Sundays off.[70]

Adani was found again to be engaged in dubious management practices. By outsourcing labour to multiple contractors, the Adani Group was able to avoid complying with state and federal laws.

Lack of pay was not the only abuse of these workers' rights. The Chief District Health Officer for Ahmedabad, Dr DC Jagani, told Fairfax Media that the living quarters the Adani Group provided for the workers were also inadequate, with poor sanitary conditions leading to multiple cholera outbreaks: 'Because there are no toilets, everyone must practise open defecation, so the ground water that is used for drinking water is being polluted and infected, and that is why we have seen so many cholera outbreaks'.

Adani's reputation for environmental destruction was not limited to India. The company was involved with several Indonesian palm oil growers, becoming one of the largest importers of the oil – a widely used product in food manufacture and consumer goods – in India. However, in 2013, Adani came under criticism from environmentalists for its association with Wilmar, whose operations had driven much of the destruction of Indonesian forests. Greenpeace, which investigated the issue, wrote that: 'Companies such as Adani which has a venture with Wilmar and Ruchi are importing palm oil every year without proper sourcing policy or commitment towards deforestation'.[71]

Adani was untroubled by Wilmar's role in forest destruction because, in 2016, he announced the formation of a joint venture with the company – 'Adani Wilmar'. At the time Adani said that 'Our current partnership with Wilmar has been successful due to a solid combination of Wilmar's strategic outlook and experience in international food business'.[72]

The Adani Group exacerbated its reputation for poor environmental practices in 2013 when it appointed Mr Jeyakumar Janakaraj to head its Australian operations. He had previously been operations manager for Konkola Copper Mines (KCM) in Zambia when, in 2010, the company was not only fined for polluting the Kafue River with toxic waste, but criticised for having wilfully failed to report it. It had disastrous consequences for the region. The pollution, which turned the river blue, left thousands of locals who relied on it for drinking water and for irrigation exposed to contamination. Some later died of liver and kidney disease.[73] In a landmark ruling in 2011, Zambian High Court Judge Phillip Musonda said he wanted to make an example of KCM for their 'gross recklessness'. He also stated that: 'The courts have a duty to protect poor communities from the powerful and politically connected. I agree with the plaintiffs' pleadings that KCM was shielded from criminal prosecution by political connections and financial influence, which put them beyond the pale of criminal justice'.[74]

Companies like Adani no doubt rationalise the process of circumventing environmental laws and regulations because everybody is doing it. Modi acted to keep the nature of his dealings with business figures like Adani beyond scrutiny. He continued to refuse to appoint an anti-corruption commissioner to the agency in Gujarat charged with keeping governments accountable and he passed legislation to render it a largely toothless organisation.[75]

Use of tax havens and scams

The Adani Group's lack of corporate ethics has seen it entangled in several scandals involving alleged tax minimisation and use of offshore tax havens, indicating a persistent pattern of denying the public purse legitimate revenues. Operating in this manner, Adani has been part of a crippling tax minimisation industry that has seen India's leading businesses stash more money in Swiss bank accounts than those from any other country. An inquiry in 2012 by the Indian Finance Ministry was unable to calculate the full extent of the problem, but noted that 'black money' was having a debilitating effect on the country.[76]

The Adani Group has been under investigation for several tax minimisation schemes. One involved the misuse of a government export incentive scheme through a complex web of internationally based front companies to engage in 'circular trading' (that is, between these front companies) in order to artificially inflate exports and then claim the financial benefits arising from the scheme.[77]

In another scam, the Adani Group was one of several companies under investigation for allegedly over-invoicing coal imports from Indonesia, ramping up the costs to ordinary Indian households and siphoning off the money abroad. According to investigations carried out by the Directorate of Revenue Intelligence:

> The modus operandi adopted was to create layers of invoicing between Indonesia and India. Intermediary firms based in Singapore, Hong Kong, Dubai and other locations were deployed to inflate the price of coal in official billing documents … the landed prices per metric tonne of coal imported from Indonesia were roughly around US$50, the declared prices in India were inflated to over US$82 per tonne which was remitted out of India through banking channels.[78]

A different scheme operated in the importation of power plant equipment.

Adani's Australian operations – based around its ownership of its Abbot Point coal port – were structured in such a way as to pay virtually no company tax in Australia. An investigation carried out by ABC economics correspondent Stephen Long discovered a complex web of offshore companies Adani established to run the Australian arm of its business that amounted to little more than corporate smoke and mirrors.[79] These comprised one based in Singapore, where the company tax rate is 15 per cent, which in turn was owned by one based in the Cayman Islands, a recognised tax haven.

Of course, Adani's tax minimisation practices were part of a larger problem of company tax evasion in Australia. In India, the authorities fared little better when they tried to crack down on similar practices. From the time allegations of Adani's tax minimisation practices first arose in the early 2000s, India's Directorate of Revenue Intelligence has been investigating the matter and getting nowhere. The allegations have 'meandered through various tribunals and courts of law', without a determination having been made. The absence of any outcome in the cases against Adani led to further allegations that the Ministry of Finance had been 'dragging its feet'.[80]

The downside of the Gujarat Model

By the end of Modi's tenure as chief minister of Gujarat, his period of administration had been criticised in five separate reports by the comptroller and auditor general – India's top auditing agency – for gross mismanagement of the State's finances, including undue benefits to certain favoured companies, including Adani.[81]

Beyond the cronyism, views are polarised on Modi's achievements as chief minister. Much has been made of the high growth rates under his stewardship of Gujarat and the electrification of all of the state's 18 000 villages shows that there was substance as well as spin behind the Gujarat Model. Yet the bright lights, new industrial facilities and improved highways failed to transform the lives of ordinary people.

'These improvements in infrastructure and governance are mainly for the corporate sector', said Indira Hirway, director of the Center for Development Alternatives in Ahmedabad. 'For other sectors, for the masses, and particularly for the poor, the infrastructure is not doing that well', she said, referring to issues such as drinking water, sanitation and social infrastructure.[82] Other observers agree. 'The dominant pattern is one of indifferent outcomes', writes Jean Dreze in the *Hindu*: 'Gujarat is doing a little better than the all-India average in many respects, but there is nothing there that justifies it being called a 'model'.[83]

Academics have labelled the results in Gujarat as 'non-inclusive growth'.[84] The State's environment was another casualty. As Modi developed his business-friendly model, the Central Pollution Control Board of India declared Gujarat to be the most polluted state in India.[85]

Modi becomes prime minister

Modi barnstormed his way to becoming prime minister in May 2014 in the world's largest ever election. Set against a stagnant economy, concerns about rampant corruption and infrastructure backlog, Modi succeeded in projecting his 'Gujarat Model' as offering a new era for India. Not only had Adani's fleet of three aircraft been placed at the aspiring prime minister's disposal, but as prime minister elect, Modi was photographed waving triumphantly boarding an Adani plane in Ahmedabad bound for Delhi, the company's colourful logo plain for all to see. Somehow, the image and the connections to big business that it revealed were subsumed in Modi's 'shamelessly presidential campaign'[86] in which his charismatic personality was on full display:

> His voice is a tuned instrument that dips conspiratorially, thunders in defiance and shifts to a sincere, matter-of-fact tone when he is doing the successful CEO routine. He seems to embody technocratic efficiency, nationalism and machismo.[87]

After Modi became prime minister, Adani was his constant companion on international visits, the only Indian businessman to be offered such a privilege. They have stayed on the same floor at hotels and eaten their meals together. The prime minister's staff were said to treat Adani 'like a boss'.[88]

On becoming prime minister, Modi adopted the same aggressive pro-growth policies that he had followed as chief minister. In the process he dropped his concern about the moral necessity of tackling global warming. In fact, it was part of a wider process of dismantling environmental protections designed in large measure to pave the way for new coal mines and other industrial projects. He no longer sought conversations about what India planned to do about global warming. Critics allege that his policies constituted a 'war on the environment'. The new BJP government equated fast growth with national pride; human rights and environmentalism were considered 'anti-national activity'.[89] The result was an alarming rise in India's pollution levels, as I discuss in Chapter 7.

From the time he emerged as an ambitious commodities trader in the late 1980s, Gautam Adani's career has been marked by contrasts. His company gained a reputation for delivering large projects on time, which has translated into great wealth for him and his company. As one of the people who have driven the liberalisation of the Indian economy over the past 20 years, he has contributed to that country's emergence as an economic powerhouse. Adani became the nation's largest private producer of electricity generated by coal. Yet Adani's reputation has been tarnished by his brushes with scandal arising out of poor corporate conduct and cronyism. Less widely grasped is his ruthless understanding of power and how it could be harnessed through networking and money; he is a political operator *par excellence.*

Why would Australian governments at state and federal level back such a rogue corporation? And why were his plans for opening up the Galilee Basin so warmly received by government and so bitterly contested by environmentalists? Without flinching, Adani walked straight into Australia's coal wars which, by the time he purchased his lease in the Galilee Basin in 2010, had been simmering for more than a decade.

CHAPTER THREE

The coal wars begin

As climate change emerged as a public issue in the early 1990s, the multinational mining corporations operating in Australia moved to shore up political support for the coal industry. They formed strong links with the media and prominent think tanks, creating a recognisable network of power promoting coal. This network was especially influential in the Liberal Party during the prime ministership of John Howard. His election in 1996 ensured that progress on climate change stalled and that fossil fuels would reign as he defended their interests with his trademark divisive politics. But growing concern over climate change ensured that Australia's position as a key exporter of greenhouse gas to the world would be challenged. The coal wars began.

It is impossible to conceive how Adani was both promoted and challenged without an understanding of this context. However, it is part of the story that has been well covered by others such as Bob Burton, David McKnight and Guy Pearse in their book *Big Coal: Australia's Dirtiest Habit* and Clive Hamilton in *Scorcher: The Dirty Politics of Climate Change*.[1] I have drawn upon these works to provide enough context to understand the Adani story. The outlines of that story are as straightforward as they are disturbing. From the mid-1990s, a campaign began that sought to promote the continual expansion of the coal industry as being synonymous with the national interest while, at the same time, downplaying the threat posed by climate change and its flow-on effects to the Great Barrier

Reef. The effort to establish this pro-coal regime involved one of the most extensive campaigns of propaganda and lies ever mounted in Australia. Exposing this power network and changing the narrative about coal have been the goals of the climate movement. Adani became a lightning rod in this long battle.

John Howard and the re-making of the Liberal Party

The Liberal/National Party government, led by Malcolm Fraser between 1975–1983, had a record of achievement on the environment. Although predisposed ideologically to support state's rights, the free market over regulation, and development of the nation's resources, Fraser's government was not hostile to environmental protection. It banned sand mining on Fraser Island, ended commercial whaling and established national parks on the Great Barrier Reef in Queensland and at Kakadu and Uluru in the Northern Territory. However, Fraser refused to intervene to prevent the Tasmanian government from damming the Franklin River, an action which helped elect his successor Bob Hawke in 1983.

Bob Hawke and the incoming Labor government were in tune with public sympathy for using Commonwealth powers to continue the work of protecting the nation's iconic environmental assets – the Franklin River, the wilderness areas of Tasmania and the rainforests of North Queensland. In the process, the government reaped the political benefits of being able to harness green preferences from the newly established Greens party, led by high-profile environmental activist Dr Bob Brown.

The Liberal Party, in opposition from 1983 until 1996, was left to ponder how it might capture a share of the public's embrace of environmental causes. As highly experienced journalist and author Paul Kelly[2] has documented, following the Liberals' defeat at the 1987 federal election, Opposition leader John Howard called for the party to rethink its stance on the environment: 'He wanted a more national approach and a firmer pro-environment stance'.[3]

During his 11 years in office (1996–2007), Howard's rethink on the environment led to significant progress on some national environmental issues. He poured $1 billion from the privatisation of Telstra into restoring the national estate. Negotiations with the Australian Democrats in 1998 led to the passage of the Environmental Protection and Biodiversity Conservation Act, which created a national framework for environmental and heritage protection. He brokered the buyback of large volumes of water as environmental flow for the Murray River. All could rightly be regarded as ground-breaking environmental reforms. Yet Howard is perceived as unsympathetic to the idea that the environment is a core responsibility of government.

In large part this perception is also deserved. His decade-long opposition to ratifying the United Nation's 1997 Kyoto Protocol fostered his anti-environment credentials. In announcing his refusal to support the treaty, Howard explained that his reasons were geopolitical, not scientific; the exclusion of developing countries from the treaty 'would put Australia at a competitive disadvantage'.[4] In 2002, Howard remained defiant in the face of strong criticism after China, Russia, India and Canada promised to sign on, leading to claims that he was slavishly following the American president, George Bush. It was less clear what Howard thought about the science of global warming. However, it is commonly understood that Howard's 'soul mates' were in the Republican party of the United States.[5] From the time of the 1992 Earth Summit in Rio De Janeiro, anti-environmentalism had taken deep root in the right wing of American politics.[6]

A similar hostility to environmentalism started to take hold in the Howard government. Howard gutted the independence of several key environmental agencies: the Australian Greenhouse Office, the National Oceans Office and the Australian Heritage Commission were abolished as independent agencies and, according to critics, became 'shells of their former selves'.[7] Howard's willingness to use the environment as a wedge issue against Labor cemented his reputation as an anti-environment leader. Howard was a tribal Liberal and this dictated that he should 'not resemble Labor in any way'.[8] For him, Labor was not just a political enemy; its very culture was an anathema. Howard wrote that saving old-growth forests – which was one of the important environmental issues of his time in government – was a 'classic case of elite urban opinion', 'the politics of symbolism' and 'feel-good politics'.[9] Howard had added the environment to his relentless pursuit of the culture wars. After his defeat at the 2007 federal election, Howard claimed that 'his conservative stance on cultural issues was one of the most important distinguishing characteristics of his period in office'.[10]

The 2004 election was pivotal in this process. Howard outsmarted Labor leader Mark Latham for the votes of timber workers in Tasmania over access to old-growth forests, sending a broader political message to blue-collar workers across the nation that he stood for their interests against 'greenies'.[11] Howard's legacy was to lay the foundations for the cultural war over coal. Abbott fully realised this potential when he came to power in 2013.

Abbott's views on climate change will be discussed later, but Howard was 'comfortable in the category of being a climate change sceptic', according to his biographer Peter van Onselen, although he was careful not to reveal himself explicitly as a climate change denier until he left office.[12]

Howard, and later Abbott, the two titans of the Liberal Party, were climate change deniers as well as political opportunists. Scholars have devoted considerable attention to trying to explain their anti-climate science beliefs. Howard's Liberal tribalism provides one clue to his mindset.

Howard's 'tribe' of right-wing Liberals views environmentalism and the desire to combat climate change as born of left-wing ideas and a threat to the values of the free market. Consequently, it must be opposed and defeated. Author and commentator Guy Rundle, writing in *Crikey*, calls such thinking a form of 'functional delusion'; Liberal Party climate change deniers know how science works, they know that catastrophic consequences are possible but they can't admit that the green/environment movement is right about global warming.[13]

Howard's anti-environment record was enhanced by the close links his government forged with the mining and fossil fuels sector. The first tangible evidence of the extent of these links emerged in June 2004, when Howard announced a policy white paper, *Securing Australia's Energy Future*, which endorsed coal as Australia's key future source of energy. The policy backed the untested technology around carbon capture and storage (CCS) of greenhouse gas emissions – effectively pumping carbon emissions from power stations and other polluters into holes in the ground – while paying scant attention to renewables and rejecting an emissions trading scheme. This was the position of the Australian Coal Association (ACA), which in the previous year set up a fund based on a levy from the industry of 20 cents on each tonne of coal to boost research into CCS. However, before long, 'financial reality kicked in and the industry turned its eyes to federal and states treasuries'.[14] The ACA lobbied Howard for several weeks to press their position and, as Richard Baker noted in the *Age*, the white paper 'was exactly what the industry asked for'.[15]

The Chief Scientist Dr Robin Batterham provided official advice on the white paper. Appointed to the part-time role by Howard in 1999, he was also chief scientist with Rio Tinto. Although a widely credentialled scientist in his own right, Batterham's continuing links with Rio while he was advising the federal government led to accusations of conflict of interest. Although a Senate inquiry in 2013 found no actual conflict of interest, it did point to the potential for one. It recommended the chief scientist's job be a full-time position under public service rules.[16]

Greens leader Bob Brown told the Senate inquiry that during Batterham's term as chief scientist, the government had cut back funding for renewable energy but had provided $340 million in direct, indirect or enhancing grants to Rio Tinto. Brown explained:

> When you look at the other side of the ledger … you find that
> the well of funding for the sunrise industries for environmental
> technology – which are based on renewable energy serving the
> whole of Australia and on energy efficiency – is basically dry.
> We have seen this extraordinary conjunction of the billowing of
> government largesse directly and indirectly to a huge company
> like Rio Tinto, whose chief technologist is Dr Batterham, at
> the same time as Dr Batterham has been the Chief Scientist
> for the government – whose role is to advise the government
> on the way forward. This gives the appearance of a conflict of
> interest.[17]

There were other concerns that the federal government's policy to lock Australia into coal had arisen out of its close links with the mining industry. The ABC obtained documentation under Freedom of Information (FOI) which showed that the government had stacked its policy taskforce – the Lower Emissions Technical Advisory Group (LETAG) – which produced the policy on Australia's energy future with representatives from the fossil fuels industry while keeping the renewable energy sector locked out of the decision making. The documents pointed out that LETAG was dominated by fossil fuel energy users and producers who worked directly with the government to develop the energy plan. It was not something that the government was keen to publicise.[18] According to notes taken by one of the executives during a LETAG meeting, the Industry Minister Ian Macfarlane stressed 'the need for absolute confidentiality'. During the Howard years, Australia was in the midst of a coal export boom. Driven by rising prices, the value of coal exports increased six-fold, from A$17.1 billion to $110.9 billion in 2011. Its share of the value of total export rose from 6 to 15 per cent.[19]

Through this industry-dominated process, Howard embraced the idea that Australia's economy rested on the supply of cheap fossil fuels and that required 'avoiding cuts in Australia's emissions for as long as possible, delaying as long as possible'.[20]

Indeed, in 2005, Australia's former chief climate change official, Gwen Andrews, former chief executive of the Australian Greenhouse Office, accused the Howard government of allowing the fossil fuel, energy and mining industries too much influence over its policies – including its refusal to ratify the Kyoto Protocol. She told the *Age* that 'she was never asked to brief Prime Minister John Howard on climate change during her four years in the role, at a time when Mr Howard was deliberating whether to ratify Kyoto'. She offered the comment in response to Howard's confirmation of Australia's involvement in a US-led Asia-Pacific coalition to tackle climate change which rejected the Kyoto protocol and instead focused on technology to make fossil fuels cleaner rather than restricting emissions from industry. China, India, South Korea and Japan were also involved. Andrews further explained:

> In my view, large energy, mining and resource interests in
> Australia had a disproportionate effect on government policy
> making with regard to energy and climate change. With
> few exceptions, they had little commitment to the concept
> of sustainable development. The arguments they used to
> influence the Government framed the debate in a way that
> pitted environmental interest against economic interest. Their
> definition of economic interest was constrained to their own
> businesses and shareholders.[21]

In fact, documents obtained at the time by the *Age* showed that big companies including BHP, Rio Tinto and Exxon Mobil 'reveal that the big companies urged the Government to put its faith in technology rather than setting emissions targets'. As journalist Richard Baker wrote in the *Age*:

> Fossil fuel, mining and energy companies are large donors to the Liberal and National parties. Between 1998–99 and 2003–04, BHP Billiton, Rio Tinto, Woodside, Western Mining and Wesfarmers donated at least $1.69 million to state and federal Coalition parties and their associated foundations, according to Australian Electoral Commission figures. Labor's federal and state organisations received $412 311 from the same companies during that period.[22]

Together with the fossil fuel industry, Howard began the process of popularising CCS as 'clean coal technology'. Even the CSIRO was compromised in the process. In 2006, Howard appointed two fossil fuel industry executives to the CSIRO board — Dr Eileen Doyle, who was Chair of Port Waratah Coal Services, and Mr Peter Willcox, who had served as the CEO of BHP Petroleum. Instead of leaving it to the coal industry to fund the technology, Howard poured millions of dollars of taxpayers' money into a fruitless quest. Critics derided the policy as a 'con job', designed to support the coal industry while avoiding putting a price on carbon. According to critics, the government knew that the technology was only in its development phase and that any large-scale application was decades away. Moreover, it wouldn't apply to Australia's, or any country's, existing coal-fired power plants.[23] Lastly, it was unlikely to attract private investment without a price on carbon: 'no sane electricity generator would choose a technology as expensive as CCS in the absence of carbon pricing'.[24] But, with a policy process politicised by the fossil fuel industry, such facts were simply inconvenient. Observing these events, Bob Brown believed that Howard's promotion of CCS 'was a political strategy that served him well … [but] hundreds of millions of dollars of taxpayers' money was poured into a hole in the ground'.[25]

Coal had triumphed inside the Liberal Party. To some commentators the Liberal Party's failure to tackle climate change, and its resort to denialism, represented the intellectual decline of the right in Australia.[26] It had departed from the more liberal tradition of European conservative parties and followed the American Republican party down the road of corporate-backed denialism, and promotion of fossil fuels. Economist John Quiggin argues that denialism in the Liberal Party (and by extension the National Party) brought together several strands of anti-intellectualism:

> For a minority of the do-nothing group, it is simply a matter of financial self-interest associated with the fossil fuel industry. For the majority, however, it is the pursuit of a tribal and ideological vendetta driven by Culture War animosity towards greens, scientists, do-gooders and so on, or by ideological commitment to a conservative/libertarian position that would be undermined by the recognition of a global problem that can only be fixed by changes to existing structures of property rights.[27]

Four interconnected centres of power propelled the Liberal Party in the direction outlined by Quiggin. Together, the mining industry, the 'big four' Australian banks, the Institute of Public Affairs and the Murdoch Press promoted climate change denialism and, more broadly, anti-environmentalism and the coal industry. The deep connections between the Liberal Party and these centres of power – discussed below – were responsible for the transformation of the Liberal Party away from its small-l liberal tradition into a party dominated by right-wing ideology.

The mining industry

The mining industry has a long history of political and cultural influence in Australia. Its power as a lobby group within the political system was formalised in 1967 with the establishment of the Australian Mining Industry Council (AMIC). The intention to lift its voice within government was no accident: a minerals export boom was in full swing and environmental and Aboriginal groups were making new demands on the government. Adopting an aggressive line against both groups, the AMIC gained a reputation for playing hardball politics. Later, the federal Labor minister, Ros Kelly, described the objective of the AMIC as 'one in which the miners can mine where they like, for however long they want ... sustaining profits and increasing access to all parts of Australia they feel could be minerally profitable, even if it is of environmental or cultural significance'.[28] In an effort to improve its belligerent public image, AMIC changed its name to the Minerals Council of Australia (MCA). Sitting alongside the MCA was, until it merged into the larger industry group, the Australian Coal Association (ACA). Together, and as previously separate entities, the MCA/ACA had close links with the state mining lobby groups and especially the New South Wales Mineral Council and the Queensland Resources Council. As a group, they represented the most powerful and politicised industry lobby group in the country; referred to variously as 'Big Coal', and as 'the carbon lobby'.[29]

Just how deeply the fossil fuel industry penetrated the Howard government was not fully revealed until 2006 when the ABC's *Four Corners* showed the documentary 'The Greenhouse Mafia'. It was based on the work of Guy Pearse, then a Liberal Party member and a former speech writer for the federal Liberal Opposition environment spokesman Robert Hill from 1997–1999. Pearse had undertaken the work for his doctoral thesis. He coaxed more than 50 anonymous interviews from key industry lobbyists who went on the record about their self-described 'mafia' representing big business polluters that had got hold of 'the keys to the [federal government's] greenhouse policy car'. Pearse told reporter Janine Cohen that he noticed the favourable treatment given to a powerful group of lobbyists from the high-energy-using industries who seemed determined to undermine the Environment Department and block any greenhouse reforms. Some of these lobbyists were previously high-level public servants in key federal departments who were subsequently negotiating with their former colleagues. It was a process Pearse described as 'playing musical chairs'. As he commented:

> There's no question that the executive directors of these
> associations have been over many years recruited, from the
> industry department in particular but other departments [as
> well], because it was felt that they had a particular advantage to
> offer those industries through improved access to government
> and government processes.[30]

The 1990s marked the beginning of the mining industry's big donations to the Liberal Party, many of them raised by Hugh Morgan, CEO of Western Mining Corporation. Morgan, a pillar of the Melbourne establishment and 'a Liberal Party golden boy', was head of the Cormack Foundation, the vehicle through which the Liberals channelled their donations.[31] Clive Hamilton has estimated that the fossil fuel lobby secretly donated almost $13 million to the Liberal Party before the 2007 election.[32] Morgan was 'a key business sounding board for the Federal Government', and frequent guest of John Howard.[33] Describing environmentalism as 'a dangerous cult' and 'religious movement of the most primitive kind', he was a key part of the business cabal working within the Liberal Party to prevent it from taking action to cut Australia's emissions.

There was much at stake for the coal industry from any moves to cut greenhouse emissions. The super-profits generated by coal exports were potentially under threat from lower share prices.

Consequently, the mining industry prepared for a 'long drawn-out fight' by developing relationships across the political system: the bureaucracy, think tanks, industry associations, scientific and economic agencies and media commentators.[34] The aim was to undermine or stall action on climate change by creating a public discourse that equated the interests of the industry with those of the nation. Australia as a quarry for foreign-owned corporations had to be protected and, in particular, 'coal was non-negotiable'; it had to 'be protected at all costs'.[35]

Morgan founded the Lavoisier Group in 2000, an organisation devoted to climate change denial. Then, in 2011, Morgan was a member of the Coalition's business group advising on its climate policy.[36] Displaying an ostrich-like mentality, the big miners avoided undertaking any studies into the vulnerability of their own operations to the risk of climate change and the need to develop policies that would help them adapt.[37] The MCA was also a lobby group that demanded billions in public subsidies for coal projects.[38] By 2013, these were estimated to be worth $4.5 billion a year – which would be less easy to justify if the industry was on a trajectory towards contraction.[39] As one of the most profitable industries in Australia, it has also received the highest rate of fuel tax credit, rebated at the full 38.143¢ per litre, and so effectively receives its fuel free of excise.[40]

Most of the big mining corporations that donated to the Cormack Foundation were also represented on the board of the Institute of Public Affairs (IPA), the leading Australian right-wing think tank. In turn, the IPA had close links with Murdoch's News Corp. Australia's 'big four' banks were also central players in this network of power. As the coal boom gripped the country from the early 2000s, the banks became major funders of Australian coal mines. They were also donors to the Cormack Foundation. In turn, the Cormack Foundation became the largest single donor to the Liberal Party, siphoning more than $40 million to it between 1999–2017.[41]

The significant links between these institutions enabled the fossil fuel industry to function as a network of power, making it inevitable that the Liberal Party would drift towards a cult-like embrace of coal and a disdain for renewable energy.

The Institute of Public Affairs (IPA)

The IPA has been Australia's most influential right-wing think tank since it was founded in 1943 by a group of prominent Melbourne businessmen, including Rupert Murdoch's father, Keith. Critics allege that the IPA 'was founded by rich men with rich men's interests at its core, albeit with obligatory nods to the national interest'.[42] From the outset, the IPA and the Liberal Party shared the same political DNA. Many prominent party members have, over the decades, also been members of the organisation and served on its board.

The IPA's brief has always been to promote the free market but, since the early 1980s, it has adopted the neoliberal version of capitalism which had become fashionable in Britain and America, pushing for privatisation, lower taxes, small government and deregulation of the labour market and the economy. In the late 1980s, it added opposition to action on climate change to this list. The IPA has not only been at the centre of climate change denialism in Australia, it is credited with having started the movement here. As academic and political commentator Clive Hamilton has recorded, people associated with the IPA travelled to the United States to be schooled into climate denialism by prominent right-wing think tanks and it has 'brought a stream of deniers to Australia'.[43] Although it has always declined to reveal its funders, it was generally recognised that, in the 1990s, the IPA was almost exclusively backed by corporate interests in the mining, tobacco, finance and gaming industries.

The IPA's espousal of climate change denialism was modelled on its American counterparts. The story of how far-right think tanks in America promoted climate denialism has been well told.[44]

However, it is worth recalling that their success was based on manufacturing doubt about the science on climate change, a lesson learnt from the long war waged by tobacco companies against restrictions on smoking.[45]

Several Australian researchers have examined the IPA's symbiotic links to this anti-science movement.[46] Elaine McKewon is among this group of researchers and has documented the IPA's hostility towards the scientific consensus on anthropogenic climate change. She dated its commencement to 1989, the year leading up to the United Nation's International Panel on Climate Change's First Assessment Report, which reviewed the most recent climate science research. In October 1989, *The IPA Review* published an unattributed editorial entitled 'The Green Messiah' claiming that concerns about the greenhouse effect were overstated and moreover, were not based on science, but were religiously inspired. According to the IPA, environmentalism – the so-called 'Green Messiah' – and its offshoot, climate science, filled the void left by the decline of traditional religion. In other words, climate science was just another form of belief. Combined with the claim that the science wasn't settled, the IPA was fashioning powerful, albeit irrational, talking points for the right's war on climate change.[47]

From this point, the IPA's attacks on the integrity of climate scientists became more frequent and direct, especially under the leadership of Mike Nahan, who became director of the IPA in 1995. Borrowing from the playbook of American think tanks, Nahan pushed the sceptical line about the science of climate change while promoting coal at every opportunity.[48] Nahan established the Australian Environment Foundation as an IPA-backed anti-environmental group, the name sounding conveniently similar to the Australian Conservation Foundation (ACF), one of the nation's pre-eminent environmental organisations. The IPA's extremist anti-environmentalist agenda gained an influential foothold in the Australian media, particularly News Corporation.

John Howard was a long-time supporter of the IPA and gave a keynote address to the organisation's 60th anniversary in 2003. After he left office he acknowledged the IPA's important influence on the Liberal Party. He said that it 'contributes very strongly to the intellectual debates on issues, and that in turn has an impact on what attitude the Liberal Party takes'.[49] This rare acknowledgement involved some re-writing of history in that Howard disavowed the IPA's calls for a radical reduction in the size of government. He had been cagey when prime minister about openly espousing climate change denialism, but out of office he 'came out'. In a 2013 speech to the London-based Global Warming Policy Foundation, which despite its name was a fraternity of climate change deniers, Howard not only dismissed scientific consensus on global warming as 'alarmist', he explained that 'he preferred to rely on his instinct, which told him that predictions of doom were exaggerated'.[50] It was a disturbing but revealing insight into the anti-intellectualism that had gripped the Liberal Party.

Towards the end of Howard's period in office, John Roskam replaced Nahan as head of the IPA. He had the classic pedigree for a conservative think tank: a background in commerce and law and close connections to the Liberal Party, together with a stint at global mining giant, Rio Tinto. Described as 'whip smart', media savvy and a zealot about taking the IPA's mission to the wider world, Roskam increased the organisation's profile, membership and media presence. He became the media's go-to spokesperson for the right, especially at the ABC. In addition to promoting the IPA's bag of neoliberal policy positions, Roskam embraced Howard's culture wars and developed close links with News Corps' widely read, and shrill, right-wing columnist, Andrew Bolt, also a vociferous climate change denier. So influential was Roskam in pushing opposition to action on climate change that Liberal insiders claim that he was 'integral in helping fuel the fire that led [in 2009] to Malcolm Turnbull's demise as Liberal leader'.[51]

The roots of Roskam's climate denialism appear to be his fundamentalist belief in neoliberalism: the primacy of the free market, the need to support economic growth and, by extension, opposition to any policies that hinder growth. According to Roskam, climate change was part of an 'anti-capitalist ideology'. Roskam has proved a skilled propagandist.[52] Academic Maria Taylor's research shows that the IPA under his leadership provided much of the 'alternative reality' about climate change; themes that were picked up as talking points by the right-wing media and by Liberal Party politicians: climate scientists were a dissent-stifling elite; climate science was a religion; environmentalism was a religion; and climate science was a left-wing conspiracy.[53]

The Murdoch media

The links between the IPA and Rupert Murdoch's News Corporation added to the tight network of anti-environmentalism that engulfed the Liberal Party under Howard and later Tony Abbott. As previously mentioned, Keith Murdoch was one of the founders of the organisation and Rupert has been one of its long-standing board members. Next to the IPA, News Corporation was one of the most influential peddlers of climate change denialism in Australia.

The *Australian* consistently misrepresented the science of climate change, undermined the credibility of eminent scientists and opened its opinion pages to provide a platform to denialists. Chris Mitchell, who assumed the position of Editor in 2002, had a 'paranoia about all things green', 'a visceral hatred of environmentalism' and a personal sense of mission about 'destroying' the Greens party.[54]

Another critic of the *Australian*, academic and political commentator Robert Manne, analysed news stories and opinion columns to do with climate change published in Murdoch's stable of newspapers during January 2004 to April 2011. He found that, of the total 880 items in the sample, only 180 accepted the scientific consensus and the need for action on climate change while 700 rejected them.[55] A separate study by David McKnight from the University of New South Wales showed that between 1997–2007, newspapers and television stations owned by News Corporation 'largely denied the science of climate change and dismissed those who were concerned about it'.[56]

Murdoch's dominating presence in the Australian media ensured that his company's views helped shape broader public opinion and opinion within the Liberal Party. He had 'a seat at the table of national politics' and political leaders knew the 'raw power' he exercised at election time.[57] In these ways, Murdoch also played a role in shaping the Liberal Party into a pro-coal, climate change-denying party.

However, Howard's willingness to fight for coal, on behalf of the party's backers, ran into some difficult political head winds.

2007: A defining year in the coal wars

The Australian summer of 2007 was a scorcher. Drought had crippled a large swathe of the country's east coast from central Queensland, through outback New South Wales and deep into Victoria. It was described as the worst drought in a millennium. Desperate farmers were going broke by the day and taking their lives in record numbers. Prime Minister John Howard urged Australians to pray for rain. It was also an election year. Despite being in power for over a decade, Howard remained the most potent conservative politician in the country. But his fortunes were waning; longevity was finally eating away at his authority and Labor had a new and charismatic leader in Kevin Rudd, the first in a decade not spooked by Howard's ruthless opportunism.

The drought, which had reduced Australia's economic growth rate the previous year by 1 per cent, had renewed public concern over climate change. The parched landscapes, the drying Murray River and urban water shortages, revealed the uncomfortable truth about climate change that Howard had steadfastly refused to acknowledge with his belligerent opposition to ratifying the Kyoto Protocol. The severity of the drought forced him to declare his doubts about the science of global warming. He was sceptical, he said, about the more 'gloomy' predictions on climate change and 'warned of the importance of not overdoing the link between drought and climate change'.[58] But he didn't say why he departed from the growing body of science that indicated just such a link. It sounded as if he had simply chosen not to believe the science.

Howard was increasingly out of step with the views of most Australians. In 2007, a Lowy Institute poll found 68 per cent of respondents agreed that global warming was a serious and pressing problem, and that 'we should begin taking steps now even if this involves significant costs'. Suddenly, renewable energy 'had plenty of public appeal'.[59] Climate change was set to dominate the lead-up to the election, with Labor announcing a target of 60 per cent reduction in greenhouse gas emissions by 2050. In the rapidly changing political climate, Rudd was looking like a leader for the future and Howard a leader whose time was up.

However, no-one predicted that the debate over climate change would quickly morph into an even more profound political rift over Australia's export coal industry.

One of Howard's first public duties of the year was to award the honour of Australian of the Year on Australia Day. It was an uncomfortable moment for the prime minister because the winner was high-profile climate activist, scientist and author Tim Flannery. A passionate environmentalist, Flannery had the gift of distilling science for a public audience and was unafraid of defending his views. He had been warning about sustainability and the risk of climate change for decades. He was a public intellectual for the environment. Only a few months before he had written an opinion piece in the *Age* in which he had castigated 'the long recalcitrance of the

Howard Government' over climate change; and his pessimism that it would only ever do 'the bare minimum to appease public opinion' because 'it was unwilling to absorb the scientific evidence'.[60] Flannery was a willing participant in the 'media game', aware that his targets were among the nation's big polluters and their supporters in government.

Nonetheless, on the day of the award, Howard graciously acknowledged that Flannery 'has encouraged Australians into new ways of thinking about our environmental history and future ecological challenges'. For his part, Flannery said that the award 'means I have an obligation to the people of Australia to continue the quest to create a sustainable future for our country and for our children'.[61]

Flannery kept to his word. Two weeks later, on 7 February he was invited on to the ABC's widely watched late-night news program *Lateline* to be interviewed by Tony Jones, its articulate and incisive host. Jones began the interview on climate change by placing Australia in the international context: the implications of the 600 power stations China and India had on the drawing board. He then angled towards his most pointed question for Flannery:

> Now, given that Australia sends to China and India huge
> volumes of the coal they are burning, could there be a time …
> where it's no longer in our national interests to export coal?

Flannery didn't blink:

> That time has already come. The social licence of coal
> to operate is rapidly being withdrawn globally, and no
> government can protect an industry from that sort of thing
> occurring. We've seen it with asbestos. We'll see it with coal.
> The reason is that, when you look at the proportion of the
> damage being done by coal now, it is significant, but that

grows greatly in the future. We have to deal with that if we want a stable climate.[62]

Flannery went on to chart his vision for Australia's energy future: replacing coal-fired power stations with geothermal energy: 'There are hot rocks in South Australia that have enough embedded energy in them to run Australia's economy for the best part of a century'. Flannery explained that coal would 'ultimately' have to be phased out but that 'first we need to build a bridge to the new energy future'.[63]

But neither the media nor the two major parties were interested in Flannery's visionary solution or his call for a planned phase-out of coal. Collectively they pounced on his statements as a call to end coal. But as journalist Jonathan Green noted of the media assault on Flannery over his *Lateline* interview: 'News Corp headkickers [had] all the opportunity they needed to take a swing'.[64] Editorials in the *Australian* criticised and distorted his views, and tabloid columnists made personal attacks on his credibility.[65] Andrew Bolt, climate change denier-in-chief for the Murdoch empire produced one of his regular diatribes mocking both Flannery and climate science. Labelling him 'Alarmist of the Year', and 'a shameless exaggerator', Bolt told his huge readership that 'high on my list is having a laugh at Tim Flannery'.[66]

Perhaps not surprisingly, Flannery sensed a conspiracy was being unleashed against him. He told Jonathan Green: 'It's a campaign. No doubt about it. My true opinions are ignored, and the effect is to smear and undermine my integrity'.[67]

The major parties wasted no time in slapping down Flannery's views. Both Howard and Rudd argued that ending coal exports would be a reckless, job-destroying measure. Howard, of course, was tied at the hip to the coal industry even though by the time Flannery sparked the debate, he had begun to shift his rhetoric more in favour of renewables, finally caught out by changing public opinion and Labor's strong pitch on climate change.

Rudd wouldn't entertain any talk against the coal industry. Labor was playing a delicate balancing act – supporting both the renewable sector and the coal industry. Still haunted by the manner in which, in the 2004 federal election, John Howard outmanoeuvred Labor leader Mark Latham to capture timber workers' votes in Tasmania, Labor rounded on Flannery as 'irresponsible', calling his plan to phase out coal 'a recipe for massive job losses'.[68] As the *Australian* noted: 'Some elements within Labor fear that by appearing too bullish on climate change, the party could push some workers' votes towards the economically hard-nosed Howard Government'.[69] Other reports suggested that nervous Labor frontbenchers were insisting that 'the future of the coal industry was safe'.[70] And so Labor continued its own form of dissembling on climate change and energy policy. It remained committed to the coal industry and its continued expansion while pushing renewable energy, as if the two positions were not mutually exclusive.

Enter Bob Brown

On 9 February 2007, Dr Bob Brown, well known to Australians for his decades-long advocacy for the environment, weighed into the debate about coal, issuing a more decisively framed call to phase out the industry. Brown had had a long history warning of climate change and battling the power of the fossil fuel industry since he was elected to the Senate in 1996. In one of his first speeches, he warned of the science showing sea levels rising by one metre, only to be confronted by the sight of both sides of the chamber 'falling about laughing'.[71]

Brown had also observed the insidious influence wielded by the fossil fuel lobby. Every day lobbyists from the various fossil fuel companies flocked to 'Aussies', 'the institutional coffee shop' for federal politicians to gather their thoughts before parliamentary business began. As Brown recalls:

> I would no sooner be sitting down with my coffee than
> there'd be someone sitting next to me. It would be a
> representative from this mining company or that mining
> company. 'Mr Brown we just want to see you about ...'.
> You were caught in the process of them wheedling their way
> in. They are there and waiting.[72]

In 2002, Brown attended the Earth Summit held in Johannesburg. With 65 000 delegates from 185 countries, including 100 heads of state, it was billed as the biggest international conference ever held. There was also a strong presence from multinational corporations. The aim of the global gathering was to reach agreements on ways to reconcile economic growth with sustainable development. Brown hoped to influence Australia's voice towards adopting an agreement to phase out the use of coal in favour of renewable energy.

On the flight over to Johannesburg was Mitch Hooke, the chief executive officer of the MCA. Striding out of first class down to Brown in economy, he was an imposing figure both physically and by reputation. Hooke had just joined the MCA, but he had been prowling the corridors of power for two decades 'defending some of Australia's most powerful vested interests against the onslaught of public opinion, twisting the arms of politicians for favourable treatment on tax, regulation and subsidies'.[73] Tall and square-shouldered, he had 'a face that looks like it's been carved out of stone and a handshake that could crush a walnut', and he liked to pepper his conversation with swear words and sporting analogies.[74] With his hand on the back of Brown's seat he said, 'Why are you wasting your time [pushing for renewable energy]; we've got this all stitched up'. He explained that he had ensured that the Howard government would work to block any progress on this issue. And, 'with a big self-satisfied smile', he trundled back to first class. The dynamics of how Hooke and Howard's Environment Minister David Kemp teamed up with other forces at the summit is beyond the scope of this work. But the end result was clear, as Bob Brown explained: 'Mitch was right. There was no progress at the summit on renewable energy'.[75] Non-government organisations cried that the summit was 'the worst political sell-out in decades'.[76]

Brown was therefore well aware of how effectively the political wagons circled the fossil fuel industry when it was publicly challenged. But straight after Flannery's entry into the debate, he had another tilt. In an article he wrote for the *Australian* titled 'Kick the Coal Habit', Brown began by pointing out the inherent contradiction of the prime minister's earnest efforts to save the Murray-Darling river system and the continuation of the coal industry.[77] Unless the nation helped tackle the worldwide pollution from burning coal, he said, politicians were wasting their breath trying to save the river system. There was, he continued, a 'simple inconvenient truth for politicians: Australia cannot address climate change without reducing our coal exports and emissions'.

Brown called on whichever party was to win the 2007 election to commit to a plan to phase out coal exports. He was careful to specify what he meant: 'That plan must be in place by the end of the next term of government ... It might take decades for the task to be completed, but the scientists are telling us that we must start immediately'. He took a swipe at both parties for 'hiding behind jobs' as an excuse for inaction. Governments, he said, have slashed jobs when they thought it was justified. And the major parties were 'living in fairyland' if they thought 'they can have an emissions trading scheme that cuts emissions and protects the coal industry'. Summing up, Brown wrote that: 'There is no doubt that the transition away from coal will be bumpy, but it will pale into insignificance if we leave the world of our children to the economic and environmental damage of coal-boosted climate change'.[78]

Brown later explained that the transition out of coal needn't be too disruptive. 'We're a wealthy country', he said, 'we can look after the miners'.

Not surprisingly, Brown fared no better than Flannery in engaging either the media or the major parties in the substance of the argument. Both 'verballed' his call for a long phasing-out period for coal, re-labelling it as a call to end coal within three years. On other occasions when Brown tried to raise the future of the coal industry he knew he was 'crossing a no-go zone' and that he'd face a hostile reception from News Corporation newspapers across the country; 'they battered me all over the place'.[79] Like Flannery, Brown saw News Corporation's support for the mining corporations as a process of 'corporate bonding'; 'they have to look after each other'.[80]

As the experience of both Flannery and Brown showed, the major parties spurned debate about the future of the coal industry. Both high-profile figures called for a long-term vision, consistent with the science on climate change. Both had their arguments misconstrued and slapped down. Idealists no doubt, Flannery and Brown's advocacy for a post-coal future was a reminder that 'the great milestones of civilisation always have the whiff of utopia about them at first'.[81]

However, the tide of events forced Howard's hand on an emissions trading policy. He announced that he would take such a policy to the 2007 election in order to match Rudd's commitment. But Howard didn't believe in the policy he presented to the people. After he lost office, the former prime minister recanted his support for the policy, conceding that it had been adopted for political reasons and that there was no longer the need for it.

The mining industry must have been worried about the drift in public debate about the future of the coal industry because in March 2007, the NSW Minerals Council spent hundreds of thousands of dollars on a TV, print and billboard campaign extolling the virtues of mining under the slogans:[82]

The coal wars begin

Jobs brought to you by mining.
A cleaner future. Brought to you by mining.
Life: brought to you by mining.

They need not have been so concerned.

CHAPTER FOUR

Coal nation:
The triumph of coal over climate

In the 2007 federal election, Kevin Rudd was unstoppable. He blitzed the November election with his chirpy personality, wonkish interest in policy, inexhaustible energy and a snappy advertising pitch – 'Kevin07'. And he had a personal story of struggle against early hardship that touched many Australians. He appeared to be an authentically modern Labor figure. Rudd's commitment on climate change was integral to his success over John Howard, and among his first acts as prime minister he signed the Kyoto Protocol. Yet, three years later his reputation was shredded when he postponed any action on introducing an emissions trading system. 'If there was a single moment when faith gave way to disillusionment', Michael Gordon wrote in the *Age*, 'it was when [Prime Minister] Rudd walked away from his response to climate change … [having] dubbed it the greatest moral challenge of our time'.[1] His decision strongly gave the appearance of a leader who did not have the very moral convictions he sought to invoke. Much ink has been spilled accounting for his change of heart and the dire consequences it had for climate politics in Australia. Indeed, Rudd's failed prime ministership quickly became enveloped in what journalist Paul Kelly has described as 'a truly tragic tale of a leader with the potential to become a great prime minister brought undone by his flaws'.[2]

Rudd might have been a flawed leader, as many have attested, but there is a parallel, and less recognised, story to his and Labor's response to climate change. Rudd was captive to the same forces that drove Howard's pro-coal agenda. Under his and later Julia Gillard's prime ministership, Labor supported expanding the coal industry as a national policy goal. Labor was responsible for the decisions that helped turn the Great Barrier Reef into a 'coal super highway' and it was Labor that approved the expansion of the Gladstone and Hay Point coal ports, crucial to the coal boom. And Labor turned a blind eye to the emerging dangers to the Great Barrier Reef from climate change and port development. While this pro-coal framework reflected Labor's traditionally strong links to mining unions, it is only part of the story; Kevin Rudd tied the Labor Party to the twin agendas of the fossil fuel industry and the mining union. The Construction, Forestry, Mining and Energy Union (CFMEU), which backed action on climate change, nonetheless forecast the continued expansion of the coal industry over the forthcoming decade, predicting jobs would grow by 55 000.[3] Despite its reputation for lawlessness, the CFMEU 'wields significant influence in both the union movement and the Labor Party'.[4] Criticised by the Greens for not advocating strongly enough for a transition for their members away from coal into renewable energy, the union is unapologetic about protecting jobs in the resource-based industries.

Rudd revealed the depth of his commitment to these agendas while he was still Opposition leader. In February 2007, he announced Labor's 'clean coal' policy: $500 million of public funds would go towards carbon capture and storage (CCS), the experimental technology promoted by the coal industry. The policy appeared to be a political strategy to compete with Howard, who was strongly endorsing this technology. Greens leader Dr Bob Brown derided Labor for getting 'caught in Howard's potentially dead-end strategy'[5] and the *Age* maintained that the policy showed Labor's real colours: 'Labor has sought to dump its environment-before-industry image by announcing new measures to help make coal environmentally friendly and protect coal industry jobs'.[6] The Howard government responded by calling Rudd's policy a 'copycat' initiative. Yet Rudd's embrace of CCS was 'the key to two of his government's big aims: joining a successful international fight to reduce global warming and continuing to be the world's largest exporter of coal'.[7]

Once elected, Rudd quickly showed the extent of his support for the coal industry. His much publicised 2020 Summit, held over 19–20 April 2008, was designed to be an 'ideas fest' to unleash bold initiatives for shaping Australia's future policy agenda. But its deliberations on climate change were heavily criticised for being 'hijacked' by the coal industry.

Anna Rose was one of the youth delegates to the summit and was allocated to participate in the climate change sub-group. She was extremely surprised to find that she was a lonely voice:

> I found myself in the climate stream with representatives of coal
> mining companies including Xstrata and Shell, yet not a single
> person from an environmental Non-Government Organisation.
> No-one from Friends of the Earth, the Australian Conservation
> Foundation, Greenpeace, Climate Action Network Australia
> or any of the State Conservation Councils. These are the
> organisations – the movement – who put climate on the
> agenda, and who did all the groundwork to make last year's
> election the world's first climate election. Why on earth would
> the coal industry be represented but not the climate movement,
> in the 'climate' stream of 2020?[8]

Rose claimed that it was clear from the outset that members of the coal industry and their 'business as usual allies' had a predetermined position to push for clean coal and more subsidies.

It was a view shared by Ben Cubby, who covered the summit for the *Sydney Morning Herald*.[9] He wrote that without any representative from the environment movement, discussion at the summit, even on relatively straightforward issues such as cutting energy use, 'met obstacles'. Summit participant Peter Coates, the chairman of mining giant Xstrata, strongly argued that as climate change became more of a reality, energy use would have to increase to help fill the gap in world food shortages and he called for 'a level playing field' for CCS technology.

With loud voices from the mining industry, and with no designated representatives from the environmental movement, the summit fizzled out as a forum to generate new ideas for tackling climate change. The status quo prevailed: transitioning away from coal mining was seen as a bad idea. There was no impetus from the government to alter this outcome. Climate Change Minister Penny Wong chaired the climate change session with Rudd observing part of the proceedings quietly from the back of the room.

The lobbying witnessed at the 2020 Summit did not let up. The *Age* reported on 10 May 2008 that some of the most powerful men in Australia, the leaders of the nation's booming coal, gas and oil companies, had been knocking on Senator Penny Wong's door or using their lobbyists to shape the Rudd government's agenda. They didn't want to wear the cost of taking action on climate change or see the value of their companies' share prices fall as a consequence.[10]

Rudd, who had by now decided that CCS 'was vital to Australia's interests', proposed a bold initiative in September 2008 with the establishment of the Global Carbon Capture and Storage Institute. It had a budget of $300 million to promote CCS projects worldwide. The prime minister summoned business leaders to Canberra for a 30-minute presentation where he unveiled his plan:

> Many were nonplussed, unsure about its aims or how it would
> be different from the CO_2 co-operative research centre set
> up under the Howard government (with almost $50 million
> in federal funds), Dick Well's National Low Emissions

Coal Council ($400 million in federal funding) or another international body set up by the US, the Carbon Sequestration Leadership Forum. 'I still have no real idea how it will work or what it will do', one chief executive said at the time.[11]

The Institute's 78 staff, based in Canberra, travelled the world seeking out projects, most in Western countries, to help fund. It was never clear why Australian taxpayers' money was to fund projects in other wealthy countries, other than the fact that Rudd had committed to making the technology work to shore up the future of the Australian coal industry. But few bothered to question why government, and not the coal industry, was spending good money after bad. It took the little-read *Green Left Weekly* to provide the pithy answer: 'The big coal industry is loath to put much money into CCS for a very good reason. It is not so stupid as to fall for its own propaganda'.[12]

In September 2009, the ABC's *Four Corners* devoted a program to CCS. Reporter Liz Jackson spoke to Howard Herzog, the principal research engineer at the Massachusetts Institute of Technology and expert in CCS technology. Jackson asked, given the progress of the technology, what were the chances CCS would achieve significant reductions in global emissions? 'Zero', Herzog said.[13] This didn't stop the Australian Coal Association (ACA) from promoting the technology on its slick website, featuring video grabs of CSIRO experts mixed in with industry spokespeople; the respected scientific agency was showing the impact of its politicisation since the Howard government.[14] By 2012, millions had been squandered and the Institute had little to show for itself. It was a dud. So, many thought, was Rudd's commitment to climate change.

By the end of 2009, and with the Copenhagen Climate talks looming, Rudd was still talking up climate change as the great moral challenge. On 28 October 2009, he spoke at the Prime Minister's Prize for Science event where he declared that 'perhaps the most wicked problem facing us as a nation and the world at the moment is climate change. It is one of the greatest scientific, economic and moral challenges of our time'. Assessments of Rudd's performance at the climate conference vary. Environmentalist Tim Flannery, who attended the talks, later wrote that Rudd 'worked hard, largely behind the scenes … to secure a deal … and his contribution was highly valued by almost everybody I spoke with'.[15]

Yet Lumumba Di-Aping, the Sudanese chief negotiator for the small African nations at Copenhagen, accused Kevin Rudd of 'leading the world in trying to kill off the Kyoto Protocol in favour of a far less onerous agreement'. He said that within a very short period of time after he arrived at the talks he began to shift his position: 'changes his mind, changes his position, he start[ed] acting as if he has been converted into climate change scepticism. All that Australia has done so far is simply not good enough'.[16]

In any event, the Copenhagen talks failed. Rudd faced his next challenge of what to do about Labor's emissions trading legislation, the Carbon Pollution Reduction Scheme (CPRS), which, in December 2009, had twice failed to pass the Senate. The politics surrounding the scheme don't need re-telling here beyond drawing out the point that Labor had bent over backwards to support polluting industries when it designed the scheme. Under the proposed legislation, the government declared it would reduce greenhouse gases by 5 per cent by 2020 and by 15 per cent if there was an international agreement, well below the 25 per cent recommended by economist Professor Ross Garnaut in his report to the Labor government, which also recommended that no free permits to pollute be given to the big polluters. Yet their fingers were all over the draft legislation.

The mining lobby led a well-funded and aggressive campaign against the CPRS highlighting their deeper involvement in the political process. Heading the campaign was Mitch Hooke, director of the Minerals Council of Australia (MCA), who was unapologetic about the industry's muscular approach. 'The new paradigm' of politics, he commented, 'is one of public contest through the popular media more so than rational, effective, considered consultation and debate'. The mining industry, he further explained, 'must spend accordingly'.[17]

Sounding much like he had resorted to the time-worn technique of propaganda, Hooke's tactic was devastatingly effective. The CPRS, he banged on relentlessly, would be a job killer, a claim roundly criticised by a range of experts.[18] Nevertheless, it scared Labor. As one senior minister complained: Hooke's 'doing doorstops every day bagging the crap out of us'.[19]

The MCA's campaigning was backed up by the ACA. It secured financial backing from the world's largest coal companies to run a multi-million-dollar advertising campaign against the CPRS titled, 'Let's cut emissions not jobs'. The campaign was devised by Crosby Textor, a prominent political consulting firm with strong links to the Liberal Party.[20]

The extent of the big polluters' influence caused an outcry in the progressive media. Writing in *New Matilda*, Ben Eltham expressed his impatience with the influence that industry was exerting on the Rudd Government:

> Can you or I get a face-to-face meeting with … Resources and Energy Minister Martin Ferguson to argue that we shouldn't have to pay for the pollution of big corporations? No, I didn't think so. But if you're Don Voelte of Woodside Petroleum, Ferguson will hop in a plane and come to you, no doubt to discuss how the Government will adjust the CPRS to make sure your multi-billion dollar LNG projects will magically qualify as 'emissions-intensive trade-exposed industries'.[21]

Tony Abbott and the triumph of Liberal Party denialism

As Rudd's efforts to promote both coal exports and climate change came under increasing strain, Tony Abbott became Liberal Opposition leader in a move that dramatically changed the future of Australian politics. On 1 December 2009 he defeated high-profile moderate leader Malcom Turnbull. The hard-right faction of the Liberal Party had thrust Abbott forward, disgusted by Turnbull's willingness to negotiate a deal with the Rudd government to put a price on carbon.

As Paul Kelly has vividly recounted, the bitter leadership struggle between Abbott and Turnbull was a contest for the identity of the Liberal Party.[22] Turnbull had been judged as 'too green' for the party and his 'folly' of negotiating action on climate change with the Rudd government risked sinking the party into a quagmire of 'disunity, indiscipline and bitterness'. Party insiders even forecast a potential split in the party. By contrast, Abbott's leadership offered the party the promise of restoring unity but at the cost of its already damaged credentials on climate change and environmentalism more broadly. With Abbott and the right-wing faction in the ascendency, the Liberal Party became a party of ideological extremism.

With his swaggering gait, barking laugh, blokey manner and stilted body language, Abbott was an unlikely political leader. He had long been seen as too erratic, conservative and unpopular to lead the Liberal Party. But what he lacked in charisma and mainstream appeal, he made up for in ambition and ruthlessness. Abbott was a quintessential political animal.

Abbott had supported Turnbull's approach of negotiating a price on carbon with the Rudd government but claims to have had a defining moment in his decision to abandon the idea. The circumstances were anything but auspicious.

On 1 October 2009, Abbott strode into a local hall in the small Victorian town of Beaumont to address the Liberal Party faithful. He was exhausted, and prone to making one of his unscripted comments; the ones that regularly attracted a headline and got him into trouble. As he lumbered through his 20-minute address, some of the faithful began nodding off until he threw out his line that 'climate change is complete crap'. Spontaneous applause erupted, crystallising Abbott's thinking on the issue. The next day in the car on the way back to Melbourne, he rang senior Liberal Nick Minchin and reported his feeling that 'the politics of this issue has really changed'.[23] Two months later Turnbull was overthrown. When questioned by journalists after he became Opposition leader about his comment, Abbott tried to walk back from it, saying that it was not 'his considered position' and 'a bit of hyperbole'.

The story embodies the baffling contradictions that lie at the heart of Tony Abbott the politician. Is he the committed conservative ideologue, or the devious opportunist willing to say anything to please an audience or grab a headline? Abbott has been, and continues to be, one of the most polarising politicians of his era and one of the most psychologically analysed. His own failed prime ministership would end in 2015 when Turnbull turned the tables on his nemesis, and has further polarised opinion about his true makeup and motivations. To his band of loyal, right-wing friends he is a complex and misunderstood figure. He is a cult hero to the right-wing commentariat for the way he trumpets climate change denialism. What motivates Tony Abbott is the subject of continuing intrigue. However, I would argue that his statements and actions on the environment reveal the competing forces in his makeup. Abbott blended the political tactics of obfuscation, opportunism and populism with a core commitment to right-wing anti-environmentalism.

All elements were on display in the leading role Abbott played in Rudd's abandonment of his policy on emissions trading. In April 2010, the prime minister rejected the option of holding a double dissolution election on the issue and effectively abandoned his policy. As Philip Chubb pointed out in his extensive examination of the collapse of the CPRS, Rudd was cowed by Opposition leader Tony Abbott, who in 2010 had released the Liberals' 'Direct Action Plan' to reduce carbon emissions which, instead of a charge on big business, proposed establishing a $3 billion fund to incentivise big polluters to tender for government funds to reduce their carbon output. Abbott used this difference in approach to target Labor:

> Abbott was running hard on what carbon pricing would do
> to the cost of living … 'the Coalition's direct action plan is
> careful, costed and capped' while the government's approach
> was a 'great big tax on everything'. He said it again and again.
> He was attempting to spook both Rudd and voters, and he was
> spectacularly good at it.[24]

Much has been, and should be, made of Abbott's long record of climate change denialism and his parallel record inside the party of swapping sides on emissions trading. After losing the leadership, Turnbull publicly castigated Abbott's 'weathervane' approach to the policy issue. Nonetheless, Abbott forged his leadership of the party by reversing his stance – henceforth he moderated his climate change denialism in order to dampen concerns in the broader community about the issue, while hardening his opposition to any scheme that put a price on carbon.

However, too much focus can be placed on trying to explain Abbott's contortions on climate change. The Liberal Party was overwhelmingly an anti-environment, anti-science and anti-climate change party by the time Abbott came to lead it. In fact, when he prevailed by the narrowest of margins over Turnbull for the leadership, he offered a secret ballot on the government's emissions trading scheme and the vote to oppose it was carried by 55 votes to 29.[25]

Thus the role played by high-profile climate change denialists including Nick Minchin, Cory Bernardi, Eric Abetz and Kevin Andrews in overthrowing Turnbull has tended to overshadow the extent of the opposition to action on climate change inside the Liberal Party. Support had been waning for years as moderate Liberal Chris Puplick, Liberal spokesman on the environment in the late 1980s and early 1990s, has observed. He claims that the Coalition parties have been in 'full retreat' on climate change since he developed a progressive response for the party to take to the 1990 election and that the party has increasingly come under the sway of the political and religious right: 'Over the course of the last 20-odd years, the Liberal Party has become anti-intellectual. It has moved away from issues of evidence and has become increasingly anti-scientific'.[26] The few prominent advocates for action on climate change in the party, including Greg Hunt, Joe Hockey and Malcolm Turnbull, either quietly repudiated their views or fell silent.[27]

Informed outsiders who had contact with the party during the Abbott years also observed this deepening reactionary culture. Renowned James Cook University coral reef scientist Charlie Vernon visited Canberra many times to brief politicians about the health of the Great Barrier Reef and was blunt in his assessments of the Liberal Party. 'I spoke in Parliament House in Abbott's time', he told a journalist, 'and there was just wall-to-wall denial about climate change, except for Malcolm Turnbull'.[28]

A study undertaken around this time by Queensland University's Institute of Social Science Research further confirmed the extent of climate denialism in the Liberal Party. It surveyed 300 federal, state and local government politicians. Asked whether the planet was warming because human activity was producing greenhouse gases, 98 per cent of Greens said 'yes' compared with 89 per cent of Labor, 57 per cent of non-aligned politicians and 38 per cent of Liberal–National party politicians.[29] Embedded in the latter group were many conservative politicians with crank views on climate change. Prominent among them was National Party Senator Barnaby Joyce, who bought into the 'left conspiracy' rhetoric about climate change, describing it as 'socialist chardonnay rubbish'.[30]

Thus, a culture of anti-science, climate change denialism and anti-environmentalism became embedded in the Liberal Party. It was not a cause of friction between the party's loosely formed factions. As the IPA's John Roskham later explained, half of all federal Liberal parliamentarians remained unconvinced about the science of climate change; these were 'solid sceptics'. The remaining 50 per cent 'feel they need to be seen to be doing something' about the issue.[31] This observation, coming from the person who had helped shape these attitudes, is both illustrative and perhaps self-serving. But even if he overstated the extent of denialism in the party, his overall assessment can't be ignored – almost nobody in the party actively promotes the need for concerted action on climate change.

The mining lobby mounts another campaign

The bruising from Rudd's capitulation on climate change was still a festering wound when the Labor government took on the miners on another front – the huge profits being made during the mining boom and the royalties regime which permitted them. In May 2010, the government introduced its Resource Super Profits Tax, through which it hoped to achieve a fairer distribution of the nation's mineral resources to the people. However, the scheme to reap these 'super profits' was based on a complex formula that defied easy explanation to the public.[32]

The big miners were incensed at this attack on their profits and mounted a campaign to overturn the legislation that mandated the new royalties regime. Run by the MCA and designed by Neil Lawrence, the advertising brains behind Labor's Kevin07 election campaign, the political heft for the campaign was provided by Mitch Hooke. Not one to shy away from a 'shitfight', Hooke had lifted the profile of the MCA with the force of his combative personality. His aggressive $22 million, 53-day advertising blitz helped cement the view that the tax was an attack on the interests of ordinary Australians. It was an unprecedented intervention in Australian politics by corporate interests.[33]

The campaign sent a chilling message to Labor; the big miners would target it at the upcoming election unless it dropped its super profits tax. Rudd's popularity suffered further from the advertising onslaught, bringing to a head the tensions festering in the party over his leadership style. These dramatic events have overshadowed another, consequential, fallout from Labor's attempts to regulate mining industry profits: big miners became major donors to the Liberal Party. At the beginning of the 2000s, political donations from the mining industry amounted to just $345 000. By 2007–08 – coinciding with the election of the Rudd government – the figure shot up to nearly one and a half million dollars. Following the fight over the mining tax in 2010, donations approached nearly $4 million. Over the decade, 71 per cent of these donations went to the Liberals and 81 per cent to the coalition of the Liberals and Nationals.[34] And these donations do not include money donated via the Cormack Foundation. The sheer scale of this involvement in the conservative side of politics raises questions about the extent to which the Liberals had been captured by the mining industry and its pro-coal, climate change denialist agenda.

Six months into his leadership, Abbott showed his ruthlessly pragmatic side. Realising the need to placate voters who believed that Australia ought to take some action to combat climate change, he softened his denialist position. In May 2010, he delivered a speech to the National Business Leaders Forum on Sustainable Development where he honed a new pitch on the issue. He repeated the typical denialist position that 'natural variations in climate have been happening since the beginning of time', but added that 'humans have influenced recent climate fluctuations'.[35]

Like Howard before him, Abbott was dissembling; he remained, like most in his party, a climate change denier. But his newly framed and more cynically nuanced position embodied in the Direct Action Plan enabled the Liberals to appear concerned about climate change while, in practice, proposing to do very little about it. Not only did critics pan the policy as 'paying the polluters', so did former leader Malcolm Turnbull who, from the party's backbench, declared: 'Direct Action is a con, an environmental fig leaf to cover a determination to do nothing' and 'a recipe for fiscal recklessness on a grand scale'.[36]

The revolving door of federal Labor

In June 2010, Rudd was deposed as Labor leader in a 'bloodless coup' that inflicted years of trauma on the party. Although opinion polls continued to give Labor a narrow lead over the Opposition Liberal Party, Rudd's leadership had been destabilised by his abandonment of his emissions trading scheme, the advertising war waged by the mining industry and his own style of leadership, which had alienated key colleagues. But the impact of the $22 million mining campaign was thought to have played a decisive role in Rudd's demise. As Mark Davis wrote in the *Sydney Morning Herald*, 'The campaign contributed significantly to a slump in Labor's electoral standing … prompting Labor MPs to replace Mr Rudd as prime minister with Julia Gillard'.[37]

Deposing a prime minister mid-term set Labor on a debilitating course of leadership struggles as Rudd nursed his wounds and plotted his return. In one of her first decisions as his replacement, Gillard 'determined to square away the miners at any cost' before the upcoming 2010 election and negotiated a watered-down version of the tax.[38] It was a stunning victory for the mining companies.

Gillard faced the electorate in August 2010, returning to office as head of a minority Labor government with Greens support. After the election Gillard reversed her pre-election pledge not to introduce a price on carbon, a change the Greens had forced upon her.

The policy was pitched to the public as a 'carbon tax', even though its scope was limited to the 1000 top polluting companies. But the term 'tax' was a gift to Abbott.

Faced with the charge of a broken promise and selling a tax that few completely understood and many resented, Gillard was in the fight for her political life. A powerful, and by now familiar, triumvirate campaigned against the law: mining companies, the conservative coalition parties and Rupert Murdoch's newspapers. A study found that 82 per cent of articles on the carbon tax in News Corporation's Australian papers were negative.[39] As journalist Julia Baird wrote in the *New York Times*:

> The heat, anger and vitriol directed at her as a leader – and as Australia's first woman to be prime minister – coalesced around the promise and the tax. It grew strangely nasty: She was branded by a right-wing shockjock as 'Ju-Liar,' a moniker she struggled to shake. The political cynicism surrounding the carbon tax certainly reduced Ms. Gillard's political capital, but it was a perceived lack of conviction in the policy itself that damaged the pricing scheme's credibility.[40]

Tony Abbott was in the forefront of the campaign against the carbon tax. Always at his populist best with a defined enemy in sight, he vowed to lead a 'people's revolt' and 'fight this tax every second of every minute of every day'. He continuously attacked the tax almost to the point of inciting hysteria, labelling it as 'toxic' and issuing absurd claims that it would end manufacturing in Australia, reduce living standards, and adversely affect Queensland's coal industry. It was, he said, 'a great big tax on everything'. At one point, he got a rock star welcome from several thousand protesters at a boisterous anti-carbon tax rally outside Parliament House. The chant of 'Tony, Tony, Tony' rose to a crescendo.[41]

Many years later, Abbott's former chief of staff Peta Credlin exposed the opportunism behind Abbott's campaign. Commenting during an episode of Sky's *Sunday Agenda* she admitted: 'Along comes a carbon tax. It wasn't a carbon tax, as you know. It was many other things in nomenclature terms but we made it a carbon tax. We made it a fight about the hip pocket and not about the environment. That was brutal retail politics and it took Abbott about six months to cut through and when he cut through, Gillard was gone'.[42]

By 2010 the fossil fuel power network was firmly ensconced. Labor had been brought to heel and its anti-mining strategy tamed, and in Abbott, the network had the best friend they could ever have hoped for. The consequences would soon prove disastrous for the Great Barrier Reef.

CHAPTER FIVE

Coal before coral:
Sacrificing the Great Barrier Reef

Late in the afternoon of 3 April 2010, the huge, 230-metre-long Chinese bulk carrier *Shen Neng 1*, with 65 000 tonnes of coal on board bound for China, slammed into an area of pristine coral reef, east of Great Keppel Island on the Great Barrier Reef, carving a 2.2-kilometre-long, 400 000-square-metre scar in an area known as Douglas Shoal. Thick black oil gushed from its hull, raising fears that the bulk carrier could break up and cause an environmental catastrophe. A massive salvage operation went into high gear but not before urgent questions were raised about what the boat was doing in a restricted zone of the Great Barrier Reef, 13 nautical miles off its set course.[1]

The political response was swift. Two days after the accident, the then Prime Minister Kevin Rudd flew over the stricken vessel and expressed his outrage over the incident to waiting media, promising a thorough review and calling for tightened regulations governing the movement of ships through the reef.

Greens leader Bob Brown also flew over the area a few days afterwards but chose tougher language to explain the disaster. He claimed that a large number of ships, including oil tankers, were moving illegally through the lane near the Douglas Shoal and authorities were doing nothing about it. It was a view backed up by local fishermen who told the media that they saw one or two big carriers a day move through the area every time they were out.[2] Brown accused the coal industry of turning the Great Barrier Reef into 'a coal super highway'. He called again for 'a radical overview of this huge export coal industry'.[3] In fact, the *Shen Neng 1* was a disaster waiting to happen. Between 1987 and 2009, 600 shipping 'incidents' were recorded in the region, and experts worried about the impact a rise in the number of super yachts visiting the reef and the growth in size of bulk carriers would have in the future.[4]

In October that year, and with the scandal over the *Shen Neng 1* a distant memory for most, Queensland Premier Anna Bligh led a Commonwealth Games bid and trade mission to India where she met with Gautam Adani about his proposal to establish the Carmichael mine. The premier was keen for discussions with the Indian tycoon because, as mentioned in Chapter 1, her government was putting the finishing touches on its *Coal Plan 2030*, a policy framework for the continued expansion of the State's coal industry.

The Plan complemented the industry's ambitious plans to triple its 2010 production levels by 2030 confident that it could exploit the surging demand for coal in Asia. Queensland became the centre-piece of the strategy. An extensive lobbying effort pressed this ambitious expansion on an already sympathetic government. Acting in tandem, the MCA and the ACA had ready access to the corridors of power in Queensland and Canberra. Together they pressed governments to expand coal mining and exports.[5] Aiding their efforts were smaller, but nonetheless, influential groups including the Energy Sullpy Association of Australia, which represented power station owners and the mining-dominated Australian Industry Greenhouse Network. Individual companies deployed in-house and external lobbyists completed what could only be described as an all-out assault to influence government policy.

Bligh no doubt reasoned that her plan for the expansion of the coal industry and the backing it received from the industry was in Queensland's interests, but she went to extraordinary lengths to advance and protect its interests. In 2009 she wrote to Greg Combet, the assistant minister for climate change in the Rudd government, demanding special treatment for the coal industry in the negotiations over the introduction of an emissions trading scheme, an intervention welcomed by the ACA.[6] Bligh also lobbied the Commonwealth to fund a futuristic coal-fired power station in Queensland utilising carbon capture and storage. The $102 million in funding was later squandered when the plan came to nothing.[7]

It was not surprising, therefore, that Bligh welcomed Adani's plans to open up the Galilee. The summary of her meeting with Adani – submitted to Parliament after her return – gives none of the flavour of the meeting. However, it did convey how keen Adani was to keep lines of communication open with her government. He asked for a high-level government contact, and also asked the premier if she would open the company's new office in Brisbane, an offer she accepted.

At the same time Bligh was paving the way for the next coal boom in Queensland, the coal seam gas industry was in a 'cowboy' phase of development in areas overlying the Great Artesian Basin. A Senate committee found 'examples of land degradation caused by seepage from extracted water storage ponds, leaking gas pipes, untreated water seeping into watercourses and erosion caused by poorly installed pipelines'.[8] The pro-development mentality of Queensland (and other resource-rich states) had created a political culture that put a low premium on the environment.

Politicians' conflict of interest over coal

As her government planned the biggest ever assault on the Great Barrier Reef's ecosystem, there was nothing to suggest that Bligh harboured any heightened concern about its fate. In fact, the sheer majesty of the reef was being lost in the dialogue about the mining boom. Bligh was not alone. With coal companies set to ramp up their exports to record levels, mainstream politicians did little to remind Australians what was at stake: the largest coral reef in the world, observable from space, and home to 'a priceless and unimaginably fragile' ecosystem: 30 species of whales, dolphins and porpoises; six species of sea turtles; 125 species of shark, stingray and skate; 5000 species of mollusc; nine species of seahorse; 215 species of birds; 17 species of sea snake; 2195 known plant species; and more than 1500 species of fish.[9] It was left largely to ordinary Australians, environmentalists and those with an economic stake in the reef to argue the case for greater protection from the fossil fuel industry.

However, it was becoming harder to ignore a fundamental question: were governments knowingly allowing corporations to profit from the demise of the reef?

All experts agreed that the outstanding universal values of the reef had steadily declined since 1981, when the Great Barrier Reef Marine Park Authority was established. The authority was charged under Commonwealth legislation to manage the fragile ecosystem within a framework of the multiple users of its vast, snake-like expanse down Queensland's coastline – farmers, urban developers, fishermen and tourists. A combination of threats from these users had degraded the reef, together with an influx from the 1970s on of the coral-devouring crown-of-thorns starfish. But new threats had emerged in the form of climate change and port development.

Alarm bells started ringing loudly in the national and international scientific community about Australia's management of the reef and the emerging threats to its survival. Scientists studying the outbreaks of mass coral bleaching in 1997–98, 2001–02 and 2006 found that bleaching coincided with increases in ocean temperatures.[10] These trends were being observed by the 'godfather' of coral reefs, Charlie Vernon, Chief Scientist with the Australian Institute of Marine Science. Vernon, who discovered, mapped and photographed coral reefs around the world, had a reputation for fierce scientific independence. He'd resigned his position as chief scientist under the Howard government because, as he explained, 'Science was being muzzled. So I left'.[11] In 2009, Vernon presented his findings on the health of the reef to the Royal Society in London with the provocative title: 'Is the Great Barrier Reef on Death Row?' Apologising to his audience for his gloomy forecast, he held little hope for its future.

As Vernon was pronouncing the demise of the reef, state and federal governments were beginning to implement plans to industrialise the iconic asset. The 'great coal rush' was in full swing with grave implications for the reef. Between 2008 and 2012, Australian and Chinese banks lent $17 billion to expand coal facilities and new liquefied natural gas (LNG) ports along the Great Barrier Reef. Among this lending frenzy was the $1 billion that went to Adani to purchase the Abbot Point port.[12] ANZ, the largest of the Australian lenders, contravened its own corporate social responsibility guidelines which, it advertised, 'will govern our business lending to sensitive social and environmental sectors'.[13]

Gladstone and Hay Point coal ports were expanded and a massive LNG plant was built on Curtis Island. Approvals granted since 2002 by the Howard government and by subsequent Queensland state and federal governments for foreign-owned corporations, including Santos, Shell and ConocoPhillips, to sell all the gas from these plants overseas, rather than reserve a percentage of gas for the domestic market, is another demonstration of the power the fossil fuel industry holds over government. The two governments were warned that problems would arise. Consequently, Australian consumers have been left competing with overseas markets for their own gas, ramping up the price of electricity, leaving the corporations to make a fortune selling at world prices.[14] Fossil fuel companies were simply pursuing their commercial interests; it was up to government to uphold the public interest.

In yet another demonstration of the industry's power over government, the coal industry also had its eyes fixed on a ten-fold increase in the capacity of Abbot Point, north of Bowen. The plans were truly ambitious: to create the largest coal export port in the world, based on the goal of opening up the Galilee Basin. The Queensland government and its North Queensland Port Authority, together with some of the biggest mining companies in the country, including BHP Billiton, Clive Palmer's Waratah Coal, Gina Rinehart and her partner GVK and, of course, Adani Mining, actively pushed for approval for this development. An Abbot Point Working Group was formed under the direction of BHP Billiton. It commissioned its own study of the environmental impacts of large-scale expansion at Abbot Point which, contrary to all other scientific advice, found that there was no substantial risk of lasting damage to the reef.[15] Shipping through the reef was set to increase four-fold between 2012 and 2032. All this expansion required major dredging operations.

These far-reaching plans for the Great Barrier Reef rarely got heard above the noise generated by federal politics and especially around Labor's ongoing leadership squabbles.

Labor's plans to industrialise the Great Barrier Reef

The Gillard government lost no time in signing off on the fossil fuel industry's plans to industrialise the reef. Heading this assault was Labor's Environment Minister, Tony Burke.

Burke had strong environmental credentials in his background. Although part of the tribal NSW right-wing faction of the Labor Party, he was part of a 'new breed of right wingers' who coalesced around Rudd's leadership aspirations in the lead-up to the 2007 federal election. He combined his interests in social justice and human rights with the environment. Before coming into government in 2007, he was an active member of the Wilderness Society and had campaigned to preserve the Daintree rainforest in North Queensland.[16] He had also learnt 'the fine art of persuasion' as a university debater and was a recognised expert in the modern art of political communication and advocacy, having established a consultancy in the field before entering politics. With his smooth, modulated voice, Burke was a polished performer. But how far was he prepared to use these skills to protect the Great Barrier Reef?

With conflict between development and the environment sparking debate on issues across the country, Burke was interviewed at the beginning of 2012 on his commitment to the environment. His values remained constant, he explained: "'It is effectively the same question", he says. "How can you make sure any developments are sustainable, sensitive to the environment and are not something we are going to look back on in 20 years' time and say, 'Why did we do that?'"'.[17] It was not quite so straightforward, argued journalist Graham Lloyd, who interviewed the minister for a profile piece. 'Labor still wears an environmental coat', Lloyd explained, 'but its core message these days is jobs and economic development'.[18]

Burke embodied Lloyd's summation of Labor's contradictory stance on the environment. The minister was quick to criticise the Queensland government's enthusiasm for developing coal ports along the reef, while failing to acknowledge federal Labor's own commitment to what environmentalists claimed was its rapid industrialisation. Prime Minister Julia Gillard embodied the same contradiction. While she had staked a great deal of her political capital on working with the Greens to introduce the controversial carbon tax, at the same time, she leapt to the defence of her government's ambitious plans for the coal industry.

Not all of federal Labor's approvals for coal projects can be discussed here. However, it is worth mentioning Burke's approval in NSW of the controversial Whitehaven Maules Creek mine, one of the largest coal mines in Australia, in the environmentally sensitive Leard Forest. Approval for the three open pit mines in the complex were fast-tracked against fierce opposition from locals who were worried about the transformation of their farming community 'into an industrial zone'. The mine threatened underground water supplies, large quantities of which were granted to Whitehaven, and it would lead to a deterioration of air quality in the region from coal dust.[19]

It was not surprising, therefore, that federal Labor backed industrial-scale development for the Great Barrier Reef. However, it seemed to take no account of critics' concerns about its potential impact. 'The sheer size and speed of port and associated development along the reef coast is unprecedented', noted the Australian Marine Conservation Society's campaign director, Felicity Wishart.[20]

Indeed, in 2011, Burke had signed off on the dredging at Gladstone Harbour, situated next to the reef, in an operation which became the 'ground zero' for poor reef management. The state and federal Labor governments insisted tough environmental regulations were in place for the operation. Most of the dredged seabed was to be contained behind a giant bund wall in Gladstone Harbour; the rest was to be dumped at a site just 400 metres from the Great Barrier Reef Marine Park. Soon after work was completed, fishermen and environmental activists reported diseased fish and mass deaths of marine life, including turtles, dolphins and dugongs. A report into the disaster, completed several years later, confirmed what locals had long known: that the bund wall design was flawed and it had leaked toxic sediments into the harbour.[21] The report was scathing of the federal Environment Department. The conditions the department set for the project were too vague to be enforced; the design of the bund wall didn't conform to world's best practice; and the department failed to adequately retain compliance records. As a consequence, the fishing industry in the harbour collapsed. Senator Bob Brown visited the city after the disaster and was horrified when a local fisherman showed him a shovel-nosed shark covered in measles-like red spots from the pollution.[22] Not surprisingly, critics claimed that the government had placed massive industrial development ahead of the health of the reef.[23]

In October 2012, Burke approved the expansion of one of the terminals at Abbot Point in response to a proposal submitted by GVK-Hancock for its Alpha Mine coal project, despite having described the Abbot Point area as 'the front lawn of the Great Barrier Reef'. Rival claims erupted over the approval process. Burke insisted that he granted the approval only after applying stringent conditions and after he had intervened over what he labelled as the 'shambolic' Queensland planning process.[25]

Activists challenged this assertion. Following access to material obtained from a Freedom of Information request, GetUp! claimed that Burke had overlooked advice issued by the Great Barrier Reef Marine Park Authority which, in 2011, had identified seven risks to threatened species from the port development.[26] Armed with this information, environmentalists argued that Burke should have ruled out the approval of the terminal 'rather than allow the company [GVK-Hancock] to undertake a lengthy environmental impact statement'.[27] In response to this claim, Burke stated that he had not seen the advice, in which case the basis for his stringent conditions remain unclear other than his access to the company's own environmental impact statement.

A subsequent Freedom of Information request highlights aspects of Burke's negotiation with Reinhart. The released materials revealed that Burke gave in to demands from her over a payment from the company of $800000 as compensation for damage to the environment, known as 'biodiversity offsets'. Rinehart complained that the amount was excessive and it was settled at $600000. But it wasn't just the reduced payment that concerned environmentalists. Bruce Lindsay from Environmental Justice explained that offsets weren't good practice because they amounted to 'giving a lump sum of cash for ecosystems that can't be compensated for'.[28]

Labor's deal with Rinehart was criticised for other reasons. Burke had also agreed to a request from Rinehart to overturn the stipulation that coal dust should not enter the Great Barrier Reef environment from the company's operations. Scientists had already publicly warned that the ramped-up industrialisation of the reef was creating dangerous levels of coal dust. As Professor Terry Hughes explained, coal dust 'has now accumulated everywhere on the Great Barrier Reef, not just near dredging sites or near the ports themselves and it is exceeding toxic levels in near-shore locations'.[29] It too killed coral and damaged marine life.

And environmentalists warned Labor that the underground water supplies of the Great Artesian Basin were threatened by the development of mega-mines with their insatiable need for water. Holding 65 billion megalitres of water, the resource is vital to inland Australia. Yet the scientific consensus maintains that the Great Artesian Basin is an ancient, closed system, at risk of being depleted by over-use. In fact in 2010, the Great Artesian Basin Coordinating Committee called for tighter regulation of mining in the region in response to increased exploration activity.[30]

Given the range and seriousness of the environmental issues involved in opening up the Galilee Basin to coal mining, Burke's approval of the first Abbot Point terminal shows flaws in Labor's approach. There was a lack of transparency and rigorous assessment. The North Queensland Conservation Council thought as much. It argued that the approval of the terminal appeared to 'have been pushed through prior to all relevant information being considered'.[31] Rinehart, backed up by the mining lobby, looked to have wielded too much power. Bruce Lindsay thought so; 'the tail was increasingly wagging the dog', he explained.[32] In effect, the approval of Abbot Point terminal showed that the system of environmental protection in Australia was seriously deficient, if not broken.

However, the Queensland Resources Council was delighted at Burke's decision. It was 'a step towards opening up the Galilee Basin', a spokesman said. Burke may have claimed that he had been striving to avoid the reef being listed as endangered by the World Heritage Committee, yet critics claim that he had approved record levels of dredging on the reef without undertaking a strategic assessment of its capacity to absorb such levels of activity.[33]

Federal Labor maintained the fantasy that Australia's export coal industry was not connected with the threats to the Great Barrier Reef. It campaigned to 'protect' the reef, but not explicitly from the consequences of its pro-development policy, which fostered port expansion and climate change. It was able to maintain this fantasy in part because of the anomaly that fossil fuels burnt overseas were not counted in a country's overall emissions. Federal Labor was in danger of reversing its proud record of using Commonwealth powers to protect the nation's iconic environmental assets, which had been especially strong during Bob Hawke's prime ministership.

The conservative parties were simply unapologetic in their continuing support for expanding the coal industry. The recently elected Queensland Premier Campbell Newman declared: 'We are in the coal business'.[34] To support the industry, his government released a far-reaching 10-year port strategy in early June, which involved dredging the seabed to create shipping lanes and dumping waste in the reef's waters, with the aim of trebling Queensland coal exports by 2030. In other words, the strategy repackaged the Bligh government's policy to industrialise large parts of the Great Barrier Reef. And the federal Opposition Leader Tony Abbott said that under a Coalition government, environmental approvals of many developments affecting the reef would be handed back to Queensland; something, expert commentators noted, that had not occurred since the 1980s.[35]

Rising concerns over the health of the reef

As the industry worked away at its plans to expand in 2012, the Australian Institute for Marine Science published a report which confirmed the worst fears of those concerned about the reef.[36] More than 50 per cent of its coral cover had been lost in the past 27 years.

It was yet another warning about its future that governments had simply failed to take into full account in their plans for expanded port development. As Ian McPhail, a former chairman of the Great Barrier Reef Marine Park Authority bluntly acknowledged, industry had been 'largely successful in lobbying governments as their principal strategy to get their way in the reef'.[37]

However, it was much harder for governments to ignore the international attention from the UNESCO World Heritage Committee (WHC). With the reef listed as a World Heritage site, Australia was bound by its treaty obligations to ensure it was protected. In 2012, the committee was celebrating the 40th year of the world heritage protection system, a visionary attempt to identify and list the world's major cultural and environmental sites. In its milestone year, the committee was itself dealing with a range of challenges as it became increasingly politicised, and experienced shortfalls in funding, exacerbated by the shock withdrawal of the United States. Nevertheless, few doubted its expertise in evaluating sites of exceptional universal value and the extent to which signatory nations were protecting them. The committee retained significant reputational power. Having sites on the World Heritage List is an inscription desired by almost all nations of the world.[38] Thus, countries attempt to do all in their power to avoid the committee classifying a site as endangered.

Yet that is what the WHC came close to doing in 2012 for the Great Barrier Reef. In March it undertook a monitoring mission to Queensland to assess the state of the reef. A draft report produced in May that year, leaked to the media, foreshadowed that the reef would be placed on the 'in danger' list unless urgent action was taken to address the committee's concerns over coal and gas expansion and port development.[39] However, the final report issued from that monitoring mission was more circumspect. It noted that while the reef continued to demonstrate outstanding universal values of beauty, composition and biodiversity, its future was at the crossroads. Noting that the iconic asset was affected by a range of current threats, it added for the first time the future threats emanating from climate change and rapid port development. These future threats, the committee noted, were of 'high concern'. It warned that an 'in danger' listing was likely unless remedial measures were undertaken. Among its recommended measures were a halt to new port developments and the creation of a long-term plan.[40]

Tony Burke welcomed the report. He used its release to criticise the Newman Liberal government's rush to open up new ports along the coast. The coal wars had made the reef a political battleground.

Federal Labor's half-hearted response

As if to remind Labor who was actually running the country, the mining industry revived its advertising campaign before the 2012 federal budget. Titled 'This is our story', the glossy, feel-good advertisements featured mine workers sharing their accounts of how the industry had changed their lives. The timing of the campaign made its message clear to the Gillard government: don't contemplate fixing the budget deficit with a revived mining tax.

Labor had another problem, too, in its relationship with the mining industry. As a result of its 'anti-mining' policies, election donations from the big miners to Labor just about dried up, giving their Liberal opponents a huge structural advantage. As experienced political commentator Bernard Keane wrote of this development, the 'long-term problem for Labor is that the habit of giving to the Liberals becomes permanent for mining companies'.[41]

Thus, Labor was in a weak position when it came to negotiating with the miners over the Great Barrier Reef. However, by the time of the 2012 advertising campaign, public opinion about the big mining companies had shifted. An Essential Research poll held in April found that 66 per cent of Australians said that they had personally not benefitted at all from the mining boom.[42]

Worryingly for the big miners, the proposition that the industry was over-taxed was rejected by a ratio of three to one. Clearly the public had started to see through the industry's feel-good advertisements. Backed by solid public support, Labor had an opportunity to press for better protection of the reef, yet it baulked at the challenge.

After the release of the WHC's report, it was left to Burke to fashion a response to the shock recommendation that the reef was at the crossroads. However, it was not until August 2013 that he announced Labor's plan to protect the reef and save it from an endangered listing. But all that Labor came up with was an updated version of its Reef Rescue program, with $137 million in additional allocated funding to address water quality issues from agricultural run-off. The program had achieved some success. But, important as this issue was, Labor had dodged addressing the new threats raised by the World Heritage Committee and Australian scientists.

Greens Senator Larissa Waters attacked the deficiencies in the plan: 'What we've seen today is Labor reannounce some old funding they announced in April, rather than tackle the key issues'. She highlighted the lack of attention given to the problems associated with 'the mass industrialisation of the reef that UNESCO was expressing extreme concern about and particularly about proposed coal ports ... where's the announcement about that?'[43] The Australian Marine Conservation Society also criticised Labor's plan for failing to come to terms with the issues of dredging, mega-port development and the shipping super highway.

In addition to ignoring the inconvenient truth about the impact of coal, federal Labor's response was also silent on protecting the economic value of the reef; the 60 000 jobs and $6 billion in national income it generated through the tourism and fishing industries.[44]

A strategy to end coal?

Environment groups had been preparing their counter-offensive to the mounting threats to the Great Barrier Reef. With the drum beats of Abbott's 'people's revolt' against the carbon tax still in the air, the finishing touches were being put on a document designed to stop the coal industry's expansion in its tracks. A bold and detailed strategy document titled *Stopping the Australian Coal Export Boom* was leaked to the press in March 2012. Written by John Hepburn of Greenpeace, Bob Burton of Coalswarm and Sam Hardy of the Graeme Wood Foundation, the strategy had the imprimatur of the broader environmental and social activist movements, having been the subject of extensive input at the first National Coal Convergence held in the Blue Mountains in October 2011. Subsequent drafts had input from organisations including GetUp!, Nature Conservation Council, Environmental Defenders Office, United Voice, The Australia Institute and Lock the Gate. These groups were among the mainstream, beating heart of progressive politics in Australia and they were calling for the biggest environmental campaign in Australian history in a bid to disrupt and delay the expansion of the industry.[45]

The strategy envisaged raising $6 million to research, organise and foster a comprehensive anti-coal campaign. As the document noted, Australia was on the verge of an unprecedented export coal boom to power a new generation of coal-fired plants in India 'with devastating consequences for the global climate'. Hoping to build on the successful grassroots campaign that restricted the spread of the coal seam gas industry, the strategy aimed to 'disrupt and delay key projects and infrastructure while gradually eroding public and political support for the industry'. The tactics included: challenging mining infrastructure and new mega mines in the courts; building political support to exclude mines from key areas such as farms, nature reserves and aquifers; increasing the perception of coal as a risky investment; and working towards removing the social licence of the coal industry. The aim was to change the story of coal 'from being the backbone of our economy, to being a destructive industry'.

Those behind co-ordinating the strategy were veterans of the environment movement. But John Hepburn's career, in particular, illustrated the transforming power of environmental ideas. His roots were in the coal industry. The son of a coalmine inspector who spent his childhood visiting mines in central Queensland, Hepburn went on to work as an engineer for a company that made components for the coal industry. As he explained to Marcus Priest in an interview for the *Australian Financial Review*:

> We have a long family connection with the coal industry and I became an activist after changing my view on the world. I basically did not have strong views at the time, but gradually started reading about the environmental crisis – someone gave me a book by [academic and environmental activist] David Suzuki. Gradually I began to understand climate change and it now drives me as an issue.[46]

Hepburn's first campaign was against sand mining on North Stradbroke Island, where he joined a blockade. And it was on Stradbroke where he first met long-time Queensland environmental campaigner, Drew Hutton. The two became friends, with Hutton drawing on his experience with the Lock the Gate campaign to play a key role in developing the anti-coal strategy.

Bob Burton was another veteran environmental campaigner who worked with the Wilderness Society in the 1990s, and went on to run SourceWatch, an American website documenting the public relations industry and corporate spin, and CoalSwarm, an online database on the coal industry funded by the Rockefeller Foundation.

Whoever leaked the document to the media, the timing couldn't have been more advantageous. The delegation from the WHC had just arrived in the country to investigate the impact of the fossil fuel industry on the Great Barrier Reef. Consequently, the media seemed ever more eager to pounce. 'Greenpeace leads a war against coal' bellowed the headline in the *Sydney Morning Herald*. The Murdoch press went into hyperbolic overdrive. Columnist and right-wing commentator, Christopher Pearson, issued a predictable 'declaration of war on coal' to headline his article: 'The operatives matter-of-factly plotting to wreak havoc on the coal industry weren't reds, anarchists or nihilists. They were eco-warriors ... going to undermine the national economy'.[47]

The chief executive of the Australian Coal Association, Nikki Williams, offered grudging respect for those who devised the strategy: 'They have outlined a very detailed and sophisticated plan for co-ordinated activity involving a number of green groups that is designed to disrupt and delay the coalmining industry', she said on the *Australian Business* program on Sky Business. 'We are concerned about it because it shows a very high level of planning.'[48] The Minerals Council of Australia described the strategy as 'economic vandalism'.

When *Stopping the Coal Export Boom* was leaked, the Labor government leapt to the coal industry's defence. Gillard led the outrage of Labor's senior ministers. 'The coal industry', she explained, 'has a great future in this country. We are seeing that future being built now. We have got to have appropriate environmental regulatory processes, of course we do, but they should always be based on fact'.[49] The pride in building the future of the coal industry was obvious in her statement, and no doubt it pitched well to traditional Labor voters alienated by the hysteria that followed her government's introduction of the carbon tax. But the claim that her government had put in place fact-based, appropriate environmental regulations is not borne out by the evidence.

Treasurer Wayne Swan articulated the same delusion. In June 2012, he decried the attacks on the industry over an advertisement Greenpeace had placed in an Indian newspaper warning about the dangers to the Great Barrier Reef from Queensland coal projects. He called the advertisement 'deplorable and obnoxious' and re-stated the federal Labor government's commitment 'to a strong investment pipeline across our resources industry', repeating the line that the government was 'determined to put in place strict environmental guidelines'.[50] However, Swan wasn't too keen on Labor being held accountable to the public through the activities of environment groups. In an effort to reduce their power and influence he threatened to remove their charitable status, an action which would erode their funding base. It was a threat later advanced by Tony Abbott when he became prime minister.

With the war over coal already under way, it was inevitable that the bipartisan approach to industrialising the reef would come under increasing attack. David Ritter's appointment in 2012 as Chief Executive Officer of Greenpeace brought an added urgency to the debate over coal and its impacts on the future of the reef and on climate change. A lawyer-turned-activist, Ritter brought well-developed communication skills to advocating these causes. Writing in the *Australian*, he acknowledged that, at the time, it was not easy to oppose the expansion of the thermal coal industry, 'but the silence of our politicians is a betrayal of our shared fate'. He said that the choice was clear: 'Australia must cease expansion of coal exports or wilfully threaten the future of our children. For our kids and our country we must act to break the silence'.[51]

Ritter was in the forefront of placing climate change activism within the historical tradition of civil disobedience campaigns for human rights. In the years to come, Adani would be the focus of just such a sustained campaign.

Abbott put in his place

Big mining money would soon help put Tony Abbott into power at the 2013 election. However, in the months leading up to his date with destiny, Abbott and the Liberals continued to serenade the far right. In April 2013, the 70th anniversary of the Institute of Public Affairs (IPA) publicly revealed the party's links to the neoliberal and anti-environmental ideas that now formed the backbone of modern Australian conservatism. Held in the National Gallery of Victoria, the occasion carried an ambience far beyond a special day for a think tank. The 'red carpet' rollout for some of the nation's most prominent billionaires, captains of industry and cultural conservatives was meant to convey the power and status of the IPA as a nationally significant political institution. As one observer quipped, if the stained glass ceiling of the gallery collapsed, 'the cause of conservatism would be [put] back a generation'.[52]

In advance of the occasion, John Roskam, Executive Director of the IPA, had compiled the IPA's '100-point wish list' designed to be picked up by an incoming Abbott government. The list envisaged a neoliberal, libertarian and anti-environmental Australia. Among its anti-environmental measures were calls to repeal the carbon tax; abolish the Department of Climate Change, the Clean Energy Fund and the Renewable Energy target; and withdraw from the Kyoto Protocol.[53]

On the night of the 70th anniversary gala event, a small group of protestors kept up a noisy vigil outside the gallery. Inside was a 'sea of dark suits topped with grey balding heads as far as the eye could see'; one of the exceptions being the presence of mining magnate Gina Rinehart, Australia's wealthiest person, with coal interests in the Galilee Basin. Rupert Murdoch graced the event with his presence, every speaker falling over themselves 'to fawn on the great man'.[54]

Abbott's speech, infused with his hard-wired Catholicism, was something of a surprise. He used it to argue that Christianity had been crucial to the development of liberalism and contemporary culture; laced with traditional Christian imagery, it became known as his 'Garden of Eden' speech. It was an attempt to impress upon the powerful that he was his own man, which, as critics pointed out, was mostly a charade. As journalist Katherine Murphy observed of Abbott's performance on the night:

> [T]he IPA has become the organisational hub for the
> renaissance of the right in this country ... The IPA and its
> fellow travellers are powerful, either through personal wealth
> or cultural influence ... Abbott couldn't ignore this group even
> if he wanted to (which of course he doesn't). Realpolitik ...
> demands a certain degree of lock-step.[55]

Photographs of the event show a deferential Abbott. One depicts him kneeling beside a seated Murdoch to talk in his ear while another shows him bending over while Rinehart whispered in his ear. He looked like 'the plutocrats' puppy', as one progressive media outlet cheekily commented on the visuals of the evening.[56]

The election was a foregone conclusion. The public had grown weary of Labor's leadership tensions between Julia Gillard and Kevin Rudd, and the media had manufactured a continuing sense of crisis about the hung parliament the public delivered at the 2010 election, despite its substantial legislative achievements. Abbott's bare-knuckle brand of politics and his sloganeering approach to issues proved decisive.

However, the choices surrounding the fate of the Great Barrier Reef were lost in the election noise. It suited both major parties for the status quo to prevail; both were locked into industrialisation. And both continued the fallacy that they did not have to choose between coral and coal; the nation could have both.

This was not what Australians thought. Public affection for the reef, especially in Queensland, was long-standing but unrecorded in recent public opinion polls. In the lead-up to the 2013 federal election, the World Wildlife Fund, through its 'Fight for the Reef' campaign, commissioned ReachTEL to conduct a poll of nine federal electorates along the Queensland coast. This showed 72.3 per cent of the 5081 people polled supported a ban on dumping dredge spoil in the marine national park and an overwhelming 74 per cent believed the federal government should have the power to stop major developments that harmed the reef.[57]

The results were confirmed a year later. The Australia Institute conducted a poll of Queenslanders which found that 63 per cent opposed projects that would increase port and shipping activities near the Great Barrier Reef and 63 per cent also opposed projects that would affect agricultural and water resources.[58]

In 2014, Greenpeace would commission ReachTEL to conduct a similar, but nation-wide, poll. Australians were asked if they agreed or disagreed with the question: 'If I had to choose between protecting the Great Barrier Reef and expanding the coal industry I would choose protecting the Reef'. A massive 85 per cent agreed with the priority of protecting the reef. Although the questions differed, the results of the opinion polls were definitive: Australians regarded the reef as belonging to the nation and not to the coal industry.

When Tony Abbott was elected prime minister in September 2013, his government introduced the most far-reaching attack on environment policies ever seen in Australia. The origins of Abbott's anti-environmentalism are discussed in Chapter 7. However, he revealed the depth of his ideological commitment as soon as he took office when he faced decisions on the approval of the Abbot Point expansion.

Abbott intended to complete the industrialisation of the Great Barrier Reef. But before any new mines could be approved, his government needed to clear the way for the massive expansion of the three Abbot Point terminals; to convert the complex into the world's largest coal port. This was the essential building block to opening up the Galilee Basin.

Greg Hunt, the Minister for the Environment, took charge of this project. Hunt had been the Liberals' long-standing spokesperson in this portfolio. Mild-mannered yet determined, he had mastered the political act of staying 'on script' to an almost robotic extent. And he had a tendency to over-hype his proposals, as if he needed convincing himself of their merit. Yet, unusually for most modern politicians, he was averse to overt displays of aggression, preferring a polite, quietly spoken way. He had had a typical 'blue blood' Liberal pedigree: Melbourne University law; Fulbright scholarship to Yale, followed by a stint at the United Nations Centre for Human Rights; and advisor to former Foreign Minister, Alexander Downer. In other words, he was a quintessential Liberal moderate.

Hunt also embraced an interest in the environment. He wrote his Yale master's thesis on regulatory frameworks to better control industrial pollution. Titled 'A tax to make the polluters pay', he argued for market-based mechanisms. The work would come back to haunt him because he was a lead author in Tony Abbott's controversial 'Direct Action' policy which, as previously discussed, was designed to attack Labor's carbon tax, proposing instead that government would pay big companies to reduce their emissions.

Behind his mild-mannered demeanour, Hunt had embraced the Liberals' radical anti-environmentalism with its disdain for science-based policy. In October 2013, newly installed as Environment Minister, Hunt was asked in an interview with a BBC news program about Prime Minister Tony Abbott's claim that UN Climate Chief Christiana Figueres was 'talking out of her hat' when she made the link between the increased severity of bushfires and climate change. The environment minister showed no shame in saying that he 'looked up what Wikipedia says' about bushfires and that it was clear that Australia had had a history of frequent events during hotter months pre-dating European settlement.[59]

Hunt's radical U-turn in policy direction on climate change and his breezy dismissal of the emerging science on the impacts of climate change clearly indicated how far anti-environmentalism had taken root in the Liberal Party, especially since Tony Abbott's ascension as leader. Nonetheless, on 9 December 2013, Hunt stunned environmentalists and many of those with an economic stake in the Great Barrier Reef by announcing that he had approved the dredging of 3 million metres of seabed surrounding the Abbot Point port which was to be dumped in the World Heritage Area. As one critic explained, if all the spoil was tipped into dump trucks it would fill 150 000 of them.

In announcing his decision, Hunt claimed that he included the 'strictest conditions in Australian history' around the decision. He also later claimed that the decision had entailed 'careful and deep review' and, more tellingly, that there was 'unequivocal advice' that the operation could be done safely.[60] Both claims were later exposed as dissembling. He and the federal government had deliberately ignored scientific advice to create the best outcome for the coal industry. Hunt gave the industry its preferred, cheaper option. A land-based alternative would have cost an additional $500 million.[61] Jon Brodie, a research scientist at James Cook University, evocatively described the politics behind Hunt's decision: 'In the end they [the coal industry] wanted the cheapest, quickest, dirtiest option at Abbot Point and that's what they got'.[62]

Hunt's announcement was met with swift and fierce criticism from those committed to protecting the reef. Dredging and dumping might have gone on for decades, but the practice no longer accorded with either public approval or the warnings from scientists, especially because the scale of the dredging was unprecedented.

The damage from industrial-scale dredging

Experts agreed that the industrial-scale dumping of dredged seabed that had accompanied the expansion of ports along the Queensland coast posed a direct threat to the reef's ecosystem. Professor Terry Hughes from the Centre of Excellence for Coral Reef Studies at Townsville's James Cook University, and an internationally recognised expert in the area, explained in an article for the widely read online magazine the *Conversation* that:

> [S]ediment from dredging can smother and kill marine species. Sediment also reduces light levels, causes physiological stress, impairs growth and reproduction, clogs the gills of fish, and promotes diseases. The extent to which this is already occurring on the Great Barrier Reef due to dredging is poorly understood.

Exacerbating the problems, Hughes argued, was poor monitoring:

> Long-term monitoring of dredging impacts so far has been woefully inadequate. Monitoring tends to focus on the short-term impacts at each inshore dredging site, rather than the longer-term effects of dumping sediment elsewhere ... In the absence of adequate monitoring, it is easy to deny the environmental impacts of dredging on the Great Barrier Reef, and to claim that they are manageable.[63]

Tourism operators were worried about declining visibility in the waters surrounding the dredging. Colin McKenzie, representing the Association of Marine Park Tourism Operators, told the 2014 Senate inquiry into the management of the reef that, following the dredging at Hay Point in 2006, visibility dropped from 15 metres to 9 metres.[64]

Apart from the direct threats posed by the dumping decision, it also sent the wrong message to the world about Australia's management of the reef. According to Professor Ove Hoegh-Guldberg, Director of the Global Climate Change Institute at the University of Queensland and a specialist in the impact of climate change on coral reefs, Hunt's decision showed that Australia was 'not really the best marine park manager in the world ... that we were cutting corners' and there was 'a risk that we could get to the point where the Great Barrier Reef is listed as World Heritage in danger'.[65]

Not surprisingly, Hughes' views were at complete variance with those of the coal industry. Michael Roche, the indefatigable head of the Queensland Resources Council, gave evidence to the 2014 Senate inquiry and re-affirmed the view prevalent in the industry that 'all dredging activities are subject to detailed environmental assessment and management ... to avoid environmental harm'.[66]

Conservationists had specific concerns about the threat to vulnerable species at Abbot Point. The Turtle Island Restoration Network, a US conservation group with links to Australia, warned that coastal development in Queensland could push several species of sea turtle towards extinction. The Great Barrier Reef plays host to six species of turtle, which are threatened by boat strikes, water pollution and the direct impact of dredging. Teri Shore, program director of the network, pointed out to Australians that

> The reef is home to some of the most amazing turtle species in the world, which rely on a healthy environment for their future. The Australian Flatback lives entirely in waters close to shore and sandy beaches, making them highly vulnerable to coastal port developments and shipping. Leatherbacks, which are also in jeopardy, live more in the open ocean where increased ship movements will take their toll through greater injury and death.[67]

Ship strikes alone had killed 45 turtles in Gladstone Harbour since the Curtis Island LNG project began in 2007, compared with an average of two a year in the previous decade.

In the spoil-dumping area there are also seagrass beds, which are home to dugongs. The 400-kilogram gentle giants of the reef's waters feed on the seagrass that dumping threatens to degrade. Once so widespread in Queensland that it would take hours for

100-metre-wide herds to pass by, the elephant-like creatures are at risk of extinction, and most of the world's remaining population live in the Great Barrier Reef.

Louise Matthiesson, Greenpeace's Queensland campaigner, crisply summed up the widespread dismay and anger in the community about Hunt's decision: 'Minister Hunt has ignored the evidence and thumbed his nose at the serious concerns of scientists, tourism operators, fishers and UNESCO about the impacts of these industrial developments and activities'.[68]

Hunt was not the type of politician to play the attack dog against an opponent. However, he had colleagues who were prepared to do so. Federal National Party Member for Dawson George Christensen described opponents of the government's dumping decision as 'eco-terrorists' and 'gutless green grubs'. In what was described as 'a bizarre speech to Parliament', he 'declared radical green groups as the greatest terror threat to North Queensland'.[69] It was the type of language that had earned Christensen the mantle of 'Australia's most polarising pollie'. He had used social media to let off 'bombshells' on the staple issues of the far right – Islam, the death penalty, gay marriage and climate change. With his big frame complimenting his outlandish opinions, Christensen is nonetheless a curious recruit to the marginal issues of the far right. Raised on a cane farm in genteel poverty, he was bullied at school and nicknamed 'the barefoot bandit' because he couldn't afford shoes.[70] Undeterred, he became a studious kid and earned a university degree in communications. However, he's forged a career dishing it out to other marginalised groups and by adopting paranoid conspiracy theories about climate change.[71]

While it's easy to pigeonhole Christensen as an extremist, nothing separated his position on developing the Carmichael mine from that of his 'moderate' colleague, Greg Hunt. Dredging would proceed as planned.

The politics of the Marine Park Authority

Once Hunt had made his decision to approve dredging, all eyes turned to the Great Barrier Marine Park Authority (GBRMPA) for its decision on whether to issue a permit for the operation. The authority's chief executive, Dr Russell Reichelt, is a well-respected scientist with a PhD in marine science and a background in studying the ecology of coral reefs. He joined the authority in 2007 as chairman and chief executive, his tenure coinciding with the greater push towards industrialisation.

From the beginning of 2014, Reichelt must have felt the pressure on him from both industry and environmentalists. The scrutiny increased when in late January a letter signed by 233 scientists arrived on his desk calling on him to reject Hunt's approval. 'The best available science makes it very clear that expansion of the port at Abbot Point will have detrimental effects on the Great Barrier Reef', the letter said.[72]

The authority was charged with the day-to-day management of the reef, and it employed considerable scientific expertise to guide its decision-making. The authority was governed by a five-member board appointed by the federal government. Although nominally independent, critics claim the authority lacked real power; its status was much the same as a government department. It is therefore vulnerable to political pressure from any number of sources: industry groups, conservationists, the GBRMPA board members and the federal environment minister.

When, on 30 January 2014, Reichelt announced that the authority had approved the application to dredge Abbot Point, the predictable storm of protest erupted. How, many asked, could the authority, with all of its scientific expertise and mandated responsibility to protect the reef, come up with a decision to dump 3 million cubic metres of dredged seabed within the Marine Park World Heritage Area? As the North Queensland Conservation Council spokesperson later told the Senate Committee inquiring into the management of the reef, 'very, very many' people in the Townsville community felt let down by the GBRMPA's decision: the agency had always been seen as 'the good guys', on the side of the reef. Following the dumping decision, it was seen 'as an agency that can be swayed by the government of the day'.[73]

With such wealthy corporate players involved and a growing voice of protest from conservation groups, the political pressure on the authority had increased dramatically. This, at least, was the conclusion of Ian McPhail, who headed the authority between 1994–1999. 'In comparison to today [2014]', he wrote, 'I faced far less pro- and anti-development pressures than my successors'. The struggle between the two forces, he pointed out, was, predictably, an unequal one:

> Pro-development forces argue strenuously at the top
> government level for approvals, leveraging the fact that their
> aims coincide with the government's need for revenue and jobs.
> In contrast, anti-development forces lack serious government
> access, instead using science … appeals to sustainability … [and
> lobbying] the UNESCO World Heritage Committee.[74]

But, in his announcement approving the dumping of dredged soil, did Reichelt overturn his own agency's scientific advice, or was he pressured to do so? Three separate investigations were undertaken, one by Greenpeace and two by the ABC. Together these indicate but don't conclusively prove the case, although Reichelt has strenuously denied that he had succumbed to political interference. He maintains that the GBRMPA's assessment was 'objective, notwithstanding its unpopularity with those opposed to coal mining expansion. The Abbot Point proposal was considerably smaller than past activities … with little impact.'[75]

In early March 2014, Greenpeace exposed some of the tensions inside the authority over the dredging issue. It released materials obtained under a Freedom of Information (FOI) request which showed that, from 2012 to August 2013, the authority repeatedly warned that the reef could be irreversibly damaged by the industry's plans to dredge.[76] In fact, as late as June 2013, only six months before Hunt made his decision, the authority stated in its advice to the federal government that the Abbot Point region of the reef was already at risk due to multiple stressors and that its recommendation 'is to refuse the proponents' application for capital dredging at the port of Abbot Point'.[77]

The ABC's *7.30* obtained its own documents under FOI and these confirmed the pressure the authority had been under. As far back as 2012, it had watered down its concerns over port developments. Whereas the authority had initially adopted a draft recommendation opposing port developments that had the potential to degrade inshore biodiversity, at its September board meeting that year, this tough line was substantially altered. It now read: 'In making decisions regarding port development, the potential impacts on inshore biodiversity should be a key consideration'.[78] In explaining the shift, *7.30* raised the possibility that two of the board's five members, former Townsville mayor Tony Mooney and the Head of the Queensland Department of Premier and Cabinet Jon Grayson had conflicts of interest because both were involved with fossil fuel companies. While a subsequent report later found no evidence of improper conduct, the revelations highlighted that ultimately the dynamics driving boards are opaque.

The ABC's *Four Corners* program weighed in to how the authority arrived at its decision to dredge Abbot Point.[79] It claimed that Reichelt himself had instigated the pathway to approval after 'he had installed a new manager over the experts who had originally advised against it'. The new manager, Bruce Elliott, later told the Senate inquiry that he was, in fact, a career public servant with no background in marine science. He explained to the committee the process behind the approval which, at face value, seemed to confirm that the proponents of the dredging had the final say, although Elliott denied this inference: '[we] worked with the proponent throughout the process ... and we required them to investigate alternatives as well. But when we got to the end of the process, the proposal we were making a decision on was for offshore disposal not for any other option'.[80]

Just how independent then was Reichelt from government? This question was raised at the end of 2014 when he and two other government officials travelled to Europe to visit prominent banks to discuss the financing of Abbot Point; they met with Deutsche Bank and Societe Generale. Both banks had vowed not to finance the port expansion after lobbying from GetUp!, green groups and the tourism industry. When the visit was later revealed in the media, Reichelt explained that it was not part of a lobbying effort but to 'provide information on the status of the reef's health'. Yet, as the *Sydney Morning Herald* wrote, the meetings 'raise questions over why Australian officials were in discussions with foreign banks relating to private mining projects, and why taxpayers were funding the trips'.[81] Reichelt later explained to Senate estimates that his briefing explored the full range of pressures on the reef.[82]

It is unclear whether Greg Hunt played a covert role in any of the processes which led to the authority changing its recommendation to him. Reichelt maintained that the decision to allow dumping was safe and was made only after Hunt imposed 'strict' environmental conditions. Yet the scientific advice appeared to be clear cut – not just from the GBRMPA but from renowned reef scientists – leading to accusations that influence was applied to overturn the authority's initial recommendation. An anonymous former board member told the ABC that 'Abbot Point highlights the agency's rubber stamp approval process and how GBRMPA acted like an arm of the [Environment] department. There was no fight'.[83] It was a view shared by Bob Brown. He maintains that the organisation came under 'huge political pressure' because it relied on government funding. Consequently, 'I didn't feel it was ever going to make a monumental stand on the [destruction of the reef] ... it should have been at war with the government in defence of the reef'.[84]

The storm of criticism following the GBRMPA's approval for the dredging and dumping operation was so widespread and sustained that Hunt was forced to back down. In November 2014, the minister announced plans to ban the controversial practice of dumping dredged soil in the Great Barrier Reef Marine Park and the ban was subsequently passed into law.[85] He trumpeted the decision as if he was responsible for a great reform rather than an embarrassing retreat from his efforts to support the coal industry. Even his attack dog, George Christensen, was on board acknowledging that he 'got it wrong' about dumping dredged soil and said that he was actively requesting that the dredged soil be relocated on land. The silence from the coal industry about the reversal suggests that it, too, had been forced to accept the realities. After all, there was a greater prize at stake for the industry's billionaire players. Environmentalists and those whose futures depended on the reef had had an important, but partial, victory.

Hunt's reversal of the dredging decision did not signal a wider move by the Abbott government to support the Great Barrier Reef; quite the reverse. Not only was it still on side with the plans to open up the Galilee Basin, it went ahead with a crippling budget cut on the Marine Park Authority which it had imposed in its infamous 'unfair' 2014 Budget. To meet its nearly $3 million in reduced funding, the authority was forced into a re-structure involving redundancies. Five directors and 12 other staff left in the 'biggest loss of expertise in the Authority's history'. The section working on the effects of climate change on the reef, which once had its own director and eight staff, was disbanded. Morale in the agency plummeted; and not just in relation to the cutbacks. The initial decision taken on Abbot Point was the last straw for some, who chose to take redundancies.[86]

Professor Terry Hughes expressed concern that GBRMPA was being 'disempowered' and that it was 'no longer the one-stop shop custom-designed institution for managing and governing the Great Barrier Reef that it once was'.[87]

The dredging issue, although overturned, was nonetheless significant for several reasons. Firstly, it was an important victory for the environmental movement, which had campaigned actively – with the support of the wider public. Secondly, this campaign had opened a window into the extent to which both the major political parties had been captured by the coal industry's plans to industrialise the reef. Thirdly, the Abbott government's eagerness to obtain a 'quick and dirty' decision on dredging revealed declining democratic norms in the country: science was swept aside, transparency was abandoned, and the Great Barrier Reef Marine Park Authority emasculated all in the name of Galilee coal, and its key champions, Clive Palmer, Gina Rinehart, GVK Reddy and Gautam Adani. Rinehart and Palmer were active climate change deniers while Adani had a shabby record on the environment in India. But, once the mining oligarchs were resigned to the amended decision on dredging they shifted their attention to Queensland, hoping to secure a quick state government approval for their mines in the Galilee Basin.

CHAPTER SIX

In the shadow of Joh: Adani and Queensland politics

The frank and fearless advice Queensland Treasury gave to the Newman government, elected in March 2012, about Adani's Carmichael mine could be summed up in one word: 'unbankable'.[1] Made public in June 2015, the timing made Treasury's advice all the more damning because, after approving the mine in May 2014, the premier had additionally announced unspecified millions of dollars of taxpayers' money to help the company build the Galilee Basin railway to Abbot Point. Campbell Newman had also announced a royalties' 'holiday' for the company as the government bent over backwards to get the project moving. Calls for an inquiry into the government's decision-making process predictably fell on deaf ears. But the revelations from Treasury, contained in materials obtained under Freedom of Information by the North Queensland Conservation Council and covered by a journalist from the *Sydney Morning Herald*, attracted headlines and outrage among critics opposed to mining the Galilee Basin. To these people it appeared that the government wanted the mine to go ahead at any cost. By the time the material was made public, Queensland voters had sent Newman packing after only one term. His government had been embroiled in repeated allegations of abuse of power, and of re-creating a style of politics reminiscent of the state's dark days under Joh Bjelke-Petersen in the 1970s and 80s.

Decision-making in Queensland exposed

Consistent with its policy of opening up the Galilee Basin, the Newman government was always going to give the green light to Adani, but it did so with a minimum of accountability and transparency. Adani had lost the race to be the first miner approved to begin operations in the region; that title had already gone to GVK-Hancock for the Alpha Coal and Alpha West mines. However, plenty of obstacles lay ahead for each of the miners to get the first shipments out from Abbot Point.

The rapid approval process accorded Adani was revealing of Queensland's culture under the Newman government. The first task was to secure Adani's status as a 'suitable operator' under the State's *Environment Protection Act 1994*. It was obtained 'without a single hiccup'.[2] Given Adani's poor track record in India, either no questions were asked about the company's reputation or the government turned a blind eye to any uncomfortable information that was uncovered; the former seems far more likely. The government's explanation for this was that it only needed to examine Adani's Australian record to validate his company's good reputation.

When the Newman government signed off on the mega-mine it did so without having sought any independent advice on the mine's environmental implications, despite widespread public concerns. However, it did sidestep objections raised by a Commonwealth scientific body. The Independent Expert Scientific Committee (IESC) had been established in 2012, in response to community agitation, to advise decision makers on the impact of coal seam gas and large coal mining projects on Australia's water resources. In a detailed report, the IESC expressed serious concerns about the groundwater impact of the Carmichael mine and was critical of the information that Adani supplied to it:

> Carmichael River will be adversely affected by a reduction in
> catchment size and reduced groundwater discharge to the river

due to drawdown, and this is predicted to increase no-flow
periods and compromise the ecosystem health.[3]

Nonetheless, the Newman government sided with the report Adani
provided, and against the experts in IESC.[4] Then in November
2014, the government proposed using taxpayers' money to help
fund the inland railway from the Galilee Basin to Abbot Point. It
made the announcement following a meeting between the premier
and Narendra Modi, who was attending a G20 summit in Brisbane
(discussed more fully in Chapter 7). The meeting which 'seal[ed] the
deal' was a reminder of the ongoing depth of the tycoon's relationship with the Indian leader.[5] Although Newman did not detail the
amount of government help on offer, he did explain that it would
come from selling government assets. Newman's Deputy and Minister for Planning, Jeff Seeney, explained the reasoning behind the
offer; it was designed to trigger the announcement from the Bank
of India to extend a $1 billion line of credit to Adani, a loan which
Modi had helped arrange with the bank.[6]

Against these big developments, the Greens continued to articulate the opposition to the mine found across the country: 'The
Liberal National Party (LNP) wanted to sell off Queensland's public
assets and give money to mining magnates, to prop up a dying
industry that was destroying the reef and climate'.[7]

Queensland Treasury was never likely to go as far as the Greens
in expressing doubts about the mine but it was, nonetheless, deeply
sceptical. The *Sydney Morning Herald*'s Lisa Cox examined hundreds of pages of correspondence obtained under FOI and it showed
a disturbing picture of how far accountability had already been sac-
rificed in Queensland under the Newman government. Treasury
officials were trying to undertake due diligence about Adani within
a government obsessed by big coal projects. The deluge of brief-
ings expressed Treasury's fear about Adani's high level of debt and
its opaque corporate structure, and because 'the group is highly

susceptible to cost shocks'. Treasury analyst Jason Wishart wrote to his director, David Quinn, expressing concern that Adani's proposed Carmichael mine was 'unlikely to stack up on a conventional project finance assessment'. Wishart also worried that the Adani Group was 'not particularly transparent' and that the company had failed to provide adequate information to 'address sources of debt and equity'. In a separate communication he wrote that Adani's continued expansion to meet its power and mine ambitions would place '[its] financial position under increased strain'.[8]

A day after Cox's revelations, the ABC's Mark Willacy, who had also trawled through the FOI documents, examined the political tensions between Treasury and Seeney.[9] Treasury was reluctant to get too close to the decision-making and, at the same time, was marginalised by Seeney and his aggressively pro-development department.

Seeney was an 'old-style' National Party MP before the merger with the Liberals in 2008 created the LNP, bringing together the two conservative forces in Queensland. A giant of a figure, both physically and by reputation in rural Queensland, he was a 'true conservative warrior'.[10] A rusted-on believer in developing the state's coal resources, he issued a continual barrage of press releases, speeches and media conferences promising 'fabulous wealth, just around the corner'.[11]

Seeney also had an ingrained affinity for the traditional, personalised ways of doing politics in Queensland. Questions were raised about his style of operating when, in 2014, he was found to have intervened to order the Sunshine City Council to re-zone a local caravan park against the wishes of the local council and his own department. The owner of the caravan park, SEQ Properties, was a 'broad supporter' of the LNP; the re-zoning added millions to its worth at the stroke of Seeney's pen. Planning experts told the ABC that Seeney's intervention was 'highly unusual and compared it to controversial interventions in local planning decisions by ministers in the Bjelke-Petersen government of the early 1980s ... [it] lacked transparency and sent a chilling message to local councils'.[12]

How much Treasury officials were aware of Seeney's reputation as a tough political operator is unclear. Cognisant that he was handling the negotiations with Adani, they feared getting trapped in a set-up of his that would provide quick approval to financial support for the mine. Of great concern was his departmental officials' reluctance to hand over to Treasury any of the relevant details and position papers relating to the government's promise of generous public support for Adani. Another Treasury official later complained that 'I suspect that we've missed the train and this [Adani's mine] will continue to be a Department of State Development-only show'.[13]

The documents made available under FOI are a revealing insight into the bureaucratic tensions over Adani at the heart of the Queensland government. But according to Tim Buckley, the director of Energy Finance Studies Australasia, and a critic of the Adani project, the documents also made for bizarre reading: 'The Queensland Treasury, you would think, would be the one doing the due diligence, would be running the numbers, checking that the substance of any transaction makes sense'.[14] But, as the materials obtained by the ABC further revealed, Seeney didn't want nosey Treasury officials involved in the details of the government's support for the project. The lead economic agency in government was 'uninvited' to some key meetings. The inference was clear. Premier Newman had given his deputy, the most aggressive backer behind the government's Galilee Basin plans, the complete authority to get the project up and running.

For a government that had come to power on an austerity drive to address high levels of debt, giving Adani virtually an open cheque seems contradictory at best. And to do so in a process that lacked due diligence and transparency was a grave risk to the State's reputation, where fears that the corrupt practices, authoritarian leadership and abuses of power that occurred during the Joh Bjelke-Petersen era would return were never far from the surface.

'Joh' dominated Queensland politics between 1968 and 1987

with pro-development, anti-environment and tough law and order policies. Parliament became a rubber stamp, the independence of the judiciary was undermined, civil liberties were eroded, and information to the public was restricted. Joh's era became a byword for corruption.

Derided by his critics as 'the hillbilly dictator' and 'the Bible-bashing bastard', his reign came to an end in a quagmire of scandal around police corruption and its links to government ministers. In 1989, a royal commission headed by QC Tony Fitzgerald investigated the scandals, recommending sweeping changes to the accountability of government in Queensland.[15]

Campbell Newman's career showed how instinctive it was for conservative governments in Queensland to revert to an authoritarian culture.

The rise of 'Can-Do' Newman

'Good luck trying to define Campbell Newman', wrote exasperated journalist Christine Jackman after accompanying the new premier on a whirlwind tour of the state's north several months after he was elected to office.[16] She had come face-to-face with his hyper levels of energy, but she didn't uncover much about his personality. The Premier had simply parried back her questions about his personal interests with a curt – 'No, I'm not answering that'. His defensiveness was unusual in a state with a reputation for populist politicians who could not only 'mix it' with ordinary people but appear to be one of them as well.[17]

Campbell Newman had a strong pedigree to enter conservative politics. The son of two former federal Liberal ministers, Kevin and Jocelyn Newman, he was a graduate of the Duntroon Military College, carrying its discipline with him into his civilian career.

Newman was a twice-elected mayor of Brisbane. As one commentator reflected on his success: 'He built road tunnels but also championed his council's decision to obtain 100 per cent of its power from renewable sources and plant 2 million trees. He voiced support for multiculturalism and for same-sex marriage'.[18] And he preferred renewable energy over coal. At a Brisbane city lord mayor's awards function, Newman spoke about his council's decision to buy electricity from green sources, saying that it was better 'than digging up huge piles of black stuff out of the ground ... [and] better in the long term for our children, our grandchildren and the generations to come'.[19]

With this background Newman was expected to be a progressive Liberal when he decided to shift into state politics. But Newman was unpredictable. He announced that he would challenge for the LNP leadership – against Seeney – in the run-up to the January 2012 state election without even holding a seat in parliament. He was parachuted in to the leadership and stood for the Brisbane seat of Ashgrove as a novice MP.

Once elected, Premier Newman's transformation was little short of amazing. He quickly reinvented himself as an authoritarian leader with a right-wing agenda on austerity, civil liberties, development and the environment. He was widely seen to be, and criticised for, re-creating the leadership style of Joh Bjelke-Petersen.[20] As academics Ann and Roger Scott commented, those who had participated in the reform of Queensland governance in the post-Bjelke-Petersen era 'may be forgiven for having thought that these reforms would be permanent'.[21] But they proved easily reversible.

The formerly progressive Brisbane mayor was an unlikely wrecker of Queensland's hard-won reputation for political reform. However, observers of his career discerned underlying similarities with Queensland's tradition of strongman leaders. Behind his 'rolled-up sleeves' approach to local politics was a 'Napoleonic' tendency to bark orders and crack the whip like a drill sergeant ordering recruits around.[22] Some speculated that this tendency reflected his military background, which had forged an ingrained preference for hierarchical structure and top-down orders. It was during his time as mayor that Newman honed his political image. As Professor Graeme Orr has written: '[it] begins and ends in the energetic "Can-Do Campbell" slogan, a slogan he has played for years as mayor'.[23] Nick Bryant, who covered Newman's successful 2012 election campaign, noticed his latent authoritarian streak. The Wilderness Society was present at one of his local electorate functions and Newman was instantly irked: 'Suddenly without warning Newman started to assail them', shouting at the environmentalists that they were 'aggressive, obnoxious and arrogant'.[24]

The *Courier Mail*'s long-standing political cartoonist Sean Leahy, who had an astute eye for the state's political culture, saw in Newman's military background the qualities that appealed to regional Queenslanders: 'We're a conservative state and we like strong, paternalistic, authoritative governments; that's ingrained in the Queensland psyche, although less so these days in the southeast. With his military background he certainly taps into that tradition'.[25]

Newman's latent domineering tendencies intensified in the transition to state politics. With his audacious take-over of the LNP leadership and his thumping electoral win, in which the number of Labor MPs was reduced to seven, his underlying personality trait came to the fore as premier. 'Can-Do' Newman became someone who 'could do' whatever he wanted. Driven, pugnacious and with an intense gaze, he grew impatient with approvals and due process that stood in the way of development.[26]

Thus the keys to Newman's transformation were his drive, self-belief and will to dominate. But the thrust of his new-found right-wing agenda owed much to his political opportunism. To cement his power, Newman 'acquiesced to LNP powerbrokers', wrote Christine Jackman.[27] Newman broke key election promises, especially around the extent of budget cuts; and his 'abrasive', 'head-strong' and 'combative' style came to define his government. The premier bristled at being labelled an authoritarian leader.[28]

Yet no less a figure than Tony Fitzgerald characterised the Newman government as little more than a quasi-democracy:

> From behind a populist facade, it engaged in rampant
> nepotism, sacked, stacked and otherwise reduced the
> effectiveness of parliamentary committees, subverted and
> weakened the state's anti-corruption commission, made
> unprecedented attacks on the courts and the judiciary,
> appointed a totally unsuitable Chief Justice, reverted to
> selecting male judges almost exclusively and, from a position
> of lofty ignorance, dismissed its critics for their effrontery.[29]

Newman shocked many Queenslanders with his quick embrace of austerity. To address the budget deficit, he sacked 24 000 public servants even though he had assured the public that savage cuts would not occur. The environment was another key area where the Newman government pursued a radical agenda, imposed without much debate. It was an area, too, where Newman broke a pre-election commitment to voters that he would protect the environment. In fact, he had invoked his father's record in stopping sand mining on Fraser Island; his credentials as a green mayor of Brisbane and the fact that he was 'exploring policy options to protect Queensland's outstanding biodiversity'.[30] But Newman set about systematically rolling back environmental laws. The cornerstone of his policy was legislation to cut back 'green tape'; his was the first Australian government to enact such a pro-development policy framework. Critics decried the measure as allowing business interests 'to ignore environmental harm to maximise profits'.[31]

Among the Newman government's measures was to gut the tighter regulations introduced in 2006 to stop rampant clearing of bushland in the state. By the end of his tenure in office, his government had overseen the clearing of close to a million hectares of bushland.[32] This process was so destructive in scale, it undermined the nation's overall ability to meet its emissions reduction targets, let alone preserve native wildlife habitat.

Climate change denialism became official government policy. Environment Minister Andrew Powell set the tone. In an interview in June 2012 he announced that he rejected climate science. He peddled the standard conservative 'sceptical' line that questioned whether humans were having an impact on climate change, a view he appeared to justify because it was 'fairly consistent across a certain percentage of the population'. When asked to comment on Powell's views, Newman described them as 'refreshing'.[33]

The government also sought to abolish the right of the community to take legal recourse against mining projects. The Mineral and Energy Resources (Common Provisions) Bill 2014 removed the right of community groups and landholders who were not living directly on a mining lease to object to proposed mines in court. This included landholders who lived downstream of proposed mega mines and whose water supply was affected.[34] The legislation was passed hastily at midnight, an action Queensland legal practitioners Stephen Keim and Alex McKean described as 'a landmark in anti-democratic abuse of parliamentary process'.[35] The two highlighted the overt political motives behind the Bill. It was intended, they wrote, to stymie 'the ability of the Land Court to scrutinise these massive projects in the Galilee, and elsewhere, [and which] has now been "disappeared" under the cover of night'. The mining lobby had worked hard to have these appeal rights removed.[36]

Among Newman's most dramatic policy reversals were those which he had promoted in his former career as Brisbane mayor: support for renewable energy and opposition to coal mining. He cut funding to the first while laying the ground to move ahead with the Bligh government's policy of expanding the coal industry. He made it clear that protecting the Great Barrier Reef came second to economic development. The science relating to the Great Barrier Reef was treated in a similarly discretionary way to that of climate change. Newman was among friends when, in November 2014, he addressed the state's peak mining body, the Queensland Resources Council (QRC) and pronounced that the reef 'is pretty healthy now'.[37]

Within six months of Newman becoming premier, there were 35 major development applications along the reef. When conservationists claimed that the level of activity on the reef was 'out of control', Newman retorted: 'We are not going to see the economic future of Queensland shut down'.[38] He not only tagged the State as being 'in the business of coal', but he linked the industry to its very future: 'If you want decent hospitals, schools and police on the beat we all need to understand that'.[39] As discussed below, this overstated the contribution the coal industry made to the Queensland economy.

Early in his term as premier, Newman had struggled to articulate his vision for the state beyond the China boom and his so-called 'four pillars' of the state's economy: agriculture, resources, tourism and construction. 'It's a good question', he told Christine Jackman in a moment of candour: 'and I can only be airy-fairy about it at the moment, to be perfectly, scrupulously honest'.[40] Without a plan for a broader economy it became much easier to double down on the push from the mining lobby. Newman overlooked the fact that the Queensland economy was overwhelmingly driven by the services sector and, seemingly bereft of alternative ideas, the Adani mine became his government's 'great hope for the Queensland economy', increasingly so as his term evolved.[41]

Thus, within months of becoming premier, Newman had undergone as complete a makeover as any politician in living memory. The moderate, progressive mayor had become the hard-edged ideological right-winger. And his 'can-do' personality had morphed into that of a strongman leader who had little affinity with democratic norms. More disturbingly, his opposition to the coal industry had given way to support for it. How real this transformation was is difficult to assess. Was Newman just an opportunist? He might have thought he needed to pitch to Queensland's traditional political culture as a right-wing, 'strong' leader and clearly he possessed some of the latent personality traits to make the switch, just as he had successfully done in promoting Brisbane's progressive urban issues.

But personality and ideology alone don't explain such a quick reversal of positions. Newman had come face-to-face with Queensland's mining magnates and their shadowy political model.

'Cash for legislation'

During the election, Newman became embroiled in an ugly undertow of power politics involving a foreign mining corporation, in what the Labor Party later depicted as the 'cash for legislation deal'. Ironically, the issue centred on sand mining on Stradbroke Island, the very mining activity that Newman's father had stopped on Fraser Island and which Newman had trumpeted as evidence of his own green credentials.

'Straddie', as the island south of Brisbane is known affectionately by the locals, is the world's second largest sand island (after Fraser Island); sand miners had operated there since the 1940s but in a relatively low-key way for many years. However, the silica in the island's sand was a valuable commodity in the production of paints, plastics, metals and cosmetics, and operations expanded so that, by the 2000s, 50 million tonnes of sand was being processed, most of it by Sibelco, a privately owned Belgian company. Environmentalists and the island's traditional Indigenous owners wanted the mining to end because of the adverse impacts on the island's ecology. In response, the Bligh government stepped in with a compromise solution that mining would cease by 2019.

Sibelco bitterly opposed the decision and sought to have it overturned. It wanted the lease extended to 2027. Budget estimates hearings held after the election revealed that the company had met on eight occasions with Labor government ministers.[42] When it didn't get its own way, the company deployed raw political force. The March 2012 election offered the company a golden opportunity to pressure the likely new premier in a seat he hadn't yet successfully contested. Among the company's goals was to have Newman agree to changing the lease arrangement before the election, presumably so that it had a veneer of democratic endorsement.

The company hired a public relations firm and ploughed over $90 000 into an aggressive advertising campaign against the decision. TV advertisements showing how much the mine benefitted the local community bombarded the airwaves 98 times during a period of a few weeks and full-page newspaper ads greeted readers with the same message. In a final show of strength, the company sent personalised letters to Ashgrove residents.[43]

Immediately after the election, representatives from Sibelco met 13 times with LNP officials, ministers and Newman himself. It later transpired that the company had prepared a paper to the minister outlining how the legislation extending the lease should be drawn up.[44] Soon afterwards, legislation was passed extending the life of the mine. The government did so even though Sibelco was in the middle of a long-running criminal trial on charges of unlawfully removing and selling large quantities of non-mineral sands. Newman's willingness to overlook the company's poor reputation simply reinforced his response to the warning Sibelco had sent his government about the power mining companies wielded in Queensland.

The local Quandamooka people, the native title owners of Stradbroke Island, sought a ruling from the State's Crime and Corruption Commission on Sibelco's intervention in the election but by the time they did so, the Newman government had gutted the powers of the Commission (see below). The newly re-formed body wrote back to the local Aboriginal group saying that it would not investigate the matter.[45] Mr Cameron Costello, CEO of

Quandamooka Yoolooburrabee Aboriginal Corporation, later gave
the following evidence to the Senate inquiry into government
administration in Queensland:

> They did not consult with us in that period up to the
> legislation. They did however consult extensively with the
> mining company and took into account its commercial
> imperatives. The Premier and his office personally intervened
> in several key decisions[.][46]

Sibelco was just one of a number of the Newman government's controversial mining approval decisions that became entangled in allegations of corruption.

Local Queensland mining tycoon Clive Palmer made major
donations to the Newman government. In 2010, Palmer was the
largest political donor in Australia, handing over $850 000 mostly to
the conservative side of politics.[47] Quirky, mercurial and with a reputation for imperiousness and for falling out with business partners,
he was a force to be reckoned with. And so, in April 2012, according
to Jeff Seeney, Palmer came to his office and allegedly said:

> 'I have paid a lot of money to get you guys elected and I have a
> lot more money to continue to do that in the future', and told
> Jeff Seeney to behave like two of the National Party's 1980s
> heavyweights – Joh Bjelke-Petersen and Russ Hinze – who
> became improperly close to business interests. ... Mr Seeney
> said that Mr Palmer wanted to bypass all the normal and proper
> assessment and approval processes 'and sought special treatment
> for (his) Waratah Coal's proposal', so it could be 'approved
> without delay' or competition.[48]

Seeney claimed that he pushed Palmer's document back across the
table and said, 'Clive we can't do business like that'.[49] When the

contents of the meeting were leaked to the press two years later, Palmer rejected Seeney's version of events and the relationship between the local mining tycoon and the Newman government curdled into a hostile feud.

Palmer's bid to gain exclusive rights to build the railway to Abbot Point were dealt a decisive blow when, in June 2012, just after Palmer met Seeney to press his case, the Newman government selected GVK-Hancock's bid to service their Alpha mine. The government had warned both billionaire miners that it only wanted one railway to service the Galilee Basin and, with fierce competition between the two bidders, the prospect of sharing the line was beyond the government's ability to negotiate. GVK India vice-president Sanjay Reddy told the press that the incoming Queensland government had asked all three proponents (Palmer, Adani and GVK-Hancock) to reach an agreement among themselves: 'So we did that, and then of course we all agreed to disagree', he said. 'So we have given all the information to government, and we are told that they will make a decision'.[50]

Palmer was 'outraged' at the decision to award the railway contract to GVK-Hancock; realising that his dreams for the Galilee were evaporating dented his ego.[51] As sources told the *Courier Mail*, Palmer had talked up his bid for exclusive rights to the railway: 'He kept saying he had all these backers and support for it. He just wanted it handed to him'. The reason was simple business self-interest; he would have been 'owner and operator of the only railway line to service the Galilee Basin, forcing rivals to be customers whose coal would have been exported out of what would have been known as "Palmer's Wharf" at Abbot Point'.[52]

He was now on the outer with a government that played political favourites. He let loose his anger at the Newman government, alleging that it had 'cooked the books' on the budget, inflating the size of the deficit to justify its austerity measures. A renowned litigant, Palmer also sued the Queensland government over the exclusive GVK-Hancock deal and played the patriotic card by complaining that the Newman government had a policy of 'favouring Indian companies'.[53]

In response, Seeney ordered an audit of Palmer's mining activities to determine his company's alleged failures to consult with Aboriginal people in its projects, and the LNP suspended Palmer's party membership. Both sides settled into taking pot shots at each other from their trenches. But Palmer's dreams of untold riches from the Galilee were turning into a mother lode of anguish for the combative tycoon.

Vitol, his Swiss partner who had agreed to buy half the coal with China Power International, had pulled out of the deal; Palmer claimed that it was at his instigation. Compounding the uncertainty further, the credit China Exim Bank offered to the project expired. In June 2012, Palmer gave a confused press conference, trying to explain the implications of these developments, but as was his custom, be breezily dismissed any doubts around the project. Only the week before he had attracted world headlines when he announced a 'memorandum of understanding' to build a replica of the *Titanic* with a Chinese shipbuilder.[54] That plan soon sank without a trace.

Palmer's plans were dealt a blow, but it was never clear that he had the capacity to pull off such a large project. However, as later events revealed, he was bent on revenge for having his plans thwarted. As author John Birmingham wrote, 'having paid good money to see Newman elected, he is now bent on spending even more to see not just Newman but his entire party extinguished'.[55] Palmer had decided to form his own political party – the Palmer United Party – which he ultimately achieved in April 2013.

In his tirade against his former colleagues in the LNP, Palmer had raised a valid point: had the Newman government undertaken any due diligence on the GVK-Hancock bid to build the railway? Palmer alleged that the Indian company was in trouble; that it had been forced to renege on constructing a coal mine in India. 'If they're not meeting their obligations in India, why does the Queensland government think they will meet their obligations here?', Palmer told the press in September 2012.[56]

On this occasion, Palmer was right; Newman's government did not appear to have undertaken any due diligence on GVK-Hancock. After all, it carried the imprimatur of the House of Hancock and was buttressed by the close relationship between Gina Rinehart and GVK Reddy. However, a closer examination of the ambitious Indian tycoon would have revealed that GVK was mired in financial trouble. Reddy's audacious gamble to become a major player in the power market in India and Asia was slowly evaporating. Besides being highly overleveraged, carrying debt of $2.8 billion with a market capitalisation of only $243 million, GVK faced a plummeting stock price, which has underperformed the Indian share price index by 80 per cent since 2010.[57] It was also behind on its final payment of over $500 million to Gina Rinehart, who gave an open-ended extension to the beleaguered company.

However, it looked as if Rinehart had backed a dud. GVK Reddy's debt had continued to balloon. Attempts to offload its assets to repay debt had fallen flat.[58] In June 2013, the *Times of India* cast even greater doubt on the company's prospects for building the mine:

Infrastructure firm GVK's $10-billion Alpha coalmine, port and rail project is uneconomical and represents an unacceptable level of risk to potential investors, says a report by the US-based Institute for Energy Economics and Financial Analysis (IEEFA). The IEEFA report emphasized that GVK has never successfully built or operated a coalmine or any business outside of India. It is overcommitted, with 16 greenfield infrastructure projects worth $20 billion across six asset classes.[59]

To add to the company's woes, local environmentalists and farmers in the Galilee Basin were challenging its plans to be the first to open in the Galilee. Later, in April 2014, they took the Alpha mine project to the Queensland Land Court, concerned over the impact the mine would have on the 8000-hectare Bimblebox Nature Reserve and on underground water supplies vital to farmers.

Land Court Commissioner Paul Smith had the weight of the Queensland government and the state's mining industry on his shoulders in coming to a determination. He was aware that the case was a 'watershed' because it paved the way for opening up the Galilee Basin to the miners. But Smith held dear to the independence of the Court and, in a surprise decision, announced that the mine should either be refused altogether or approved only on condition that the company engage in 'make good arrangements' with affected farmers. But GVK never acted on the requirements; locals soon believed that the Alpha mine was dead.[60]

However, graziers in the Galilee hadn't seen off GVK-Hancock's Kevin's Corner mine. Bruce and Annett Currie owned a 25 110 hectare beef property situated 60 kilometres north of Jericho that adjoined the proposed mine. In 2013, the Currie family, along with other farmers, objected to GVK-Hancock's application for Queensland government approvals – a Mining Lease and Environmental Authority – on the basis that the mine threatened their groundwater:

> Our grazing enterprise is totally reliant on access to groundwater. We are a direct neighbour to this proposed mine, so when GVK Hancock modelled groundwater drawdown that extends roughly 4km into our property, but stopped short of showing us anything less than a 1 metre water drop, we were very concerned. The fact they did not include our property or bores in their bore survey shows disregard for the impacts on local farmers and neighbours.[61]

The Curries would wait a year and a half for the decision.

While these events with GVK-Hancock were playing out, relations between Palmer and the Newman government soured even further when the contents of the 2012 Seeney–Palmer meeting were made public in August 2014 under FOI. Palmer rejected Seeney's account, sued the Newman government for defamation and called it corrupt. Seeney referred Palmer to the Crime and Corruption Commission, alleging that he tried to influence government decisions. While nothing came from either legal challenge, the allegations surrounding the Palmer–Seeney meeting offer revealing insights into Queensland's free-wheeling political culture under Newman: accusations flew wildly about corruption among key players and the public was none the wiser.

What Adani made of these events is unknown. He might have seen the similarities with Indian politics – governments negotiating with selected mega-rich business figures behind closed doors. Doubtless encouraged by the wounding bar-room-style political brawl between one of his main competitors and the Queensland government, he couldn't have failed to notice the personalised decision-making style of the Newman government and its lack of transparency and accountability. Insider political negotiations were his forte. And two of his main competitors had fallen by the wayside.

In pursuit of his pro-development ethos, Newman had ignored the problems other states had experienced. Similar powerful mining forces operated in NSW and, as its Independent Commission Against Corruption (ICAC) warned in 2013, the arrangements at the state level relating to the licensing of coal mines 'provided an opportunity not found in other parts of government for individuals to engage in corrupt conduct'.[62]

The tangled web of corruption

The cosy, secretive and self-serving way in which Queensland mining companies sought to exert influence over government decisions was not, on the surface, especially unusual. For decades Australian state governments had been caught up in corruption-type scandals over their crony relationships with big business. Cronyism involves preferential relations between government and business in which the former bestows favourable deals on the latter outside full consideration of the public interest, independent assessment and/or competitive tendering processes. In return, governments are 'rewarded' with sizeable election donations and potential post-political careers with companies or their lobbyists. As mentioned, Adani had been a beneficiary of such a system in India.

Increasingly, such relationships are seen as corrupting the democratic process, which is supposed to be transparent, accountable and conscious of the public interest – not an arm of the corporate world. Both India and Queensland's democratic processes have been affected by these practices, resulting in decisions on development projects that critics claim work against the public interest.

Such a process is referred to an 'institutional corruption' to distinguish it from 'personal corruption' – handing cash to politicians – for which there is no evidence under the Newman government.

Queensland's notoriety for institutional corruption under the Newman government has been set out in two reports compiled by the progressive think tank The Australian Institute.[63] The material compiled in these reports comes from government documents, the electoral commission annual returns of political donations, details of the close connections between senior bureaucrats and companies, and individual case studies of mining companies' lobbying activities. Together they highlight a systematic pattern of mining interests securing favourable decisions from the government. As the authors of one of the reports noted of the mining projects they studied:

all gained extraordinary access to government ministers and extraordinary outcomes. These outcomes included legislative changes to removed environmental protections, federal and state governmental approval of projects despite serious environmental concerns, and even retrospective approval of illegal mining activities.[64]

There is no generally accepted term to depict a government that allows democratic norms to be fashioned by, and for, vested corporate interests. To describe such a system as 'corrupt' and/or 'cronyism' has its own definitional problems.

Over the past two decades, scandals involving the influence of money on political decision-making have unfolded in several states at a steady pace. As mentioned, Queensland had its own royal commission into the corrupt practices of the Bjelke-Petersen government. In Western Australia the former premier, Brian Burke, has been the subject of two official inquiries over his business dealings.[65] Tasmania has been dogged by claims that both the major political parties were too close to forestry company Gunns Ltd, the state's biggest company and its largest political donor.[66] And New South Wales has been wracked by the corrupt activites of Labor MPs Eddie Obeid and Ian Macdonald, both of whom are currently serving prison sentences.[67]

All state governments are vulnerable to corruption scandals because historically they have placed the highest priority on developing their primary resources. Courting big corporations often leaves them prone to being captured by them. Granting licences for companies to exploit valuable state-owned primary products such as forestry, mining and fishing involves large transfers of assets from public to private hands in a process that necessitates the highest standards of accountability and transparency on the government's part.[68] But good governance is often lacking at the state level.

Where then does Queensland fit today into this schema of

corruption? Environmental journalist Graham Readfearn, in a research paper for The Australia Institute, points to a key difference from other states when he writes of 'a systematic web of access and influence for fossil fuel companies'.[69] This web of influence in Queensland under both Bligh and Newman saw government captured by the industry for special deals; the difference between the two governments lies in the extent of the capture and the greater lengths to which Newman went in undermining democratic norms.

The influence of miners in the state was such that it resembles what some analysts refer to as a 'shadow government'. Used across a range of contemporary examples of corruption scandals, a 'shadow government' is said to exist when politicians and selected, influential business figures facilitate private control over public resources, causing institutional decay of formal government structures.[70] The concept has been used to explain the widespread shift to the privatisation of government services in Great Britain over the past several decades, which involved transferring massive wealth to private companies in a process shrouded in secrecy.[71]

By its very nature, a 'shadow' government is hard to define – the network of interests that constitute its power and how these might be linked and organised are kept secret. For some, the concept might seem too nebulous. For others, it might simply resemble the more established concept of the organised lobbying industry. Yet the example of the Queensland mining industry shows that it forged deep, symbiotic links with government in ways that were designed to facilitate favourable outcomes for the industry in a system of limited accountability. In this sense, the mining industry was a 'shadowy' partner with government. The lack of an upper house might make Queensland more vulnerable to the shadowy influence of corporations.

How then did this system operate in Queensland?

Queensland's 'shadow government'

In January 2015, when most Queenslanders were enjoying their summer break and otherwise disconnected from politics, the powerful QRC was busily engaged in interfacing with state politicians. It used Twitter to tell MPs what their individual electorates gained out of the mining industry in terms of jobs and money spent on goods and services. In what had become a time-honoured mining industry practice, the QRC provided the MPs with a type of economic modelling that inflated the benefits of mining, but which had been discredited by the Australian Bureau of Statistics and the Productivity Commission.[72]

How many of the MPs used the incorrect data to provide 'talking points' in their electorates is unknown but the attempt at such blatant, self-serving promotion had become a chief weapon in the mining industry's ongoing campaign for hearts and minds, especially in the face of what they feared was a rising tide of anti-coal community sentiment fostered by the broad coalition of environment and community-based groups. The QRC's modus operandi was to reshape information into propaganda.

The QRC is a key component of this system of unaccountable power. The organisation has symbiotic links to its national counterpart, the Minerals Council of Australia (MCA), and the Australian Coal Association (ACA) and to fraternal state bodies, especially the New South Wales Mineral Council. Among its most recent members are GVK-Hancock and Adani Mining. In NSW and Queensland, 'coal mining is the main mining game by a big margin' for the mining lobby.[73]

Each of the peak mining bodies are funded by national and international mining companies, the latter wielding enormous influence, especially export coal corporations. The board of MCA includes BHP-Billiton, Rio Tinto, Xstrata Coal Australia, Anglo American and Peabody Energy – all with major interests in coal. In August 2013, the ACA announced that it was going to be subsumed into the MCA, effectively creating a dominating presence in the expanded lobby group. As journalist Mike Seccombe wrote, '[r]epresentatives of the biggest polluters on the planet now run the show [at the MCA]'.[74] In fact, the merger proved to be a smart move for the coal industry. With the environment movement gunning for it, there was a strategic advantage in lodging itself in the main peak body, from which it could exercise a controlling influence and with many times the budget to exercise its power.

The era of 'Big Coal' had arrived. Anti-coal campaigner Bob Burton has estimated that together, the mining industry's peak bodies pulled in more than $100000000 between 2012 and 2014 to press their case for coal.[75] Acting separately and in concert, 'Big Coal' exercises its power in three main ways: recruiting senior government officials to its ranks; lobbying in the corridors of power; and as a public relations machine promoting its pro-coal propaganda.

As the 'shadow government' in Queensland, 'Big Coal' has achieved enormous success. It has shaped the pro-coal narrative driving the state's politics, extracted enormous public subsidies for its projects, shaped policy to pave the way for its ongoing expansion, intervened directly in the political process when its interests were threatened, and fended off public concerns about its impacts on the Great Barrier Reef and climate change.

Newman, like Anna Bligh before him, had to deal with the reality of 'Big Coal's' powerful hold on the state. Whether they believed it or not, both leaders parroted the industry's PR line that coal was the lifeblood of the Queensland economy. Together, political leaders and the coal industry created a distorted picture of its contribution to Queensland. This was revealed in a survey of Queenslanders published by The Australia Institute, which found that Queenslanders believed the industry employed 10 times more people than it actually did and that its contribution to the State's revenue was five times greater than it was in reality.[76] The survey was part of a report on the state's coal industry, which showed that it was among the state's smallest employers (1.2 per cent of overall employment) and contributed a modest 4 per cent to government revenues. As the report noted, the Queensland coal industry 'makes a lot of noise … it is the mouse that roars'.[77]

The industry's 'roar' had produced the biggest government subsidies to the mining industry of any state in Australia. Not surprisingly, the mining industry prefers this issue be kept out of the public discussion as much as possible because public handouts to an otherwise wealthy industry do not seem a rational response by government and they undermine the argument jointly advanced by government and industry that the coal industry makes a vital contribution to the State's revenue base. However, studies that The Australia Institute has undertaken show that Queensland taxpayers' subsidies to the mining industry totalled $9.5 billion between 2008–09 and 2013–14. In the latter year, these were equivalent to the amount government spent on disability services and capital expenditure on hospitals.[78]

In fact, the provision of social services in Queensland suffers as a consequence of the subsidies given by governments to the mining industry. Social services in Queensland are under-funded in comparison with other states. As The Australia Institute wrote: 'Queensland's Treasury makes it clear that part of this problem is the state's continual spending on assistance for the mining industry. State-funded mining infrastructure comes at the expense of schools and hospitals'.[79] Opening up the Galilee only exacerbated how much the state budget was skewed towards subsidising mining. Independent research showed that the Queensland government had spent $2 billion of public money in assisting the expansion of Abbot Point without any economic assessment of the spending.[80] Such analyses of Queensland government spending contradicted Newman's assertion about the importance of the coal industry to Queensland's revenue base. The reverse was also true; mining redirected precious public monies away from the provision of essential services.

The QRC was instrumental in pushing to open up the Galilee Basin. For many years the council was headed by Michael Roche, who provided the organisation with consummate insider status. In fact, Roche was a classic example of the revolving door of government insiders who moved into the mining industry, providing a seamless symbiotic working relationship between the two. Roche had enjoyed senior management roles with the Australian Stock Exchange in Sydney before entering the government sector in Canberra as a senior executive in the Department of Prime Minister and Cabinet. He then headed to Queensland in various senior roles, including Deputy Director General in the Queensland Cabinet Office. He also served on the boards of the ACA and the MCA, thus cementing relationships and expertise across the interface between government and the mining industry. The growth of that interface helped give the industry its power.

Loopholes in the already weak laws governing the operation of lobbyists underpinned the QRC's ability to operate behind the scenes. Peak bodies like it were exempt from the register of lobbyists and therefore were not required to disclose their interactions with government.[81] How the organisation went about pushing its views in the corridors of power for opening up the Galilee and for the benefits extended to Adani cannot be known, but are easily inferred.

Nonetheless, the QRC also maintained a high public profile under Roche's leadership. Its annual function attracted hundreds of supporters in mining, business and politics. The organisation also ran media advertising campaigns that pushed the industry's distorted views of the benefits of coal mining. It staunchly maintained that any attempts to halt port development along the Great Barrier Reef amounted to, in Roche's words, a 'political anti-resources agenda'.[82] In April–May 2014, it teamed up with the state government to produce a 'Reef Facts' campaign that included TV advertisements and a website.

The $2.4 million campaign was mounted to address two

political problems. Firstly, the government's own polling in South East Queensland confirmed the results of previous polls: the public was worried about the health of the Great Barrier Reef. The polls recorded high levels of distrust about what the government was telling people along with their concerns that environmental interests were coming 'a clear second' to the government's economic agenda. Secondly, the government was concerned about the World Heritage Committee's impending decision on the status of the reef. Together, the government and QRC went on the front foot to counter what they perceived as the campaign by conservationists to 'trash' the government's reputation as manager of the reef.[83] Teaming up with the mining industry – and the perception this might create – did not bother the Newman government; rather it seemed they were partnering with a natural ally.

The pitch driving the 'Reef Facts' campaign was that the Great Barrier Reef was not under threat from global warming, dredging nor shipping traffic. It misleadingly claimed that these were the findings from the Australian Institute of Marine Science, citing one of its papers published in 2012, which found that most coral loss resulted from cyclones (48 per cent), crown-of-thorns starfish (42 per cent) and global warming-induced coral bleaching (10 per cent). In other words, the coal industry was having little or no impact on the reef.

Yet the QRC and the Newman government had misrepresented the scientific paper in question and, more broadly, the scientific consensus on the state of the reef. The Marine Institute's paper only set out to examine three of the disturbances to coral and prefaced its findings by pointing out that risk factors to the reef included dredging and coastal development, including ports. Moreover, the authors emphasised the future threat from global warming: '[r]egional policies cannot protect coral reefs from global-scale risks due to climate change-associated heat stress and intensifying tropical storms ... Mitigation of global warming and ocean acidification is essential for the future of the GBR'.[84]

However, Roche pronounced the campaign a great success: 'Since the start of the campaign, there has been a three-fold increase in visits to the Queensland Government's Reef facts website with thousands more visitors to the QRC's Working Alongside the Great Barrier Reef website'.[85] Inside government and in the public realm, the QRC continued to aggressively push the line that there was no direct scientific link between coal mining and climate change.[86] The reef was safe, it said.

Roche was just one example of the ever-spinning revolving door of senior government bureaucrats quietly transferring to senior roles in the mining lobby and helping to keep the industry embedded in government. Senior officers in government and industry move back and forth between positions, undermining public confidence in the independence of government in its dealings with the mining industry.[87]

This 'revolving door' allows former mining sector employees to be involved in assessing mining industry projects for government. It also raises the prospect that government staff may have an eye to future employment in the mining industry when making decisions, or that they take with them sensitive government information when they switch over. The arrangement is designed to suit both sides.

Jeff Seeny's Department of State Development was headed by David Edwards, who, before accepting the position, was a senior manager with the company GDH, which provided consultancy services to the resources sector. Edwards became known as the Newman government's 'chief bureaucrat for corporate boxes', such was his ability to pick up high-quality seats at major sporting and theatre events.[88] He was part of a custom in the Newman government (and no doubt others) of holding high-level private meetings with coal company executives and others because such meetings were classed as 'in-house' and didn't require disclosure on official registers of lobbying. As the *Courier Mail* reported: 'The free tickets [given to Edwards] have been offered by a vast array of different business sectors, from mining companies with multi-billion dollar deals that hinge on government approvals to firms of lawyers, insurers and consultants'.[89] In fact, so common were these forms of lobbying that Queensland's regulatory framework for lobbying was undermined. One expert told a state parliament inquiry into the practice that the current regulations '[catch] 20 per cent of people who actually lobby'.[90]

Edwards had a 'working dinner' on an evening in February 2013 with Sanjay Reddy and his wife Pink Reddy: the $345 bill, including a $99 bottle of Shiraz, was charged to the Queensland taxpayer because, Queensland government officials later explained, it helped to 'develop and maintain working relationships' between GVK and the department. The meeting was to discuss 'rail investment'.[91]

Such commonplace practices as sharing dinners and football matches take on a different meaning when government is in control of sensitive mining projects and is charged with protecting the public interest. The occasions suggest a degree of intimacy between the two sectors, potentially compromising the public interest. As Hannah Aulby and Mark Ogge, researchers at The Australia Institute, comment: 'By contrast, organisations that advocate for the public interest are rarely awarded this degree of access'.[92]

David Moore was an example of an industry lobbyist who came to work at the highest levels of government, only to return to lobby for the mining industry. Director of the firm Next Level Holdings, he came to work with Jeff Seeney in the lead-up to the 2012 state election and returned to his company after the election, where two of his clients were GVK-Hancock and Adani.[93] Next Level Holdings assisted Adani with government backing for the rail line to Abbot Point.[94] Adani also hired a media communications consultant who had formerly been senior media advisor to Seeney, and another who had served as senior advisor to prime ministers Kevin Rudd and Julia Gillard.

Media communication was a key strategy for Adani. Through

his media consultants, he embarked on several television campaigns, as journalist Anna Krien reported:

> In 2013, a television commercial for Adani Australia was
> broadcast across the state. A warm European woman's voice
> asked, 'What does Adani mean to Queensland? A fresh
> stake in the global economy … Adani means 10 000 jobs
> for Queensland workers [cue to image of young man in
> hi-vis vest unspooling cables, smiling boyishly] … Adani
> means $22 billion in royalties and taxes invested back
> into Queensland communities [cue hospital corridor and
> stretchers].'[95]

Yet another consultant hired by Adani had only recently left the position of chief executive of North Queensland Bulk Ports, the location of Adani's coal ports.[96]

In other words, Adani played the insider political game required of corporations in contemporary politics and especially in Queensland. There was no shortage of lobbyists, with excellent credentials, to choose from. Greens MP Jeremy Buckingham found at least 20 senior officials recruited by the Newman government that had shifted between the resources sector and government without any cooling-off period. This included the premier's chief of staff, who had previously worked for the Queensland Gas Company (QGC). While there was nothing illegal about any of this activity, it was so opaque that it is impossible to determine what had been offered to whom and whether any strings were attached.

Buying influence or buying decisions?

The mining industry was not content with being embedded in the Newman government. It sought to buy the loyalty of the party as well through a cascade of political donations. The 80s witnessed the emergence of an 'arms race' in election spending in Australia; 'war chests' funded by corporate Australia.[97] Changes to the electoral laws made by the Howard government (2006) and the Newman government (2014) significantly wound back the limited but hard-won reforms of previous governments and made transparency at the Commonwealth level and in Queensland that much more difficult to establish.

The Howard government lifted the level at which donations had to be disclosed from $1000 to $10 000, adjusted for inflation. In effect, this meant that a corporation or an individual could secretly donate up to $80 000 spread across the eight state/territory branches of the party. Critics alleged that the changes would increase the chances of corruption and make transparency more difficult. As the *Age* reported on 23 May 2006: 'according to one former Howard Government adviser, corporate money does have an impact. "Staff and MPs are encouraged to engage with donors. Not a week would go by without hearing the phrase, 'They are a good supporter'",
he said'.[98]

Newman modelled the Queensland donation laws on the Howard government's, lifting the limits imposed by the Bligh government to the same level as the federal government which, in 2014, was $12 800. The government further relaxed the donation laws by exploiting the gap between what is legally a donation to a political party and what could be classified as a fee for a good or service, which was not covered in the new laws. As political commentator Bernard Keane wrote: 'such lack of transparency is ripe for exploitation by party mates seeking to obtain access and influence'.[99]

Consequently, Queensland was at the front line in this election 'arms race' and the state's mining corporations willingly obliged by funding the party generously. Even before the Newman changes, the LNP had become the most bankrolled political party in Australia, bringing in $17.5 million in donations, just edging out the NSW branch of the Labor Party for the top spot.[100]

Adani Enterprises was one of the donors to both the LNP and the Liberal Party of Australia, handing over a total of $70 300, according to official receipts. The company also obtained 12 meetings with Newman government ministers in 2013–14, including numerous meetings with Jeff Seeney.[101] Officially declared donations were only part of the tsunami of corporate and especially mining donations flooding the LNP. Mining companies offered in-kind support as well. This had created a potentially serious conflict of interest. In the lead-up to the 2012 state election, the public had no suspicion that an LNP official with close ties to the mining industry was developing the LNP's environment policy. Only in May 2014 was it revealed that James Mackay had been directing the government's environmental policy development since 2012. During the election Mackay worked full time for the LNP while also being paid $10 000 a month by the company QCoal, which was owned by the reclusive billionaire Chris Wallin, one of the LNP's biggest donors.[102] When questioned, Newman rejected the charge of conflict of interest because Mackay had disclosed his links with the company to the party. Again no law or regulation had been broken.

To cement its relationship with the corporate sector, and its donations, the Newman government established QForum in the lead-up to the 2012 state election. It was designed, in part, to skirt the electoral laws to increase the level of undocumented donations while providing a venue for confidential meetings with corporate executives. The LNP reassured corporations that joining QForum 'does not constitute a donation or membership of any political party'. A loophole in the electoral act allowed political parties to provide 'subscription services'. The organisation was advertised as 'the place for strategic engagement and policy discussion in Queensland' in the LNP annual report. Journalist Amy Remeikis conveyed some of the flavour of its cosy, shoulder-rubbing culture:

Members are invited to speak to 'business leaders and policy makers together to develop the ideas that are making Queensland an even greater state with even greater opportunity'.

It is structured into different programs – the LNP Corporate Observers programs takes place at the same time as the party's major events 'providing a unique opportunity for business to engage with the Party's organisational and policy leadership, MPs, Senators and Councillors in one place at one time'.

The Leaders' Club, known as the 'forum for the captains of Queensland business' has limited membership which is gained through either invitation or referral.

'This is an exclusive forum for high level policy discussion and networking with political leaders from all three levels of government'.

In effect, QForum provided a system that allowed executives to pay for private access to ministers.

Under Newman, unprecedented amounts of money sloshed around the political system, much of it unaccounted for. Secret dealings between company executives and government were institutionalised. And corporate lobbyists worked the corridors of power with little regulatory oversight about the nature of their dealings. Changes to the electoral laws increased the amounts of undeclared donations and retained loopholes to preserve the anonymity of government relations with business.

Newman bolstered his system of 'shadow government' by weakening, some said emasculating, the Crime and Misconduct Commission. In the midst of its joint campaign with QRC on the Great Barrier Reef, the government introduced legislation to rename the commission to the Crime and Corruption Commission. The changes removed the need for bipartisan support to appoint its head, and to allow its appointed head the sole power to direct that a matter not be investigated, and to increase the threshold of what constituted official misconduct. The changes were widely seen as trashing the legacy of the Fitzgerald inquiry, including by Tony Fitzgerald himself[103] and by Doug Drummond QC, the special prosecutor who helped convict officials in the wake of the inquiry. He claimed the changes posed 'the real risk of moneyed interests acquiring benefits which they shouldn't legitimately acquire' in Queensland. In other words, the commission had become 'an unmuzzled watchdog'.[104]

The changes were necessary to help the Newman government fend off increasingly loud calls for inquiries into its approval for several controversial mines, which were also linked to large donations from the companies concerned. Tony Fitzgerald was one of the rising tide of Queenslanders who thought that the Newman government had debased democracy:

> The Government plainly had a mandate to pursue its
> preference for development over the environment. However,
> it's at least questionable whether it exceeded its mandate by so
> radically weakening environmental protection and approving so
> many controversial projects, breaking pre-election promises and
> benefiting Liberal National Party donors.[105]

However, such was the tightly drawn veil of secrecy surrounding his government's relationship with the mining sector, and in the absence of a Fitzgerald-style inquiry, the extent of the corruption is impossible to fully assess. Nonetheless, Adani was one of the biggest beneficiaries of the Newman's style of government.

At the January 2015 state election voters sent Newman packing. Labor leader Annastacia Palaszczuk had performed little short of a political miracle, returning Labor to government after its own shattering defeat four years earlier. Adani needed to ensure that the new premier backed its project, and hired lobbying firm Next Level Strategic Services in February 2015. The ABC's Stephen Long analysed the Queensland register of lobbyists and found that Next Level undertook 33 lobbying contacts for Adani, more than double the contact reported by any lobbyist on behalf of any other client. Next Level met '24 times with the Queensland Labor Government to push Adani's interests, eight times with the Opposition, and once with the mayor of Townsville'.[106] Over the next few years Palaszczuk gave Adani almost everything it sought. Significantly, the Carmichael mine was declared a 'critical infrastructure project' – a status never before granted to a mining project – and which exempted it from a range of planning controls and legal objections.

A master of insider, crony politics, Gautam Adani had played his hand adroitly in Queensland. But there was a bigger stage still to conquer; he also required ongoing support from the Abbott government. The company probably couldn't imagine how enthusiastic Abbott was about supporting coal.

CHAPTER SEVEN

The Abbott government and 'standing up for coal'

After the Abbott government was elected in 2013, one of the first acts the Minister for the Environment Greg Hunt undertook was to ring Tim Flannery, head of the Climate Commission, to inform him that the agency was being abolished. Flannery was expecting the call. Abbott had campaigned on closing the commission, which the Gillard government had created to monitor climate change in Australia and to provide information for the community. As Flannery later explained to the *Saturday Paper:* 'Not only did they abolish it – we knew it was coming – they took down the website, on which millions of dollars had been spent, and [which] was being used by people like teachers, farmers and other groups around Australia'.[1] It appeared as if the government was trying to expunge official recognition of climate change. As experienced journalist Mike Seccombe commented, the Abbott government 'and its backers in the fossil fuel industry just don't like anyone talking about climate change'.[2]

But the demise of the commission was merely part of the most systematic attack on environment policy ever undertaken by any government in the nation's history. Abbott acted on his signature campaign issue to abolish the carbon tax; the event was recorded in a photograph showing him clapping his colleagues in a triumphant gesture as if they had pulled off an historic victory, which in fact they had. Australia became the first nation to abolish legislation to deal with climate change. However, Abbott's targets were wide-ranging: Australia's contribution to international efforts to deal with climate change stalled; renewable energy was demonised and subjected to funding cuts and a reduced target; hundreds of jobs were cut from the federal Department of the Environment; savage cuts were dealt to environmental groups; action to address the decline of the Great Barrier Reef was marginalised in favour of its industrialisation; science policy was jettisoned; protection of the nation's water resources was weakened; and highland national parks were opened up for cattle grazing. As Seccombe wrote: 'the Abbott government is way out in the right field on the environment, even by comparison with past Coalition governments and conservative governments overseas'.[3]

This culture of anti-environmentalism, climate science denialism and pro-coal advocacy was responsible for Greg Hunt's quicktime approval of the Carmichael mine . It was later challenged and briefly overturned in the Federal Court before being reinstated in an amended form (see Chapter 10).

Abbott envisaged that Australia would become an 'international energy superpower'. As he told an Asian Society dinner on a visit to Houston in April 2014: 'Australia should be an affordable energy superpower, using nature's gifts to the benefit of our people and the wider world'.[4] What he meant, of course, was a fossil fuel/coal superpower. Abbott had simply picked up an old line run by John Howard when he tried to sell the same slogan to the public in 2006, without getting any political leverage from it. But when Abbott repackaged it for the Houston audience, it attracted widespread media interest in Australia. The slogan encapsulated Abbott's anti-environment agenda and its binary mindset: his government would embrace coal and fossil fuels and cast the environmental movement as the enemy.

Abbott's anti-environmentalism

Locating Abbott's views on the environment are like trying to make landfall in a fog; what appears clear one moment quickly becomes obscured the next. Contradiction came easily to him. He once tried to philosophically define conservatism as inherently connected to conservation; both involved 'keeping the best of what we have'.[5]

Just after Abbott rolled Turnbull to become leader, Bob Brown paid him a courtesy call. Brown was not surprised when Abbott 'looked straight at me and said, "I am an environmentalist!"'. 'I did not roll my eyes or argue', Brown later explained. 'I had heard the like before. The CEO of Tasmania's Hydro-Electric Commission, after flooding Lake Pedder and at the height of the controversy over damming the Franklin River, maintained that he was an environmentalist. So have a string of other dam-builders, loggers and gougers of the Earth'.[6]

Brown was aware that Abbott had been repeating this absurdity for years. Abbott seemed to think that mere repetition of the claim meant that audiences would believe him.

After he became Opposition leader, Abbott delivered a speech on the environment to the Sydney Institute in which he tried to spruik his green credentials. He declared that 'it's a good conservative principle that each generation should aim to leave the planet in better shape than we found it'. Concern for the environment had been part of his childhood and adolescence, he explained:

> As a child exploring the bushland near the family home, a
> teenager canoeing down New South Wales' coastal rivers, a
> student trekking through the wilderness to Sydney's west or,
> these days, as a surfer and volunteer firefighter, I have always
> had a strong consciousness of environmental values and an
> appreciation of the need to protect the one planet that we have
> to live on.[7]

The difference he had with the contemporary green movement, he explained, 'is about how best to preserve the environment, not the importance of the task'. His approach was based on 'practical environmentalism' rather than the sort of grand moral statements issued by Kevin Rudd.[8] However the term 'practical environmentalism' – also used by John Howard – left plenty of scope for interpretation and side-stepping. And, as his actions as prime minister showed, Abbott's assault on environment policy was ideologically and politically driven.

Abbott brought his warrior mentality to the task of white-anting Australia's environmental policy framework. Out of step with 21st-century thinking about the environment, Abbott's views were forged in another era, by conservative Catholic mentors who opposed environmentalism and who upheld the divine command for humans to subdue nature to serve human ends.

These views were shaped by two influential mentors; the first was the dour Catholic Cold War warrior BA Santamaria, whom Abbott idealised. Santamaria was a polarising figure, just as his protégé became. His dogged pursuit of Communist sympathisers inside the Labor movement helped split the party in the early 1950s. But Santamaria also had a grim view of Western permissiveness. He was disdainful of the emerging social movements of feminism, gay rights and environmental activism. Explaining his views on the latter towards the end of his life Santamaria said: 'When I speak of that [the environment] it's sort of a deep attachment ... [but] I don't want to make a fetish of it, or a science out of it'.[9] Young recruits like Abbott, drawn into Santamaria's staunchly conservative Catholic movement, were expected to devote their lives 'in a grand battle to save civilisation' and to do so without compromise.[10]

Abbott later came under the tutelage and friendship of another polarising, conservative and authoritarian figure. George Pell, the outspoken and controversial former Cardinal of Sydney, and currently senior Vatican Treasury official, is a climate change denier and anti-environmentalist. His views have been at odds with more recent Vatican teaching which, since at least 1990, has endorsed the view that destruction of the environment and (more recently) climate change are serious threats.[11] Brushing the Vatican aside, Pell used his influence and bulldog-like personality to become an influential figure in the debate about climate change in Australia.

In a 2011 address to the British Global Warming Policy Foundation, Pell argued that the community's concern for climate change and the environment were symptoms of the West's 'pagan emptiness' – a Western fear when confronted by the immense and basically uncontrollable forces of nature. Without religion, he thought, people would inevitably be frightened of something. Perhaps, pondered Pell, they're looking for a cause that is almost a substitute for religion.[12] His claim was a standard trope in climate change denialist literature.

In a long, rambling speech, Pell went on to declare his belief that environmentalists harboured 'anti-human claims' before trotting out the standard denialist critique of climate science, an account described by experts in the field as 'dreadful', 'utter rubbish' and 'flawed'.[13] Abbott has made no secret of his closeness to Pell and of seeking out his guidance, and Pell was effusive in praising Abbott's leadership.[14] On environmental issues, the two share the same views.

However, appeals to religious teachings alone don't account for Abbott's war on the environment. His campaign blended into his alpha male personality, which journalist and author David Marr has so vividly described.[15] Encouraged by his family to believe in his destiny, Abbott grew up with a romantic and grandiose view of his place in the world. Imbued with a powerful determination 'to stand for old ideas and old authority', and 'against the political tide',[16] Abbott became a warrior for fossil fuels and sought to slay the dragon of environmentalism.

Like any Liberal politician, Abbott had an acute sense of the forces shaping conservative opinion on climate change: the so-called 'shock-jocks' of the corporate media. Alan Jones, Ray Hadley, Andrew Bolt, Miranda Devine and the like have done 'a very good job of linking climate change to bongo-playing, weed-smoking hippy lefties'. The hijacking of the climate change cause by this group has 'played perfectly into the hands of the big polluters'.[17] Tony Abbott understood the emotional appeal of the shock-jocks' rhetoric and, as one commentator bitingly conceded, saved the fossil fuel industry 'millions in lobbying expenses'.[18]

However, the shock-jocks were only one of the centres of influence promoting fossil fuels that Abbott latched on to. As previously mentioned, before coming to power he paid due deference to Murdoch and to the Institute of Public Affairs (IPA). Not surprisingly, he gave the mining industry a seat at his government's table. Anne Davies from the *Sydney Morning Herald* found a similar interconnected network of power at the federal level as had existed under Campbell Newman in Queensland. AGL Energy was just one of the companies that played 'revolving door' politics between government and the industry:

> AGL tends to favour in-house representation in its dealings with politicians. The current head of government relations is Lisa Harrington, who was until 2013 a senior adviser to Mike Baird [then NSW State Treasurer]. She replaced Sarah McNamara at AGL, who went back to work in the Prime Minister's office with her old colleague Peta Credlin whom she knew from her days in Communications minister Helen Coonan's office. McNamara was Abbott's policy adviser on resources for a year and is now chief of staff to the federal minister for industry (and resources) Ian Macfarlane. Shaughn Morgan, AGL's manager of government and external affairs, has similarly impressive credentials on the Labor side. He was an adviser to NSW Attorney General Jeff Shaw in the 1990s and worked with Adam Searle, now Labor's NSW resources spokesman.[19]

And behind the scenes was the guiding hand of the Minerals Council of Australia (MCA) and its state counterparts, especially the Queensland Resources Council (QRC) and the New South Wales Minerals Council. Greens leader Christine Milne tried to call out Abbott's connections to the fossil fuel power network. In a speech at the National Press Club in April 2014, she termed the network surrounding the Coalition as an 'Abbott, Murdoch, Rinehart collaboration directed and promoted by the Institute of Public Affairs'.[20] The press duly reported her speech but did not investigate whether, in fact, her assertion that Australia was being run on behalf of a group of oligarchs had merit. Independent member for New England Tony Windsor felt that the issue of donations in the Abbott era needed investigation. With the relationship between Gina Rinehart and Nationals leader Barnaby Joyce in mind, he told federal parliament:

> If a mining magnate does want to relay money to a particular
> political party because of some favour that might be granted
> at some future date, they can do that without being traced
> through a whole range of funds and associated entities that
> the major political parties currently have. This is an issue that
> needs to be explored very closely, because we could be moving
> towards an American system where money does buy favour and
> where money does lobby for particular policy changes.[21]

Windsor wanted Rinehart to clarify her interest in the seat of New England:

> Does it have anything to do with coal seam gas on the
> Liverpool Plains? Does it have something to do with the water
> trigger, the amendment to the *Environmental Protection and
> Biodiversity Conservation Act* that is currently before the Senate?
> Senator Joyce, who is a candidate in New England, was part of

the delaying tactics to prevent that amendment getting through
the parliament the week before last.[22]

As mentioned, the core of Abbott's thinking on the environment
was the common, religiously inspired, anthropocentric idea that
the economy takes primacy over the environment and, as prime
minister, Abbott expounded this view many times. On one occasion he declared that while there was only one habitable planet,
which 'we should try to protect', humanity 'shouldn't sacrifice the
economy just to save the environment'.[23] On another occasion
he said: 'We don't support, as a government and as a coalition,
further lock-ups of our forests. We just don't support it. We have
quite enough national parks. We have quite enough locked-up
forests already. In fact, in an important respect, we have too much
locked-up forest'. His comments were delivered to a timber industry dinner in Canberra where he also confirmed his government's
request to the World Heritage Committee to delist 74 000 hectares
of Tasmania's World Heritage area to open it up for logging.[24]

While such views are common in sections of the community,
they were out of step with mainstream thinking about sustainability
and the environment. As critics argued, Abbott's views represented
the antiquated thinking that nature should be made available for
humans to exploit; and, more latterly, as a resource to increase business profits and a mantra in neoliberalism's commitment to growth
and a deregulated free market. Cheap fossil fuel energy was the cornerstone of Abbott's vision for Australia.

The Abbott government was not only uninterested in examining the short-sightedness of this vision, it took active steps to sup-
press contrary views. His government was explicitly anti-science.
The government abolished the position of Minister for Science as
a discrete portfolio and slashed research budgets, leaving scientists
feeling that their discipline was 'being systematically removed at all
levels'.[25] Abbott had riled the scientific community who were 'bitter

and angry' at the cuts of more than half a billion dollars to the country's esteemed scientific institutions, including the Commonwealth Scientific and Industrial Research Organisation (CSIRO) and the Australian Research Council.[26] Certainly critics believed that anti-science positions had been taken to a level never seen before in Australia.[27] Environmental scientists, in particular, expressed dismay at the Abbott's government's policies describing them as 'an environmental train wreck'. Some felt that they were 'screaming in the dark' to convince the government to adopt a more sustainable course.[28]

Well-known climate change deniers were appointed to official government positions. Abbott appointed Maurice Newman to chair his business advisory panel. Newman's ideas on climate change have been described as 'crazy'.[29] His many rogue statements on the issue include the paranoid-sounding conspiracy theory that climate change was a hoax led by the United Nations to end democracy and impose authoritarian rule.[30] In another outburst, he asserted that people who used the term 'denier' to describe those who deny the science should themselves be described as 'global warming Nazis'.[31]

Abbott appointed fossil fuel executive and climate change denier Dick Warburton to head a review of the renewable energy target in a move reminiscent of the old adage about the fox in charge of the chicken coop. The prime minister was known to be close to prominent denier Ian Plimer, Professor of Geology at Adelaide University who, as mentioned, was an advisor to mining magnate Gina Rinehart, herself an avid climate change denier. Abbott also developed links to Bjorn Lomborg, an internationally prominent campaigner against action on climate change. Before the Abbott government was elected, Greg Hunt revealed that Lomborg's 'modelling' was a centrepiece for the Coalition's Direct Action policy. As political scientist Michael Holmes writes:

> Lomborg's particularly dangerous form of climate denial is to
> begrudgingly accept the science while producing economic

models to say that global warming is really a minor issue. He is famous for using economic modelling as a mercenary gun for hire, saleable to governments and jurisdictions requiring climate inaction, climate distraction, or just straight-out climate crisis denial.[32]

Until the election of US President Donald Trump in November 2016, there wasn't a government anywhere in the Western world, or beyond, that sought advice from such a cabal of anti-science 'experts'. Australia's future was indeed being radically reshaped.

'Coal is good for humanity'

Having established his intention to develop Australia into a fossil fuel superpower, and a laggard in developing renewable energy, Abbott felt the need to create the economic and moral case for this vision. Abbott's address at the opening of the Caval Ridge Mine in central Queensland in October 2014 did just that. Abbott had intended to sharpen his case for coal because he wanted to flag his opposition to the Chinese government, which had just imposed a harsh, 6 per cent tariff on imported coal as part of its long-term plan to reduce its use. Coal, the prime minister declared, had a big future. Then he produced the media headline that helped define his vision for Australia: 'Let's have no demonisation of coal. Coal is good for humanity, coal is good for prosperity, coal is an essential part of our economic future, here in Australia and right around the world'.[33]

In May 2014, addressing an MCA dinner he attacked the coal industry's critics. The tone of his speech was as revealing as its content:

I want you to know that you are not in hostile territory; you are here amongst people who want you to flourish and if there is one message that I can give you this evening, it is

that this government wants you to succeed, because when
you succeed, our country succeeds. It's particularly important
that we do not demonise the coal industry and if there was
one fundamental problem, above all else, with the carbon tax,
it was that it said to our people, it said to the wider world,
that a commodity which … is our biggest single export,
somehow should be left in the ground and not sold. Well
really and truly, I can think of few things more damaging to
our future.[34]

Some thought Abbott had gone too far in spruiking coal in this way. As respected journalist Laura Tingle observed: Abbott 'has for one reason or another appeared to tip more and more of the government's political eggs into the coal basket. It's been a nightmare for the industry because Tony Abbott has now made coal a deeply political issue'.[35]

Abbott government ministers also took up the 'moral' case for coal. The claim that it was 'good for humanity' was repeated many times by senior ministers. Greg Hunt, for example, claimed that Australian coal would be 'providing electricity to up to 100 million people in India [who] can be lifted out of poverty where there can be electricity for schools and hospitals'.[36]

Several points can be made about this attempt to create the moral case for coal. Firstly, the coal industry devised the two slogans commonly used by Coalition politicians. As Graham Readfearn has documented, US coal giant Peabody energy first laid out the 'moral' case in a 2010 speech at the World Energy Conference – coal would help the poor and 'clean coal' would help reduce global emissions.[37] There were dangerously ill-informed components to these claims. Coal contributed to the premature deaths of millions of people around the world as well as lifting the poor out of poverty through access to coal-fired power manufacturing jobs. China had shown how rapidly this model could be developed but at an enormous cost to its environment and the health of its people. Abbott's ministers' practice of ignoring the growing understanding of the global ill-effects of coal amounted to wilful ignorance. In sum, Australia's coal industry was involved in exporting climate change and causing growing numbers of premature deaths. Nevertheless, the inflated and misleading claims about the benefits of coal were picked up and promoted by the Australian Coal Association (incorporated into the MCA in 2013) and the New South Wales Minerals Council. Their line that coal could end global poverty 'became the industry's favourite PR line' and the pitch was repeated parrot-like by the Abbott government.[38]

World Bank president Jim Yong Kim didn't support the Abbott government's claims about coal. He said a rise in average temperatures of 2°C would leave millions of people trapped in poverty. In 2013, the bank had stopped funding coal-fired power plants. In fact, in the previous five years it had doubled its financial support for renewable energy projects such as off-grid household solar in Bangladesh and Mongolia, wind farms in Turkey and geothermal projects in Kenya. In announcing the bank's policy, Kim declared: 'we wanted to make clear that a two degrees Celsius warmer world would be a disaster that we have to avoid'.[39]

In July 2015, Oxfam Australia reported that coal is 'not good for humanity'. It concurred with the World Bank: for the world's poor, 'renewable energy solutions offer a much more affordable, practical and healthy solution than coal'. It claimed that the Australian coal industry had been falsely promoting coal as 'the main solution for increasing energy access and reducing poverty around the world'. And it made the larger point that denialists in the Howard and Abbott governments had simply refused to countenance: 'the world's poorest people are made even more vulnerable through the increasing risk of droughts, floods, hunger and disease due to climate change'. Australia, Oxfam concluded, 'must rapidly phase out coal from its own energy supply and as a wealthy developed country, do far more to support developing countries with their own renewable energy plans'.[40]

Independent experts in India didn't support Abbott's claim that Australian coal would be good for India's poor either. EAS Sarma, a former secretary of India's Ministry of Power, argued that 'Australian coal doesn't make sense for us – but renewables do'. Rejecting the push to develop the Carmichael mine to export coal to India, Sarma argued that adding new-generation coal capacity largely benefitted existing affluent customers because many villages are beyond the reach of the electricity grid, and the pollution from coal plants disproportionately affected the poorest. Hence, local-scaled renewables were the only answer.[41]

There was more than a whiff of colonialism in Abbott's thinking on India's energy future. He conveniently overlooked the growing concern in India about the nation's alarming rise in air pollution levels. While India's cities were enveloped in pollution, Australia's national interest, as defined by Abbott, was synonymous with that of the big mining corporations.

There is no indication that Abbott ever briefed himself on India's air pollution, but the trends were clear. As its growth rates rocketed under the liberalisation of its economy and the privatisation of its power plants, successive Indian governments had turned a blind eye to reports warning of an atmospheric crisis, a toxic brew of dangerous gases, to which pollution from coal power plants was a major contributor. Governments unwilling to confront vested interests had ignored at least 15 studies undertaken between 2000–2015.[42] However, from 2013 onwards, the problem had become a national crisis: estimates then showed that Indians were dying prematurely in the hundreds of thousands each year. Then, based on data gathered in 2015, the respected medical journal the *Lancet* found that there were 2.5 million premature deaths in India from air pollution. Worldwide, it found that 9 million people died prematurely in 2015 from air pollution, representing 16 per cent of all deaths.[43]

The very coal rush that Abbott was supporting in opening up the Galilee was attracting international concern. In November 2014, just weeks after Abbott uttered his slogan that coal is 'good for humanity', the *New York Times* reported that Australia's coal rush 'could push the world into irreversible climate change and make Indian cities, already among the world's most polluted, even more unliveable'.[44]

Not surprisingly, this message failed to penetrate the mental wall of climate change denialism and anti-science that Abbott had built around his government.

The campaign against renewables

If it was moral to use coal, then renewable energy must be an enemy. On coming to power, Abbott signalled that his government was preparing to slash the Renewable Energy Target (RET) of 20 per cent set by the Rudd government. Abbott said a cut was necessary to complement his plan for Australia to be 'an affordable energy superpower'.[45] He regretted that the Howard government had ever established the modest 2 per cent target in the first place.

However, the long-drawn-out negotiations to reduce the RET were accompanied by ideologically driven statements so irrational they laid bare the government's real agenda of squeezing the sector in favour of the coal industry. Treasurer Joe Hockey set the tone. In the lead-up to the government's first budget in May 2014, he unleashed a personal tirade in an interview on Macquarie Radio against the turbines operating outside Canberra and being used to supply Sydney's desalination plant. Hockey surprised most Australians with his unvarnished views: 'If I can be a little indulgent please, I drive to Canberra to go to Parliament, I drive myself and I must say I find those wind turbines around Lake George to be utterly offensive. I think they're just a blight on the landscape'.[46] It was a line repeated many times by Abbott, who described wind farms as 'visually awful'.[47]

Only a few months into his prime ministership, Abbott initiated 'a hostile review' of the RET. As mentioned, he appointed former Caltex chairman and climate change denier Dick Warburton to undertake the review, which became a co-ordinated attack on the industry. Fossil fuel lobbyists such as Matthew Warren's Australian Energy Council (AEC), the IPA, and online anti-renewables 'hate site' 'Stop These Things' joined in the Abbott government's attack on the renewables industry.[48] In fact, on one occasion, Abbott went on Alan Jones' radio program and said eight times that he wanted to stop 'these things' (wind turbines) – an uncanny reference to the website.[49] The MCA kept up a running attack on the renewables sector, shamelessly complaining about subsidies it received. The Abbott government's eventual 20 per cent cut to the national RET diminished the sector's prospects but led to a public backlash against the government.

The RET was one of the three main pillars of renewable energy policy developed under the Rudd and Gillard governments in negotiation with the Greens. The other two were the Clean Energy Finance Corporation (CEFC), which funded projects around Australia, and the Australian Renewable Energy Agency (ARENA), which fostered innovation in the area. The Abbott government's attempts to abolish both agencies failed several times in the Senate, whereupon it stripped each of funding.

Uncertainty around the national policy framework had caused renewable energy investment to collapse by 90 per cent over the preceding 12 months, more than 2500 people lost their jobs, and Australia lost valuable time to transit out of its own domestic dependence on ageing coal-fired power stations. Abbott was killing the renewable energy sector while it was booming in other parts of the world and while Australia continued to be powered by a 'clapped-out old energy fleet that belongs in the Eastern Bloc'.[50] A representative from the renewables sector accused the government in July 2015 of waging 'an aggressively ideological agenda' because 'solar and other renewables are competing with coal, and Abbott is intent on protecting that industry'.[51]

Renewable energy wasn't the only area the Abbott government targeted with funding cuts. Environmental organisations that advocated renewable energy and/or actively opposed the Abbott government's industrialisation of the Great Barrier Reef were subject to savage cuts in the 2014 Budget. These groups included the Environmental Defenders Offices, the Great Barrier Reef Marine Park Authority and Land Care.

The 2014 Budget also cut the program – Grants to Voluntary Environment and Sustainability and Heritage Organisations – designed to assist state conservation councils and their member groups, as well as hundreds of grassroots groups throughout the country, with grants of between $2000 and $77 000. It had been in operation since 1973 and was vital in providing a grassroots voice to environmental issues. As one spokesperson told the *Guardian*: 'This will have a dire impact. It's starting to look like [the Government] are trying to silence environmental organisations'.[52]

Australia's backsliding on climate change

Defending the coal industry inevitably brought the Abbott government into conflict with international efforts to deal with climate change. The government intended to wind back Australia's efforts, consistent with the goal of promoting Australia's export coal industry. Abbott intended to abolish another government agency dealing with climate change – the Climate Change Authority – which the Gillard government had set up as part of the package of initiatives negotiated with Greens leader Christine Milne.

Independent of government, the purpose of the authority, as envisaged by the Greens, was to provide government with independent advice on how to lower emissions through recommending an appropriate greenhouse gas emissions target.[53] Milne was aware that there was a gamble to this approach because everything depended on appointments to the board and the Greens could negotiate only three members; the government had the choice of nominating the remaining six. However, the board comprised people with high-level expertise. Former Reserve Bank head Bernie Fraser was the authority's chair and its board had eight other high-profile members, including the chief scientist Ian Chubb, the former head of the Australian Industry group Heather Ridout, academic economist John Quiggin, and high-profile public policy academic Clive Hamilton.

Abbott's efforts to abolish the authority also ran into opposition in the Senate. Meanwhile, the authority produced a draft report that was highly critical of the Abbott government's position on climate change.[54]

Abbott's confrontation over climate change intensified over preparations for the G20 meeting to be held in Brisbane in November 2014. The meeting occurred at a pivotal moment in both the domestic and intergovernmental debates on climate change. The Paris climate talks – set for December 2015 – were expected to produce a binding international agreement to limit temperature rises to 2°C. Prior to the G20 meeting, American president Barack Obama had negotiated a separate bilateral agreement with the Chinese government on their respective countries' contribution to reducing greenhouse gases. Moreover, the Intergovernmental Panel on Climate Change had not long released its latest synthesis on climate change science, warning that without urgent action, global temperatures would rise by more than 2°C, the accepted outer limit for avoiding dangerous climate change.

In Australia, the Great Barrier Reef Marine Authority had also released its latest Outlook Report and it contained a stern warning for the government about action on climate change which, it said:

> remains the most serious threat to the Great Barrier Reef. It
> is already affecting the Reef and is likely to have far-reaching

consequences in the decades to come … The extent and
persistence of these impacts depends to a large degree on
how effectively the issue of rising levels of greenhouse gases is
addressed worldwide.[55]

Unmoved by any of these calls to action, the Abbott government
sought to ensure the issue of climate change would not be discussed
at the G20 meeting, despite the fact that it had been on the agenda
at previous gatherings of the body. As hosts of the meeting, the
Abbott government had some control over the agenda and for the
best part of a year, it lobbied to keep the issue off the table with the
flimsy justification that it wanted the meeting to focus exclusively
on economic issues.

But his efforts to wish away climate change reached farcical levels when a growing body of international leaders including
Barack Obama, United Nations Secretary-General Ban Ki-Moon,
Pope Francis and Britain's Conservative Prime Minister David Cameron joined in calls to put climate change on the agenda. Forced to
concede the issue, the Abbott government nonetheless made sure
that on its G20 meeting website, the words 'climate' and 'sustainability' were absent from the official wording. Economic growth took
centre place in the government's pitch for the meeting.

Barack Obama was the drawcard in Brisbane and he took the
Abbott government's climate change denialism head-on. Addressing an enthusiastic crowd of 1000 students and dignitaries at
Queensland University, the president put climate change at the
centre of his concerns to be addressed by the global leaders gathering in the city. He called on young Australians 'to pressure politicians to resist vested interests and tackle global warming'. And he
highlighted the plight of the Great Barrier Reef in a personal way,
acknowledging the reality that most Australian politicians shied
away from. Obama claimed that the 'natural glory' of the reef was
threatened. He wanted, he said, to be able to bring his daughters

out to experience the reef and 'I want them to be able to bring their daughters and sons to visit and I want it to be there 50 years from now'.[56]

Abbott and his ministers were blindsided by the speech. Abbott was said to be 'privately seething'.[57] Once Obama had left the country the Abbott government made a frontal attack on his 'call to arms' speech. As Lenore Taylor wrote in the *Guardian*:

> Tony Abbott and senior ministers were deeply angry at Barack
> Obama's show-stealing climate change speech during the G20.
> We know because they have been briefing News Ltd columnists
> to that effect all week – including graphic accounts of how
> they rang up afterwards and yelled at state department officials
> for failing to give a 'heads up' that the president was going to
> 'dump on' the PM.[58]

Digging themselves in deeper, Foreign Minister Julie Bishop sought to slap down Obama's concerns about the Great Barrier Reef by saying that the reef was not in danger, and publicly called into question the briefing given to the American president. She contacted the US Secretary of the Interior to 'correct the record'.[59] Trade Minister Andrew Robb backed up the foreign minister and concurred that the president had been 'misinformed'.[60] The combined reaction was a telling illustration of the culture inside the Liberal Party: their anti-science, anti-climate change fixations and their willingness to break with the country's closest ally.

During the G20 discussions, Australia preferred to team up with Canada's Conservative Prime Minister Stephen Harper, who had forged a close friendship with Abbott. Their shared ideology included 'a desire for an emissions-packed future where Canada's dirty tar sands and Australia's coal fuel their nations' respective economies for decades to come'.[61] Together they intended to make a stand to limit action on climate change.

But Abbott and Harper were outgunned at the summit. For his part, Abbott left world leaders bemused by his official speech, in which he focused on domestic policy issues, including his government's proposed co-payment to visit the doctor. As one satirist commented on Australia's embarrassing moment on the world stage: 'Abbott might just as well have been talking about parking meter problems in his home electorate of Warringah'.[62]

After difficult discussions, the final G20 communique included a significant passage on climate change, despite Abbott's impassioned defence of the coal industry. He had made his own call to arms during these closed-door discussions by declaring that he wanted to 'stand up for coal'. But, as the *Sydney Morning Herald* reported, Australia had been forced to back down on its attempts to stifle global action on climate change:

> After much wrangling, the final leaders' communique includes
> a recommendation for nations to commit funds to the UN's
> Green Climate Fund that Prime Minister Tony Abbott
> opposes. According to sources, a clear majority of leaders –
> including US president Barack Obama – argued for stronger
> language in the communique on climate change, to the
> apparent chagrin of Mr Abbott.[63]

Australia had been left isolated.

Meetings with Modi

While the G20 meeting itself was a disaster for the Abbott government, it had spin-offs for its plan to press ahead with opening up the Galilee Basin. The presence of Indian Prime Minister Narendra Modi gave impetus to these plans. India had been Abbott's first overseas visit as prime minister and the gesture paid diplomatic dividends as the two leaders struck up a personal rapport. Modi's visit to Brisbane provided plenty of photo opportunities showing how well the two got on. Together they envisaged taking the India–Australia relationship to a new level. Trade between the two nations was lacklustre and both leaders saw opportunities, particularly for Australian exports of coal, uranium and services. Modi expanded on these themes when he addressed the Australian parliament.

> There are few countries in the world where we see so much synergy as we do in Australia. India is a nation of more than a billion seeking development. Australia is a developed country of a few million people and vast resources. I see Australia as a major partner in every area of our national priority, providing skills and education to our youth, a roof over every head and electricity in every household ... energy that does not cause our glaciers to melt, clean coal and gas, renewable energy and fuel for nuclear power ... India will be the answer to your search for new economic opportunities.[64]

The commitment to increase imports of coal complemented Abbott's vision of Australia as an energy superpower. For his part, Modi had been under pressure to prioritise coal over uranium. Indian businessmen were lobbying for coal: 'With two-thirds of India's power stations fired by coal, and latest data showing that half of them down to a week's stock, tapping into Australia's coal reserves is a more pressing need than accessing uranium'.[65]

Modi came to Brisbane prepared to act. A meeting was arranged in Brisbane between him; Gautam Adani, who came over especially for the meeting; Queensland Premier Campbell Newman; and the chairperson of the government-owned State Bank of India (SBI), Arundhati Bhattacharya. Modi had asked her to come to Brisbane. They struck a deal. SBI would provide a A$1 billion loan to Adani to develop the mine and, as mentioned, the Queensland government offered to raise the funds, through the sale of public assets, to construct the railway to Abbot Point. Newman was desperate to get the project rolling because, by this time, Adani was the last man standing who was willing to take the risk on developing the Galilee.

However, in India the reaction to the deal was altogether different. A storm of criticism erupted in the media that this was another example of Indian crony capitalism: Modi had intervened to help his close friend Adani with a business deal. Opposition parties and environmental groups claimed that Modi had pressured SBI, a claim that Bhattacharya rejected.[66] There was no direct evidence of such pressure but critics pointed out that this was likely the case. In the first instance, the deal was struck at the same time as global banks – Citigroup, Morgan Stanley, JP Morgan Chase, Goldman Sachs, Deutsche Bank, Royal Bank of Scotland, Barclays, Credit Agricole and HSBC – had decided to stay away from funding the project for environmental reasons. Secondly, Adani's gross debt had risen from US$11.5 billion to US$13.5 billion in the six months to September 2014, raising questions about its capacity to service the interest on the loan.[67] In any event, many Indians felt that the 'SBI-Adani episode is a public relations disaster for the bank'.[68]

Arundhati Bhattacharya was asked whether the bank shared concerns environmentalists had raised about the project and she explained that: 'Queensland's government have clearly said that there is no environmental issue ... the threat to the Great Barrier Reef is much more from the star fish attack'.[69] Newman, it appeared, either hadn't read the Great Barrier Reef Marine Park Authority's latest report or failed to disclose its warnings to the SBI chairperson.

For Modi the deal represented a convergence of interests. He was able to assist his friend and party donor, Adani, while also responding to the pressures from Indian business groups to lift coal imports. And he was working to fulfil his development model for India, which remained focused on coal-led economic growth. He was replicating China's strategy for posterity but relying on the private sector to do the job.

However, Modi's deal with the SBI to fund the Carmichael mine soon unravelled. Responding to political pressure in India, the bank walked away from the deal. It had also undertaken its own assessment of the project following the G20 meeting the previous year, including a site visit to Queensland. According to documents obtained under Freedom of Information:

> 'The credit guys (at SBI) are not comfortable with the project', said one of the sources. 'Nothing is moving on that project.' A second source said on Friday that SBI weighed factors including poor coal prices and the lengthy timeline of the $7 billion coal project before turning down the loan request. Many Queensland coal mines are running at a loss. But Adani's Australian project has also been hit by political and environmental opposition, amid protests over the potential impact to the Great Barrier Reef. Adani has said it met a string of environmental conditions. 'It is a challenging project', said the second source. 'The bank has to look at foreign exchange risk also.' While the final decision has been keenly awaited, few in the industry had expected the SBI to press ahead with what would have been the largest ever loan granted by an Indian state bank for an overseas project. But the confirmation brought relief to some investors at a time when India's state banks are under pressure to clean up their balance sheets and to carry out tougher due diligence after years of profligate lending.[70]

Adani's shaky business plan

The SBI's decision to ditch the Carmichael mine should have been yet another signal to the Abbott government that the project was on shaky ground. Yet because of its commitment to making Australia a fossil fuel energy superpower, the government would not let up in its efforts to open up the Galilee Basin. This ideological fervour blinded the government to the risks of both the project itself and Adani's capacity to deliver it. As the SBI's withdrawal revealed, Adani's Carmichael mine represented a huge gamble for the company. Firstly, the price of coal was in a state of flux in 2013–14 and threatened to undermine the business model propping up Adani's 'pit-to-plug' strategy. And international banks were increasingly being warned off the project. However, Adani had already invested heavily in the project and as opposition grew, it began to look like a project too big to fail as far as Adani was concerned.

If the mine were stopped, Adani would lose the estimated $3 billion he had already spent on the project: half a billion to purchase the lease from Linc Energy; $2 billion on the purchase of the Abbot Point terminal; and another half a billion on preliminary drilling and site works.

Yet economists had long been arguing that the mine was financially unviable, and that this would eventually defeat Adani's attempts to get it going. An independent assessment of the Carmichael mine undertaken in 2013 came to this conclusion. Tim Buckley and Tom Sanzillo from the US-based Institute for Energy Economic and Financial Analysis compiled the report. Both former private sector financial analysts, they switched to promoting renewable energy to super funds and governments as better long-term investments than coal. Such a strategy was said to represent 'the new face of anti-coal activism', bringing the language and financial expertise of the banking and investment sector to the debate over climate change and energy.[71]

Buckley and Sanzillo found that Carmichael coal would be 'a high-cost product in a low-priced coal market'. They estimated Carmichael coal would cost over US$95 a tonne whereas the market price for coal in In India was US$30 per tonne.

India is facing an enormous financial and political challenge to convert its existing coal-fired power plants to more efficient and lower emitting technology. The coal industry was increasingly championing new technology as a potential answer to the economics of opening up the Galilee, hailing newer, lower emission technology as a new lease on the use of coal for baseload power. The International Energy Agency states that the newest plants are 40 per cent more efficient than the older plants, yet to call them 'clean' is misleading; they are still more polluting than gas-fired power plants.[72]

In the meantime, India continued to have the world's dirtiest power plants, reflecting not just the dominance of old coal power technology, but lax regulations and enforcement. Even the most inefficient and polluting plants are permitted to operate.[73] It is a system made for an opportunistic operator like Adani. He can use higher grade coal for new technology plants while selling poorer quality Galilee-sourced coal into the country's existing 'dirty' power grid.

In fact, it has been suggested that Adani intended to export lower quality coal from the Galilee into India's old technology plants. Stephen Long from the ABC found sworn evidence from one of Adani's Australian court cases that the company intended to produce two products: a low-ash product suitable for premium markets in Asia and an unwashed, high-ash product – producing more pollution – bound for India.[74]

As Abbott continued to promote his moral case for coal and fight action on climate change, Adani faced uncertain prospects in securing finance for his mega mine.

Creating a Northern Australian 'slush fund'

The Abbott government was so keen to open up the Galilee that it developed a 'slush' fund to use taxpayers' money to facilitate development of the region. Every effort was made to cloak these plans in a broader strategy of appealing to the nation-building goal of opening up northern Australia.

Conservative politicians had, for generations, dreamed of northern Australia as the next frontier for economic development. Gina

Rinehart had been trumpeting her call to create a special tax-free zone for investors. The Liberal Party's favourite policy think tank, the IPA, had been promoting the same proposal. In fact, as the IPA itself acknowledged, it had been working hand-in-hand with Rinehart's lobby group, Australians for Northern Development and Economic Vision, to call for the establishment of a Northern Special Economic Zone with lower taxes and a reduced regulatory burden.[75]

Responding to these overtures, Abbott had released the Coalition's policy on northern Australia in the lead-up to the 2013 federal election. In a 48-page detailed policy document, the future government highlighted both the opportunities and obstacles confronting the north. It sought to develop the region's agricultural, energy, tourism and services sectors in order to propel the region's and the nation's growth.[76] The policy document pledged that the Coalition would develop a white paper to chart the future course of Coalition policy and to an audit of northern Australia's infrastructure needs.

Abbott was committed to the policy. It complemented both his pro-growth and fossil fuel superpower goals: 'Mr Abbott believes the north holds the potential to "double Australia's agricultural output", draw in some 2 million international tourists annually, and build a new clean and efficient energy export industry which the Coalition believes has the potential to add $150 billion to the Australian economy'. He supported the call for tax incentives to develop the north.[77]

Once in government, Abbott moved to have both the audit and the white paper completed. Titled *Our North Our Future*, the document was imbued with appeals to nation-building. It spoke of the challenge of encouraging northern Australia to 'grasp its full potential and become an economic powerhouse' by promoting a business environment conducive to investment. It proposed that a new northern Australia infrastructure projects pipeline would be managed by a Northern Australian Infrastructure Facility.[78] Whatever the merits of the policy, the thinking inside the Abbott government was clear-cut, if not fully publicly declared: the facility was being created with a focus on opening up the Galilee.

Before the agency was even created, Treasurer Joe Hockey acknowledged to the media 'that Indian company Adani, which plans to build Australia's largest coal mine, might receive taxpayer money from the Northern Australia Infrastructure Facility to help build a rail line from its Carmichael mine in central Queensland to coal terminals at Abbot Point'.[79] Behind the scenes, senior government ministers Josh Frydenberg and Matthew Canavan, both pro-coal enthusiasts were planning to establish the Northern Australian Infrastructure Facility as an agency with the flexibility to make good Hockey's frank admission. However, it was left to the Turnbull government to complete the work.

Quashing dissent

As opposition to the Carmichael mine grew, Abbott considered ways to shut down the dissent over the project. The list of environment groups campaigning about Adani started to number in their dozens. Abbott was seething over the legal challenges environment groups were making to delay the expansion of coal exports through the Great Barrier Reef. But how to curb the activities of environment groups?

Liberals and right-wing groups had been thinking about this problem at least since Greenpeace's strategy paper, *Stopping the Australian Coal Export Boom*, was leaked to the press in 2012. In the same year, Liberal Nationals Senator Matthew Canavan took exception to a statement Greenpeace made to a Treasury Inquiry into tax concessions in which it outlined its activism: 'We have blocked trains, occupied Lucas Heights, trespassed at the Lodge, illegally raised banners ... amongst many other activities. These activities have never been for any other purpose than the public benefit and in furtherance of core purpose and values'.[80]

By 2014, the Federal Council of the Liberal Party, federal ministers, Coalition MPs, the MCA, the IPA and the Murdoch press were targeting the advocacy role of Australia's environmental non-government organisations (NGOs).[81] The plan to silence them was simple: remove their tax-deductible charitable status. This was moved as a motion at the Liberal Party's 2014 federal conference by right-wing Tasmanian MP Andrew Nikolic. He named the Wilderness Society, the Australian Conservation Foundation, the Bob Brown Foundation and the Environmental Defenders Offices as engaging in 'untruthful, destructive attacks on legitimate business' and characterised their work as 'political activism'. Nikolic claimed NGO activism was at odds with his state's 'future prosperity', that NGOs were engaged in 'boot camps' and that their activism was 'illegal'.[82] The motion was carried. Both Liberal and Nationals MPs wanted a 'cleansing' of the Department of Environment's list of organisations that could receive tax-deductible donations.

In April 2014, the government established a parliamentary inquiry into the issue. The committee went through the motions of calling for submissions – of which hundreds were made – but with the government in control of the inquiry, the majority recommendation to withdraw charitable status was a foregone conclusion.

Matt Canavan made a detailed submission to the inquiry, which provided Liberal members with all the justification they needed to act. He had undertaken his own research into the issue, trying to establish the extent of the problem. He surveyed 106 environment groups and claimed that 61 per cent had 'an endemic culture of politicisation' including opposition to the use of fossil fuels. Fifty per cent of the organisations Canavan surveyed had used legal action to 'thwart or delay government approvals for development'. According to Canavan, this exceeded the spirit of the legislation that provided tax-deductible status for charitable organisations. In his mind, to comply with the law on charities, environmental organisations should be limited to 'practical initiatives' such as tree planting, land rehabilitation and wildlife preservation.[83]

However, freedom of speech was at stake. Environmental groups believed the proposal was designed to strip them of their ability to campaign against mining projects. This was the stated aim of the MCA. It maintained that these organisations 'seem to be pursuing an ideological objective of stopping Australia's fossil fuel projects'. The council argued that the right to free speech 'should not be conflated with an entitlement to tax-payer funded political activity'.[84]

Environmental groups argued that no distinction could be drawn between their on-ground and advocacy roles in protecting the environment and they had the law on their side. In 2010, the High Court had ruled that groups with tax-deductible status also have the right to engage in political debate and advocacy. Summing up the judgment, Peter Burdon, senior lecturer in law at Adelaide University, wrote:

> The judgement described the freedom to speak out on political
> issues as 'indispensable' for 'representative and responsible
> government'. Moreover, the court pointed out that there is
> no general rule that excludes 'political objects' from charitable
> purposes. Instead, the key consideration is whether the
> organisation 'contributes to the public welfare'.[85]

Quite apart from the question of law, the groups promoting the crackdown showed shameless hypocrisy. The lobbying activities of mining companies were tax-deductible. In fact, the industry spent $484 million on lobbying governments between 2005 and 2015, costing the federal Treasury $145 million in lost revenue. The NSW Minerals Council, whose activities included expensive PR campaigns promoting coal, also had tax-deductible status, claiming $18 million each year.[86] Donors to the IPA were able to claim tax deductions. And News Corporation paid little tax. As the *Australian Financial Review* pointed out on 11 May 2015, the Australian Taxation Office 'has only one company in its highest risk category for tax avoidance – Rupert Murdoch's News Corporation. Four years ago, 13 of the country's biggest companies were in Q1, the ATO's highest-risk category for tax avoidance, but now only News Corp Australia remains, reflecting what is described as a secretive, aggressive approach to the ATO'.

The public did not support the Abbott government's noisy efforts to quieten environmental groups. In another demonstration that his government ignored public opinion in favour of vested interests on environmental issues, a Fairfax poll in September 2015 showed 70 per cent of Australians opposed removing charitable status to this sector.[87] The fight over this issue would simmer for several years.

Abbott's plan to sell out the reef

In the meantime, the Abbott government had its turn at masquerading concern about the health of the Great Barrier Reef. Having told the G20 – and the broader international community – that the Great Barrier Reef was not in danger in the short term, the Abbott government released a future-oriented plan in March 2015, although a draft had been released for public comment late in 2014. The Reef 2050 Long-Term Stability Plan had been compiled for mainly political reasons. The World Heritage Committee (WHC) was set to meet in June that year to consider whether the reef was 'in danger'. The committee had at its disposal the grim warnings from the Great Barrier Reef Marine Park Authority (GBRMPA) in its latest outlook report. While it commenced on the optimistic note that the ecosystem still possessed the universal values of a world heritage area, its findings and conclusions indicated that the reef was entering a critical phase. An increasing number of its diverse habitats were assessed as being 'in poor condition'; more than half the region's biodiversity had deteriorated since 2009.[88]

This has meant that 'the grade of "good" is borderline with "poor" and is likely to deteriorate further in the future'. Overall, the reef 'continues to face a combination of extremely serious challenges ... Without promptly reducing threats, there is a serious risk that resilience will not be improved and there will be irreversible declines in the Region's values'.[89]

Reacting to these developments, the goal of the Abbott government's plan was to reduce pollution running onto the reef, including targets to reduce nitrogen by 80 per cent and a 50 per cent cut in sediment by 2015.[90] The plan also set up a Reef Trust with $100 million in funding to enable landowners to continue the work of reducing chemical run-off into the reef's waters. Abbott released the plan with much rhetorical fanfare, talking the talk on how much he and his government were concerned about protecting the reef: 'We're making our position clear right around the world: this is a number one priority of the Australian government to protect the Great Barrier Reef ... we are all conservationists ... the last thing I'd want to do as prime minister is anything that would compromise the reef'.[91] By now, Abbott had made an art form of separating his words from his actions, as if he lived in parallel universes.

Sidestepping the GBRMPA's findings, Foreign Minister Julie Bishop embarked on an international diplomatic 'onslaught' to convince the member nations comprising the WHC that the reef was not in danger. It was a campaign of misinformation and diplomatic intimidation. How could Bishop misrepresent the truth about the reef? After all, as a lawyer she was noted for her determination to 'get to the bottom of her brief' and her willingness to take the advice of senior departmental officials.[92] But, at the time, she was noted as a staunch defender of Abbott and behind the polished media performances and stylish, coiffured appearance lay a hard political operator. Glimpses of this were revealed publicly in the 'death stare' eye contact for which she was notorious. But her Liberal values were opaque. Journalists found her lacking a policy framework and elusive to pin down.[93]

To avoid the reputational and economic damage from an 'in danger' listing, Bishop, along with Greg Hunt, mounted a military-style diplomatic campaign to avert a political disaster. A dedicated taskforce was set up in the Department of Foreign Affairs to co-ordinate the flow of misinformation. Ambassadors in all 21 member countries were enlisted in the lobbying effort and Bishop, along with Hunt, racked up $400 000 between them travelling to nearly all of the member countries.[94] In meetings with her foreign counterparts, Bishop carried a message that misinformed and was designed to frighten foreign governments. An 'in danger' listing would, she warned,

> send a message around the world that even if you meet all of
> the criteria set out by the World Heritage Committee, there is
> still a risk that they will place an area on the in-danger list. It
> would have significant implications for Australia but it would
> also set a very dangerous precedent for countries who don't have
> the opportunity to take the action that Australia has. Every
> country that has an environmental icon that activists seize upon
> would be at risk.[95]

Bishop exceeded her reputation for playing hardball politics. The WHC folded, reviving concerns over its lack of immunity to international political gamesmanship. It had been duped. Jon Day of the Centre of Excellence for Coral Reef Studies at James Cook University analysed the Abbott government's report to the WHC in an article for the *Conversation*.[96] Day, who had also been an Australian delegate to the WHC between 2007 and 2011, argued that in compiling its report to the WHC, the Abbott government had 'been very selective regarding which facts are presented and which facts are ignored'. He then listed six ways in which the government had pirouetted around the truth. His central claim was that of the 41 separate elements that the government claimed collectively demonstrated that the reef was in overall good condition, 60 per cent showed a deteriorating trend compared with their condition when the reef was first placed on the World Heritage List in 1981. Moreover, the government's report had ignored the threat posed by climate change and exaggerated its claim to have responded to all of the WHC's previously raised concerns.

Of course, driving Bishop's diplomatic frenzy was the threat to the government's plans for expanding the coal and fossil fuel industry along the reef. Like federal Labor before it, the Abbott government suffered from the delusion that Australia could continue to expand its coal industry and protect the reef. Scientists repeated their warnings to government that this was impossible. The Australian Academy of Science advised in a draft of the plan that there was 'no adequate recognition' in it of the importance of curbing greenhouse gases.[97] As Abbott said on the release of the plan, it was 'important to continue to strengthen our economy'. While he added that a strong economy and environment 'go hand-in-hand',[98] to his government, like the Rudd/Gillard Labor governments before him, the economic argument meant expanding coal into the Galilee Basin. The problem for both parties was that their concern about the reef was reactive; it was a priority only when its status appeared threatened.

The same 'functional delusion' applied to the Abbott government's approach to the Paris climate talks. Abbott had shifted his rhetoric on the issue since his 'climate change is crap' speech in 2009. He now told reporters that he took climate change 'very seriously'. But, in reality, his core views had changed very little and his actions demonstrated the low priority he gave to the issue. In addition to wielding the axe against all the pillars of climate policy in Australia, he declined an invitation by UN Secretary-General, Ban Ki-Moon, for world leaders to attend a summit in New York in September 2014 'to bring bold measures to cut greenhouse gas emissions'.[99] And experts continued to argue that the government's Direct Action policy was incapable of producing the required large cuts in emissions.

In December 2014, Bishop headed off to attend preliminary UN climate talks in Peru. Before she left, a poll conducted by Fairfax showed that 60 per cent of Australians believed that Direct Action left Australia with an inadequate response to climate change.[100] But Abbott was deaf to the concerns of the majority of Australians. His approach was to do whatever he could to halt the rising tide of global opinion in favour of a binding climate agreement. Abbott insisted that trade minister and global warming sceptic Andrew Robb 'chaperone' Bishop to the talks, a move which infuriated the foreign minister. As Mark Kenny wrote in the *Sydney Morning Herald*, 'His inclusion is being seen as a signal to those within the Coalition in favour of more ambitious emissions reduction targets that Mr Abbott remains opposed to ramping up policy even as the rest of the world positions to do so'.[101]

Bishop didn't only have Robb to worry about as she arrived at the talks. The Climate Action Network of Europe, an NGO that compiles The Climate Change Performance Index, rated Australia near the bottom of its list of countries for action on climate change.[102] Although Bishop pledged that Australia would work towards a legally binding treaty in Paris, her performance at the talks earned no fewer than three 'Fossil Fuel Day Awards' for blocking progress on the talks, principally for her opposition to pledging any money to the Green Climate Fund set up to help developing countries mitigate the effects of climate change. The awards were judged by the Climate Action Network.

In advance of the Paris talks, the Abbott government committed Australia to a target reduction of between 26–28 per cent in its greenhouse gas emissions by 2030, but achieving the target through Direct Action was another challenge altogether. The target placed Australia at the lower end of international commitments to tackle climate change. But removing the carbon tax and replacing it with Direct Action left the Abbott government with a bitter legacy: a framework that saw Australia's emissions continue to rise while around the globe emissions were flatlining or falling in comparable countries. As the *Guardian* reported in August 2017: 'The figures reveal a clear trend of increasing greenhouse gas emissions since the carbon tax was repealed in 2014 – a trend that runs counter to Australia's international commitments'.

But by the time these results were available, Tony Abbott had lost the leadership of the Liberal Party; a second sitting prime minister had been removed by a vote of their party-room colleagues. However, unlike Kevin Rudd, Australians were overwhelmingly in support of removing him from office.[103]

CHAPTER EIGHT

Malcolm Turnbull:
The price of power

On the evening of 13 September 2015, Malcolm Turnbull drove his Volvo station wagon a short distance from Parliament House to fellow Liberal Party member Peter Hendy's house in Queanbeyan, where a small group of colleagues had gathered to plot a leadership coup against Prime Minister Tony Abbott. As journalist Pamela Williams later wrote of that night: 'Turnbull was in striking distance of a dream that had shaped his life'.[1] Just a year earlier, Turnbull's chances of returning to the Liberal leadership had been rated as next to zero. However, Abbott's leadership had floundered: the community outcry against his government's 'unfair' 2014 Budget never subsided; his stream of gaffes attracted ongoing ridicule; the unforeseen re-introduction of knights and dames misread the mood of the country; and the venom directed against Peta Credlin, his controlling chief of staff and proxy 'first lady', had earned the ire of his colleagues. Abbott's leadership was widely seen as terminal. Yet, the stakes on the evening of the 13th were high. Would the numbers in the party room hold as expected? Tearing down a second sitting prime minister was a dramatic step.

There were few surprises when Malcolm Turnbull fronted the media the next day to announce his intention to challenge Abbott. Turnbull had prepared his case to the public like the well-briefed lawyer he was. As justification for his grab for power, Turnbull cited

30 consecutive news polls which the government had lost. The benchmark came to haunt the new prime minister and was an early indicator of his poor political judgment. But he promised a different style of leadership to Abbott's:

> We need a style of leadership that explains those challenges
> and opportunities, explains the challenges and how to seize the
> opportunities. A style of leadership that respects the people's
> intelligence, that explains these complex issues and then sets out
> the course of action we believe we should take and makes a case
> for it.[2]

And in a direct swipe at Abbott, Turnbull said: 'We need advocacy, not slogans. We need to respect the intelligence of the Australian people'.[3]

Tellingly, Turnbull was vague on the issues he intended to champion as prime minister, leaving the impression that the leadership change was more about style than substance. And what about climate change? Did the wealthiest man ever to grace the office of prime minister intend to go back into battle on his signature issue? It quickly became apparent that, behind the scenes, Turnbull had paid a high price for attaining the leadership. The National Party was 'seething' over the 'political assassination' of Abbott and, in return for their support, Nationals leader Warren Truss demanded a written pledge that Turnbull would not change existing policy on climate change (that is, he would not put a price on carbon) or on same-sex marriage.[4] Many in the Liberal Party also insisted on maintaining the status quo on these issues.

The leadership coup to tear down Abbott quickly morphed into political folklore: Turnbull had sold his soul to obtain the prime ministership. The man who, in his own mind, was destined to become prime minister had put ambition before principle. His trajectory is almost a metaphor for modern politics. But just how accurate is this narrative? It is an important question for what it tells us about Turnbull himself, the character of the Liberal Party and the ongoing saga of the attempt to open up the Galilee Basin.

At the outset Turnbull seemed a natural fit for the office. Indeed the public largely welcomed the shift to someone who, unlike Abbott, seemed to possess the gravitas for the job. Turnbull had fashioned an appealing public image: progressive, erudite and a smooth media performer. And, in 2015 the public still largely saw him as principled. After all, he had staked his previous tenure as leader of the Liberal Party on a robust endorsement for action on climate change. Less well understood was Turnbull's background as an aggressive corporate lawyer and ruthless merchant banker.

Turnbull hasn't just kept the promise not to alter climate change policy; he has embraced the entire conservative pro-coal, pro-Adani, anti-science and tepid climate change agenda. In other words, there's been little difference between Turnbull and Abbott on these key issues. Crucially, Turnbull has maintained these positions despite the growing risks to Australia and to the earth from his government's support of both the expansion of the coal industry and of Adani as a company. Like Abbott, he placed climate change deniers and fossil fuel executives in key government posts.

How could Turnbull change his position as easily as a snake shedding its skin?

Turnbull as climate change champion

Malcolm Turnbull championed climate change with seemingly fierce conviction when, in 2007, he became John Howard's Minister for the Environment. Climate change, he said, was 'an enormous challenge and probably the biggest one our country faces, the world faces, at the moment'. He mounted a deeply personal attack on Peter Garrett, Labor's high-profile recruit, himself an environmentalist of long standing who had made an uneasy transition from iconic rock star to federal politics. Turnbull ridiculed Garrett as an idealist who 'tries to change his spots all the time' and who had 'abandoned almost all of the positions he has had in his life – or has purported to abandon them'.[5] In Turnbull's characterisation, Garrett was simply an opportunist without the courage of his convictions.

Turnbull went on the attack again in 2009 for the cause of climate change. He wrote an opinion piece about new Liberal leader Tony Abbott's adoption of Direct Action to combat climate change. 'Any suggestion', he argued, 'that you can dramatically cut emissions without any cost is, to use a favourite term of Mr Abbott, "bullshit". Moreover he knows it'. Then he took a swipe at his party's culture: 'Now politics is about conviction and a commitment to carry out those convictions. The Liberal Party is currently led by people whose conviction on climate change is that it is "crap" and you don't need to do anything about it'.[6]

Turnbull was still in fighting mode during the 2010 federal election campaign. He strode onto the stage of a packed Sydney Town Hall at the launch of *Beyond Zero Emissions Stationary Energy Plan*, a report demonstrating the technical feasibility of moving Australia to 100 per cent renewable energy. He was to make a speech in support of the plan. By now he carried the aura of a climate change martyr, not least when he was introduced at the launch as a 'pariah' inside his own party. Turnbull welcomed the description as 'distinctly' a privilege.[7] Playing to the loud applause, Turnbull said the country had to get to a situation 'where all or almost all of our energy comes from zero or very near zero-emissions sources. We as a human species have a deep and abiding obligation to this planet and to the generations that will come after us'. Turnbull also considered 'clean coal' in this speech and dismissed the concept as a mirage: 'Despite all of the money and all of the hope that has been put into carbon capture and storage there is still, as of today, not one industrial-scale coal-fired power station using carbon capture and storage'.

In 2011, delivering the Virginia Chadwick Memorial Lecture to a predominantly Liberal audience, Turnbull was still in martyr mode. He declared that a war was being waged on scientists by 'those opposed to taking action to cut emissions, many because it does not suit their own financial interests'. And, in a frank admission, he took a shot at the power wielded by the mining industry:

> Mr Turnbull said parties with vested interests were trying to muddy the waters on climate science to prolong the export of coal, comparing their actions to tobacco companies distancing the connection between smoking and lung cancer. 'It is undoubtedly correct that there has been a very effective campaign against the science of climate change by those opposed to taking action to cut emissions, many because it does not suit their own financial interests, and this has played into the carbon tax debate'.[8]

As these interventions show, there were few more passionate advocates in parliament for action on climate change – and the challenges involved in shifting from fossil fuels to renewables – than Turnbull. Few others in politics had his combination of charm, ruthlessness, advocacy skills and limitless access to a largely adoring media. A few years later, a new Turnbull emerged as prime minister. He had fallen in behind the anti-science and pro-coal forces that dominated both the Nationals and Liberal parties.

The real Malcolm?

Turnbull has always projected a strong presence in any gathering. 'The air crackles with a self-assurance and a sense of risk', commented Phillip Adams, one of Australia's iconic broadcasters and columnists, from his long observations of the famous and powerful.[9] Turnbull has always seen himself as a man of destiny: destined to be fabulously wealthy and to become prime minister. He has freely admitted that he always wanted to be where the action is.[10] As almost everyone who has followed his career attests, Turnbull had a rare combination of qualities that enabled him to achieve his twin ambitions. Along the way he burned through friends and colleagues, networked among the most powerful moguls in the country, led the failed Republican campaign under heavy criticism for his leadership skills, became a committed Catholic and continued to stoke media interest in his political aspirations.

Elected to the wealthy Sydney electorate of Wentworth in 2004, Turnbull was finally within striking distance of his goal when, in 2009, he succeeded in toppling Dr Brendan Nelson, the leader the Liberals chose to succeed Howard after the party lost office in 2007. On his exit from politics, Nelson felt he needed to set the record straight. He asserted that Turnbull had more than just a healthy ego. His comments were reported in the *Sydney Morning Herald*:

[T]he former medical practitioner feels the need to diagnose Malcolm Turnbull's condition. Says Dr Nelson: 'You need to look up narcissistic personality disorder. There's about 5 per cent of the population who are born with narcissistic traits, and about 2 per cent have narcissism. He's got narcissistic personality disorder.[11]

Perhaps Nelson felt he possessed the medical qualifications to offer such a diagnosis. But others had made similar assessments of Rudd and, later, of Abbott. The age of political psychology had arrived and leaders are now more psychologically scrutinised than they have ever been. In the case of Turnbull, the question has become whether he is driven by anything greater than himself. His biographer Paddy Manning reports a conversation Turnbull had in the late 1970s with *Sydney Morning Herald* journalist David Dale. Turnbull announced to Dale that he wanted to be prime minister by the time he was 40.

'For which party?' asked Dale. 'It doesn't matter', responded Turnbull.[12] For Manning the central question about Turnbull's restless interest in politics was what he stood for.

However, for many observers of politics, Turnbull stood for the small-l liberal tradition of the Liberal Party – the party of Malcom Fraser's era – that, under the leadership of Howard and then Abbott, atrophied in the face of rising conservative populism. Turnbull played to his progressive image, appearing monthly on the widely watched ABC program *Q&A* dressed in a fashionably cut leather jacket, an image used to 'charm us all into believing that he wasn't like any other member of the Liberal Party'.[13]

Prominent academic and commentator on Australian politics Robert Manne believed Turnbull sat squarely in the small-l liberal Fraser tradition with his support for gay marriage, republicanism, multiculturalism, Indigenous recognition and action on climate change, along with a disavowal of growing economic inequality.[14] Manne offered a flattering profile of Turnbull in a 2012 article for the *Monthly*. He sincerely believed that Turnbull was bravely swimming against the tide of conservative populism in the Liberal Party. He later recanted this assessment with a *mea culpa*: 'I now realise what a fool I was'.[15] Nonetheless, there were signals in his conversations with Turnbull for the profile that puzzled Manne at the time, namely, a nagging doubt that Turnbull wasn't quite the figure he wanted him to be. If Fraser and Howard represented different trajectories of the Liberal Party, Manne wrote, 'Turnbull seems to genuinely admire them both'.[16]

Turnbull's image as a progressive conservative with green credentials remained largely intact when he announced to the nation his intention to challenge Abbott. However, not all were convinced that the 'old' Malcolm had survived. And there were those who questioned the authenticity of his green credentials. As a merchant banker, Turnbull had bought into logging operations in the Solomon Islands which, for decades, had seen their forest resources over-exploited. As Howard's Environment Minister, Turnbull had approved the controversial Gunns Ltd pulp mill in Tasmania, amid fierce opposition from environmentalists, under pressure exerted by the prime minister. Turnbull's assurances to locals that he opposed the mill were quickly jettisoned.[17]

Becoming prime minister in September 2015 invited another round of scrutiny. Michael Brull, writing in *New Matilda*, critiqued the authenticity of Turnbull's liberalism. Firstly, he raised the issue of Turnbull's allegiances, pointing out that he had wielded 'extraordinary power' before politics, working closely 'with some of the most rich and powerful men in Australia'. As a consequence, Turnbull 'is likely to represent well the interests of the rich and powerful, who will ultimately serve as his base. The business lobby is excited and they have good reason to be'.[18]

Brull argued that, as a consequence of his social position, Turnbull's progressive views were politically shallow, limited to safe issues which avoided 'any major form of social change'. Secondly, Brull examined the dark side of Turnbull's character. Turnbull's ideals, he argued, were 'outweighed by his commitment to pursuing power'.[19]

Robert Manne agrees: 'Without repudiating his earlier views', Manne wrote, 'Turnbull would never have become prime minister of Australia'. But he, too, saw elements of Turnbull's character in the ease with which he made the transformation. As a barrister by training and inclination, causes for him 'are quasi-clients that he voluntarily and serially embraces with the kind of sincerity barristers must routinely muster in court'.[20]

Lawyer, refugee advocate and former Liberal Party member Greg Barns has a more sympathetic interpretation. He believes that, in his heart, Turnbull remains a small-l liberal, 'but he's had to cut his cloth to suit his position in what is now a pretty hard-core, right-of-centre party'.[21] Barns offers an important perspective: Turnbull's problem is not just about him, but also with the culture of the party he has chosen to lead. But there's been no escaping Turnbull's own fall from grace in the eyes of most Australians.

Perhaps not surprisingly, Turnbull has shown little insight into his own predicament. He continues to hit out at those who, he claims, lack moral fibre. In February 2017, it was Labor leader Bill Shorten's turn. Turnbull labelled him a 'fake' who 'doesn't have a fair dinkum bone in him'.[22]

Even in the Machiavellian world of politics such policy backflips as Turnbull has shown on the environment demonstrate an unusual degree of ideological flexibility. Like a clever barrister, Turnbull can master whatever brief he needs to.

Turnbull's Orwellian shift

As English novelist and essayist George Orwell lamented in his 1946 essay, 'Politics and the English Language', the use of language had become 'ugly and inaccurate because our thoughts are foolish, but the slovenliness of our language makes it easier for us to have foolish thoughts'. And, he argued, slovenliness was a powerful political tool: 'Political language ... is designed to make lies sound truthful'. On climate change, Prime Minister Turnbull has shamelessly borrowed from Orwell's insight. His transition from climate change crusader to climate change coward happened within days of him becoming leader.

On 5 October 2015, Turnbull dismissed the challenge Labor had set him to develop a bipartisan approach to developing a renewable energy target. Shorten said that the steep drop-off in investment in renewable energy in Australia was an international anomaly that must be fixed. He pointed out that, in the past year alone, clean energy investment had risen by 8 per cent in the United States, 12 per cent in Japan and 35 per cent in China. 'In Australia, however, under the Abbott government's overtly pro-fossil fuel/anti-renewables stance, it went backwards by 35 per cent'. While two million jobs in the sector had been created worldwide, Australia had shed 2300 full-time positions.[23] Labor's answer was to develop a commitment to a 50 per cent renewable energy target even though it lacked specific details on how it proposed to reach the target. But the man who previously helped to launch the report on zero emissions went on the attack. Shorten, Turnbull said, was 'reckless' in advancing a 50 per cent target when a 'reduction in emissions you needed could come more cost-effectively from carbon storage, by planting trees, by soil carbon, by using gas, by using clean coal, by energy efficiency'.[24]

Turnbull had fallen in line with the Coalition's talking points, which it shared with the fossil fuel industry. He described those who advocated transitioning out of coal as 'delusional'. Direct Action, the Coalition's climate change policy, which Turnbull had once described as 'fiscal recklessness on a grand scale', was now a 'resounding success'. And he repeated the coal industry's discredited claim that stopping exports of Australian coal 'would be of no benefit to global climate whatsoever' because Australian coal was cleaner.[25] Journalist Lenore Taylor wrote in the *Guardian* that Turnbull's pro-coal advocacy required 'all his rhetorical skill to bridge the gap between what he knows is true and what he has to say to appease his party'.[26]

Senior government ministers continued to spruik the Carmichael mine using disputed and/or discredited claims. Campaigning in North Queensland ahead of the July 2016 federal election, Attorney-General Senator George Brandis recycled the assertion that the project would generate 10000 jobs – an assertion that evidence from Adani's own consultant in the Land Court in 2015 had shown was false (see Chapter 10). Senator Matthew Canavan excitedly told the media that the Adani project would 'deliver billions in taxes', overlooking the investigations into Adani's tax minimisation schemes.

But on 1 July, days before the election which narrowly returned the Turnbull government, central Queensland resident Kristy Harling, a former Rio Tinto worker, asked what politicians intended to do to curb the job crisis within the region on ABC's *Q&A* program. 'Central Queensland needs help now and residents are suffering because of the lack of a transition program for the region. With all this talk of jobs and growth, what are your plans for central Queensland to ensure it is not littered with ghost towns?' she asked. She later told the press that 'neither party has put forward a campaign that addresses the problem'. 'I think it's rather naive to continue to hold on to coal. I think it's important we think outside the box so we can prepare the workers for that transition when it does happen', she said.[27]

Such calls for an innovative approach to the problems of central Queensland fell on deaf ears. The government simply doubled down on adding new slogans to its pro-coal lexicon. Energy policy should be 'technologically neutral' which, as environment journalist Graham Readfearn pointed out, was 'absurd and should be seen as code for "we don't have the courage to take on our detractors". They are phrases designed to pander to people who go out of their way to claim "coal is good for humanity"'.[28]

The pitch to 'clean coal' and away from renewables became embedded in the Turnbull government's entire approach to Australia's pressing energy and climate change needs. Turnbull wasn't that much different from any of the recent Australian prime ministers who 'have faced major challenges regarding the gap between Australia's role as a major exporter of coal and its fluctuating ambitions to help tackle climate change'.[29] But, unlike Abbott, Turnbull remained sensitive to criticism about where his true values lay. He hit back at suggestions that his own mansion's 'large personal rooftop solar and battery system sends a message contrary to the government's endorsement of "clean coal"'.[30]

The Turnbull government's renewed pitch to clean coal continued to defy the experts. In June 2017, David Hilditch, who for

12 years was commercial manager with the Carbon Capture and Storage Co-operative Research Centre established by the Rudd Labor government, told the ABC that the technology was unviable, saying that 'there are no examples where it has worked on a fully commercial basis'.[31] Yet government ministers continued to push the technology.

It was becoming increasingly difficult for the Turnbull government to parry community concern about climate change with its hyped-up promotion of 'clean coal'. Soon after he became prime minister, Turnbull attended the Paris climate talks. Several weeks before his departure, he received yet another demonstration that the so-called coal wars were increasingly part of the concerns of mainstream Australians. Sixty-one prominent Australians including Wallabies star David Pocock, three former Australians of the year, and eminent scientists and economists, along with Anglican Bishop George Browning, pressed Turnbull to stop any new coal mines and to put an international coal moratorium on the agenda of the forthcoming Paris climate talks.[32]

Backed by green and social action organisations, the 61 eminent persons signed an open letter featured in full-page advertisements in Fairfax Media newspapers, calling on the host of the December talks, French President Francois Hollande, and Mr Turnbull to oppose new coal developments – including the Carmichael mine in Queensland's Galilee Basin.

The signatories addressed the issue that Australia's two major political parties had long chosen to ignore: 'It is not just the fossil fuels a country burns for its own energy that matters, but those dug up for export to others'.[33] Turnbull issued a swift response to the 61 eminent Australians. Employing the claim that 'coal is good for humanity', Turnbull warned 'against driving the world's poor into "energy poverty" by clamping down on coal'. His comments drew acclaim from the coal industry.[34] Turnbull went off to Paris to do everything he could to protect the coal industry. But before his departure, he took another swipe at climate change policy in Australia.

Unable to scrap the Climate Change Authority as the Abbott government had intended, the Turnbull government restructured the agency in October 2015 with the appointment of five new board members. Bernie Fraser had already resigned over his disagreement with the Coalition's low emissions target. The new appointments included Wendy Craik, a former head of the National Farmers Federation and Productivity Commissioner who headed the agency; former Howard government transport minister John Sharp; and chief executive of the Australian Chamber of Industry and Commerce Kate Carnell, who also had served as Liberal chief minister for the ACT. She had been 'a feisty critic of climate change policies … [and] once accused clean energy investments of "destroying jobs" rather than creating new ones'.[35] Rounding out the new appointments were economist Danny Price, and Stuart Allison of Bid Energy. Both Price and Allison had advised the Coalition government on Direct Action.[36] All the new members had declared that climate change was an important issue and said they accepted the science. They joined the three existing board members – appointed under the previous Labor government – public policy expert and ethicist Clive Hamilton, climate change scientist Professor David Karoly, and economist Professor John Quiggin, who 'were outnumbered'.[37]

Critics argued that the government had 'stacked' the authority with appointees who supported the Coalition.

Climate change laggards

The 2015 Paris Climate Change Conference was set to be a pivotal moment in the long struggle to reach a meaningful international agreement on climate change. The geopolitical stars were finally in alignment, principally because the two largest emitters of greenhouse gas, China and the United States, had separately struck a deal to drastically lower emissions. The goal of the talks was to reach agreement to keep rises in global temperature to below 2°C. But in signing up to the global accord, Turnbull and his Environment Minister Greg Hunt tried hard to spruik Australia's contribution to reducing emissions when, in fact, they ensured that Australia not only continued to lag behind the international effort, but formed an obstacle to meaningful progress.

Critics panned the government's stance in Paris as 'duplicitous'. As Hannah Aulby, a clean energy campaigner for the Australian Conservation Foundation, pointed out, the government 'has been using every trick in the book to make our targets sound good'.[38] In fact, Australia continued to be ranked the worst performer in the Organisation of Economic Cooperation and Development (OECD) on climate change and among the worst overall in the world.

The first day of the talks started badly for Turnbull and Hunt. At the last minute, they snubbed an invitation to join a 40-country campaign to remove fossil fuel subsidies. Conservative Prime Minister of New Zealand John Key formally presented the Fossil Fuel Subsidy Reform Communiqué to Christiana Figueres, Executive Secretary of the UN Framework Convention on Climate Change (UNFCCC), on behalf of the Friends of Fossil Fuel Subsidy Reform, saying fossil fuel subsidy reform is the 'missing piece of the climate change puzzle'. Key noted a crucial fact; one-third of global carbon emissions between 1980 and 2010 were driven by fossil fuel subsidies. By some estimates these totalled more than US$500 billion per year. The subsidies acted to keep the price of fossil fuels artificially low and Key said eliminating them could provide 15 per cent of the effort to meet the 2°C target. 'As with any subsidy reform, change will take courage and strong political will'.[39]

Australia had lost a key ally in international climate change politics. Canada's Stephen Harper, a close friend of Tony Abbott's, had lost the recent Canadian election to Justin Trudeau. As one observer noted, the new progressive prime minister 'gave a commitment that Canada would do an about face and sign up to the 40-country push to remove fossil fuel subsidies, apparently it was all too much for Turnbull, who was unwilling to face down opposition from the conservative forces in his party room'.[40]

Turnbull's performance didn't get any better. He stood on the stage and crowed about ratifying the second commitment period of the Kyoto Protocol. As Greens federal MP Larissa Waters pointed out, this meant nothing more than that Australia would meet its current 'measly' 5 per cent target in climate pollution reduction to 2020.[41] And that took no account of the government's plan to open up the Galilee Basin to unleash yet more coal onto the world's market.

Malcolm Turnbull also announced in Paris that Australia would double investment in clean energy innovation over the next five years, although as Larissa Waters said, 'While this sounds very exciting, it's completely at odds with the Turnbull government's plan, reiterated only in the same week [as the Paris Conference], to abolish the two government bodies driving clean energy investment and innovation' – the Australian Renewable Energy Agency (ARENA) and the Clean Energy Finance Corporation (CEFC) as Abbott had attempted to do the previous year.

There was yet another exercise in double-speak in Paris. Australia had to find a way of committing to help developing countries deal with the impacts of climate change while continuing to oppose Obama's Green Climate Fund. Turnbull announced that the government would direct some of its aid budget to this task without acknowledging the country's aid budget was already at an historic low because of the current government's savage cuts.

Perhaps the most challenging criticism of the prime minister's performance came from the leader of one of the smallest nations attending the conference. President Anote Tong of Kiribati, a clutch of coral atolls and isles in the Central Pacific, took aim at Australia's continuing expansion of coal exports, bristling at Prime Minister Malcolm Turnbull's 'silly argument' that they 'would make not the blindest bit of difference to global emissions' because importers would simply seek new suppliers. Tong reversed the argument: 'I think what they should be doing is not doing it, and encouraging the others not to do it, rather than have a competition to do it', Tong said. 'They should not be competing to do it [by saying], "If I don't do it, he'll do it"; they should be saying, "If I don't do it, he won't do it"'.[42]

The Turnbull government's determination to pursue its pro-coal agenda was not just a risk to Australia's international reputation on climate change, it also posed a potential risk to the stability of the nation's financial system. In yet another example of the government's binary mindset, it overlooked a peer-reviewed report highlighting that there had been no official examination in Australia of how climate change might affect the nation's financial system, despite the Bank of England and other central banks around the world having undertaken significant work in this area. At stake was the possibility of Australian banks being exposed to stranded carbon-intensive assets, such as the many coal mines they had financed. Ten per cent of the loans of Australia's 'big four' banks were found to comprise potentially stranded asset risks. And the banks' loan books were loaded up with mortgagees likely to be affected by climate-damaged coastal dwellings. Such risks 'could spread through the entire financial system'.[43] But a decade and more of climate change denialism and slavish compliance to the fossil fuel industry and pro-coal media had made it easy to overlook such warnings.

The government not only sought to diminish the threats climate change posed to iconic places like the Great Barrier Reef, it also sought to forestall public alarm about these threats. In early 2016, the government lobbied to have references to Australia removed from a report on climate change jointly published by the Union of Concerned Scientists and UNESCO. One of the authors of the report, Adam Markham, was shocked to learn of the missing material on Australia when the report was published. Indeed, when the Australian Department of Environment saw a draft of the report, it objected, and every mention of Australia was removed by UNESCO. The government was worried that adverse publicity about the Great Barrier Reef, in particular, would harm tourism. It didn't share Markham's view that:

> Rather than have a negative effect on tourism, I think this information would have helped galvanise the international community to want to reduce greenhouse gas emissions to the level where we might be able to reduce the impact on the [Great Barrier Reef] in the long term.[44]

Conservationists cried that the government had engaged in a 'cover-up'. Will Steffan, emeritus professor at the Australian National University and head of Australia's Climate Council, and one of the scientific reviewers of the axed section of the report, said Australia's move was reminiscent of 'the old Soviet Union'. Indeed, no sections about any other country were removed from the report.

Explaining the decision to object to the report, a spokesperson for the Department of the Environment told the *Guardian*: 'Recent experience in Australia had shown that negative commentary about the status of world heritage properties impacted on tourism'. The timing of the intervention appears to have been decisive. The request for removing references to Australia had been made in early 2016 at the time when world heritage forests in Tasmania were on fire, the Great Barrier Reef was being hit by coral bleaching, and the CSIRO was sacking climate scientists due to budget cuts. It was then that the Department of Environment had 'conveyed' to UNESCO its concerns about the contents of the draft report.[46]

As has been discussed, for decades Australia's approach to climate change had been shaped by lobbying from fossil fuel interests. But under the Abbott and Turnbull governments, the interests of the coal industry had become institutionalised as an arm of

Australia's foreign policy. The Department of Foreign Affairs and Trade (DFAT) actively supported expanding coal-fired power plants in South-East Asia. The decline in the demand from China prompted discussions between Australian government ministers and representatives from the coal industry. In 2016, Austrade began assisting Vietnam to develop a coal import strategy. The result was a significant lift in coal-fired power generation at the expense of developing the country's renewable potential, especially in solar and wind power.[47]

In the case of Thailand, Australia supported the plan developed by the state-owned Electricity Authority of Thailand to develop six new coal-fired power plants, some of which were set for environmentally sensitive areas and which were opposed by local villagers.

In Vietnam and Thailand, the Australian government turned a blind eye to the implications of such projects in raising global greenhouse gas emissions to enhance the development of the Australian coal industry.[48] The Turnbull government undertook similar trade missions to promote coal, among other trade opportunities, to India. At one level this could simply be seen as a normal part of government trade missions. But at another level, Australia's active promotion of coal continues to undercut international efforts to reduce global greenhouse gas emissions and acts as a restraint on Australia's willingness to lead on climate change action.

Turnbull also maintained the wider assault on environment policy begun under Abbott, whose savage cuts to environment programs continued to have an impact. The Turnbull government's future projections planned to reduce environment spending to less than 60 per cent of 2013–14 figures despite continued warnings that 'climate change was altering the structure and function of natural ecosystems, and parts of Australia's natural estate were in poor or deteriorating condition'.[49] By comparison, mining companies were receiving twice as much in fuel tax credits as the Turnbull government's total budget for environment and biodiversity programs.[50]

Modi's coal-fired approach to Paris

Australia wasn't the only country whose contradictory approach to the Paris climate talks was mired in dependence on coal. India's Prime Minister Narendra Modi engaged in the same rhetorical dance on climate change – promising action while keeping the nation firmly in the fossil fuel age. As the Paris talks were about to begin, the International Energy Agency produced a report with a stark warning: 'Surging consumption of coal in power genera-tion and industry makes India, by a distance, the largest source of growth in global coal use'.[51] Potentially good news for Adani, but bad news for the planet. As the *Economist* wrote of these develop-ments on the eve of the Paris talks, 'Every so often a country comes along whose economic transformation has a vast impact on the world's climate system. For the past generation that country has been China. Next it will be India ... [it] is on the way to becom-ing the biggest contributor to increases in greenhouse gases within 15 years'.[52]

India had become a threat to international action on climate change. Under Modi's policies of rapid economic growth, India had emerged as the world's third largest emitter of greenhouse gas. Intransigence on its part could derail any commitment to keeping global rises in temperature to a maximum of 2°C. With the opening up of the Galilee Basin – primarily for Adani's exports to India – Australia stood to be a willing participant in any future breakdown of the Paris agreement.

In the lead-up to the Paris talks, Modi was under increasing pressure to deliver ambitious targets to reduce emissions. However, he drew on the same argument China had used for decades: it was morally wrong for the country not to be allowed the opportunity to use fossil fuels to develop. 'Coal is not an obsession for India', he said, 'it is a compulsion'.[53] But as the climate talks approached, and under pressure from American President Barack Obama to be a constructive player in Paris, Modi stated an intention to follow 'a cleaner path than the one followed hitherto by others at a corresponding level of economic development'.[54]

While Modi mapped out an ambitious pathway for the growth of renewable energy, this would not lessen India's dependence on coal, which has been projected to continue for the next 30–40 years.[55] Between 2010 and 2015 India had installed one-quarter of the world's new coal-burning capacity.[56] It is walking wide-eyed into the polluted environment that China – and the West beforehand – had created.

India is trapped in a 'coal conundrum'. By prioritising development at all costs, based on using dirty coal energy as baseload power, it had, by 2015, 13 of the top 20 most polluted cities on the planet. Modi saw no alternative; domestic pressures from a rising population hungry for jobs meant that coal use would have to rise. Even the grand plans for growing solar risked being undermined by India's 'rivers of red tape' and its dysfunctional power market.[57]

Yet any rise in global temperatures risked having severe impacts on India's poor. The country's reliance on the monsoons – already being disrupted by climate change – to feed its vast population meant potential catastrophe for the millions living in rural areas. The challenge for India is immense, but potentially capable of being met: 'It can attempt what no country, rich or poor, has so far managed, which is to skip the deadliest and messiest stages of economic growth and forge a new green path'.[58] But, as matters stood in 2016, this was not the path India was forging.

Establishing the Northern Australia Infrastructure Facility

In March 2016, the Turnbull Government brought to fruition the plans, developed in the previous Abbott government, to establish the Northern Australia Infrastructure Facility (NAIF) with $5 billion in funds. As previously mentioned, it was meant to oversee the economic development of Northern Australia, although few doubted that its top priority was to open up the coal developments in the Galilee Basin and to give favourable consideration to allocating a $1 billion loan to Adani to construct the railway to Abbot Point.

Just how much Adani relies on obtaining the loan has been the subject of ongoing speculation. Company statements that the project is not conditional on the loan sit oddly with the government's determination to offer one to the company. Former Liberal leader and Professor of Economics John Hewson has studied the unfolding debate and observes that the loan is likely critical to Adani: 'It could be accepted by potential financiers as low-cost, high-risk "quasi equity". It would also effectively hand Adani a monopoly position in a standard gauge rail, in turn creating monopoly conditions at Abbot Point'.[59] Others have speculated that Adani's strategy has been to obtain a loan and go back to the State Bank of India – where they can leverage political connections – and say they have the support of the Australian government.

Based in Cairns, the NAIF Board is surrounded by supporters of the mine from mayors of the regional cities of Townsville, Mackay and Rockhampton. The region has suffered from the recent downturn in mining, a crippling drought and the effects of Campbell Newman's slashing of public sector jobs. But in Townsville, especially, the biggest blow came with the collapse of Clive Palmer's Queensland Nickel with the loss of 800 direct jobs and thousands more supporting jobs. Unemployment in the region shot past 10 per cent. According to Townsville mayor Jenny Hill, suicide rates had increased, families were torn apart and drug and alcohol crime rates had risen. 'The town is just full of disheartening stories', she told the *Queensland Times*.[60] It is not surprising then that many in the region saw the conflict over Adani in class-based terms. A bumper sticker read: 'Don't take my coal job and I won't take your soy latte'.

Critics, though, questioned whether NAIF could make a properly assessed decision on the use of massive public funds for the mine. The ethical investment firm Market Forces wrote in a submission to a Senate inquiry into NAIF that it was:

> being distorted to suit political agendas. We believe that
> the intent of the Federal Government to pursue further
> development of coal projects at all costs is a key motivation for
> the establishment of the NAIF and also heavily influencing its
> decision-making processes.[61]

The conservative Productivity Commission has slammed the NAIF. The commission said that it appears the fund is being guided by political priorities rather than established commercial discipline and there is a danger the projects it champions will fail to cover their costs, let alone service their debts.[62]

Several factors gave weight to claims of politicisation. Firstly, and as many submissions to the Senate inquiry formed in 2016 to examine NAIF complained, NAIF was created with a 'stark lack of transparency'.[63] Although its charter requires NAIF to take the public interest into account when allocating loans, its decision-making processes are shrouded in secrecy. It doesn't have to consult the public in arriving at decisions and its processes are not made public. As The Australia Institute pointed out, 'NAIF does not have internal policies and procedures for application and assessment. The Minister says that there is "not really a formal submission or application process" but "discussions that occur"'.[64]

Secondly, in the absence of high levels of accountability, NAIF is free to embrace a 'high-risk appetite'; that is, funding projects that may not be viable and/or whose proponents may not be able to repay the loans, even though these are offered on very generous terms.

Thirdly, NAIF was spared other aspects of good governance, namely the need to take climate change into account when making decisions. As the Institute of Energy Economics and Financial

Analysis wrote in their submission to the Senate Inquiry, company directors are increasingly understanding that climate change risks need to be a major focus of any board's agenda.[65]

Finally, the professional expertise of appointees to the NAIF Board was 'skewed towards mining rather than the diversified industries that are critical for the future of Northern Australia'.[66] In fact, almost all seven members of the Board had direct links to the mining industry, raising questions about possible conflicts of interest. The three mostly strongly connected are:

- Sharon Warbarton: Gold Road Resources, Fortescue, Dalrymple Bay Coal Terminal, Roy Hill Mine.
- Khory McCormick: Minter Ellison Lawyers, who act for: Rio Tinto, Minerals Council of Australia, Queensland Resources Council, Abbot Point Coal terminal, Adani, GVK-Hancock.
- Karla Way-McPhail: Undamine (which contracts to Xstrata, Glencore), Coal Train.[67]

This issue was publicly raised on at least one occasion when the ABC revealed that NAIF board member Karla Way-McPhail held an interest in mining companies and was a Liberal National Party supporter who had attended party fundraisers.[68] A day after she was questioned about her potential conflict of interest, Ms Way-McPhail went on the record as an enthusiastic backer of the Adani mine, describing it as a 'vital' coal project and 'a huge boost' to central Queensland.[69]

Adani applied for a loan through NAIF in November 2016 but failed subsequently to lodge an investment case for the loan as if this was unnecessary. By applying to NAIF for funding, Adani has effectively conceded that it will struggle for finance, given the rules of NAIF require it to lend only to projects that would not otherwise have received finance from established sources.[70] But NAIF itself has struggled to get its act together. In its first two years of operation, the board spent $500 000 per year on its board fees and racked up over $300 000 in travel costs, even though it had only met four times and had lent no money.[71]

One of the baffling aspects of NAIF's work was why it continued to delay any approval of funding to Adani when it was clearly predisposed to approving the $1 billion loan sought by the company. Part of the reason was the struggle within the agency of how to reconcile Adani's poor corporate reputation. Emails obtained in early November 2017 by Market Forces show officials in NAIF apparently in doubt about how to reconcile a clause in its legislative requirement that 'must not act in a way that is likely to cause damage to the Commonwealth's reputation' and Adani's history in India. Much of the content of the emails had been redacted, concealing the exact nature of their concerns and deliberations. However, one email dated 24 November 2016 had the subject line 'NGBR [North Galilee Basin Rail] Project – Proponent's environmental track record'. Attached to the email was a Greenpeace briefing paper titled 'Adani's record of environmental destruction and non-compliance with regulations'.[72] Any approval to Adani may therefore be open to legal challenge.

NAIF was also extremely sensitive to accountability through Freedom of Information (FOI) requests. In January 2017, it rejected an FOI request by Greenpeace about the number and location of its meetings on the basis that its directors had been subjected to 'substantial cyberbullying' and protests outside its Cairns office. Such information, it argued, should be kept secret.[73]

Coal-friendly appointments

NAIF and the Adani loan had key senior backers in the Turnbull government. When Greg Hunt was moved on from the Environment portfolio, his replacement Josh Frydenburg was also given the energy portfolio, creating the new Energy and Environment

Ministry. The potential for synergy between the two areas carried the risk that the new department would be dominated by the energy sector. That prospect became clearer when Frydenburg fronted Andrew Bolt's *Sky News* program. He stated: 'I certainly believe in the moral case that Tony Abbott and others have put that our coal, our gas, our energy supplies do lift people out of energy poverty, and that's going to be an important theme of my term in this role'. After the interview, Bolt described the minister as the 'New Mr Coal'. Shortly after Minister Frydenberg's appointment was announced, the Australian Petroleum Production and Exploration Association put out a glowing media release. The Queensland Resources Council Executive Director Michael Roche did the same.[74]

Frydenberg's critics took exception to his appointment. Nikola Casule, climate and energy campaigner at Greenpeace, said Frydenberg's appointment was a 'huge blow' to the Great Barrier Reef: 'For Malcolm Turnbull to appoint a minister who still believes that there is still a strong moral case for coal even during the worst coral bleaching in the Great Barrier Reef's history shows contempt for the Australian public'.[75]

Minister for Resources and Northern Australia Matthew Canavan was not only pro-coal and pro-Adani, he was also an ardent climate change denier. Considering himself well read in the scientific literature, he wrote that since the 2009 Copenhagen climate conference:

> The risk of dangerous climate change has reduced …
> Accordingly it holds that the policy action we should take in
> response should be less ambitious, less costly and less binding
> than what was envisaged at Copenhagen.

Further, he argued that:

There is no clear global solution to this issue. We should instead
let nations make their own decisions about how to respond
in a cooperative and flexible manner. The evidence that there
is dangerous climate change is not as strong and we should
therefore not impose large costs on the global economy.[76]

His views represent the same binary mindset that has driven the
Coalition for years: if the science is wrong then coal can rule. Consequently, he was keen to announce that the government was going to
back a $100 billion investment target to expand the Australian coal
industry. Firing a verbal volley against environmentalists calling for
a halt to new mines, Canavan said it would be 'hypocritical to stop
coal production for exports on the grounds that developing nations
should not use fossil fuels to drive their economic growth'.[77]

Turnbull moved to elevate advice from the coal industry,
appointing Sid Marris as his climate and energy advisor. Marris left
his role as head of climate and environment at the coal industry
lobby group, the Minerals Council of Australia, to join Turnbull's
staff. Marris had worked for the Minerals Council since 2008, after
spending 16 years at the *Australian* newspaper.[78]

At the same time as Marris' appointment, information sur-
faced based on the Australian Electoral Commission's annual figures on political donations that politicians and their parties derived
$77 million from undisclosed sources, leading an expert at Mel-
bourne University to claim that: 'Australia's political donation laws
are among the most lax in the world. Large organisations can influence political policy without any of us knowing anything about it. It
is a really easily corruptible system'.[79]

Just as the flow of unregulated money into the system was perfectly legal, so too were ideologically partisan appointments to sensitive government positions. The Turnbull government overruled
an independent selection panel to appoint the chairwoman of the
MCA to the ABC board. Perth-based Dr Vanessa Guthrie had more

than 30 years of experience in the mining and resources industries, holding a variety of senior executive roles at Alcoa, Woodside Energy and Goldfields Limited. In justifying the appointment, Communications Minister Mitch Fifield said that Guthrie had the 'requisite skills' to be on the board, despite not making the final list of recommendations put forward by the Nomination Panel for ABC and SBS Board Appointments. As reported in the *Sydney Morning Herald*, her appointment was seen in the ideological context of the coal wars. Her five-year appointment came 'amid heated political debate about the role of fossil fuels and renewable energy in Australia', and followed government criticism of the public broadcaster's coverage of coal mining and energy security:

> The government has been fiercely critical of the ABC's coverage of energy, with Resources Minister Matt Canavan accusing it in December of running 'fake news' as part of a campaign against the proposed Adani coalmine in Queensland. The ABC was also accused of bias against the NSW Shenhua coal mine proposal but was cleared by a review. The Institute of Public Affairs – which has spawned a number of Coalition MPs – claims the ABC has a 'systemic bias', giving the renewable energy industry favourable coverage but showing hostility towards coal and other fossil fuels. In an interview with the *Australian Financial Review* last year, Dr Guthrie attacked social media activism against fossil fuels, taking aim at 'inner-city smashed avocado eaters' for unfairly targeting coal and the minerals industry more broadly.[80]

Turnbull, Guthrie, Fifield, Canavan and Frydenberg had all converged in a frenzy of climate change denialism and pro-coal promotion in the year after the Paris climate change accord. Conservatives in Australia remained unrepentant. Australia's export coal industry continued to have a disproportionate impact on global climate change while the government defended its meagre greenhouse gas reduction target. As a 2016 report from Greenpeace pointed out, the rapid growth in Australia's fossil fuel exports shows its overall contribution to global climate change is getting worse, not better: 'This year, Australia will export a billion tonnes of carbon dioxide (CO_2) in its coal – more than it plans to save domestically between 2020 and 2030. If its coal exports grow by over 60 per cent, as the Australian Government projects, the resulting increase in carbon emissions will erase the benefit of Australia meeting its Paris target nearly seven times over'.[81] The simplistic retort from the government was that our coal is cleaner.

Even though the contribution of Australia's export coal industry received little media coverage, the blowback against the government for its climate change policies continued to simmer. In June 2016, John Hewson joined the chorus of criticism over the Turnbull government's climate and energy policies. At a rally in Turnbull's Eastern Sydney electorate of Wentworth, Hewson gazed out at a sea of placards and launched a damaging attack on the Liberal Party's record. He condemned short-term politicking over climate change as a 'national disgrace'. He criticised 'a conscious attempt by the Abbott Government to wipe out the renewable energy sector', and attacked John Howard, who he said 'admitted in London that he'd played short-term politics deliberately' with policy around emissions trading. Hewson said the Turnbull Government's emissions reduction target was 'about half of what it ought to be if you're going to actually take the challenge of climate change seriously'.[82]

The revolving door between government and the mining industry continued to spin. Sophie Mirabella, a former high-profile federal MP, was head-hunted by Gina Rinehart and given the title General Manager of Government and Media Relations. The appointment created some 'interesting ripples' for the Liberal Party. The reason was clear enough: 'Sophie is obviously extremely well-connected in both government and business at a national level', a senior

Liberal source said. 'Gina Rinehart wouldn't have employed her if she wasn't.'[83]

Walking through the revolving door was an equally influential figure, retired senator Ian Macfarlane. He slipped quietly into the position of chief executive of the Queensland Resources Council. With his gravelly voice and direct manner, Macfarlane was the perfect fit for the bulldozing operational style long practised by the council. He lost no time lobbying his former party on the need to construct a new fleet of coal-fired power stations for Australia.[84]

Transparency International – the organisation that tracks corruption among the governments of the world – increasingly had Australia on its radar during the Abbott/Turnbull period of office. In 2017, it found that the practice in Australia of politicians becoming lobbyists is 'particularly common', with 191 of 538 lobbyists registered as former government representatives. It called for stricter 'cooling off' periods before politicians could enter the lobbying industry.[85] In practice, defining what is and isn't a lobbyist makes it a particular challenge to delineate regulations in this area. But the figures provided by Transparency International highlight the urgency of doing so. Increasingly, politics in Australia is being regarded as merely an apprenticeship for lucrative business careers.

The Climate Change Authority splits

The Abbott and Turnbull governments had put the architecture for Australia's coal future in place piece by piece. Among the last pieces of the policy framework was the finalisation of the way in which the government intended to meet its Paris commitments. As mentioned, this had been given to the Climate Change Authority – recently 'stacked' with Coalition supporters. Months of discussion and compromise followed as the authority painstakingly worked through the complex issues.

Behind-the-scenes harmony among the board members had evaporated. For Clive Hamilton, the new appointees had changed the authority's character. It was now 'dominated by people who want action, but too much action'. As time wore on, Hamilton realised that 'Turnbull was drifting away from any meaningful action on climate change'.[86] The government had already ignored the authority's call for much deeper cuts to emissions of between 40–60 per cent on 2000 levels by 2030 in the lead-up to the Paris talks. However, by the time it released its *Special Review of Australia's Climate Goals and Policies* in August 2016, the split among the board's members about the degree of climate change action required had led to two separate reports – Clive Hamilton and David Karoly prepared a minority report. Their disagreement with the majority report was summed up in the following argument:

> We believe that the effect of the majority report will be to sanction further delay and a slow pace of action, with serious consequences for the nation. Those consequences include either very severe and costly emissions cuts in the mid-to-late 2020s, or alternatively a repudiation of Australia's international commitments, and free-riding on the efforts of the rest of the world. As we see it, the recommendations of the majority report are framed to suit a particular assessment of the prevailing political circumstances. We believe it is inappropriate and often counterproductive to attempt to second-guess political negotiations, especially for a new and uncertain parliament. The unduly narrow focus of the majority report, seemingly based on a reading from a political crystal ball, has ruled out policies, such as a strengthened renewables target and stronger land clearing restrictions, that have a proven capacity to respond most effectively to the nation's climate change goals.[87]

Coal takes centre stage

The pro-coal forces propelling the Liberals for decades culminated in a second front at the beginning of 2017. Not only would the Galilee Basin be opened for exports to India and South-East Asia, new coal-fired power stations were set to boost Australia's domestic energy market. There was a perverse logic to the policy: if Australia was set to unleash more coal onto the market it made 'sense' to link this to the domestic energy market.

On 1 February, Turnbull gave an address to the National Press Club in which he outlined the government's strategy. Turnbull acknowledged that the government had invested $590 million in clean-coal technology since 2009, despite Australia not having a high-efficiency, low-emission power station. But this didn't stop the prime minister from trying to create the case for 'clean coal'. 'The next incarnation of our national energy policy should be technology-agnostic', he said.[88] Environment and Energy Minister Josh Frydenberg joined the promotional campaign: 'Australia, as the biggest coal exporter in the world, should be looking at how we can roll out similar technologies', he said. As Lenore Taylor wrote, the Turnbull government 'has a particular need for doublespeak' on clean coal technology. Having campaigned to end a tax on carbon, 'it found it convenient to claim the discovery of the climate policy equivalent of a free lunch'.[89]

The day after Turnbull's National Press Club speech, Treasurer Scott Morrison outlined how the government intended to fund the rollout. He would not rule out using money set aside in the CEFC to construct a new generation of coal-fired power stations. 'Coal is a big part of the future under a Coalition government and clearly that's not the case under the alternative', Morrison told the ABC. 'It's the Clean Energy Finance Corporation – it's not the wind energy finance corporation.'[90] Critics were alarmed to say the least.

Behind the scenes, the MCA and its chief executive, Brendan Pearson, who had occupied the position since Mitch Hooke's departure in 2014, had pressed hard for the policy. Pearson had large shoes to fill. After his departure from the MCA, Hooke was awarded an Order of Australia (General Division) for his services to mining. Preason soon showed that he possessed similar fighting qualities as his predecessor. The MCA conducted a 'no holds barred campaign for new coal power stations to be built in Australia'.[91] Described as 'a loyal servant' of the coal and mining industries, Pearson was a 'strident' activist for coal. As a source told the *Financial Review*: 'I think his view was that if you let [the environment] movement win on coal then they'll tick that box and move onto the next thing, and I think that drives his strident activism'.[92]

Weeks after Turnbull and Morrison declared their revamped agenda for coal, the tensions in the Climate Change Authority came to a head with the resignations of Hamilton and Quiggin; Karoly decided to stay in the organisation until his term expired. Both Hamilton and Quiggin cited the government's failure to take global warming seriously, its 'perverse' support for coal, its continuous attacks on renewables and the fact that it was 'beholden to right wing anti-science activists in its own ranks and in the media' as reasons for their resignation.[93]

How did Turnbull make sense of these developments? Was he in a fugue-like state dissociating from his former self, or did he simply accept the brutal realities of power? Or, as Brendan Nelson intimated, was Turnbull likely to be the sort of leader overly enamoured with being prime minister? It's hard to discern which one, or combination, of the possible interpretations explains Turnbull's role in promoting the very policies he had previously and explicitly disavowed.

By the early months of 2017, tensions over energy policy and the Adani mine had been simmering for seven years. Straddling both the Abbott and Turnbull governments were three separate, but interlinked, campaigns to stop the mine: the campaign over native title (see Chapter 9); the environmental campaign in the courts (see Chapter 10) and the campaign waged by activists to force banks to disavow funding Adani (see Chapter 11). Together these campaigns intensified the war over coal and the Carmichael mine.

CHAPTER NINE

'This huge black hole':
The fight over native title

I t's hard to imagine a more uneven political contest. A small, but committed, group of Aboriginal people from the Wangan and Jagalingou traditional owners of central Queensland has been locked in a bitter struggle with the Adani Group since 2011 over the rights to their lands on which the proposed Carmichael mine is to be situated. And, of course, alongside Adani stand the Queensland and federal governments, not to mention the Indian Prime Minister Narendra Modi. As the fight has gone on, the Wangan and Jagalingou people have attracted their own influential supporters – and considerable public support – opening up a broader contest over the *Native Title Act 1993* itself and the rights of Indigenous people to control their future in the face of the 'coal rush'.

The significance of the Wangan and Jagalingou's case can't be underestimated, although it is not the first time in the modern era that Aboriginal people have opposed big mining developments on their land. In the early 1970s, the Noonkanbah people in the Kimberley region of Western Australia blazed a trail for self-determination, even though their struggle was quashed by the Liberal government of Sir Charles Court with a contingent of police. More recently, the Gomeroi people of NSW stood alongside farmers, celebrities and environmentalists to oppose the controversial Maules Creek mine, which threatened to destroy a number of their sacred sites. In 2013, the Goolarabooloo people of the Kimberley were part of a broader community campaign which successfully fought off plans to build one of the largest gas plants in Australia at James Price Point, a move that would have industrialised the remote and pristine Kimberley coastline.

However, the Wangan and Jagalingou's struggle against Adani has been an important test case of the native title legislation in Australia. Bitterly opposed by conservatives when prime minister Paul Keating introduced it in 1993, the legislation was widely heralded as ending the legal fiction of *terra nullius*, which had unjustly dispossessed so many Aboriginal people and had allowed governments control over those Aboriginal groups still living on their country. But the *Native Title Act* was always a compromise in what it offered Aboriginal groups seeking their native title rights. The Wangan and Jagalingou's struggle is not just a significant legal hurdle to Adani's plans to develop the Galilee Basin, it has also revived the debate about Aboriginal sovereignty because 'No means no' has been the theme of the Wangan and Jagalingou's fight against the mine. They regard it as the most important fight over land rights since Mabo because it challenges the central limitation of the *Native Title Act* – the right to veto development.

Heading this David versus Goliath struggle is 57-year-old Adrian Burragubba, an internationally recognised didgeridoo musician and educator, as well as a long-standing campaigner for Indigenous rights. A traditional law man, he 'has knowledge that was passed onto him through the elders of his father's people when he was a small boy. They taught him the law'.[1]

There is a sad irony to Burragubba's family background. His grandfather was part of several generations removed from their traditional lands, initially by pressure from gold miners who arrived in central Queensland in the 1860s turning out gold from the region for decades afterwards. Thousands of prospective miners flocked into the Wangan and Jagalingou country 'to rape our land'.

Burragubba's family was put into church-run missions which 'were like concentration camps. They wanted Aboriginal people out of the way. So you couldn't leave them. The Police would take you back if you did'.[2] Those who refused to leave the land were murdered. For Burragubba this history is a living thing. Because no government has ever apologised for the dispossession and the murders, the Wangan and Jagalingou are, according to him, 'in a state of undeclared war'.[3] And now the miners want to come back.

Burragubba heads up the Wangan and Jagalingou Family Council, the community's governing body. His grey beard, stern countenance, and imposing physique give him the air of a natural leader. He also has a powerful way with words. In describing the impact of the mine on his people's traditional country, he says that 'Our land will be disappeared'. The mine would 'tear the heart out of our land', with devastating impacts on their native title:

> [our] ancestral lands and waters, our totemic plants and
> animals, and our environment and cultural heritage. It would
> pollute and drain billions of litres of ground water and
> obliterate important spring systems. It would potentially wipe
> out threatened and endangered species. It would literally leave a
> huge black hole, monumental in proportions, where there were
> once our homelands. These effects are irreversible.[4]

Initially reluctant to take on the role of fighting to stop Adani, members of the Family Council thought Burragubba's naturally outspoken personality and his background as an entertainer and cultural ambassador gave him the capacity to take their cause to the wider public.

Of critical importance to the Wangan and Jagalingou is the threat the mine poses to their most sacred site: the Doongmabulla Springs. Experts agree that the springs would die if the process of draining the underground water to service the mine's operations depleted the aquifers feeding them. But the mine would also have other invasive impacts: infrastructure for power, fuel and water supplies would be built, along with a waste disposal facility, a coal handling and processing plant, a heavy industrial area housing concrete batching and hot mix bituminous plants, as well as fuel storage facilities. The mine would also create a massive stockpile of rock waste. The promise of rehabilitation seems impossible to believe.

Burragubba has taken groups of Wangan and Jagalingou on visits back to Country. As a traditional elder and leader, he sees it as his mission to inspire his people to reconnect with their culture and land and 'why this is so special and worth fighting for'.[5]

As their opposition to the mine grew, members of the Wangan and Jagalingou have exposed the weaknesses of Australia's native title system. Burragubba and his group have dared to challenge the closed system of fossil fuel power in Australia. As the group explained:

> We are fighting to protect our land against the extreme power
> and wealth of the Adani Group – a massive global corporation
> – and against the state and federal governments that actively
> support the fossil fuel industry in pursuit of coal exploration
> [on] our sacred traditional lands for private shareholder profit.[6]

It is a daunting struggle, not just because of the forces of government and miners. The Wangan and Jagalingou have been met with mostly 'deadly silence' by other Aboriginal groups. Burragubba sees his struggle against Adani as one of fighting for true sovereignty, whereas he sees Aboriginal groups generally as trapped into the cycle of the native title system: 'They hold the position that they have nothing else and native title is their only way out'.[7]

For Burragubba, the fight with Adani has exposed the limitations not just of the land rights system but of Aboriginal people's lack of real sovereignty. 'You can't get self-determination', he says, 'by relying on a mining company to give you something'. He is insulted that, as a traditional elder and leader, neither Adani nor Australian government officials have ever paid him the respect of face-to-face meetings. 'I shouldn't have to talk to hired lawyers', he explains.[8]

Profits before marginalised people

It is not surprising that Adani would, ultimately, adopt a strategy to manipulate a native title settlement with the Wangan and Jagalingou community. As shown in Chapter 2, Adani's business model has regularly ridden roughshod over poor communities in ways that showed little regard for their future wellbeing. And Adani was part of a culture in India that paid little regard to the rights of the country's tribal peoples. In circumstances that are strikingly similar to Australia's Indigenous people, India's diverse tribal communities, comprising 8.6 per cent of the population, have suffered a history of discrimination, marginalisation and impoverishment, despite a provision in the Indian constitution that they require special consideration.

Many tribal-inhabited regions in India are rich in mineral, forest and water resources and, consequently, they come into conflict with large-scale development projects. As an official government report noted in 2014: 'Laws and rules that provide protection to tribes are being routinely manipulated and subverted to accommodate corporate interests'. Tribal protests are frequent and are met 'with violence by the State's paramilitary forces and the private security staff of the corporations involved'.[9] The conflict over access to tribal land intensified after India's economic liberalisation, when the state-owned Coal India Ltd stepped up its appropriation of forested tribal lands to mine coal. As a consequence, many thousands of tribal people were displaced and thrown into bonded labour.

There is no evidence that Adani ever briefed himself on the importance of culture to the Wangan and Jagalingou. The closest Burragubba came to an opportunity to educate the company was a brief meeting with Adani's cousin and company executive, Samir Vora. He was intrigued and somewhat taken aback by the Dreaming stories Burragubba told him, as if it was the first time he had heard about Aboriginal culture. But Burragubba felt that Samir's hands were tied and that 'he didn't really want to hear our side'.[10]

Australia's faulty native title system

As mentioned, the Wangan and Jagalingou are representative of those Aboriginal groups most affected by colonisation, rounded up and displaced from their lands by racist policies. Yet, despite the history of dispossession, its members have maintained strong cultural and physical connection to their land. In 2004, the Wangan and Jagalingou registered to have their land rights recognised under the 1993 *Native Title Act*, the first step towards recognition of full native title. This cumbersome process of validation hadn't been completed by the time Adani began to show an interest in their land, and still hasn't. Nevertheless, registration conferred on the Wangan and Jagalingou certain rights in relation to future activities that might have an impact on their land.

However, the *Native Title Act* confers limited real power on Aboriginal groups. Principally, this is because it provides no right of veto over development projects and, while it makes provision for compensation through royalty-style payments, such an outcome is not mandated. The Act stipulates the need for a process of negotiations to be held 'in good faith' between companies and communities in order for them to reach an Indigenous Land Use Agreement (ILUA), although the term itself is ambiguously defined. For these reasons, the process is often heavily stacked against Indigenous claimants to native title.

The Special Rapporteur for the United Nations noted, in his 2010 report on Australia, limitations that are relevant to the Wangan and Jagalingou struggle with Adani: ILUAs often undermined

Indigenous rights because the terms were kept secret, legal representation for communities was often inadequate and the interests of governments were often at odds with those of Aboriginal people.[11] If negotiations fail to reach an ILUA, companies can approach the National Native Title Tribunal (NNTT) for a determination. Yet, the arbitrating body 'rarely decides that a mining lease cannot be granted'.[12] As Anthony Esposito, Burragubba's political advisor, bluntly puts the case against the NNTT: 'It's an instrument of state in the service of miners and other developers'.[13]

In short, the Wangan and Jagalingou were acutely aware that they entered negotiations with Adani in a weak bargaining position. They were also aware that 'many Indigenous communities' in similar circumstances 'feel they have no satisfactory choice' but to come to an agreement with mining companies.[14] Experts in native title agree. ILUAs 'are very hard for Indigenous people to resist. The native title regime provides very limited protection, such that Indigenous people are often forced to take a poor ILUA deal, rather than risk ending up with nothing at the National Native Title Tribunal'.[15] A recent report in Western Australia confirmed these findings. It highlighted that Aboriginal groups face significant barriers to leveraging real benefits from their native title rights because of their weak bargaining position, which is inherent in the legislation.[16]

Whatever the merits or otherwise of the native title process, the point here is that members of the Wangan and Jagalingou community resented what they regarded as '[t]his biased and unfair process'.[17] They chafed at the restricted right to negotiate with companies and they were incensed that striking an ILUA did not require their informed consent. They could simply be railroaded by the legal process.

An imposed agreement

Adani Mining negotiated with the Wangan and Jagalingou community over the three mining leases that comprised the Carmichael mine. Negotiations on the first of the leases commenced in May 2011. To enter the native title system, the so-called claimant group (in this case the Wangan and Jagalingou community of 400 people) had to appoint 'applicants' to the negotiating process. In the case of the Wangan and Jagalingou community, their representative body, the Wangan and Jagalingou Family Council, appointed the applicants. The council comprised two representatives from each of the 12 ancestral families that make up the Wangan and Jagalingou community. In all matters pertaining to the group, the council reached decisions by consensus or, if that was not achievable, then through a majority vote.[18] In 2011, the claimant group appointed seven applicants to represent their interests. At this stage of the process Burragubba was not among them.

Negotiations were tense from the beginning. In the first six-month period, Adani Mining gave the Wangan and Jagalingou just two weeks to agree to its 'best offer' ILUA despite the immense impact on their native title rights. When they asked for more time to address the issues, 'Adani Mining's lawyers informed us that if we did not agree to its timeline, it would refer our negotiation to the NNTT (in other words we could get no deal), and threatened that the Queensland government could use a process of compulsory acquisition of native title for the rail infrastructure'.[19]

Tensions escalated when the Wangan and Jagalingou appointed a new legal team to strengthen their representation. When the new legal team sought to include a 'life of mine services' contract, which would provide long-term benefits to the community in the form of jobs and business opportunities, the rift between the two parties began to widen. The request for a 'life of services agreement' indicates that there was support among the seven-member Wangan and Jagalingou applicant negotiation team to make a settlement with Adani if the terms of the agreement were satisfactory. Adani's conduct became 'rigid and unwilling to consider additional terms of agreement'.[20] Consequently, the company rejected the inclusion of a life of mine services contract. On this basis, the Wangan and Jagalingou claimants declined the ILUA on offer, unconvinced of the benefits it would provide to the community and with ongoing fears about the damage to traditional lands.

With the lapse of the stipulated period for negotiations, Adani was now within its rights under the Act to approach the NNTT, where the company could be reasonably sure of gaining approval for the lease. However, while this process was in train, the company began moves to undermine the authority of the Wangan and Jagalingou Family Council by suspending negotiations with it while beginning correspondence with the mine's supporters. As tensions in the Wangan and Jagalingou community rose, just which members of the community had authority to negotiate on their behalf became a critical issue. Adani was aware that not all the mine's supporters were registered members of the Wangan and Jagalingou claimant group. The company adopted the divide and conquer tactic to advance its interests. However, despite some differences in the Wangan and Jagalingou claimant group, there was agreement that talks with Adani collapsed because the compensation on offer was 'wholly deficient'.[21]

Predictably, in May 2013, the NNTT granted the first mining lease to Adani. According to Adrian Burragubba, the tribunal 'decided against our arguments regarding lack of good faith in negotiations'.[22] Burragubba believes that an agreement should never have been struck in the first place because Adani had not secured funds to build the mine.

However, according to lawyers from Clayton Utz, the firm representing Adani, the matter was decided on the evidence:

> The Tribunal found that, although for the purposes of considering the impact of these matters the Tribunal assumes that the native title rights and interests asserted in the claim exist, the native title party must bring evidence of how the grant of the mining lease will impact on these rights. This will necessarily require evidence of the current exercise of these rights. As the native title party did not produce this evidence, the Tribunal was unable to make findings that the grant of the mining lease would have an effect on the enjoyment of the registered native title rights and interests.[23]

It is difficult to fully assess the reasoning behind the tribunal's decision because not all submissions made to it are publicly available. What is clear is that both the Queensland government and Adani stressed the economic benefits of the mine and the NNTT agreed, and found that the mine would not deny the Wangan and Jagalingou access to their native title rights, despite clear evidence, raised also in environmental court challenges against the mine (see Chapter 10), that building the mine risked destroying the Doongmabulla Springs.

In October 2013, Adani resumed negotiations with the seven-member claim group in relation to the remaining two mining leases and proposed an ILUA covering the remainder of the mine site. During the 12 months of these negotiations, the divisions in the Wangan and Jagalingou community intensified; divisions, in part, stirred by Adani. Changes of personnel for the second round of negotiations intensified these. Whereas a seven-member team had represented the Wangan and Jagalingou in the first round of negotiations, this had been reduced to three for the subsequent round. The team comprised Patrick Malone and Irene Simpson, who had both been members of the first round, and Adrian Burragubba, who was appointed for the first time. His appointment proved decisive because of his resolute opposition to the mine, his leadership skills and his determination to represent the wishes of the Wangan and Jagalingou community through its Family Council.

During these negotiations Malone and Simpson agreed to negotiate with Adani. As Burragubba later explained, although the pair opposed the mine, they nonetheless 'favoured an agreement with Adani Mining, apparently because their understanding of certain legal advice led them to believe that opposition to the Carmichael mine was futile and an agreement with Adani Mining would provide benefits not otherwise attainable'.[24]

Explaining her decision to negotiate with Adani, Simpson said that '[T]here was majority support in a vote of the native title applicants [that is, her, Malone and Burragubba] to go ahead with negotiations. It was legal and there is huge support in the mob because it will bring jobs'.[25]

Burragubba continued to reject the offer Adani was making. The compensation on offer, he said, was 'a pittance'; his view was that the agreement signed by Simpson and Malone was made under duress; the 'few minimum wage jobs in a dying industry' were not what his people deserved. The Wangan and Jagalingou, according to Burragubba, were simply being offered 'crumbs by Adani'.[26] In fact, he claimed figures supplied by Adani showed that it planned to pay Wangan and Jagalingou workers just $35 000 a year.[27] By this stage, Adani regarded Burragubba as a troublemaker and sought to exclude him from meetings it arranged with Simpson and Malone.

Whether Simpson and Malone had the authority to strike an ILUA with Adani became the key sticking point with the Wangan and Jagalingou. Burragubba claimed that the two were prohibited from doing so without the consideration and approval of the Wangan and Jagalingou Claimant Group. A meeting to this effect was held in October 2014, where 200 from the Claimant Group attended and formally rejected negotiating an ILUA with Adani.[28] In doing so, the Claimant Group upheld the Wangan and Jagalingou Family Council 'as the representative and decision-making body of our people'.

It further authorised Burragubba as the council's chief spokesperson, along with Murrawah Johnson, appointed to represent the views of the community's younger generation.

Murrawah, an emerging charismatic leader in her own right, had become an activist for her community through her attendance at the October 2014 meeting when, at 22 years of age, she was entitled to vote on the ILUA issue for the first time. As she later explained:

> I was one of the people that stood up – the whole thing was orchestrated by Adani to acquire an ILUA by 3pm … And I think that might have been a contributor to how they got the no vote.
>
> I was going through the proposal and I stood up and said, 'Where's the environmental impact statement?'
>
> And they said, 'What?'
>
> And I repeated, 'Where's the environmental impact statement? This is supposed to be the largest new mine in the world'.
>
> And I was told to my face in front of 200 people, 'That's none of your concern'.[29]

The fake controversy over Wangan and Jagalingou support

The Wangan and Jagalingou community's fight over national title had attracted little media attention until the community made a second decisive rejection of an ILUA deal with Adani. But in twice rejecting a deal, the Wangan and Jagalingou had elevated their fight to a contest over native title itself and the rights of Indigenous people to self-determination. The *Australian* seized on the growing significance of the struggle and claimed that the community was being manipulated by outside left-wing groups. 'Green activists', one of the paper's senior reporters, Michael McKenna, wrote, 'are behind an 11th hour bid to scuttle … [the 2014] land-use agreement'.

McKenna concluded that the deal only fell apart 'after anti-coal activists bankrolled Adani opponents within the Indigenous group, who then voted against supporting the mine'.[30]

It is true that the Wangan and Jagalingou attracted support from a range of progressive groups, including the Australian Youth Climate Coalition and GetUp!. Both promoted the Wangan and Jagalingou cause on their websites and helped raise funds for legal challenges, and awareness about a petition the Wangan and Jagalingou were circulating among the public to present to the Queensland government. Support for the Wangan and Jagalingou also came from Graeme Wood, the millionaire creator of the Wotif.com travel accommodation site and a supporter of the Greens. Wood offered the Wangan and Jagalingou Family Council an office at his Brisbane headquarters. Wood explained that he was 'totally passionate' about stopping mines in the Galilee Basin 'because it's just an absurdity. It's the destruction of the world as we know it. It's about greed versus the future of the natural world'.[31]

In 2016, the *Australian* again restated its claim that 'outsiders' and 'foreigners' were using the Wangan and Jagalingou for their anti-coal agenda. Emails leaked by WikiLeaks revealed that the US-based Sandler Foundation funded the little-known Australian-based environment group The Sunrise Project, which offered the Wangan and Jagalingou financial support and scholarships if they continued to oppose the Carmichael mine. The Sunrise Project was headed by John Hepburn, a former staffer with Greenpeace. The emails had been plucked from the tranche of materials WikiLeaks had obtained in October 2016 from John Podesta, the chairman of Hillary Clinton's presidential campaign.

The *Australian* claimed the emails showed the Wangan and Jagalingou and The Sunrise Project had reached an agreement only weeks after the 2014 meeting which rejected any ILUA with Adani. The information in the emails further revealed that The Sunrise Project was offered help from another non-government group,

Human Rights Watch, on ways to keep intact the former's tax-exempt charity status because 'the mining companies seem to own the Liberals (in Australia) and they play very dirty'.[32] An advisor to Burragubba told the *Australian* that no agreement with The Sunrise Project had ever been signed.

The lack of confirmation about its claims of outside interference didn't stop the *Australian* from pressing its case. The paper fumed in an editorial that the details of the links between The Sunrise Project and the Wangan and Jagalingou community confirmed its fears that Australia was a key target in a 'global, no-holds-barred war against coal which has set a priority of shutting Adani out of Queensland'. This was an affront to Australian democracy, the paper argued: 'We should decide what mining projects are opened up in the country and the circumstances in which they open'.[33]

Hepburn shot back at the *Australian*'s attempt at whipping up a conspiracy theory. He said that it was no surprise that Clinton's senior advisor would seek a briefing on the ongoing expansion of coal mining in Australia, given Clinton's commitment to implementing the Paris climate agreement. Hepburn couldn't resist highlighting the contradiction in the *Australian*'s argument about foreign influence:

> They're [the *Australian*] saying that we need to guard our
> sovereignty from environmental organisations, when the
> mining industry in Australia is 80% foreign owned. They put
> tens, if not hundreds, of millions of dollars into a massive
> public relations machine … They have incredible influence.[34]

To bolster its editorial line that Australians should be shocked about 'foreign influence' in the debate about the coal industry, the paper commissioned an article from Brendan Pearson from the Minerals Council of Australia, itself funded in large part by foreign-owned mining companies. His demands that the Wangan and Jagalingou should fully disclose their sources of funding was supported by the Queensland Resources Council, which also had representatives from foreign companies on their board.

The reporting was a classic beat-up designed to serve Murdoch's flagship newspaper's own ideological agenda. The heart of the dispute involving the Wangan and Jagalingou was not which likeminded groups they reached out to for support, but whether the Wangan and Jagalingou should be given the right to informed consent for a massive disruptive project on their land. Burragubba had made this very clear. It was, he stated, a fight for the 'right to free, prior and informed consent, including our right to give or withhold our consent to a proposed destructive project … on our traditional lands'. 'If we reject a proposed project', he further explained, 'our "no" does not mean "no". Instead, it means the decision is taken out of our hands'.[35] And the larger point here needs emphasis. If the native title system had so comprehensively failed Aboriginal people, where else could they turn for support other than by linking up with the larger political struggle against the mine?

Another fruitless native title hearing

Following the October 2014 meeting when the Wangan and Jagalingou community voted down negotiating an ILUA with Adani, the company went back to the NNTT to have their second licence application approved, again without the consent of the community. This was duly ratified in April 2015. Burragubba had emailed the tribunal with the statement that 'our lawyers were asked to tell the tribunal that we can no longer participate in these proceedings', although he did spell out to the tribunal that 'at no time has the Wangan and Jagalingou Claimant Group, through its own determination, consented to the proposed mine or any of its component parts. The Wangan and Jagalingou Family Representative Council's objection is a broader one that goes to the heart of our rights as an

Indigenous People, and the issue of obtaining our free, prior and informed consent for matters affecting our traditional territories'.[36]

The flaws in the NNTT process were becoming clear for all to see. What happens when 'applicants' don't want an ILUA at any cost? The short answer was that the tribunal had to find a way to provide Adani with one. In the second NNTT hearing, Burragubba claimed that Adani used Simpson and Malone's support for granting the mining lease as evidence of the wider Wangan and Jagalingou community's support 'despite those two members acting outside their mandate and not representing our people's wishes'.[37]

The tribunal, which did not carry out its own independent investigations on the claims that came before it, again found that it was 'unable to conclude that there will be any (or any significant) impact on the ability of members of the native title claim group to access the area ... or to carry out rites, ceremonies or other activities of cultural significance'. It upheld the claims of Adani and the Queensland government 'that the grant of the proposed leases will serve the public interest by contributing to 'developing and maintaining a mining industry that generates very considerable export income, employment opportunities and wealth for the local, State and national economies'.[38] It accepted, at face value, the figures Adani supplied indicating that the mine and rail developments would create over 10 000 jobs in Queensland; a claim that had been repeated to the point of a mantra by both the company and the government, and which Adani's own experts had testified were false (see Chapter 10).

But cracks started to appear in the Wangan and Jagalingou's small group that did support the mine. Following the NNTT's second determination, Patrick Malone, one of the two Wangan and Jagalingou applicants who had been in favour of an ILUA with Adani, expressed doubts about his involvement. He told the media that the NNTT process 'was skewed in favour of miners and governments for his people to have a hope of winning the day'.

He preferred that the mine didn't go ahead but was resigned that it would, so he was 'trying to get the best results for his people'.[39] In other words, he felt the full constraints of the native title system.

The Wangan and Jagalingou escalate their battle

After their second loss in the NNTT, Burragubba and Johnson opened up multiple fronts in their battle with Adani and the Queensland and federal governments. By now, both were seasoned campaigners and media performers. In March 2015, they arranged a media conference outside Queensland's Parliament House and announced that they were going to present a 'Declaration of Defence of Country' to the Speaker, Peter Wellington. It was a classic, but effective, media stunt; the 'Declaration' merely affirmed the Wangan and Jagalingou community's opposition to the mine and their intention to continue to fight for their rights, and it issued a call to arms to 'other Australians and the world community' to join them in their fight.[40] Johnson was photographed handing the 'Declaration' to Wellington while that evening Burragubba was invited onto the ABC's *Lateline* program to discuss their cause.

In late May, the pair announced their intention to mount a 'World Banks Tour'; a trip to North America, Europe and Asia to try to block Adani's access to funds. They intended to remind banks of their human rights obligations and, no doubt, of the potential damage to their reputations from ramped-up protests against the mine.[41]

While in North America, Burragubba and Johnson visited the First Nations People of the Canadian Province of Alberta to hear about their struggle against the mega-tar sands project. As Burragubba explained to the Australian media before departing overseas, the Canadian visit was about building solidarity between Indigenous people across the globe and to 'draw inspiration from our individual battles'. Indeed, the parallels between the two Indigenous groups were disturbingly similar.

About 23 000 Indigenous peoples from 18 First Nations and six Métis settlements live in the oil sands region in north-east Alberta, comprising an area about twice the size of Tasmania. The extracting and refining of the oil, which sits within 100 metres of the ground surface, is on such a huge scale that it has been described as the largest industrial project in the world.[42] In the process, 775 000 hectares of boreal forest, acclaimed as one of the planet's ecological treasures, have been cleared or degraded.[43]

Described as being as thick as peanut butter, tar sands require an environmentally destructive process to extract the oil. After the forest cover is removed, the bitumen is stripped off and transported in trucks the size of three-storey buildings to industrial 'cookers' where toxic chemicals separate the heavy crude from the bitumen. The end product has been labelled by critics as 'the dirtiest fuel on the planet'.[44] In a relatively short time, the region's pristine boreal forests, clean rivers and lakes had been turned into 'a devastated eco-system of deforestation' and for the First Nations people, a 'slow industrial genocide'.[45] Toxic chemicals have entered the First Nation peoples' traditional food sources, causing an alarming rise in the level of cancer among them.

First Nations people had been leading a growing resistance movement to the project when Burragubba and Johnson visited. However, they were as powerless as the Wangan and Jagalingou had been to stop the combined power of corporations and government from destroying their land. Indeed, Canada's treaty arrangements with its Indigenous people – long seen as a model for Australia's First Peoples – does not guarantee the right of veto over developments. Just as in Australia, the 'national interest' takes precedence:

Consultation is just that, telling a community a project is being proposed that may or may not have impacts to a First

Nation and the recognition of its Treaty rights. As of yet, there is no legal framework within the Constitution of Canada that recognizes the principles of Free, Prior and Informed Consent (FPIC) for the right of First Nations to say 'No' to a proposed development.[46]

The First Nations people had witnessed their government hand over the responsibility for environmental monitoring to corporations, only to see that no real monitoring took place. Like the Wangan and Jagalingou, the First Nations people of Canada were calling on their government to uphold the 2007 UN Declaration of Indigenous Rights. As each was aware, both Canada and Australia (along with the United States) had held out against signing the treaty because they were concerned about the ramifications of legalising an Indigenous right to a veto over development projects. Both subsequently signed the treaty but did nothing to formally ratify it into national law. Not surprisingly, the Wangan and Jagalingou had much in common with the struggles of their counterparts in Alberta. As Murrawah Johnson explained to Chief Allan Adam of the Athabasca Chipewyan First Nation: 'We are here because we also believe making strong relations with First Nations around the world is essential to the fight with the fossil fuel industry'.[47]

Adani's 'skulduggery'

On 25 June 2015, not long after Burragubba's and Johnson's visit to Canada, the Wangan and Jagalingou community met to reconsider the structure of their Native Title Claim Applicant Group, then only three members, two of whom (Malone and Simpson) had, according to the Wangan and Jagalingou Family Council, 'violated their mandate to act on the instructions of our people'.[48] The intention was to make the Applicant Claim Group fully representative of the Wangan and Jagalingou community by increasing its size from three to 12 – one each from the 12 ancestral families. The meeting was held at the Tavernetta Function Centre in the Brisbane suburb of Carseldine.

In what was described by Michael West, a journalist for the *Sydney Morning Herald*, as 'an Adani ambush', the company bussed in 150 people and paid for their food and accommodation for three days, in an attempt to force an ILUA.[49] 'We saw the buses turn up and we were wondering what was going on', Burrabugga later explained. In effect, Adani had tried to stack the meeting with people not formally associated with the Wangan and Jagalingou community. However, Adani's 'cunning stunt' backfired as West explained: 'They [the company] hadn't counted on their 150 votes changing their minds after impassioned speeches from the likes of Burragubba'. For his part, Burragubba saw the whole episode as simply part of the 'tactical skulduggery' Adani had been engaged in for years.[50]

Adani also made a number of misleading public statements in an attempt to win over public approval in its native title dealings. Adani told the media in 2015 that Burragubba was not authorised to speak on behalf of the Wangan and Jagalingou and that his company was 'dealing with all of the duly authorised representatives' when this was clearly not the case. The company also publicly rejected claims that the Wangan and Jagalingou community opposed the mine when, in fact, a majority of the community had twice voted against it.[51] The company also echoed the claims in the *Australian* that negotiations with the Wangan and Jagalingou community broke down after the intervention of paid activists. Burragubba was particularly incensed by the company's assertion that they were being manipulated. 'Whilst we have reached out to the broader community for support', he replied, 'we absolutely retain our autonomy to decide with whom we collaborate and it is extremely offensive that Adani Mining would suggest that we are not making our own decisions'.[52]

In October 2015, the Wangan and Jagalingou, having suffered two blows in the NNTT, appealed to the United Nations for assistance. Burragubba and Johnson sent a closely argued 38-page letter to Ms Victoria Tauli-Corpuz, the Special Rapporteur on the rights of Indigenous People at the UN Office of the High Commissioner for Human Rights in Geneva. The crux of their argument was that the approval of the Carmichael coal mine in Australia was in violation of human rights law as it applied to Indigenous people and which was expressed in a range of core UN human rights treaties. This body of international law, the pair argued, recognised their right to free, prior and informed consent, including the right to give or withhold consent on resource projects. As they further pointed out, Adani had consulted with their community in bad faith 'as it has attempted to undermine and interfere with our institutions of representative decision-making'.[53]

In addition to citing specified UN covenants on civil and political rights to which Australia was a signatory, Burragubba and Johnson noted the findings of the Australian Human Rights Commissioner, who argued that Australian governments had interpreted their obligations under international law to consult with Indigenous peoples as little more than a duty to tell them 'what has been developed on [their] behalf and what will eventually be imposed on them'.[54]

Noting that Australia had failed to enforce international law in respect of Indigenous people, Burragubba and Johnson made a heartfelt plea to Tauli-Corpuz to further investigate the issues they had raised by coming to Australia and meeting with them, and 'by sending an urgent appeal to the Australian government expressing your serious concern that the human rights of our people are being violated through the approval of the Carmichael Coal Mine'.[55]

Having targeted banks and appealed to the UN, the Wangan and Jagalingou decided to appeal to the Federal Court in Brisbane. In November, David Yarrow, a lawyer for Burragubba, alleged in his application for a hearing that Adani had provided the NNTT with false claims about the mine's economic benefits in what amounted to a distortion of the Native Title Tribunal's decision-making process.[56]

The Wangan and Jagalingou's legal challenge was just one of several attempts to stop the Carmichael mine in the courts. Those mounted by environmentalists are examined in the next chapter. Together, these legal challenges not only rattled the Queensland government and the conservative media, but Adani personally.

In early December 2015, Gautam Adani made a rare appearance in the Australian media. He was 'fed up', he said 'with relentless opposition' to his Carmichael project. In an even rarer acknowledgment of his insider political dealings, he was reported as 'asking authorities to stop entertaining objections to the mine'. He sought from the federal government 'a law banning activists seeking judicial review of environmental approvals already granted by the Australian authorities'.[57] Here was a 'foreigner' meddling in Australian politics calling for democratic rights to be wound back, but the *Australian*, for one, couldn't see the contradiction over its own hype about 'foreigner' interference in the Wangan and Jagalingou case. In fact, the newspaper ended the year with an erroneous dig at Adrian Burragubba, now its latest bete noire activist opposing the fossil-fuel agenda. In an article about the impending Federal Court case, the paper did its best to discredit Burragubba's leadership of the Wangan and Jagalingou. He had 'lost the support of his clan'; he had 'faced a revolt by his fellow native title claimants'; he was 'single-handedly delaying the final approval of the project' and he was 'backed by green groups'.[58]

It is little wonder that the *Australian* and the Queensland government were so incensed over the Wangan and Jagalingou campaign. In December 2015, Anthony Lynham, Queensland's Minister for State Development, Natural Resources and Mines, was forced to acknowledge that he could not issue the mining lease until the Wangan and Jagalingou case was resolved by the Federal Court. Burragubba's persistence had, for the time being, forced the Carmichael mine into an impasse.

In April 2016, a group claiming to represent the Wangan and

Jagalingou met and voted 294–1 in favour of an ILUA with Adani. Patrick Malone, who was part of that agreement, claims that under the agreement 7.5 per cent of the jobs in the construction phase are for Wangan and Jagalingou people. Malone, who went on to be employed by Adani as a co-ordinator of Aboriginal cultural issues, supported the mine for the jobs it would provide traditional owners. However, Burragubba is challenging this agreement in the Federal Court.[59] At the time of writing this judgment hasn't been handed down. Whatever the outcome, the Wangan and Jagalingou's struggle has highlighted the unfinished business of native title in Australia.

CHAPTER TEN

The legal challenge from 'greenies'

During the Abbott and Turnbull governments, environment groups proved just as persistent as the Wangan and Jagalingou in using the legal system to challenge the mine. Together, the legal challenges against Adani reveal deep flaws in Australia's legal framework to protect the environment in an age when global warming is set to mount the greatest threat to the planet's ecosystems. Revealed also is the willingness of conservative politicians to clear the legal path for corporations to pursue fossil fuel projects despite the seriousness of this threat.

In 2015, the Mackay Conservation Group (MCG), an environment group largely unknown outside the regional Queensland city of Mackay, temporarily stopped the Adani juggernaut in the courts by winning a case over the need to protect threatened species at its mine site. The federal court challenge the MCG mounted was as bold as it was potentially risky. Submitted initially to challenge approval for the mine over the impact of climate change on the Great Barrier Reef, the group later widened their grounds for appeal to include threatened species and Adani's poor track record on the environment.

The MCG was part of a broader strategy in the environmental movement to use the law to frustrate or stop fossil fuel projects, a tactic successfully used in the United States. As Lisa Cox wrote in the *Sydney Morning Herald* at the time of the MCG challenge: 'Australia is under siege from a new kind of eco-warrior, one with a manual and money for legal challenges designed to endlessly frustrate economic development'.[1] Conservatives decried such a strategy as an abuse of the legal system. The coal wars had entered a new phase.

However, for conservation groups the legal strategy carried risks. It consumed scarce resources and potentially crippling costs could be awarded against them. Such groups needed powerful allies to mount these challenges. Yet, for the MCG, the Carmichael mine represented a direct assault on its core organisational concern: protecting the Great Barrier Reef from climate change and from the coal industry's invasive operations.

Represented in court by the Environmental Defenders Office of New South Wales (EDO NSW), the victory was quickly overturned by federal government action. Yet the ramifications were far-reaching. The MCG's legal challenge was the first of several made by conservation groups against the mine; those mounted by Land Services of Coast and Country Inc and the Australian Conservation Foundation are discussed below.

The MCG's temporary victory brought a ferocious blowback from the Abbott government. In a sign that the coal wars were heating up, Abbott and Attorney-General George Brandis used cries of 'lawfare' and 'vigilante litigation' to denounce those in the conservation movement who took action to try to stop the big development projects that were central to the vision of Australia as a fossil fuel energy superpower.[2]

The Mackay Conservation Group and its case

Situated on the edge of the Great Barrier Reef, Mackay has for generations been known as the 'sugar capital of Australia'. More recently, it has been transformed into a major coal exporting hub due to its close proximity to the rich Bowen Basin deposit. The MCG had been in existence for 30 years when it took up the case against Adani.

The MCG works with local residents, farmers and fishermen 'to make sure that their knowledge, connection to place and their livelihoods are not shoved aside in the coal rush'. Adopting a community development approach, they seek to empower 'frontline communities' who daily face the challenges of living close to the coal industry. 'Together we are powerful' is their slogan.[3] 'We're a small environment group, but we have a very long and proud history of defending the environment in our region', explains MCG co-ordinator, Ellen Roberts.[4]

MCG members worry about a future built around coal and affected by climate change. They lament the lack of state and national leadership to forge a different future for North Queensland. The MCG believe there's been a failure to prepare the regional community for the changes in the local economy that will result from the inevitable downturn in coal. Instead of a clear analysis of the shifts in global energy use, 'we see a denial of the problems facing the industry and support for even more new coal projects'.[5]

The MCG Management Committee did not make its decision to undertake the litigation lightly. As Michael Williams, the president of the organisation's board, wrote: 'All litigation in the Federal Court has the potential to incur costs, which means we have to pay the other side's hefty legal bills if we lose. However, we knew that the approval of Australia's largest coal mine with all of its massive environmental impacts was not something that we could let go by unchallenged'.[6]

In the beginning, the MCG appeal against Environment Minister Greg Hunt's approval of the mine was based on a single argument: that he had failed to consider how the burning of the coal from the Carmichael mine would contribute to global climate change and further adversely affect the Great Barrier Reef. The MCG hoped that, if they won the court case, 'this would change the way that coal projects were assessed in Australia'.[7] For such a small group, the MCG had grand ambitions.

Their legal representatives, EDO NSW, based their legal challenge on Section 136 of the *Environment Protection and Biodiversity Conservation (EPBC) Act (1999)*. Introduced by the Howard government to form the legislative centrepiece for the protection of the Australian environment, the Act stipulates that assessments must take into account international principles of ecological sustainability. Therefore, logic followed, where projects have an impact on areas of national environmental significance, 'consideration must be given to concepts such as the needs of future generations and the precautionary principle'.[8] Accordingly, the EDO NSW argued 'that these principles necessarily require Hunt to consider the climate change impact of emissions from the burning of coal when deciding whether to approve a mine licence'.[9] Effectively, the MCG appeal was a test case on the implications of coal mining for global warming. As Samantha Hepburn, Professor of Law at Deakin University, pointed out, case law in this vexed area was mixed. In 2006, court rulings on the need to take into account greenhouse gas emissions from mining split both ways; one found that these were too indirect to be taken into account while the other found that they did come into the scope of the EPBC Act.[10] In both cases the courts took the issue seriously.

Environmental law and its prospects

Using the law to protect the environment is not a new practice. Nonetheless in 2015 it was still relatively undeveloped in Australia, especially on big issues such as climate change.

Public interest law on behalf of the environment began in the United States in 1970 with the foundation of the Natural Resources Defence Council (NRDC). It has grown from a group of law students and attorneys at the forefront of the emerging environment movement to 2.4 million members and 500 lawyers, scientists and policy experts. Together, these people work on both policy and programs to advance the cause of the environment as well as litigate in state and federal courts to influence compliance with the Clean Air and Clean Water Acts, along with other environmental legislation. The NRDC is seen as a relentless group of lawyers and scientists. Their example has inspired like-minded groups around the world.

In Australia, the EDO NSW Inc was formed in 1985 and this led to similar organisations being set up in other states. In 1996, these organisations came together as the Australian Network of Environmental Defenders Offices, bringing together the nine community-based environmental legal centres 'to protect the environment through legal challenges and become an advocate for community members who work on behalf of the environment'. The NSW EDO works on multiple, diverse court cases each year, including international whaling, climate change, planning, water supply and cultural heritage. It also publishes *Impact National Journal of Environmental Law*. Within the EDO network, climate change law has emerged as a sub-specialty of environment law, as it has elsewhere. The turn to the courts by environment groups in Australia is largely a consequence of inaction on climate change at the national level.[11]

The EDO NSW was concerned about the 'foundering' of environmental protection in Australia over the previous decade, and especially since the Abbott government handed over federal environmental approvals under the EPBC Act to the states and territories.[12] Australia's most iconic natural and cultural assets were under greater threat from development.

When it took on the MCG case, the EDO Network was still reeling from cuts to its funding the Abbott government imposed in its first budget. The network was stripped of $12 million in public funding. EDO Queensland principal solicitor, Jo-Anne Bragg, 'suspected the government has been swayed by the resources industry' to weaken their role. The timing of the cutbacks was significant; as Bragg observed, it came 'at a time when Queensland was considering massive port expansions near the Great Barrier Reef and enormously contentious coal projects'.[13] More broadly, the EDOs had run a number of landmark court cases for community groups across Australia including high-profile cases against new coal mines, pollution of rivers by power stations, residential planning and the impacts of coal seam gas developments on local water resources.

It wasn't just the recent deep cuts to funding that made the MCG case a difficult one. Critics argued that judges, especially on big resource projects, were affected by the cultural mindset that favoured development. As prominent environmentalist academic Ian Lowe wrote: '[I]t is presumed that developments which are economically desirable will go ahead unless there is an absolutely iron clad case that there will be outrageous environmental impacts which even the most benighted judge in an environment court cannot accept'.[14]

Even though the system was stacked in favour of corporate development projects, the MCG's appeal worried the industry. The chief executive of the Queensland Resources Council (QRC) Michael Roche claimed the case was part of a co-ordinated environmental strategy to close down the coal industry and pointed to Greenpeace's 2012 *Stopping the Australian Coal Export Boom* strategy. Roche believed that environmental groups, often funded by wealthy benefactors, exploit the legal system: 'It's time for our governments to step up and close the loopholes that enable these actions and the resulting negative impacts on our industry, not only in Queensland but right across the country', he said. 'For as long as these loopholes exist, highly motivated and well-funded activists will exploit them.'[15] Roche overstated the degree of co-ordinated efforts to end the coal industry, while completely ignoring the industry's own exploitation of the political system. While MCG did receive funding for its challenge from the activist organisation GetUp! and the Queensland Conservation Council, Ellen Roberts explained that taking legal action against Adani was a separate matter for each group.[16]

The case against Adani grows

Having lodged its case against Adani in January 2015 on the grounds that the impact of climate change would worsen the prospects for the Great Barrier Reef, three months later the MCG expanded its appeal. Ellen Roberts told the press that the appeal now included Adani's poor environmental track record. She said that Greg Hunt was aware of Adani's record in India but relied on the company's self-assessment submitted for the project, which highlighted that it has a good environmental record overseas: 'We really need to look at what kind of companies we're inviting into Australia and can they be trusted to operate those projects ethically and in accordance with the law', she said, adding that 'the only way Greg Hunt could issue an approval was to try to brush it under the carpet'.[17] And then in May 2015, the MCG found that Hunt had ignored advice from his own department about the impacts on two threatened species in the Galilee Basin: the yakka skink, a reclusive species of lizard; and the nocturnal, frog-eating, ornamental snake. In all, they proceeded with three grounds for the appeal.

After weeks of hearings, approval for the mine was set aside by consent of the parties after the judge found that Greg Hunt had not properly considered advice about the yakka skink and the ornamental snake. As no judgment was brought down, a determination was not made on the other grounds raised by the MCG. Adani blamed the court ruling on a 'technical legal error' by the federal department, while the QRC said 'legal loopholes' had paved the way for anti-coal activists to delay billions of dollars in investment and thousands of jobs.[18] Neither was sympathetic to the judgment about threatened species.

Nor was the prime minister. Tony Abbott, ever the coal warrior, seized on the judgment, claiming that it was 'tragic for the wider world' if legal safeguards were allowed to stall large mining projects, adding people have grounds to be 'angry' that a court overturned approval for Australia's biggest coal mine. He went further by saying that: 'As a country we must, in principle, favour projects like this'.[19]

However, the president of the New South Wales Bar Association, Jane Needham, made the obvious, but necessary, retort: 'The comments [by Abbott] demonstrate a lack of understanding of the independent role of the courts in our democracy. It is critical that our courts make decisions on the basis of the legislation they are charged to interpret and the facts of each individual case before them'.[20]

A few days later, Attorney-General Senator George Brandis announced that the government had 'decided to protect Australian jobs' by removing Section 487, which allowed third-party groups to appeal environmental approvals, from the EPBC Act. He argued that the provision 'allows radical green activists to engage in vigilante litigation to stop important economic projects'. He further claimed that the Act provides 'a red carpet for radical activists who have a political, but not a legal interest, in a development to use aggressive litigation tactics to disrupt and sabotage important projects'. Their ultimate aim, he asserted, is to use the courts for political purposes, 'bringing developments to a standstill, and sacrificing the jobs of tens of thousands of Australians in the process'.[21] However, there was no evidence that any such widespread 'aggressive litigation' was actually occurring.

As Attorney-General, Brandis is duty bound to defend the rule of law and, in his case, he is fond of describing himself as 'a classical liberal with a very deep belief in the rule of law'.[22] Yet, like all attorneys-general, Brandis was also a politician (he retired from politics in 2018 to become High Commissioner to the United Kingdom) and the conflict between the two roles produced contradictory views about the operation of the law. Possessed of a high self-regard and a dictatorial style, Brandis attracted sharp criticism for abrogating his principled position on the law when it suited him. He engaged in 'a bitter brawl' with Solicitor-General Justin Gleeson SC, restricting access to his legal expertise which, Gleeson complained, curtailed his ability to offer the government fearless legal advice.[23] Gleeson subsequently resigned. Brandis was further criticised for 'stacking' the Commonwealth's Administrative Appeals Tribunal with 'failed Liberal candidates, unemployed staffers and party donors'; some of the positions attracted salaries of $300 000.[24] The tribunal acts as an independent review of a wide range of decisions made by the Australian government.

Brandis strongly supported the Carmichael mine, arguing that it was the 'best shot at economic prosperity in the future'.[25] Thus, it was with his political hat on that Brandis led the attack on Section 487, because the case for removing it was weak. However it was consistent with Abbott's anti-environmental stance in general and reflected the pressure the government was under from the mining industry and right-wing think tanks, which had been loudly calling for the scrapping of Section 487.[26] And, more specifically, observers of Australian energy policy, including Richard Dennis from The Australia Institute, argued that the changes were promoted 'to help the Carmichael mine'.[27]

Whatever its motivations, the government met with stiff opposition. Cristy Clark, a lecturer in law at Southern Cross University, argued that the proposed changes to the Act would seriously curtail 'the scope for public interest litigation in defence of the environment' as well as 'curtail the rule of law'. As she pointed out: 'The Adani case was settled after Hunt conceded he had failed to abide by the law in granting the approval – that is, he rushed it. The judgment merely requires the government to abide by its own laws. Hunt is free to re-approve the mine within weeks'.[28] This was, in fact, what happened. In October 2015, Hunt re-approved the mine with new supposed safeguards for the species concerned.

Brandis' heavy-handed action sparked a wider debate about the operation of the EPBC Act and its capacity to protect the environment. An investigation carried out by two journalists from the *Guardian* found that there were no grounds for believing that environmental groups were misusing the courts to pursue their own agendas. They found that between 2000 and 2014 only 2.2 per cent of projects that required federal government approval under the EPBC Act were knocked back. However, as the journalists discovered, this high rate of approvals masked a flawed system that wasn't guaranteed to protect the environment as envisaged in the Act. In the first instance, the process favours developers because they submit environmental impact statements for assessment, written by consultants and paid for by proponents. The Department of the Environment then examines these reports:

> 'A lot of it comes down to the ethics of the consultant,' says a
> former environment department staffer who asked not to be
> named. 'Some behave more ethically than others, who are put
> under pressure to tell a story that the proponents want to tell.
> Department people are generally junior public servants who
> sit in Canberra and never go to these places they are assessing.
> They can have the wool pulled over their eyes.' Critics have
> argued for a merit-based system, including an independent
> body to examine the claims of proponents on environmental
> impacts. But others insist the EPBC Act ... is robust legislation
> that can either be a heavy stick or a feather duster, depending
> on its application.[29]

Conservationists saw the shortcomings in this system. As Ellen Roberts said about the MCG's temporary win: 'We're really concerned that it has taken a legal action by a community group to show up the flaws of the process, to show the fact that Australia's environmental laws aren't being followed by Greg Hunt'.[30] Sue Higginson, the principal solicitor at the EDO NSW, further explained: 'The law requires that the minister consider these conservation advices so that he understands the impacts of the decision that he is making on matters of national environmental significance, in this case the threatened species'.[31]

The implications were clear; any changes in the area should be towards strengthening the Act and its implementation, not taking a stick to conservationists because the Adani project was held up by ministerial sloppiness. But this line of reasoning was lost on both Brandis and Abbott.

The MCG victory produced a ripple of confidence in sections of the environmental movement that the end of Adani's mine was in sight. John Hepburn, former Greenpeace activist and founder of The Sunrise Project, sent an email to one of its funders, the US-based Sandler Foundation. The tone of the email was upbeat: 'The Adani Carmichael mine and the whole fossil fuel industrial complex', he wrote, 'is in its death throes'. In his exuberance, he wrote that he was 'going to buy a few bottles of bubbly' to share with the other environment groups fighting Adani.[32]

While Hepburn's optimism was misplaced, there were other ramifications from the MCG case. It put a dent in Adani's reputation in the financial world. Adani himself was reportedly 'privately fuming' over the MCG appeal because it added further uncertainty around the Carmichael mine, which was 'likely to further spook banks and investors who are already being targeted by green groups for investing in fossil fuel projects'.[33]

Outspoken North Queensland National Party MP George Christensen met with Adani representatives in Australia after the judgment came down and told the media that: 'They [Adani] are sick of spending money and getting no results and you can't blame them, in fact you wouldn't blame them for walking away from Australia'. Speaking from the other side of the ideological divide, he took a swipe at the MCG and their supporters: 'The green movement is out there saying, "We've done this on behalf of the community", but who in the community actually gave them the authority to go and act on their behalf?'[34] Apparently, Christensen hadn't read the opinion polls, which registered overwhelming public support for protecting the Great Barrier Reef.

A minnow takes on the giant

If the MCG was an undersized outfit to take on Adani, then Land Services of Coast and Country Inc (LSCC) was positively tiny. It has no website nor any means of generating publicity. It has no recognisable membership and no funds. Operating out of a small flat in South Brisbane, its financial return in 2014 revealed a profit of 99c on revenue of $40, with $2035.09 cash in the bank and liabilities of $2034.20.[35] Its only identifiable spokesperson is Derec Davies, an activist with a low public profile. Yet it secured the services of the EDO Qld to mount several court challenges against Adani. Its shadowy status outraged the *Courier Mail*:

> Derec Davies has sought to delay billions of dollars' worth of mining projects in central Queensland, a region reeling from high unemployment. With the support of the taxpayer-funded Environmental Defender's Office, his two small incorporated bodies – Land Services of Coast and Country Inc and Coast and Country Association of Queensland Inc – have waged 'lawfare' against both Adani's Carmichael mine and billionaire Gina Rinehart's proposed GVK Hancock mine at Alpha through the Land Court, Supreme Court and Court of Appeal.[36]

So, who is Derec Davies? Before he formed LSCC in 2013, Davies had been the Brisbane co-ordinator of Friends of the Earth (FoE). Driven by an opposition to 'corporate neo-liberal globalisation', FoE combines concerns about environmental justice, social justice and economic welfare into its agenda. Its radical edge also comes from its commitment to direct-action protest as a necessary catalyst for change.[37]

Set up in Australia in the early 1970s, a FoE chapter was also established in Brisbane. However, the northern branch limped along with few members until it was formally dissolved in 1984. Re-formed in 1996 with a renewed commitment to grassroots activism, it sought to look beyond the 'reformist' agenda of the mainstream environment movement.[38] Derec Davies cut his teeth as an activist in this radical environmental fringe group. As co-ordinator of the newly re-formed Brisbane chapter, he worked with Aboriginal groups opposed to the Carmichael mine and fought the approval given to Xstrata's Wandoan mine. In line with FoE's 'climate justice' policy, he told the media that the coal industry 'was on their last legs trying to extract as much as possible before they get trodden over by the renewable transformation'.[39]

Davies had achieved brief notoriety in November 2011. Putting FoE's philosophy of direct action into place, he locked himself onto a Gladstone port corporation dredge after being ferried into the harbour on an inflatable speedboat, and unfurled a banner which read 'Save the reef, halt dredging'. He was charged with causing $35 000 worth of damage and appeared in the South Brisbane Magistrates Court in January 2012, where magistrate Jim Herlihy dismissed the damages claim, upholding Davies' right to protest: 'This court is not in the business of closing down genuine protests'.[40]

Seemingly abandoning his direct-action approach, Davies moved on to create his new organisation and to use the courts to continue his anti-coal campaign. In this capacity, he mounted a challenge against Gina Rinehart's Alpha Coal project, winning acknowledgment that it could not proceed without taking into account the groundwater needs of neighbouring farmers.

Over a six-week period in mid-2015 and with a legal team of six lawyers, the EDO Qld went into battle for Coast and Country in Queensland's Land Court before President Carmel MacDonald. They sought a judicial review of the Queensland government's approval of the Carmichael mine, objecting to it on the following grounds:

- The impacts to groundwater and impact on the one-million-year-old Doongmabulla Springs.
- The impacts to the largest remaining population of the Black Throated Finch, and the Waxy Cabbage Palm.
- Adani's economic assessment and over-estimation of jobs and benefits to Queensland.
- The mine's carbon emission contribution to climate change and impacts on the Great Barrier Reef.

The Land Court does not possess the power to reject a proposed development, but any unfavourable recommendation made a project less likely by adding to community concerns. Jo-Anne Bragg, one of the lawyers on the EDO Qld team, explained that: 'The crucial part of this case is that there will be independent experts, some of which have been engaged by the community group, as well as experts engaged by Adani. This is a very important element, because those experts will have to debate in an open court'.[41] In effect, Adani and his mine were on trial.

Derec Davies explained the reasons behind taking court action:

In our opinion, the Queensland Department of Environment and Heritage Protection has made an error of law. The department cannot just ignore those laws that will allow the big end of town to develop a huge, polluting coal mine that will create catastrophic environmental harm both now and into the future. We say the Queensland Government's decision to approve this mine is flawed. It requires the scrutiny of a court of review.[42]

As significant as all the grounds comprising the challenge were, Davies and EDO Qld were especially committed to testing the law on climate change. As EDO Qld solicitor Sean Ryan had said: 'Our question was whether Australia's federal environmental laws protected our Great Barrier Reef from its most serious threat – climate change'.[43]

With the MCG case still being considered in the Federal Court, media interest in some, but not all, of the grounds brought by LSCC was high. However, one area of little interest to the media was the fate of the Doongmabulla Springs, the spiritual home of the Wangan and Jagalingou peoples, outlined in the previous chapter. The hearing exposed serious flaws in both the application of the EPBC Act by Environment Minister Greg Hunt and the limitations of the judicial approach in assessing big mining projects.

The evidence of experts from both Adani and LSCC were in agreement on matters relating to the springs: they were ecologically significant and in danger of being destroyed by the Carmichael mine. 'Exceptional ecological value' was the term agreed by both sides. The springs supported a large area of wetlands with many unique species, several of which were threatened with extinction, including the black throated finch.[44]

President MacDonald expressed her concern that 'given the exceptional ecological significance' of the springs, 'I consider that the lack of direct investigation or modelling [by Adani] is concerning'.[45] She found that the impact of the groundwater supplies by the mine was a direct threat to the springs with 'consequent serious environmental damage'.[46] In fact, 'If the springs dry up completely, the spring wetlands will be lost and all spring-dependent species including the rare plant species endemic to the wetlands will be eradicated'.[47]

In other words, a regional ecological disaster would potentially unfold in central Queensland, one which Greg Hunt had either overlooked or failed to sufficiently investigate. But such a prospect was not sufficient grounds for MacDonald to prevent the mine from going ahead. She thought 'an adaptive management approach' would suffice.

Curiously, the fate of the black-throated finch fared better in

MacDonald's findings. Again, expert evidence submitted by both sides agreed that the bird was endangered. The approval of the mine meant it was left to an uncertain fate because the development would strip it of considerable habitat. MacDonald came to the bird's rescue:

> I am satisfied from the evidence that there will be serious or irreversible environmental damage to the continued survival of any BTF in the mining lease area from the proposed mine because there will be a complete loss of any BTF habitat within the open cut pit area and related infrastructure areas. As I am satisfied that there will be serious irreversible damage ... it is necessary that preventative measures be taken to control or regulate the certain threat of environmental damage if the mine proceeds.[48]

However, on the larger issue of global warming and its flow-on impacts to the further destruction of the Great Barrier Reef, Mac-Donald accepted the evidence of Adani's experts. She had previously rejected climate change arguments against Xstrata's Wandoan mine proposal in 2012.[49]

In the LSCC case, MacDonald's reasoning showed the inadequacies of the law in dealing with climate change. MacDonald accepted the expert evidence – including from those appointed by Adani – that the expected 2°C of warming will have significant impacts on Queensland including: a decline in the Great Barrier Reef; increased flooding and severe cyclones; increase in heat-related deaths and disease; increased droughts; and a rise in sea levels. Professor Hoegh-Guldberg, who gave evidence to the federal parliamentary select committee into management of the Great Barrier Reef, discussed in Chapter 5, repeated his warning to the Land Court that 1°C of warming is dangerous to the reef and 2°C would cause 'large scale changes'.[50] However, MacDonald rejected that these grim predictions had anything to do with the CO_2 levels emanating from the Carmichael mine. She sided with Adani's experts that coal from Carmichael would not make any difference to the equation on climate change because, if the demand for coal continues to be strong, it will simply be sourced from elsewhere. As EDO Qld solicitor Jo-Anne Bragg explained, this argument had been strenuously resisted in their presentation to the court:

> We say, as a matter of law, that argument is simply irrelevant.
> It is just as if someone tried to argue that water pollution
> from a proposed sewage treatment facility should not be given
> weight during assessment because another facility with equal
> water pollution impacts might be built somewhere else instead.
> The fact remains the proposed facility would still have serious
> impacts that need to be considered and assessed. Just because
> the harm would be no worse than the alternative, does not
> make the harm non-existent.[51]

But, as previously mentioned, under UN processes, only the country that burns coal is responsible for the emissions it generates.

The LSCC case offers a revealing insight into the ongoing political and institutional weaknesses in dealing with climate change in Australia. According to Prime Minister Abbott and some of his senior ministers, the need for policymakers to consider climate change in their decisions constituted vexatious litigation. MacDonald treated the issue seriously but the LSCC case was not to become a groundbreaking one in regard to climate change.

While the hearings around environmental issues attracted little media interest, a frenzy erupted around the questioning of two of Adani's company representatives about the economic benefits of the mine. The first to appear before the court was Rajesh Gupta, the company's financial controller. This was the first time Adani had been required to publicly account for his claims, widely made in

TV advertisements and on the company's website, that the project would deliver 10 000 jobs and $22 billion in taxes and royalties. As discussed earlier, this had been transformed into a political mantra by state and federal governments and extensively circulated in the media. Michael West, covering Gupta's evidence for the *Sydney Morning Herald*, described his performance when cross-examined by EDO Qld lawyers as ranging from 'unconvincing to embarrassingly vague and forgetful'.[52]

In an unexpected move, Gupta pulled the rug from under the company's claims of $22 billion in revenue. Under cross-examination he accepted that the real figure was $7.8 billion in revenue to the state – a $14 billion disparity.[53] He later tried to recalculate the amount to $14 billion.

Gupta's performance only got worse on the issue of tax because he all but admitted that the company would explore ways to minimise its tax, as the *Guardian* reported:

[Gupta] repeatedly declined to say whether it would take advantage of a common ploy used by mining companies, revealed in a recent senate inquiry, of using 'marketing hubs' in lower tax jurisdictions like Singapore to sell coal to and reduce the profits realised and taxes paid in Australia.

Gupta, under cross-examination from barrister Saul Holt, acknowledged that Singapore-based Adani Global Private, the 'parent entity' of Australia-based Adani Mining, was set up for 'coal trading'. But he said he couldn't comment on whether Adani Mining in Australia would sell all its coal to its Singapore parent. 'We can't comment on that. We'll not necessarily … be selling to them. We might sell to the customers directly as well,' Gupta said. 'It's not illegal.'

Holt said, 'Are you planning to use Adani Global Private Limited in Singapore as a trading hub to reduce – optimise, lawfully and legitimately – the corporate tax you pay in Australia?'

Gupta replied: 'What I can say is that we have done the calculation of taxes based on the profit we'll be generating in Australia, and we'll be paying the taxes on that basis.'

Holt: 'You didn't answer my question. Are you planning to use Adani Global Private Limited as a trading hub? Let's break it down?'

Gupta: 'I'm sorry, I can't answer that question'.[54]

Other experts called by LSCC thought the likelihood of Adani paying any tax was unlikely. Financial energy analyst Tim Buckley told the court: 'Because of the collapse in the coal price, because of the massive coal discount and because of the cost structure, the mine, in my forecast, is actually going to lose money', Buckley said. 'Therefore it actually won't pay tax.'

With the media still reeling from Gupta's appearance, Dr Jerome Fahrer, a consultant to Adani, and a former Reserve Bank economist, further damaged the company's claims about the economic benefits of the mine. Fahrer, who worked for Allen Consulting, had been recruited by Adani to model the economic benefits of the Carmichael mine. In his submission to the Land Court, which was only made public when he was questioned about it during the court hearing, he stated that: 'Over the life of the project it is projected that on average around 1464 employee years of full-time equivalent direct and indirect jobs will be created'. In fact, Fahrer went on to be critical of previous modelling done by another firm, which used a different method to arrive at the figure of 10 000 jobs. He described the assumptions made in the modelling as 'extreme and unrealistic'.[55]

And so Fahrer blew a big hole in the company's claim about 10 000 jobs. Under cross-examination during the hearing, he agreed that, relative to total employment in Queensland, the increase in jobs from the project would be 'very small', emphatically repeating that '[i]t's not many jobs. We can agree on that ... Not many jobs ... No argument. Not many jobs', and going so far as to say, 'Again, the benefits of this project are not about jobs; they're about incomes'. In fact, Fahrer admitted that the total number of jobs would be 1206 in Queensland and 1464 in the rest of Australia.[56] Fahrer also accepted that the royalties the project generated would be much less than the company's projections. Several years later, Fahrer still stood by his findings: 'While the mine will create jobs directly and indirectly ... those jobs will be drawn from other industries. So the net number of jobs created is quite small'.[57]

Another of Adani's experts, John Sanderson, who had worked in the fields of financial analysis and energy for 20 years, had an even more dire warning for the Court: '... this is an extremely risky project ... everybody knows that, I admit that'.[58] It is notable, too, that Adani produced no evidence of any financial backing for the project.

In her report, Carmel MacDonald accepted the thrust of the adverse evidence about the mine's lower than projected economic benefits. In what amounted to a damning assessment of Adani, she wrote that 'the applicant has overstated certain elements of the benefit of the mine'. She found that the figure of $7.485 billion 'is the applicant's most recent estimate of royalties'. She accepted that Fahrer's figures on employment were accurate. The result, she wrote, 'is that the benefits of the project are likely to be less than modelled by Dr Fahrer'.[59] However, MacDonald still found that the economic benefits of the mine outweighed the environmental concerns. LSCC lost their case, but they could lay claim to a moral victory.

Derec Davies was disappointed with the result but was on strong ground when he said that it had taken legal action from conservationists to establish that the company had 'grossly inflated' the purported economic benefits of the mine and that this highlighted a 'huge problem' with government scrutiny of mining proposals. 'It's highly problematic that we don't have government agencies that undertake and scrutinise this work and it's really reliant on organisations or landholders or companies impacted by the proposed development to have to undertake this themselves.'[60] In light of these revelations, Davies said that it was an opportunity for governments to review their support for the Carmichael mine.

The call for a thorough reassessment of the mine is an important point to consider. At the very least, the Land Court hearing not only put Adani on trial but his backers in government as well. Serious shortcomings in the environmental approval process were shown up, including that the Abbott government was initially more concerned about giving the go-ahead to the mine than fulfilling its responsibilities under the EPBC Act. Equally, it is a shortcoming of this Act that it does not explicitly require governments to consider the dangers posed by climate change in protecting threatened species and biodiversity. The case also exposed the culture of 'development at all costs' inside the Abbott government when it came to fossil fuel projects. Writing in the *Saturday Paper*, Mike Seccombe summed up this mentality. 'The coal industry', he wrote, 'uses flawed economic models to persuade gullible governments to approve new mines and expansions, grossly inflating employment benefits and ignoring profitability questions'.[61]

However, from the perspective of the mining industry, the Land Court hearing was an unmitigated victory. Michael Roche felt vindicated: 'This judgment is a comprehensive rejection of the activist argument against this huge job-generating project, it's rejected the activist arguments around the financial viability of the project, it's rejected the activists' arguments around the issue of climate change'.[62]

The Australian Conservation Foundation's case

There was one last throw of the dice in the public interest law campaign against the Carmichael mine, this time mounted by the Australian Conservation Foundation (ACF). It has a proud record of more than half a century of advocating for the environment. Independent and non-partisan, it sees itself as committed to changing the paradigm of Australian politics: 'We take on the big structural challenges that stand in the way of change – the laws, policies, institutions, decisions and practices – to create a system that does right by people and nature'.[63] The ACF also had helped pave the way for public interest environmental law. In 1989, it challenged a Commonwealth decision granting export woodchip licences. The Federal Court found that the organisation had a 'special interest' in the issue permitting the challenge to proceed. The case 'famously extended the ability of public interest groups to challenge decisions made by government'.[64]

The ACF decided to challenge the federal government's approval of the Carmichael mine under the EPBC Act, cognisant that the MCG case had not brought down a finding on the impact of the mine on global warming and that the LSCC case, which did consider this issue, was heard in a lesser court. The action coincided with the Senate's rejection of the Abbott government's attempts to remove the right of community groups to use the EPBC Act to mount environmental appeals, Abbott's so-called 'lawfare' changes. A Senate inquiry into the change highlighted starkly polarised community opinion on the issue. Submissions to the inquiry in support of removing Section 487 came only from industry lobbyists – the Minerals Council of Australia, the Business Council of Australia, Ports Australia and the South Australian Chamber of Mines and Energy. Every other submission opposed the bill, including farmers, lawyers, academics and environmental groups.[65]

With the rights of community groups under the EPBC Act intact, the ACF proceeded hoping that an appeal under the Act in the Federal Court could result in a groundbreaking decision:

> ACF took the case because a challenge to the Carmichael
> decision on climate change grounds stood to be a very
> significant environmental law case in Australia. It had the
> potential to set important legal precedents, incorporating
> climate change considerations into the EPBC Act and
> importing some of the strong language of the World
> Heritage Convention into domestic law.[66]

In other words, the case could set a precedent which would force the federal government to consider the impact of fossil fuels on World Heritage listed environments, making it harder to secure approval for coal and gas projects.

Samantha Hepburn thought such a case could be argued. She pointed out that the EPBC Act specifically requires the principles of ecologically sustainable development to be taken into account when assessing matters of national environmental significance and 'the minister must evaluate not only how the land will be impacted, but also broader issues relevant to intergenerational equity'.[67]

Heard before Justice Griffith in the Federal Court in Brisbane on 3 and 4 May 2016, the ACF's case boiled down to the alleged failure of the Minister for the Environment Greg Hunt to correctly consider the likely impact on the Great Barrier Reef of pollution from coal burnt in India. In legal terms, it was a tough case to argue, as Elizabeth McKinnon, one of the ACF's lawyers on the appeal, explained:

> We always knew that these cases are very difficult to win. The
> serious limitation of environmental laws in Australia is that one
> can only challenge the Minister's decision on process, not on
> merit. This is called 'judicial review'. In essence, this means that
> the Court won't say 'Minister, you got it wrong'. The only thing

it will be willing to say is 'you followed the wrong legal process when you made the decision'. That is why there is such a low rate of success for these kinds of cases.[68]

In fact, a judicial review of a minister's decision is not only a very narrow procedure, it is the only avenue available under the relevant sections of the EPBC Act. Legal experts describe it as 'like trying to fight in a straight-jacket'.[69] The federal government had the advice of the solicitor-general to give weight to its arguments. In documents supplied to the Federal Court, Hunt denied he failed to consider the impacts of coal on the reef when approving the mine. As the solicitor-general explained, Hunt considered but dismissed the claim that the burning of the coal 'would be a substantial cause of climate change effects' and would have 'no impact on matters of national environmental significance'.

The minister reasoned that whether the burning of the coal would make climate change worse depended on whether it would increase the total amount of coal burned globally. But he noted there were a 'raft of factors' that could affect how much coal was burned globally, including whether the coal from the mine displaced other coal and whether it was dealt with within various national emissions targets.[70] In other words, he used the same 'tortured logic' used in the LSCC case. Effectively, this would allow any emitter of CO_2, no matter how large, to deny the causal link between their actions and global climate change. As McKinnon politely wrote after the judgment was handed down in August 2016: 'Sadly, the Judge found that this was a legitimate decision-making process under the section of the EPBC Act and thus no error of law was made'.[71]

Considering all three legal cases outlined above, the hopeful assessment of a few years ago that the law 'stands to make a very important contribution to managing climate change' has not proved to be the case in relation to the Carmichael mine.[72] The applicants confronted the limitations of the EPBC Act to specifically address the impacts of climate change. As the Australian Human Rights Commission's review of the Act pointed out: 'With regard to climate change, the *EPBC Act* was passed prior to Australia's adoption of the Kyoto Protocol and Australia's Carbon Pollution Reduction Scheme. As a result, there is currently no trigger or mechanism under the EPBC Act for addressing issues affected by climate change'.[73] But as Tristan Edis, writing in the *Business Spectator*, commented, 'the logic of having our environmental approval law blind to climate change no longer makes sense'.[74] His point was echoed by Kelly O'Shanassy, the chief executive of the ACF who, in the wake of the decision, called for the 'next generation of environment laws' that explicitly deal with the impacts on climate change from coal mining.[75]

Unmoved by such reasoning, the Turnbull government welcomed the Federal Court decision, as did their fraternal backers in the mining industry. The indefatigable and media-savvy Michael Roche could always be relied upon for a pithy quote. The ACF had prosecuted a 'nonsense case', he said.[76]

It later transpired that the prospects for the black-throated finch were poor. The 'offset strategy', approved by the federal environment minister in response to a recommendation from the LSCC to protect the fragile status of the species, allocated land outside the mine site to 'offset' the loss of habitat from the development of the mine.

Yet, the BTF Recovery Team, a group made up of experts dedicated to the bird's survival, obtained Adani's documents under freedom of information laws and compiled a report which it sent to the federal environment minister in 2017. This showed that 'the conditions attached to the approval of Adani's proposed mine do not protect against the bird being wiped out and that the habitat proposed in offset areas is of lower quality compared to the mining areas'.[77] The researchers described the strategy as akin to 'spinning the roulette wheel' on the bird's survival. It is the fate of just one small, pretty orange and black bird, up against the development of a mega mine. Yet its extinction would add to Australia's record of having the highest rate of wildlife extinction in the world. It is a crisis, experts have warned.[78] However, the black-throated finch was merely 'a technical hitch' in Greg Hunt's swift re-approval of the mine in a political culture infused with pro-development and anti-environmentalism.

Thus, after three court cases, the wisdom of the law upheld the legality of the Carmichael mine with its 'carbon bomb' potential to destroy a unique ecosystem in the Galilee Basin, threaten already vulnerable species and contribute to the further destruction of the Great Barrier Reef. And this in return for modest, at best, employment and returns in revenue to the State.

CHAPTER ELEVEN
The banks under attack

In May 2014, Paula and Peter Samson of Perth closed their account with the National Bank, after a 35-year association, in protest over the bank's exposure to the polluting fossil fuel industry. 'We are worried about climate change', Paula Samson, a retiree, told the *Sydney Morning Herald* in an interview. 'The only way to make a change is to take money out of the fossil fuel industry. On a small scale, we need to be doing this.'[1] The Samsons were part of a growing environmentally driven divestment movement in Australia that targeted all institutions with large investments in the fossil fuel sector. Operating globally, impetus to the movement in Australia had been provided by Bill McKibben, American environmentalist, academic and founder of activist organisation 350.org. His speaking tour and media appearances spread his message that Australia and the world needed to stop investing in carbon-intensive industries.[2]

From these inauspicious beginnings emerged one of the most widely supported environmental campaigns in Australian history. Combining social media activism with traditional forms of protest activity, the campaign targeted Australia's 'big four' banks and their funding of the fossil fuel boom. Forcing the banks to renounce funding for the Carmichael mine was a focal point of this campaign. This deployment of 'people power' against one of the key pillars of the economy was as audacious as it was uncertain; nothing on this scale had ever been attempted.

The divestment movement was a new front in the war on coal. Driving it was the pressure exerted by concerned citizens, investors and students, signifying that it had now become part of the mainstream political discourse. The aim of the movement was equally straightforward: taking away the industry's social licence – 'turning fossil fuel firms into social pariahs, just like big tobacco'.[3]

From 2013, the divestment movement took off in Australia. As Bill McKibben reflected on its progress three years after it began, Australia had more divested institutions per capita than any other developed country, and second only in number to the United States. Institutions which had divested from fossil fuels included a large number of local councils around the country, superannuation funds, universities, churches and health institutions – all pledging to shift their investments away from coal, oil and gas.[4] According to one academic study, divestment is playing an increasingly significant 'disruptive innovation' role in strengthening support for rapid de-carbonisation.[5]

A fierce reaction emanated from predictable quarters. As clean energy commentator Giles Parkinson stated, the reaction was 'as though someone had committed treason against Team Australia. Or at the very least against Team Coal'.[6]

Australia's 'big four' banks were a particular target of the divestment campaign because of their deep involvement in funding coal and gas projects. Yet none of the 'big four' banks – Westpac, ANZ, National Australia Bank (NAB) and the Commonwealth Bank (CommBank) – entertained the idea of divesting from fossil fuels. Quite the reverse; they dug themselves in to resist the campaign. As the Australian Bankers' Association explained, the banks did not expect a significant shift in customer numbers due to the environmental campaign. 'Banks will not stop lending to the fossil fuels industry today, but will continue to assess community views into the future', a spokesman explained.[7]

Banks therefore became a target in the anti-coal war. In fact, the war against the 'big four' over their involvement in fossil fuels pre-dated the onset of the divestment movement. Greenpeace was among the first environmental groups to raise community aware-ness about the involvement of Australia's 'big four' banks in the coal industry. Its 2010 report, *Pillars of Pollution: How Australia's Big Four Banks are Propping Up Pollution*, was the first systematic anal-ysis of the flow of funds from the banks into coal mining and the consequences for climate change.

The 'big four' were 'financing the coal industry which is fuel-ling pollution and making global warming worse. The impacts of climate change are being felt throughout Australia and the Pacific region, home to the banks' customers. Australia needs to undergo a clean energy revolution, and the big banks have a vital role to play'.

The report highlighted the central contradiction for Australian banks; that despite Australia having among the most abundant sources of clean energy in the world, they continued to pour 'your savings' into coal while ignoring the environmental consequences of the pro-jects they financed. To mask this contradiction, Greenpeace claimed, the banks engaged in 'spin' about their efforts in sustainability.[8]

To complement their report, Greenpeace commenced a 'dirty banks' campaign and singled out ANZ as the dirtiest bank with the most invested in fossil fuels. In October 2010, several Greenpeace activists scaled the ANZ Queensland headquarters and unfurled a giant banner 'ANZ: We Pollute Your World'.[9] The 'dirty banks' cam-paign continued into the following year. Activists rode Melbourne trams, merging with morning commuters, wearing dust masks branded with an adapted ANZ logo and wearing t-shirts reading 'ANZ – we pollute your world'. Photographs of the protest were shared on social media. Similar movements were being waged in the United States and Europe in what amounted to a global campaign against coal.[10]

Small, but important, signs that the 'big four' were sensitive about their involvement in coal emerged alongside Greenpeace's campaign. In that year, ANZ removed from its website the boast that it was the largest funder of coal in the country and in the same year, Greenpeace reported that Westpac had insisted on a confidentiality clause as part of a finance deal for a coal-fired power station so that its name could not be revealed, for fear of reputational damage.[11] Also in the same year, the online newspaper *Crikey* reported that the banks 'are now also coming under intense environmental scrutiny over the impact of their lending practices'.[12] Business and environmentalists around the world had their eyes on Australia, as the world's largest coal exporter. 'In this global attack on the future of fossil fuels, Australia has become the frontline', reported the *Australian*.[13]

Plans to open up the Galilee Basin occurred just as the anti-coal movement started to gain momentum. The confluence of these developments had implications for Adani; it was inevitable that both Adani and potential financiers of the Carmichael mine would become a target of this movement. This included both national and international banks. Banks in the Northern Hemisphere had been lobbied by both Australian and international environmental organisations and, from 2013, a steadily growing number disavowed any funding of Adani. When two of the biggest American banks – Citi and JB Chase Morgan – notified their intention not to finance the project, they cited their opposition to funding any resource projects that were within a world heritage area or would significantly degrade a critical natural habitat.[14]

Australia's 'big four' had no such commitments, even though they professed to have embraced the principles of sustainability. Environmentalists thought they needed to be pressured into taking action. This occurred in a fragmented and disjointed way, with the involvement of a wide range of activist organisations operating across three overlapping campaign strands. Firstly, banks were under pressure to become part of the divestment movement. Customers were targeted to withdraw their funds from the 'big four' and place them in financial institutions that had already declared that they were not involved in the fossil fuel industry. Secondly, environment groups campaigned to try to force the big banks to disavow any investment in the expansion of the coal port at Abbot Point, as part of the existing environmental campaign to save the Great Barrier Reef. Lastly, environment groups specifically targeted the 'big four' not to fund the Carmichael mine. Each group decided where in this field of activity it would devote its resources. Some campaigned across the three strands. The overall strategy was confusing. Was the emphasis on the long-term goal of ending coal or the shorter-term goal of stopping Adani, or both? What the campaign against the banks lacked in coherence, it made up for in sheer commitment and awareness raising. There is little doubt that the banks needed to be pushed to consider their responsibilities to climate change. Theirs was a struggle between corporate reputation and the bottom line.

Australian banks and the funding of Adani

Australia's banks were likely to be a crucial link to the eventual funding of the Carmichael mine. Several reasons impelled them towards the project. Firstly, the 'big four' together provided 75 per cent of funding for fossil fuel projects in Australia between 2007 and 2017. This totalled approximately $80 billion loaned to coal, oil and gas projects in Australia since January 2007.[15] Secondly, the pressure on Australia banks intensified because, by 2014, nine of the top global funders of coal had declared that they would not be involved in Adani's Australian operations. Thirdly, if Adani could obtain a major global financier, it was likely to be conditional on having an Australian partner. According to Tim Buckley from the Institute of Energy Economics and Financial Analysis:

> when global banks are looking at projects in Australia, they
> look to the Australian banks who have the on-the-ground
> knowledge, on-the-ground feel for the project, to come out

and endorse a project. Then the international banks can
piggyback effectively off the local knowledge, and effectively,
due diligence of the big Australian banks.[16]

Fourthly, unlike their counterparts in the Northern Hemisphere,
the 'big four' Australian banks were reluctant to walk away from
investing in coal and, up until 2015, hadn't professed any concern
about climate change and the fate of the Great Barrier Reef; quite
the reverse. They were well and truly behind the fossil fuel industry, having backed a succession of big coal projects in NSW and
Queensland and the industrialisation of the Great Barrier Reef.

Lastly, the banks were under political pressure not to renounce
funding to Adani. According to media reports, 'officials within the
federal government have made calls to the major banks to assure them
that the expansion of Abbot Point will not pose a risk to the Great
Barrier Reef'.[17] This led to claims from environmentalists that both
state and federal governments were showing preferential treatment
towards the big miners, claiming that banks are now under pressure
to fund the new mines. Not that they needed much convincing; the
'big four' were embedded in the fossil fuel power network.

Countervailing environmental pressures existed as well. For
years, the banks had 'greenwashed' their active involvement in fossil
fuels, and especially coal, with shallow statements about their commitment to sustainability. As one academic critic has observed:

> Disclosure by banks on exposure to coal projects tends to be
> reactive, with bank websites and annual reports revealing very
> little hard information about their approach to investment in
> carbon intensive sectors … banks seem more focused on setting
> targets for paper consumption and the carbon emissions of
> running their offices and branches, than the more important
> issue of the carbon intensity of the projects they lend to.[18]

The 'greenwashing' by Australia's banks through promoting sustainable practices reached a risible level when, in 2014, Westpac was voted the world's most sustainable company at the World Economic Forum in Davos, Switzerland. Westpac CEO Gail Kelly was in attendance at the event to receive the award, saying that 'Westpac had been recognised for its commitment to social, environmental and economic responsibility'.[19] The mainstream Australian press cheered the company for the global recognition it had received, ignoring the most obvious contradiction: how could a company that was actively involved in funding climate change through its extensive support of coal projects be considered a paragon of sustainability? Only, as journalist Simon Butler wrote, by inverting the meaning of the word 'sustainability'.[20]

Butler pointed out that the award was adjudicated by Canadian media firm Corporate Knights, whose idea of sustainability did not fit the generally accepted criterion of meeting the needs of the present without compromising future generations. Rather, Corporate Knights worked to a definition that held to: 'creating more wealth than we destroy ... Sustainable firms are those doing the best job at creating net wealth – economic, social, and ecological – as compared to their peers'. As Butler argued, this definition prioritised the needs of private businesses to generate higher returns. While corporations inevitably viewed their role in this way, it had little to do with the concept of sustainability: 'Corporate efforts to hijack the term "sustainable" and use it to justify business-as-usual are hardly new, but they are pervasive – helped along by mainstream media that typically reports on such greenwash as legitimate news, without critical comment'.

However, in the lead-up to the Paris climate talks in December 2015, all of the 'big four' felt obliged to announce policies supporting the goal of limiting global warming to less than 2°C. While the policies appeared to be strongly worded, 'none of the banks have backed up their statements with concrete commitments to reduce lending to coal, oil or gas activities'.[21]

Taking on the banks

The challenge to shift the banks away from Adani – and ultimately away from fossil fuels – has to be one of the toughest challenges ever taken on by community-based organisations in Australia. It occurred at a pivotal time. The anti-coal movement had started to gather momentum by the time Adani purchased his lease in the Galilee in 2010 and progressive politics was rapidly being reshaped by social media and the digital revolution. Progressive groups had been handed a tool of unparalleled potential. New online activist groups had emerged during the 'noughties' that were committed to environmental and human rights values and to holding corporations to account. But would the new tools be sufficient to take on one of the pillars of the Australian economy?

The environment groups pitted against the combined weight of the 'big four' were a diverse lot. This reflects the hydra-headed nature of Australia's environment/activist movement. 'Old', established organisations like Greenpeace and the Australian Conservation Foundation (ACF) stood alongside newly formed – and social media focused – organisations such as GetUp! Dozens of groups had a stake in campaigning against the banks, each with different histories, memberships, geographic affiliations, philosophies and campaigning strategies. In recent environmental battles, diversity had been a strength.[22] The crowded space surrounding anti-bank activism is, in itself, indicative of the depth of community feeling about the role of the 'big four' in funding this activity. Together, the various groups brought a formidable array of skills and human and financial resources. The anti-coal movement had grown substantially since Bob Brown and Tim Flannery had together pitched the issue into the political debate in 2007. By 2013–14, it was common knowledge that funding was the key issue for Adani's plans for the Carmichael mine.

Outweighed in terms of political power and influence, the environment groups fighting the banks had strengths other than their diversity. The raw people power behind these groups is formidable. It's hard to calculate precise numbers. However, in 2014, Greenpeace estimated that the 11 groups it co-ordinated for one of its campaigns against the banks represented 2.2 million members.[23] Although the list includes some of the biggest conservation/activist groups in the country, many others with an interest in the anti-coal, anti-Adani campaigns were not included on that occasion. And given that groups such as GetUp!, 350.org and One Million Women grew rapidly, it is certain that the total number of involved people concerned about Adani grew to be well above the Greenpeace estimate, although it is not clear how many considered themselves actively involved.

With membership comes money and the biggest of the environment groups had considerable funds at their disposal – raised increasingly through small-donation online funding drives. This financial clout helps explain why the Abbott and Turnbull governments were determined to remove their tax deductibility status. Again, a total figure is difficult to pin down, but an investigation undertaken by the *Australian* – as part of its coverage of the debate on the tax-deductible status of environment groups – found that over the previous decade, $685 million had been raised through the combined resources of Greenpeace Australia Pacific, WWF Australia, Friends of the Earth (Australia), The Sunrise Project, the Lock the Gate Alliance, 350.org Australia, the ACF and the Wilderness Society.[24] As this figure didn't include GetUp! – which has proved adept at fundraising – a total figure is also likely to be much higher.

There is also the intangible element to the power wielded by all social movements, especially the modern environmental movement. Collectivist in nature and altruistically driven, its campaign against the banks was propelled by people dedicated to changing the world. And banks, which were coming under increasing scrutiny for their lending practices and excessive profits, were vulnerable to a values-based campaign of pressure. According to Andrew Ure, managing director of Ogilvy Earth, a public relations consultancy specialising in environment and community issues:

> Activists are increasingly clever about who they target – rather than attack the people involved in operations, they've gone after the consumer-facing organisation because it's more vulnerable to public pressure … the public, particularly Generation Y, now expects businesses to consider their impact on the environment and community and any consumer-facing business is vulnerable to this sort of activist pressure at any time.[25]

Campaigning in the digital age

Boiled down, this was a timeless contest between corporate and people power. Nevertheless, it was an environmental campaign like none before. Typically, environmental campaigns are geographically located, aiming to save a particular place from development, and are usually directed at a single entity: government or one big company. The campaign against the banks was broader than place, even though saving the Great Barrier Reef and the spiritual home of the Wangan and Jagalingou peoples were key focal points. It was also centred around addressing the global challenge of climate change and the responsibility of coal-laden countries like Australia to take a leading role in the debates and action. Moreover, there wasn't just one entity to fight but two powerful sectors of the economy – banks and their links to mining corporations. Lastly, the presence of a foreign-owned and based company added to the complexities of the struggle to get the banks to walk away not just from Adani, but from coal as a source of energy. The diffusion of targets explains why different groups concentrated their energies in different ways.

Social media became the driving force behind the campaigns waged by the various groups. Of course, over the past decade, employing the internet to harness people's passions for political causes had become well established. Connectivity in modern political activism now moves with the advent of new tools: Twitter and Instagram complemented and, in some cases, superseded 'established' technologies such as Facebook and Flickr. Never has it been easier or speedier to share information, raise awareness, harness protest activity, petition an organisation, raise funds and attract new members. But what does all this activity amount to? Has 'clicktivism' replaced real-world activism, or enhanced the latter?[26] Academic Anne Coombs injected a note of caution into the debate. 'The power of the technology', she writes, 'has made that seem more tantalisingly possible than ever':

> It has spawned a whole new professional class of online campaigners and given new tools to more traditional organisers. And it has made possible a degree, and a scale, of co-operation and collaboration never seen before. In the ten years since the online campaigning organisation GetUp! started, much has changed in progressive activism.

But, she points out, '[w]hen sympathies are engaged by so many causes, how important is any one of them?'[27] Other critics of social media activism question whether it has transformed civil dissent and protest into 'feel good' events that don't achieve much change, while others point to the possibilities it has provided to create 'visual activism' based around the transmission of shared images that make it increasingly difficult for those in authority to 'look away'.[28] Whatever its actual impact, there is little doubt that social media activism has enabled far more people to be engaged in political action without having to invest large amounts of personal time.[29]

The power of social media in focusing on the banks was demonstrated early in the campaign. In 2013, ANZ faced 'a storm of protest on social media' over its environmental record a week after a hoax that drew public attention to the bank's investment in coal mining. A fake press release purporting to announce that ANZ Bank had withdrawn from the Maules Creek coal mine tricked the stock market and temporarily wiped nearly 9 per cent off the value of Whitehaven Coal. The hoax prompted an investigation by the Australian Securities and Investments Commission and the person responsible for the hoax, anti-coal activist Jonathan Moylan, later faced court over his actions. Despite the official anger directed at Moylan, social media suggested public sentiment 'is firmly holding ANZ's feet to the fire' for its decision to invest in the mine. As the *Australian Financial Review* reported:

> Both ANZ's Australian and New Zealand Facebook pages are filled with criticism from members of the public angry about the mine, which environmentalists say would destroy up to 2000 hectares of koala habitat, disrupt fertile agricultural land and generate huge amounts of greenhouse gas emissions. Most of the activity is on Facebook but there is also negative commentary on Twitter.[30]

ANZ ignored the comments. But the head-in-the-sand approach exacerbated its poor image, according to Andrew Ure:

> the bank should use social media to communicate its ethical investment position and how it interprets the Equator Principles, a set of voluntary standards to help banks identify and manage the social and environmental risks associated with the direct financing of large infrastructure projects such as dams, mines or pipelines.[31]

While the banks were slow to utilise social media to get their message out, groups like GetUp! and 350.org deal directly with consumers. With half a million followers on Facebook, GetUp! has an unrivalled opportunity to engage in what Liberal Party official Andrew Bragg describes as 'intimate communication': 'You like "a page" such as GetUp!, and they can talk to you directly on your newsfeed when you're anywhere in the world with your smartphone. It literally follows you around. The organisation which is being "liked" is also given a treasure trove of data about the community of people that have clicked "like"'.[32]

Data is crucial in the new digital world. Facebook provides age, gender, location and other data points, such as other interests, to 'liked' organisations. As Bragg notes, this is 'incredibly valuable because it permits direct targeting of voters based on their interests and preferences as collected in real time'; it is 'better than running a $2 million TV advert during the 6 pm news'.[33]

Opportunities to connect with like-minded people are enhanced by the instantaneous nature of the communication across time and space. Political messaging has been given a new potency. In 2016, GetUp! organised an online petition to save the Great Barrier Reef. Started by an 11-year-old girl named Sophia on GetUp!'s citizen-led site CommunityRun, it received a response from its target: international celebrity Ellen DeGeneres. DeGeneres, the voice of tropical fish Dory in the environmental-themed film *Finding Nemo* and its sequel *Finding Dory*, issued a statement of support. Environment Minister Greg Hunt subsequently sent a series of tweets to DeGeneres outlining the efforts of the government to protect the reef. As political scientist Ariadne Vromen, who has studied the power of social media in politics, explained: 'This example shows just how much political engagement in Australia has changed over the past decade. New organisations have taken the lead in channelling the citizen voice into politics'. She adds that similar to sibling organisations internationally, 'GetUp! uses a storytelling and emotion-laden approach to structure its campaigns and public messaging. This creates a shared, positive narrative that is more likely to lead to collective action than negative, adversarial politics'.[34]

All the organisations involved in the anti-bank campaign

operated extensive websites with easy access to online forms to petition the banks. Donations and recruitment of new members were
linked to such ready-made story-telling actions.

Yet despite the power of social media, 'old'-style non-violent
direct action also remained a cornerstone of the campaign against
the banks, but was now linked into social media to inspire current
and future members. In 2013, GetUp!, Australian Youth Climate
Coalition (AYCC) and the ACF organised the National Day of Climate Action, attracting 60 000 people who participated at the ral-
lies, held in capital cities and in more than 130 towns and regional
centres. While not directed at Adani, such protests contributed to
the awareness raising that later propelled action against the 'big four'
banks.

The banks were the target of a number of direct action protests. On 22 October 2014, for example, 80 people from a range
of climate and environment groups occupied ANZ headquarters in
Docklands, Melbourne, calling on the bank to disinvest from fossil
fuels. The event was held in solidarity with the Pacific Islands and
12 'Pacific Warriors' were part of the 'occupation'. The 'Pacific Warriors' shared traditional songs that 'echoed through the building and
silenced the space'. They then shared 'the depth and pain of how the
changing climate impacts their sense of culture and belonging'. As
the organisers later wrote of the impact of the event:

> These headquarters house 6500 ANZ employees, many of
> which stood out on the balconies and listened to the speeches,
> stories and spontaneous choirs that sprung up. We occupied the
> space for eight hours, until we thanked the ANZ employees for
> their patience and exited the building spreading our message to
> the media outside.[35]

Co-operation among the groups was a semi-regular feature of the
campaign. Trying to save the Great Barrier Reef from development

brought groups together to pool resources. On 9 September 2014, for example, a coalition of 12 groups, including GetUp!, Greenpeace Australia Pacific and the ACF wrote to the 'big four' asking them to stop investing in large coal and port expansion projects that damage the Great Barrier Reef. They also took out a front-page advertisement in the *Australian* newspaper. It was 'a bold statement of intent', according to a spokesperson from GetUp!.[36]

By the beginning of 2015, progress on the campaign had been slow; the combined weight of non-violent direct action and a strong social media presence had produced little movement in the banks. Some groups ramped up their non-violent activities. Throughout 2015, protesters gathered at Commonwealth Bank branches in capital cities around Australia, forcing the bank to temporarily close a number of the branches. On 19 May 2015, protesters from 350.org peacefully occupied the Commonwealth Bank's headquarters in Melbourne, an event that created wider media interest. Charlie Wood from 350.org was on hand to provide the message:

> The Commonwealth Bank says it is the 'People's Bank'
> yet the people are calling on them to say NO to carbon
> bombs like the Galilee. We've emailed, petitioned, had
> meetings and moved our money, yet CommBank still stays
> silent. Unless they heed our call and say no to coal mine
> and port expansions on the Reef, they face a creative and
> unrelenting community campaign … and should be ready
> for nationwide protests.[37]

Protesters subsequently occupied the Sydney headquarters. 350.org's Krista Collard explained that they 'have been trying to talk with CommBank for years now and basically every time members of the public, members or concerned residents bring this up, they've been shielded from talking to anybody that has any decision making power'.[38]

ANZ branches were also the location for novel protest activity to attract wider social and traditional media coverage. In June 2015, four people dressed as giant native animals descended on the ANZ bank's North Sydney branch asking for loans for new homes after theirs were 'destroyed' by an ANZ-funded coal mine. A spokesperson explained that: 'A koala, a possum, a kangaroo and a parrot all walked into the bank in full business suits to ask for a home loan and remind ANZ what it has done. These animals will continue to remind ANZ of how damaging coal is until they commit to never finance Galilee Basin coal mining projects'.[39]

Social media was crucial in enabling activist organisations to be flexible, speedy and unpredictable in organising non-violent protest. Volunteers were essential to this strategy. Most of the organisations involved in the anti-bank campaign had active volunteers among their many online members. Along with 350.org, the AYCC deployed a small army of its 120 000-strong membership to its 'adopt a branch' campaign, involving visits to local branches to talk with branch managers, staff and customers. As AYCC representative Ella Weisbrot explained: 'We met Westpac branch managers in every one of its 300 branches in NSW. We met with them twice – up and down the east coast. We also met with 100 NAB managers in one week – asking them to speak to their members and called on CEOs to cancel funding for coal ports'.[40] The campaign attracted widespread attention with media coverage across TV, radio and print – including being dubbed 'extraordinarily successful' by the *Australian Financial Review*.[41]

Tim Flannery believed that the local branch campaign was effective: '[n]ews of the visits soon reached headquarters and Westpac ... [became] fully aware of the extent of community opposition'.[42] While, as discussed below, NAB became the first bank to reject any funding for Adani, it would be another three years before Westpac came out publicly in opposition to funding the Carmichael mine. Westpac adopted a policy to 'stonewall, ignore and be as ambiguous as possible' in the face of the campaign. As one commentator noted, the bank believed that:

> The protests involve a small number of people (perhaps 60 at the protest this Monday outside the Westpac HQ) and the online campaigns don't seem to have gained much traction. Westpac execs have presumably decided that the majority of their customer base doesn't give a damn so neither should they.[43]

However, inside the bank the pressure of the campaign was having an impact. Like an army under siege, internal debate 'raged' over whether the bank should support Adani, without declaring its position either way.[44]

Undeterred by the slow progress in forcing all 'big four' to confirm their positions, in 2015, AYCC unfolded a campaign to provide new ATM screens. Across the country, staff at banks arrived at work 'to find hundreds of your ATMs have been updated with new screens telling your customers that you could use their savings to risk the reef and the climate'. Launching the campaign, AYCC national co-director Kirsty Albion said in an open letter to the banks that: 'Today we are declaring these projects should be placed on a "black-list", on behalf of 110 000 young Australians'.[45]

There was an even more direct tactic used by anti-bank volunteers in the effort to hold the banks to account. Attendance at the annual general meetings of the 'big four' continued the shareholder activism movement that had, for several years, sent ripples of concern through the corporate world in Australia and overseas. As the *Sydney Morning Herald* reported: 'Environmental groups rightly want to hold banks accountable to their rather vague public support for fighting climate change, and many do this by asking tough questions about financing of big polluters at the banks' annual general meetings'. Such face-to-face grilling, along with other non-violent direct action, may have been partly responsible for the sudden fall in the banks' lending to coal mining which, in 2016, had declined by at least $1.6 billion over the previous year. However, as the *Sydney Morning Herald* reported: 'It is difficult to know just how much this is because of deliberate policy action, as opposed to swings in the economic cycle'.[46]

Traditional media continued to be a source for promoting the campaign against the banks. In fact, the campaign had succeeded in becoming a mainstream issue in the news even when comparatively small events were organised. Thus, the *Age* covered the 2014 'Divestment Day' protest in Melbourne, which targeted major banks that continued to invest in new coal, oil and gas projects. With fewer than 100 people taking part, it hardly ranked as a major community event. However, there was undoubtedly wider community interest in the issue and the Melbourne protesters had a simple and compelling message. They donned t-shirts proclaiming: 'My bank chose fossil fuels so I chose another bank'. Across Australia, 1000 bank customers were persuaded to switch banks from the 'big four'.[47]

Coverage by traditional media was important in continuing to re-state the case against the banks to the audience beyond high social media users. ABC *News* gave extensive coverage to a small protest outside the Sydney headquarters of the Commonwealth Bank organised by 350.org. Organisers were given ample opportunity to boost their message about the banks:

> The 350.org campaigner for Sydney, Isaac Astill, said the
> group was urging the bank to divest from the Galilee Basin
> coal mines and the Abbot Point coal port expansion located
> near the Great Barrier Reef. 'The Great Barrier Reef provides
> 69 000 jobs, it's a $6 billion industry and it's one that will be
> there forever and ever as long as we preserve the Great Barrier
> Reef', he said. 'Eleven international banks around the world
> have responded to this campaign and ruled out investing in

Abbot Point. Of the big four, CommBank have become the
front runner when it comes to funding Abbot Point'.[48]

Continuous tracking of the money banks invested in fossil fuels was
an important part of the campaign. This task fell largely to Market
Forces, an organisation that emerged to be an influential player
in the anti-banks campaign. Proudly affiliated with Friends of the
Earth, it established a reputation as a provider of ethical investment
advice and was regularly quoted in the press. Its mandate was to
work across the financial sector, tracking institutions that were damaging to the environment. The data it collected made it possible
for individual customers to track where their particular bank was
investing in the fossil fuel sector.

Among its activities, Market Forces also listed on its website the
names of 34 national and international companies linked to Adani
with a single electronic form enabling a simultaneously delivered
message: 'Given the services your company offers, I am concerned
that you may be approached to support Adani's plans to mine and
export coal from the Galilee Basin in Queensland ... And every
company that helps this nightmare become a reality would be partly
responsible for the environmental and climate devastation the Carmichael project stands to inflict'.[49]

A range of other groups lent ballast to the campaign. The Australia Institute, for example, released an ongoing stream of research
reports – a number already cited in this book – which focused on
the economic issues surrounding the Adani mine and which helped
undermine any claim the banks had to finance it. Director Richard
Dennis was widely quoted in the traditional media discussing the
institute's work.

The above is just a small sample of the range of activities
mounted to try to force the banks to declare their hand on Adani.
Business groups in general observed the campaign and began to fret
at the impact it was having on the banks. Before being appointed

as acting director of the federal Liberal Party, Andrew Bragg was the Menzies Institute's Enterprise Policy Unit director. In this capacity he bemoaned that businesses were not fighting back against social activist groups: 'The anti-business forces are becoming increasingly adept at creating campaign organisations', he said. Moreover, activist groups 'were much more effective in targeting their arguments directly to consumers using social media platforms such as Facebook, while business groups were often largely talking to themselves'.[50]

Bragg also made a surprising admission about the newly levelled political playing field:

> business was 'traditionally not collectivist in nature', which made it hard for it to mobilise forces like activist groups could. 'But these days anti-business groups know how to go directly to the consumer', he said. 'They are the modern equivalent of talkback radio as they are talking directly to their audience. But there is no business organisation that is able to do that'.[51]

John Roskam, head of the right-wing think tank the Institute of Public Affairs, made a similar admission about the shift in political power towards social media activist groups. 'The Liberals now fear GetUp!', he wrote, 'nearly as much as the ACTU'; and 'The capacity on the left to mobilise grassroots activism has always been admired from afar by the Liberals. In recent years that's turned to fear'. Roskam wanted to make a point about the current Liberal Party; he lamented that it was too ideologically tame to attract passionate advocates to its cause: 'Any Liberal who knows anything at all about politics will come to the conclusion that there's no way a non-left wing version of GetUp! can be developed to assist the Liberal Party'.[52]

However, Roskam was out of touch. A more muscular ideology wasn't the answer to the Liberals' failure to mobilse grassroots activism. He failed to realise a central point about social activism and its campaign against coal. Increasingly, it had the support of mainstream Australians, including many traditionally conservative-minded farmers. Cliff Wallace of Maules Creek, New South Wales, was one farmer who arose early most mornings while 'a rag-tag army of anti-coal activists camped in tents and tee-pees on his land to catch a few more hours sleep'. He was happy to host the protesters because he shared their views. Wallace is particularly worried about the impact the mine will have on his farm's groundwater and says he is 'deeply saddened' by the disruption to the region's animal habitats. Wallace was a part of the diverse social movement concerned about the impact of coal both in Australia and globally. As one commentator observed: 'Taking on Australia's powerful coal sector was once left to environmentalists like Greenpeace and the World Wildlife Fund, but now the anti-coal movement is attracting wider support, from farmers to banks and investment funds striving to be seen as ethical investors and not contributing to global pollution'.[53]

The Commonwealth Bank – the first to shift

The Commonwealth Bank was the only bank with direct links to the Carmichael mine acting as an advisor to the project. Adani has been a client of the Commonwealth Bank since it was part of a syndicate in 2012 that provided a $2 billion debt package to support Adani's ownership of the Abbot Point coal export port on a 99-year lease. That loan was refinanced in 2013, but with several other banks dropping out, it left the Commonwealth Bank to provide a far greater share of the debt. 'As an adviser, Commonwealth Bank was in line to be a leading lender to Adani's Carmichael mega coal mine', said Julien Vincent, lead campaigner with Market Forces.[54]

From these developments, it was clear that the Commonwealth Bank saw the project as viable and likely to go ahead. It might not easily have been able to walk away from any future involvement in the mine. When the announcement came on 4 August 2015 that the

Commonwealth Bank had ceased its role as an advisor to the Carmichael mine, the bank declined to elaborate on the circumstances
of its role. But Michael West and Lisa Cox, writing for the *Sydney
Morning Herald*, reported that sources inside the bank said that the
environmental controversy surrounding the Carmichael project was
a factor along with the project's financial risk.[55] However, the bank
refused to rule out funding the project and continued to have links
with Adani. Pressuring the bank into a full retreat would take a more
sustained effort. For its part, Adani wasn't going to let environmentalists claim a win. It asserted that the bank hadn't walked away;
rather Adani had terminated its services.[56]

The National Australia Bank pulls out

The others in the 'big four' were closely watching these events. The
action taken against the Commonwealth Bank had sent a powerful
message to the sector. A month after the Commonwealth Bank's
decision to terminate its role as advisor to Adani, the NAB made an
announcement of its own. In September 2015, it made a definitive
statement that it would not be involved in financing the project. Of
all the banks, NAB had the least exposure to fossil fuel investment.
Cameron Clyne, a former chief executive of the bank, told the press
that Australia's powerful addiction to coal as a source of energy and
growth was 'economically reckless'.[57]

That view was shared, in part, by the board, which, in declaring that they had no intention of funding Adani, also said that 'it
wanted to take a leading role in developing renewable energy'.[58] The
problems of funding for Adani continued to multiply. It was not just
that one Australian bank had publicly declined to become involved
in its project, but that NAB's decision added to the number of banks
globally that had declared their intention not to become involved.
The decision was described as 'a bombshell' to Adani.[59]

The NAB's decision was also a slap in the face to Prime Minister

Tony Abbott who, just the week before, had claimed that business leaders who were not prepared to advocate for Adani were 'playing games with our economic future'.[60]

In fact, the NAB's decision provoked a polarised response. 'While NAB is getting hailed by twitterers as the saviour of the reef, I've received emails and calls from almost every coal client I've got', James MacGinley, the director of natural resources at NAB's institutional bank, explained to Richard Gluyas of the *Australian*. NAB chief executive Andrew Thorburn and other senior executives scrambled to reassure coal industry customers that the bank still supported them. As Gluyas reported from sources in NAB: 'No one is happy about NAB bowing to NGO [non-government organisation] pressure. We're in damage control now, with Andrew Thorburn and other senior execs making calls to various aggrieved clients'. NAB was apologetic about 'breaking ranks' but said it 'may have learned our lesson today'.[61]

Another propaganda campaign for coal

With the campaign against the banks starting to make an impact, the Minerals Council of Australia (MCA) grew increasingly worried. BHP was one of the council's most influential members and Mike Henry, the head of the company's coal division, issued a warning in September 2015: 'It would be fair to say that as we stand here today, in the court of public opinion, the "no coal" camp has been more effective. Anti-coal activism has been building momentum over many years'. Henry urged the sector to unite to fight back.[62] Others in the sector were also pessimistic about the falling public support for the coal industry. Darren Walker, from Queensland-based U&M Mining, acknowledged to a mining conference in June 2015 that the shift in public opinion about coal mining had made operating in today's environment more difficult: 'groups and activists with an anti-coal agenda had made significant strides in recent years'. Paul

McLeod from Risk Communications Australia drew the attention of the conference to the public relations success of the disinvestment campaigns.[63] Based on these comments, one of the environmental movement's strategies to change the image of coal appeared to be working.

A counter-attack was organised in the first week of September 2015 when the MCA unveiled its latest advertising campaign, around the 'benefits' of coal. Dubbed 'The Little Black Rock' campaign, television screens and social media were blitzed with the 'endless possibilities' of coal. A spokesman for the coal industry said that the campaign will 'provide a balance to the less than factual arguments often put forward by anti-coal activists'.

'Isn't it amazing what this little black rock can do', began the MCA's advertisement: 'creating light and jobs', 'delivering $6 billion in wages for Australians', 'reducing emissions by up to 40 per cent' and, in a very 'ocker' touch, the public was reminded that there would be 'no coldies without coal'.[64]

However, the MCA had underestimated both public opinion and the power of social media. Its campaign was mocked on social media: 'The campaign began to trend and became the butt of many jokes on Twitter'. As one industry expert explained: the risk to any brand 'is that as soon as you hand the hashtag to the general social media public, you're then losing control'.[65] Not only did the campaign backfire, it was rated as 'PR fail of the year'.[66]

The MCA's campaign was also undermined from an unexpected source. Alan Jones is Sydney radio's most powerful broadcaster. He is a friend not just to the Liberal Party but to Abbott as well. He has made a career out of launching verbal missiles into the political debate, but his right-wing views made him the last person likely to appear on an advertisement funded by environmental activists. Jones had railed against the science of climate change. Yet he teamed up with Lock the Gate, the anti-coal seam gas activist organisation, to make a television advertisement which was shown during the same period as the MCA's 'Little Black Rock' campaign.

Despite his unlikely presence, Jones brought an earthy credibility to the campaign. The son of a coal miner and farmer, he had genuine sympathy for the plight of farmers and for the need to protect productive farmland from coal mining. He worried about the impact of the Carmichael mine on farmers' access to water from the Great Artesian Basin.

Jones had already given Abbott a verbal dressing-down on his program. In July 2015, he told his listeners that the Abbott government's approval of the Shenhua Watermark coal mine, in the farming district of the Liverpool Plains in New South Wales, was 'disgraceful', 'beyond belief', and tantamount to the government selling its soul to mining.[67] Few politicians came off the better from one of Jones' rants. But he was an irresistible conduit to Liberal voters, who were now exposed to his anti-coal outpourings.

Jones was outraged at the prospect that Adani would be given a government-backed loan. As his intense gaze beamed into television sets around the country for the advertisement, Jones took aim at both the Abbott government and the recently elected Queensland Labor government headed by Annastacia Palaszczuk: 'How is it that Australian governments are committed to Adani when no bank in the world will lend them money? I'm saying to Adani and the governments of Australia, if you think we are that stupid, you need to think again'.

It's hard to assess the impact of Jones' one-off intervention. However, business groups believed that the advertisement resonated: 'His intervention creates another difficult frontline battle for the Abbott government, turning the Coalition supporters, who are generally Jones' listeners, against the prime minister and other senior cabinet ministers on this issue'.[68]

The ANZ's turn

By October 2015, another bank announced stricter rules for lending to coal projects. ANZ – the bank with the biggest exposure among the 'big four' – set stricter rules for lending to coal-fired power stations. Only the latest generation of coal technology would be funded. Although the announcement didn't specifically prevent lending to Adani, the bank declared that it was going to change its activities to be consistent with the need to limit rises in temperature to 2°C and it committed $10 billion in funding for renewable energy.[69] It was also the first time one of the banks had definitively stated that climate change is occurring. These statements meant that, in practical terms, ANZ was a non-starter for the Carmichael mine. In its climate statement, ANZ conceded to the public pressure it had come under: 'We understand some of our stakeholders view our financing of fossil fuel industries as a material risk and in direct conflict with our stated position on the need to reduce greenhouse gas emissions'.[70]

Observers agreed. Writing in the *Australian Financial Review*, Matthew Stevens wrote: 'Adani is the target of a global campaign by an increasingly potent anti-coal lobby that has pushed a fleet of serious international banks to publicly boycott lending to a new generation of Queensland coal'.[71]

Westpac and the Commonwealth Bank were the last two of the 'big four' to hold out on declarations of intent regarding funding for Adani. As mentioned, the Commonwealth Bank had responded to pressure and ceased acting as Adani's advisor to the project, but otherwise hadn't ruled out financing it and Westpac maintained its 'stonewalling' until the beginning of 2017.

Adani always maintained that he didn't need the involvement of the Australian banks and speculation simmered away that the company would turn to China to finance the mine. Moreover, by 2016, both the Queensland Labor government, led by Annastacia Palaszczuk and the Turnbull-led government committed Australia to funding the mine through the National Australia Infrastructure Facility. Thus, as important as the campaign against the banks was, on its own it was insufficient to stop the mine. A more co-ordinated, focused and energetic campaign was needed. By the end of 2016, several groups and individuals were coming to the same conclusion. The foundations of #StopAdani were being laid.

GetUp! gets going

GetUp! was already the most influential progressive activist organisation in Australia when Paul Oosting replaced Sam McLean as national director in 2015. Unrelenting and intense in its campaigning, the organisation tended to burn through its leaders every 3–4 years since its foundation in 2005. Oosting inherited an organisation with a membership in excess of 800000 and a string of high-profile campaigns on health, refugees and the environment. Oosting built on GetUp!'s record with his ability to combine innovative strategy with aggressive campaigning. Like activists the world over, he is driven by a deep ambition to make a difference, to break open the vested interests that run politics.[72]

Oosting was raised in the cauldron of Tasmanian environmental politics. He was a child living with his parents in Wesley Vale, 'on some land with chooks and sheep', when, in the late 1980s, the state-government-backed proposal to build the Wesley Vale pulp mill galvanised the local community into a pitched battle to stop the mill. The successful campaign forged the career of Greens leader Christine Milne.[73] Oosting's parents had thrust themselves into the campaign, with seven-year-old Paul absorbing some tough lessons:

> There was also at times a real sense of fear because my dad
> would often put up placards in our front paddock and at night
> people would come and smash up the property and signs. I
> have very vivid memories of one particular moment being s—

scared, holding my cricket bat and going out the front when
Dad was out there to scare them off. I also remember the issue
really creating angst in the primary school.[74]

Fifteen years later, the Tasmanian government backed Gunns Ltd
to build another world-scale mill in the state, this time in the picturesque Tamar Valley. Oosting walked off the streets and into The
Wilderness Society (TWS) office in Hobart and offered to volunteer
for six months as part of the campaign to stop the mill. Eventually,
the organisation scraped enough money together to offer him a paid
job and Oosting played one of the leading roles in stopping the mill.

Showing an early flair for edgy political stunts to increase
awareness, Oosting teamed up with Vica Bayley, the director of the
TWS, to perform a pantomime on the lawns of Parliament House
in Hobart in 2007. The pair masqueraded as then-Gunns boss John
Gay and then-premier Paul Lennon, rolling around in a double bed
plotting a 'sweetheart deal for a special mate'.[75] However, campaigning against Gunns was not for the faint-hearted; the company sued a
group of protesters in an infamous case of corporate misuse of power,
known as the Gunns 20 case. Oosting joined GetUp! in 2011.

The 2016 election was a turning point for GetUp!. Oosting
and the team devised a strategy to target hard-right members of the
Turnbull government and is credited with playing a role in having
three MPs voted out in big swings. Apart from the media attention
the campaign attracted, and the hostility it generated from Liberal
politicians, the strategy had flow-on effects for GetUp!'s role in the
fight against Adani. The 2016 election had been a distraction from
its anti-Adani campaign and a general air of complacency had crept
into the organisation's thinking on the issue. As Oosting explains,
the campaign against Adani 'lost focus' during 2016 and not least
because of 'the vibe that the project was probably on its last legs'.[76]

After the 2016 election the organisation realised it needed an
enhanced national-based political strategy to fight the Carmichael

mine in place of its previous focus on external agencies such as international banks and the World Heritage Committee. This was seen as a means to counter the increased support for the mine that both the Palaszczuk and Turnbull governments were offering. But what shape would such a strategy take?

GetUp! went into a process of reflection on where it was headed as an activist organisation. The 2016 election showed that it could mount a potent political campaign, but it sought to increase its effectiveness to bring about policy change. To facilitate this thinking, Oosting arranged for consulting firm NetChange to provide advice.

Headed by Jason Mogus and Tom Liacas, NetChange focused its work on building social change movements. Its 2016 report, *How progressive campaigns are won in the 21st century* went 'like wildfire' through the environment movement.[77] Mogus and Liacas had studied advocacy campaigns worldwide that, over the previous decade, had achieved significant impact. They identified one group of campaigns that had performed exceptionally well, which they termed 'directed network campaigns'. These were identified as being: 'Led by a central body that frames and co-ordinates energies towards shared milestones but also leaves a fair amount of freedom and agency to grassroots supporters and a diverse network of inside and cross-movement allies'.[78]

Oosting and the GetUp! team were attracted to the model of a directed network campaign. They wanted to increase GetUp!'s own 'people power' capacities while developing stronger alliances with like-minded groups. As Oosting explained: 'We can't match it with the big parties on advertising budgets, but we could see the power of people being our key asset'.[79]

GetUp! planned to strengthen its political influence through adopting the directed network campaigns model. Their change in direction was timely, because others were moving in a similar direction. In late 2016, former Greens leader Bob Brown called Geoff Cousins, president of the ACF and high-profile campaigner, against both the Tamar Valley pulp mill and the plans to industrialise the Kimberly coast. They shared their concerns that the campaign against Adani lacked a coherent and focused framework.[80]

From this diverse set of conversations, plans were laid to form #StopAdani, one of the most significant environment groups ever formed in Australia.

CHAPTER TWELVE

The end game?

The involvement of both Bob Brown and Geoff Cousins in creating #StopAdani brought two of Australia's most high-profile environmentalists to the forefront of the fight against the Carmichael mine. With contrasting and unique experiences in the environmental movement, they helped bring other groups into the newly formed 'network', and their presence helped make it clear 'that this was going to be a nationally focused campaign'.[1] In characteristically blunt fashion, Cousins explained that the anti-Adani campaign comprised 'bits and pieces of activity that is not producing a result'. Both he and Brown 'pushed to get all the groups to come together'.[2]

Brown, of course, is a veteran campaigner and former leader of the Greens who, since retiring from federal parliament in 2012, has continued his environmental activism principally through his Bob Brown Foundation. I had known Brown when I was a journalist in Tasmania in the early 1980s, covering his first campaigns to protect Tasmania's old-growth forests from the state's relentless wood chipping industry. We hadn't met for 30 years when I asked him to launch my book, *The Rise and Fall of Gunns Ltd*, in Hobart in early 2015. He had lost none of his charisma. The assembled audience delighted in his address, a mix of self-deprecating humour, understated references to his long career, passion for protecting the environment and flashes of his still infectious smile.

Since that event I've watched as Brown resumed campaigning against moves by the Tasmanian government to open up the Tarkine

Wilderness in north-western Tasmania to logging. In January 2016, he and three others were arrested under Tasmania's recently enacted anti-workplace protest laws, a blatant attempt by Will Hodgman's Liberal government to stop environmental activism.

As he did on the Franklin River campaign, Brown understands the opportunity to use the High Court to win environmental battles and he took the Tasmanian government's draconian legislation to the High Court. In a landmark decision, the court found that attempting to stop protests against development was at odds with the implied right in the Australian constitution to freedom of political communication. The legal victory was fought not by a high-profile firm, but the small Hobart firm of Browne and Fitzgerald, long-standing legal advisors to Bob and his partner, Paul Thomas.

Since his retirement, Brown has lived in a secluded part of southern Tasmania where the rolling green hills of Paul's sheep farm meet the calm waters of Randalls Bay with its picturesque rocky shoreline and inviting views across the D'Entrecasteaux Channel to Bruny Island. The day I visited in early November 2017, Bob and Paul had just finished shearing the last of the sheep. Over lunch Bob reflected on his life after politics, a process he described as regaining his soul after decades in the cauldron of parliament. As the afternoon wore on the phone rang several times: journalists wanting comments from Bob on various issues. He remains actively engaged. And, as his recent arrest attests, has lost none of his campaigning zeal.

We discussed his long involvement in the anti-coal campaign and his role, along with Geoff Cousins, in assisting the #StopAdani movement. He was buoyed by its potential, but nothing suggested then that the movement he had helped unleash was close to bringing about the likely demise of the Carmichael mine. At the end of the interview, I asked him what his response would be if the Adani mine did proceed. He said simply that he has made plans to lead a cavalcade of cars up to central Queensland, where he has built links with the traditional owners. His Bob Brown Foundation recently awarded Adrian Burragubba 2017 Environmentalist of the Year.

Cousins doesn't have Brown's longevity in the environmental movement nor his credentials for direct action. But in the past five or six years he has emerged as one of the movement's most skilled and influential strategists. After taking a lead in several high-profile campaigns, Cousins became president of the Australian Conservation Foundation (ACF) in September 2014. His unlikely journey into environmental activism had little to do with his successful career in commercial advertising, but he has brought with him the skills and contacts he acquired in the corporate world.

In 2014, I interviewed Cousins for *The Rise and Fall of Gunns Ltd*. At the time, his contribution to the environmental movement had attracted considerable media interest. He already had a high profile in business circles, earning a reputation as one of the most experienced advertising brains in the country.[3] For 20 years, Cousins had been a senior executive with what was then Australia's most powerful advertising agency, George Patterson. He has also been a director of James Packer's Publishing & Broadcasting Limited and the Seven Network. In 2006, he was 'bulldozed' onto the Telstra board by the Howard government to help it sell its $8 billion privatisation of Telstra to the public.[4]

How had such a corporate heavyweight, a quintessential insider, a confidant of former prime minister John Howard, changed sides? Cousins has been disarmingly open in answering the media's questions about his journey from corporate titan to environmental crusader, but what intrigued me was how elements of his 'corporate personality' remained deeply embedded but redirected to his new cause.

In conversations I shared with him on this, and on my book on Gunns, it was apparent that Cousins relishes a battle and, like any successful businessman, he likes to win. But he brings to these new battles over the environment the skills and mindset of the corporate world: experience in running complex strategic business campaigns, an understanding of how boards and CEOs think and behave, a relentless focus on achieving outcomes, and unrivalled access to the boardrooms around the country. He blends these skills with a rich, baritone voice that can cut through to the media or a town hall meeting along with a commanding physical presence. Although Cousins is the first to reocognise the importance of grassroots activism, it is also the case that activists have never had such a powerful corporate voice in their corner.

In the battle over the Gunns pulp mill in Tasmania's Tamar Valley, activists had, over many years, taken the fight up to Gunns and transformed their protest into a national cause. Greens leaders Bob Brown and Christine Milne had taken it into the federal parliament. Cousins and the Wilderness Society's Paul Oosting worked at lobbying the financial institutions backing Gunns. The campaign against Gunns broke new ground in the sophistication of its strategy. Cousins was instrumental in laying out a plan, in league with the company's major financiers, for a coup against the Gunns board; effectively throwing out its old, pro-old growth logging, 'greenie'-hating CEO and board members and replacing them with a new CEO and board membership. Nothing as audacious as this had ever been attempted by the environmental movement and, although Cousins' efforts to end the saga of the pulp mill were only one part of a long and determined community-based campaign, I had talked to numerous people in the Tamar Valley who regarded him as one of the heroes of their struggle.

At the time I was writing the Gunns story, friends in the Kimberley region of Western Australia began recounting Cousins' involvement during 2011 to 2013, in the campaign to stop Woodside's $30 billion Browse Basin gas project at James Price Point, north of Broome. Cousins had quickly shifted from helping to stop Gunns, on to a new fight to save one of Australia's pristine coastlines from industrialisation. He was instrumental in working the boardrooms and pulling together a group of high-profile supporters to back the campaign. In the end, community action prevailed over government-backed corporate power and the Kimberley coast was saved.

In an ironic twist, Cousins' elegant house in Sydney's elite Point Piper stands just up the road from Prime Minister Malcolm Turnbull's. The two have developed into hardened opponents, an antipathy originating from the campaign Cousins waged against Turnbull over his role as minister for the environment in the Howard government which approved the Gunns pulp mill. On billboards and leaflets, Cousins depicted Turnbull as 'The Minister Against the Environment'. Turnbull accused Cousins of engaging in 'corporate bullying'. But applying pressure is the basis of Cousins' strategic view of environmental campaigning: 'You've got to find the pressure points and keep pushing at them until you get a response'.[5]

As I was leaving his house after our mid-November 2017 interview, Cousins had been buoyed by the state election result in Queensland and the blow this had inflicted on the federal government's plan to hand Adani a loan through the National Australia Infrastructure Facility (NAIF). But he wasn't confident that victory had been won. He was involved in other power plays to halt the mine and these hadn't yet come to fruition when we met. His parting words were that, if necessary, he'd try to organise shareholder activism in India to take action against Adani.

Yet, a few short weeks later, all the main pillars propping up Adani – the 'big four' banks, the NAIF, the mining lobby and Australia's two major parties – had either fallen or were cracking badly. It would be extremely difficult for Adani to rise from its position at the end of 2017. So how had the pillars fallen so quickly in the second half of 2017?

Confronting Adani in India

Before speaking to Bob Brown in late 2016, Cousins had already resolved to take action of his own to try to intensify the focus on Adani. In March 2017, he travelled to India to try to intercept Annastacia Palaszczuk's planned trip to meet with Gautam Adani and his board, as part of a goodwill promotional tour to show her government's support for the Carmichael mine. Cousins had several objectives for his trip, including a plan to intercept the premier on her arrival in Gujarat state where she, and the several regional Queensland mayors travelling with her, were to have lunch with Adani. As Cousins explains: 'I didn't think Adani felt in any way concerned about their situation in Australia and that it was not impacting on their reputation in India. That is what I wanted to disturb'.[6]

It was a tricky operation; Cousins wasn't sure anything would come of it. He didn't have the details about the premier's itinerary and, in any event, trying to intercept such an official visit might risk arrest and/or deportation. For these reasons, he decided to go as an individual and not as president of the ACF. Cousins realised that he needed 'to have some message from Australia and not just me running around'. Within a week, and in concert with his wife Darleen Bungey, the ACF and The Sunrise Project, they received support from 91 prominent Australians to endorse an open letter. Among the list were well-known authors, artists, musicians, traditional owners, former politicians, environmentalists, scientists and academics.

However, Cousins scored a major publicity coup by enlisting the support of former Australian cricket captains Ian and Greg Chappell, whose involvement would generate interest in the Indian media. Cousins met Ian in a pub and over a beer secured his involvement. The presence of the Chappell brothers, and especially Ian, also generated interest in the Australian media about the trip. Ian had surprised many people with his previous outspoken stance on

Australia's treatment of refugees. As Ian Chappell later explained, it was 'worthwhile' if joining with his brother Greg thrust the issue into the public spotlight in cricket-loving India: 'You realise as a former Australian captain that there are times when you have a louder voice than a lot of other people [and] there are times to use that louder voice'.

His views on Adani, he explained, were the culmination of years of taking an interest in climate change, in part due to the influence of his wife, Barbara-Ann:

> I've got a wife who is one, intelligent, two, she's got a scientific mind, and three, a very strong social conscience. She's been on about climate change for 20 years, probably before most others, so I'm hearing about it regularly and obviously can make up my own mind.[7]

The open letter made three points for Adani to consider: firstly, that the Carmichael mine would contribute to climate change and threaten the Great Barrier Reef; secondly, that coal is killing millions around the world; and thirdly, that the mine lacked wide public support in Australia.

The letter was ridiculed by federal government MP George Christensen. Always good for a media-grabbing outrageous quote, he railed against the signatories as 'elitist wankers' trying to wipe out job opportunities for struggling Queenslanders. In a statement Christensen said: 'Styling themselves as "prominent Australians", these elitist wankers include investment bankers, CEOs of major corporations such as Telstra, pretentious literati, professional activists and has-been celebrities'.[8]

Cousins was accompanied on the trip to India by three other people, none of whom he had met before and all of whom travelled separately to reduce the risk of attracting unwanted attention from the authorities. The three joining Cousins were: Imogen Zethoven from the Australian Marine Conservation Society; Lindsay Simpson, a tourism operator from the Great Barrier Reef; and Bruce Currie, a grazier from central Queensland. They were armed with the results from a recent poll commissioned by the Australian Marine Conservation Society which found that 63 per cent of Australians agreed with the statement that 'the best thing for Australia would be for Adani to invest in large-scale solar power stations, rather than a coal mine'.[9]

The group landed in Ahmedabad, the capital of Gujarat, and the headquarters of the Adani Group. Their first task was to meet with Indian villagers in Mundra and Hazira, areas which, for years, had been affected by Adani's operations, as discussed in Chapter 2. As they discovered, the plight of the villagers had worsened since Adani's operations first moved into their area. The land Adani had claimed had extended out further into the sea, making access to the their fishing grounds even more difficult. To Bruce Currie, the visit to these villages 'sent a shiver up my spine':[10] The farmers and fishermen:

> Told me familiar stories of a big company that gets its foot
> in the door by promising local jobs and a boost to the local
> economy, but at the end of the day doesn't really give a damn
> about their community ... I met a date farmer ... who lost
> the entire 10 acres of crop due to coal dust ... What worried
> me most of all were reports by farmers and pastoralists of their
> groundwater being polluted and watercourses blocked.

What he saw, Currie believed, 'made me even more worried about the risks to Queensland's water security if Adani gets a foothold here'.

While still in Ahmedabad, the four protesters delivered the open letter to Adani headquarters and had what Cousins later described as a 'productive meeting' with senior Adani management. Later the group held a press conference on the footpath outside the company's headquarters. It was one of several tense moments in the trip. They were told that it was illegal to hold a press conference in the street and, consequently, they were risking arrest. A huge contingent of security people were present, and Cousins asked one of the group's Indian minders whether they were police or a contingent from Adani security. He was told that it didn't matter; 'they were one and the same thing'.[11]

The group managed to deliver their message to the media: 'We are in India to tell Adani that Australians do not want this coal mine. Coal is a dirty, dying industry that is bad for Australia, bad for the Great Barrier Reef, bad for our health and bad for our future. We welcome Adani's investment in solar, but we do not welcome investments that damage GBR and our country. The future of India is dependent on solar energy and not coal'. The press conference received front page coverage in a number of Indian newspapers. But Adani himself remained characteristically belligerent in the face of the protest, saying that it was motivated by a small group of 'misled' people.

The group then confronted the reality that they had no idea where the premier was going to meet Adani. They did not know if she would be meeting with him in his home town. Had it not been for a tip-off from an Australian journalist covering Palaszczuk's visit, their efforts would likely have been in vain. However, armed with the information that she would be arriving the next day at the airport in Bhuj, not far from Adani's operations in Mundra, Cousins and Imogen Zethoven hastily took to the road for the seven-hour drive from Ahmedabad. Killing time in the airport attracted the attention of police because it is normally difficult to get into an Indian airport without a valid aeroplane ticket, necessitating some fast explanations as to why they were waiting around without valid tickets. But, as luck would have it, just as they managed to convince the police that they needed to leave the airport, they saw an official black limousine arrive; the door flung open and, with a gaggle of media alongside, Cousins saw his chance. In an instant he manoeuvred around, stood in front of the open door and said: 'Welcome Premier'. With cameras clicking furiously, the image was transmitted around India and back to Australia. 'We got massive coverage in India', Cousins explained.[12]

In New Delhi, the group met with a former Indian minister for the environment, Jairam Ramesh, who had instigated several prosecutions against Adani, and who told them that: 'I have prosecuted Adani many times. They never met their environmental conditions in India, why do you imagine they would do so in Australia?'. Ramesh also raised a theory as to why Adani was set to import huge amounts of coal from the Galilee Basin when the Modi government had recently announced its intention to phase out imported coal. Although Ramesh had no evidence to prove his theory, he nonetheless believed that the coal from the Galilee 'will probably come into India, be re-classified as Indian coal and then re-exported to Pakistan and just through that process Adani will make another fortune'.[13]

The Australian press also covered the trip and gave the four travellers positive feedback that they had injected new energy into the campaign against Adani. In the longer term, there were other spin-offs from the trip. Cousins was approached by ABC *Four Corners* journalist Stephen Long, who wanted to do a story on Adani's operations in India but who was having trouble convincing management that he had sufficient contacts in the country to warrant the resources needed to make the program. Cousins furnished Long with the contacts he had made and Long obtained approval and travelled to India to start work.

In the meantime, Cousins travelled to Canberra for the launch of #StopAdani.

#StopAdani formed

On 22 March 2017, Bob Brown officially launched #StopAdani with 13 other environmental groups including the Bob Brown Foundation, the ACF, 350.org, GetUp!, the Australian Youth Climate Coalition, the Seed Indigenous Youth Climate Network and the Australian Marine Conservation Society, although that number would grow to over 30 groups and include Greenpeace, One Million Women, Friends of the Earth and many state-based and regional conservation councils. The alliance called for:

- Urgent and serious action to cut carbon pollution.
- A complete withdrawal of the Adani Carmichael mine, rail and port project.
- A ban on new coalmines and expansions in Australia.
- An end to public subsidies for polluting projects.

However, the strategy called for a multi-faceted campaign targeting the only two remaining Australian banks that had not disavowed funding Adani; the Queensland and federal government's support for a loan to Adani through the National Australia Infrastructure Fund (NAIF); and Adani's reputation both internationally and at home. Groups would share research, communications and strategic thinking and build a website from which local groups could draw down campaign materials. The name #StopAdani itself was settled on after doing the rounds of the groups involved. Brown said the groups were 'drawing a line in the sand with Adani, just as previous generations did with the Franklin River dam'.[14]

#StopAdani quickly became the brand name of the opposition to Adani and its Carmichael mine. Brown persuaded the savvy organisers to adopt a decidedly low-tech form of advertising – a car bumper sticker. A few thousand were printed and were snapped up immediately.

Some doubted whether the various organisations would give

up their own territory, but that doubt dissipated almost immediately. The ACF and GetUp! shifted stopping Adani to become the number one priority of their respective organisations, rather than having it as simply part of their broader involvements. As Cousins explained, once the organisation got rolling 'people started to see the force of it'. Extensive phone hook-ups between the participating organisations started occurring 2–3 times a week. ACF, along with other organisations, put volunteers on the ground in North Queensland, training activists to facilitate local community action.[15]

The impact on the ground was immediate. In just seven months, more than 160 local #StopAdani groups had formed across Australia. These groups started taking action in their communities – actively lobbying local members of parliament, holding public meetings, and spreading the word about why Adani's coal mine should not proceed. In turn, these local groups organised hundreds of events and activities in their communities.

The creation of #StopAdani was unprecedented in several ways. It linked up more environment and community-based organisations under the one banner over the entire country than had ever occurred before. It unleashed a plethora of creative and innovative strategies that helped cement Adani as a toxic brand name. And, in the process, #StopAdani helped push the fight against the company into a genuine nationally based mass movement.

The Indian media was drawn into the size and intensity of the campaign. Writing in the influential business magazine, the *Wire*, Kabir Agarwal observed the vibrancy and dynamism of the anti-Adani campaign:

Earrings, caps, t-shirts, socks and bandanas with the words 'Stop Adani' printed on them have become more common than one would imagine on the streets in Australia. Creative videos have been put together expressing strong displeasure with the mine and Adani. Artists have written and performed

songs highlighting the dangers that the mine poses and the
importance of speaking out against it. Graffiti on streets
and in public toilets convey an adverse and contemptuous
view of Adani's efforts to mine coal in Australia. Pictures of
Adani on massive billboards accompanied by words such
as 'destruction' and 'exploitation' can be seen at prominent
places in cities.[16]

However, not every activist group sought affiliation with the new
organisation. In January 2017, as #StopAdani was in the process
of being formalised, a new organisation was recruiting members.
Galilee Blockade was established as 'a secretive network' of activists
laying the groundwork for a campaign of direct action against Adani
across the country. It was the pointy end of the environment movement. Among their ranks were veterans from past iconic environmental campaigns who were willing to risk arrest for the cause. In a
short time they were reported to have enlisted 11 000 supporters. In
cities along the east coast the group recruited criminal lawyers who
agreed to be on hand if legal support was required.[17] Organiser Ben
Pennings, a veteran environmental activist who had sailed on the
Rainbow Warrior at age 20, warned that if called upon, his organisation could deliver the largest contingent of direct action protesters
in Australian history.

In formal and informal ways, the anti-Adani cause was captur-
ing the public's imagination. Yet the energy sparked by #StopAdani
has proved impossible for organisers to control. Local groups around
the country popped up bearing the name but some had little or no
formal affiliation with the official body.

Geoff Cousins received a call from 'a very senior politician' worried about a #StopAdani protest group which had occupied his electorate office. He was not in attendance at the time but his son was
and the politician wanted Cousins' help to get the people out. After
making a few calls, Cousins called the concerned politician back

and had to inform him that he couldn't find out who the group in his office was or how to contact them. He explained to the politician that he:

> must understand that this is no longer a nice neat group of half a dozen big environment groups sitting in a room. Many of the new groups have formed of their own accord and use the Adani brand name … we don't even know who they are. This is now a true movement of the people and it's not all being centrally directed.[18]

Increased protest activity soon followed the formation of #StopAdani. Among their first goals was to increase the pressure on Adani generally, but especially on Annastacia Palaszczuk's government to renounce her support for providing a loan to Adani through the NAIF. With an eye to the next state election, the ACF and GetUp! announced in early June 2017 that they would 'bombard' federal MPs with phone calls, pressure international banks to rule out funding and investigate a possible legal challenge should NAIF approve a loan. GetUp!'s Sam Regester said that the activists' 'No 1 priority' was stopping the NAIF loan.[19] In fact, by the beginning of June 2017, GetUp! volunteers had made 50 000 scripted calls into Queensland marginal seats; each volunteer having been supplied with instructions on how to conduct phone calls with voters to galvanise opposition to the Adani project.[20]

In June 2017, the international activist group SumOfUs announced that they were raising money via their 1.5 million online supporters to erect a huge billboard in Palaszczuk's electorate with the message: 'If you donate today, Palaszczuk won't be able to miss the fact that community opposition to Adani's mine is as big as ever – and that if the mine gets built, it will cost her votes'.[21] The organisation had also run a 'spoof' anti-Adani advertisement on social media that clocked over half a million views.

Newly trained activists for #StopAdani began popping up at

political meetings. On 11 July they interrupted the premier's town hall meeting in Cairns chanting 'no, no, no' in opposition to the mine. As the *Courier Mail* reported:

> [T]he Premier told them jobs were vital and coal mining would not cease in Queensland: 'Coal is going to be part of our energy mix for many years to come', she said.
> 'Rubbish', the protestors howled in reply.
> They later interrupted the meeting by bursting into song.[22]

Palaszczuk's support for the Carmichael mine had a farcical element to it. The premier had recently announced a plan to fight climate change and help save the Great Barrier Reef through a program to decarbonise the Queensland economy through increasing commitment to renewable energy while, at the same time, turning a blind eye to the coal that would be burnt in India, which would ultimately undermine her policy.[23]

Publicly at least, Gautam Adani wasn't worried about the protests. He responded to the ramped-up campaign with characteristic fighting words: 'We have been challenged by activists in the courts, in inner-city streets, and even outside banks' but insisted that the company remained committed to the project.[24] For his part, Prime Minister Malcolm Turnbull wasn't showing any signs of rethinking his government's support for the mine either, continuing to laud it as 'a boon for Australia'. And, in April 2017, Turnbull visited Modi on an official visit to India where he recommitted his government to the Carmichael mine.

Westpac folds

While activity in Queensland ramped up, the organisers of #StopAdani also wanted to complete the campaign it was waging against the 'big four' banks.

On 9 April 2017, Australia's business and political elite gathered at Carriageworks, the renovated Eveleigh Rail Yards turned arts hub, with its vast interior space providing an ideal venue for large community events. There were few more prestigious occasions for the big end of town than Westpac's 200th birthday celebration. But CEO Brian Hartzer, who had been paid $6.7 million in salary the previous year, hadn't foreseen that the occasion might be disrupted by a large anti-Adani contingent. After all, over the previous three years, Westpac had dismissed the anti-bank protests as insignificant.

The bank spared no expense to entertain its hundreds of elite guests, among them coal prankster and Treasurer Scott Morrison. As they were making their way to the venue, #StopAdani activists deployed social media to encourage supporters to join them. Hundreds turned out on the driveway of the venue to greet the well-heeled guests with chants of 'Stop Adani'.

Shaun Murray was one of two activists who managed to evade security and gain access to the main event. No one knows how this breach occurred, however it is thought that they followed members of the orchestra in, wearing similar black shirts and trousers, which fooled people into thinking that they were official staff.[25]

As the guests enjoyed the fine wine and food, everyone's attention was suddenly drawn to a noise from the ceiling. Murray had managed to scale the scaffolding on one wall, where he proceeded to unveil a #StopAdani banner and then lock himself onto the railings. The banter and socialising stopped as organisers fretted about how to get him down. A cherry picker was quickly brought into action and rumbled its way between the tables, its distracting 'beep-beeping' sound adding to the growing restlessness of the guests. But the operator couldn't force Murray to budge. With the event quickly turning into a shambles, Murray was able to shout above the rising din and denounce Westpac for failing to rule out funding Adani. Looking down on the glitterati, he bellowed: 'All you have to do is look at what's happening on the Great Barrier Reef to see the impact of global warming on our environment and society'. A clearly rattled Hartzer got up onto the stage and told the guests that the bank was not funding the mine and implored the guests not to listen to 'fake news'.[26] Amid the hubbub, one of the country's top CEOs was heard having a word in Hartzer's ear to the effect that the company would have to bring forward its new climate change policy.[27]

After holding forth for 90 minutes, Murray was pulled down by members of a police sea and rescue squad. The Twittersphere lit up: 'I just crashed Westpac's 200 birthday ball with@shaunmurray76'. The protest was all over Facebook. As a night of celebration, Westpac's 200th birthday bash was ruined; the use of such an audacious disruptive tactic could have come straight out of Greenpeace's 2012 strategic manual for bringing an end to the export coal industry. As Glenda Korporaal noted in the *Age*: 'the Westpac issue highlights how business in Australia has been caught out when it comes to social activism in 2017'.[28]

A few days later, Hartzer announced the bank's stricter new climate policy, which effectively ruled out funding Adani, with its poorer quality coal. Part of the announcement was a planned lift in funding renewable energy. Minister for Resources and Northern Australia Matt Canavan was not impressed, describing the bank as 'wimps' for failing to stand up to environmental activists. He was right in one respect: Westpac, the most defiant of the 'big four', had folded in the face of pressure. Michael Bones, a writer for the website 'Future Super', wrote: 'The change of heart for Australia's second largest bank is not altruistic. Westpac has been targeted by a sustained campaign from customers, climate-concerned citizens and environmental #StopAdani banner'.[29]

It was the Commonwealth Bank's turn next. It came under fire on two fronts. Activists declared that they would 'go to war' with the bank over revelations made public in early May 2017 that Adani used a Commonwealth Bank account to make a $1.6 million deposit to the Queensland government for a water licence approval. The outcry

from groups including Greenpeace and 350.org showed how successful the anti-bank movement had been in turning Adani into a toxic
brand because there was no suggestion that the deposit was part of
any future funding arrangement. However, green groups seized on
the information to allege the existence of 'secret links' between the
company and the bank. Months of pressure followed involving an
estimated 100 000 Australians before the bank publicly declared in
August that it had ruled out lending any money to Adani.

All four big banks had now been tamed and tethered; none
would be reaching out to Adani. To claim this as a singular victory
for the environmental movement may be overstating their impact;
as mentioned, a range of factors were affecting the relationship of
the 'big four' to the coal industry. But the likelihood is that one or
more of the banks would have been part of any funding consortium
assembled by Adani. Several of the 'big four' were already tied up
with Adani in Abbot Point and otherwise heavily involved in funding Australian coal projects. Therefore, on balance, the anti-bank
campaign was instrumental in pushing the banks to distance themselves from Adani and to announce stronger climate policies. Those
inside the fossil fuel industry acknowledged as much.

But the banks' problems didn't stop there. Just after the Commonwealth Bank's August announcement, two of its 'mum and dad'
shareholders, Guy and Kim Abrahams, launched a case against it,
arguing that the bank had breached the Corporations Act for failing
to adequately disclose the risk climate change posed to its financial
position in its 2016 annual report.

Like all companies, banks were coming under increasing pressure to report on their risk profile in relation to climate change and
the 'big four' had failed to comply with the new reporting standard.[29] This is not surprising given their continued deep involvement
in funding fossil fuel projects. A lawyer for Environment Justice
Australia predicted that the Federal Court action would be a test
case with potential far-reaching repercussions.[30]

The Minerals Council of Australia has its wings clipped

Along with the 'big four' banks, the Minerals Council of Australia (MCA) had been one of the staunch pillars supporting the Carmichael mine. By 2017, MCA had consolidated its reputation as a ruthless and effective lobbyist for the mining industry and especially for the interests of corporations mining coal. Increasingly, critics of the organisation are using an analogy with America's NRA (National Rifle Association) to account for its power and influence. The NRA is able to control the political agenda to advance the interest of its members in ways that act against the national interest.

The parallel with the NRA is threefold. Firstly, the raw power that the MCA unleashed against the 'anti-mining' agenda of the Rudd/Gillard Labor governments sent a chilling message to the political system in general. Secondly, the campaigns against Labor consolidated the power relationship between the MCA and the Liberal/National parties, and there were claims that the Liberals in office under Abbott and Turnbull had been captured by the money and influence it wielded. Thirdly, the MCA's relentless propaganda campaigns promoting coal had distorted the debate about the impact of Australia's export coal industry.

In fact, the MCA broke ranks with other corporate interests and, in a submission to a recent parliamentary inquiry into political donations, conceded that it made donations and attended party fundraisers to gain access to politicians.[31] Corporations had long maintained the fiction that they engaged in these activities to support democracy. Why the MCA decided to puncture this myth is not clear. With the MCA under pressure on a number of fronts it was, perhaps, a deliberate poke in the eye to remind politicians of how the game is played.

As the industry's chief promoter of coal, the MCA was coming under increasing scrutiny from the environmental/activist movement. By the beginning of 2017, the pressure exerted by these forces brought to a head tensions between the organisation's largest donors, especially BHP. The issue came down to a stark but simple choice: could the 'big Australian', whose investment in coal had been wound back in recent years and who backed the new dictates on limiting greenhouse gases, continue to support such a reactionary organisation?

The extent of this dilemma was exposed in a study by The Australia Institute. Analysing media reports in the 12 months to September 2017, it found that the MCA featured in 1594 Australian news stories mentioning coal, three times more than for any other mineral. As the institute pointed out, this continued aggressive promotion of coal did not reflect the interests of the majority of the MCA's 45 members, only a handful of which had a direct interest in coal mining.[32] As previously discussed, much of this recent evangelism for coal – and its parallel denial of climate change – was attributable to the MCA's director, Brendan Pearson.

As one of the MCA's two major funders (along with Rio Tinto), if BHP withdrew from the peak lobby group it would be a blow to the MCA's power and influence inside the Liberal Party. A split had already opened in the organisation. AGL – Australia's biggest emitter of greenhouse gases – had left the previous year over differences on climate change and energy policy. AGL had already announced its intention to transition out of coal, which earned the company a stern rebuke from Prime Minister Malcolm Turnbull.

The MCA was on Geoff Cousins' list of targets in the revamped anti-Adani campaign. Playing to his strengths as the 'corporate assassin' of the environmental movement, in early September 2017, Cousins arranged a meeting between himself and Andrew Mackenzie, CEO of BHP. As he explained, 'What I can do in the mix is a bit different from everybody else'. Retaining his connections in big business, Cousins has 'a different level I can get to'. In a long conversation with Mackenzie, already under pressure from investors' concerns about the 'big Australian's' lacklustre performance, Cousins highlighted the sharp differences in policy between the MCA and BHP on climate change. He also raised the issue of the MCA's push to remove tax deductibility status from environmental organisations. He asked Mackenzie whether he was comfortable with Brendan Pearson's efforts to publicly push this position and whether Mackenzie had considered the risk to BHP's reputation from being associated with attempts to quell free speech.[33]

Mackenzie insisted that BHP was trying to be a good corporate citizen, to which Cousins replied: 'Unless you get out of the MCA you are going to get constant pressure from the environment movement'. Cousins followed up with a letter to Mackenzie outlining the various issues on which the two organisations differed and the consequences for BHP from its continued membership of the MCA.[34] It was a test of strength between the two organisations. With 17 per cent of its funding provided by BHP, the MCA needed BHP more than 'the big Australian' needed the MCA.

As if to confirm that the MCA blinked first, two weeks later, Pearson left the lobby group, but not before further pressure was placed on BHP over its links to the MCA. A small group of shareholders associated with the Australian Centre for Corporate Responsibility had put together a resolution ahead of BHP's annual meeting set for November, asking the miner to review its membership of the MCA, claiming the 'inconsistencies between our company's policies and the MCA's lobbying positions are clear'. BHP agreed to conduct the review, including examining where its positions differed from that of the lobby group, and announced it would publish the results before the end of the year. The company subsequently put out a statement that it opposed the government's long-standing push to deny tax-deductible status to environment groups. Its new stance forced the Turnbull government to wind back its campaign, having earlier in the year sent letters to environment groups foreshadowing the start of tougher guidelines.[35] As the *Sydney Morning Herald* noted, the campaign 'lost traction after BHP indicated it would oppose such curbs'.[36]

The significance of these developments was clear. Not only had the MCA been put on notice by its largest and most influential funder, BHP had also arranged for Pearson to depart. As Phil Coorey wrote in the *Australian Financial Review*, when Pearson stepped down, 'it was universally accepted to be a consequence of pressure by BHP. It supports in-principle the adoption of a clean energy target which the government is furiously re-working to accommodate pro-coal forces in its ranks'.[37]

Pearson had his supporters inside the fossil fuel power network. Nationals leader and Deputy Prime Minister Barnaby Joyce vented his frustration at BHP for shafting Pearson. He claimed that the company had allowed itself to be hijacked by anti-coal activism. Pearson, lamented Joyce: 'had to contend with an incredibly well-organised and highly-funded green campaign which I believe is fundamentally at odds with the economic prosperity of Australia'.[38] And, signifying that it had lost none of its verve for fighting the coal wars, the *Australian*'s outspoken right-wing columnist Janet Albrechtsen wrote: 'We lost a valuable voice last week when Brendan Pearson was effectively shoved out of his job as boss of the Minerals Council of Australia by those who prefer feel-good corporate bromides and green myths over energy facts and figures'.[39]

The defenders of the export coal industry failed to appreciate the structural shift that Pearson's departure signified in the debate about coal and Australia's energy future. Caught in the cult of coal, they couldn't see that coal was becoming increasingly at odds with the interests of corporate Australia. Journalist Ben Potter summed up the shift taking place in corporate boardrooms. As an anonymous source told him: 'BHP got their man ... BHP and Rio Tinto were never comfortable with his [Pearson's] coal advocacy'.[40] Nevertheless, BHP was playing something of a double game. It continued to derive a small, but important, part of its revenue from coal, but it appeared to believe that it wasn't worth the damage to its public relations to continue to openly promote the industry. With public acceptance of coal waning and the costs of renewables continuing to plummet, both big miners came to see that promoting coal, and the MCA's role in it, were 'lost causes'.

In something amounting to a threat, BHP announced in its review at the end of 2017 that it would withdraw from the World Coal Association and quit the MCA in 12 months' time unless the council backed away from its high-profile lobbying for the coal industry.[41] These were further clear signs that the anti-Adani forces were having an impact. Rarely has corporate Australia been forced into such concessions and in such a public manner.

Northern Australia Infrastructure Fund is nobbled

When #StopAdani was formed, the Northern Australia Infrastructure Facility (NAIF) was high on its list of targets. So when Annastacia Palaszczuk called a Queensland state election for 25 November 2017, Adani and the Carmichael mine were guaranteed to be among the prominent issues. The Liberal National Party opposition backed the mine to the hilt, as did Pauline Hanson's right-wing populist party, One Nation, which was expected to perform well in its founder's home state. But no-one expected the extent to which the mine would dominate the election and shape its outcome.

The premier was forced to walk a fine line between support for the project in North Queensland and opposition to it in key inner-city Brisbane seats. But she also needed to tread carefully in her own party. Deep divisions within the government over the mine had continued to bubble away since her unlikely election win over Campbell Newman in 2015.

When she was elected, few Queenslanders knew much about her. In fact, she is the quintessential political operative: the daughter of a state Labor MP, a background in student politics and law, and roles as a Labor political advisor before standing in her MP father's Brisbane electorate in 2006. With this background she was destined for a political career. As one journalist has written, her 'career is one dominated by a devotion to education and to the craft of politics'.[42] Her image as a woman with a warmth of personality and an aversion to risk-taking was an appealing contrast with Newman's abrasive, crash-through style. Some thought her a 'plodding performer' as a minister in the Bligh Labor government[43] and, consequently, nothing suggested that she would seriously take on the power of the Queensland resources industry. As premier she played much the same political game as all politicians in the major parties have done – reassuring voters that everything was being done to protect the Great Barrier Reef while supporting the massive expansion of the coal industry.

During the 2015 election, Palaszczuk had criticised Newman for 'throwing a bucket of taxpayers' cash ... at one particular company [Adani]'.[44] Following her election win, the new premier quickly offered Adani unlimited access to the underground water of the Great Artesian Basin and the status of critical infrastructure project. In 2016, her government wrote to the Commonwealth suggesting they look into funding the railway line through NAIF; then in May 2016, Deputy Premier Jackie Trad refuted that suggestion only to be contradicted the following day by Treasurer Curtis Pitt, who said the government's position was to support NAIF funding to the project.[45] In fact, in November 2016 he told state parliament that since the government came to office 'we have been working closely with the Commonwealth government to facilitate ... the NAIF ... in North Queensland'.[46]

Labor was torn by an ugly left–right factional fight over the Carmichael mine. War raged between Palaszczuk's pro-Adani right faction and Trad's anti-Adani left faction.[47] Tensions spilled out into the public when Cabinet tried to resolve a royalties deal for Adani. With the company threatening to walk away from the project, Palaszczuk was forced to bring in Labor's Mr Fix-It, David Barbagallo, described as a 'political head kicker' with 'business nous'. As he calmed the tensions inside the party he was in contact with Adani, meeting with their lobbyists, Next Level Strategic Services, twice in the first two weeks in the job.[48] They did a deal which gave the company a discounted rate on royalties in the early years of production but which, over the long term, would require it to pay the full amount of royalties. A classic compromise had been reached from Palaszczuk's initial position (the same as former Premier Campbell Newman) to grant a royalty 'holiday' to the company.

Renewed questions were raised about how much change had occurred in Queensland under Palaszczuk's government. From being a critic of Newman's support for the mine, she became one of its prime advocates and she maintained close links to the state's mining industry and its lobbyists. In August 2017, she arranged for Cameron Milner, a director with Next Level Strategic Services, to come into Labor headquarters to help run her re-election campaign.[49]

Milner has been described as 'one of the most experienced and best-networked players in the Queensland ALP'. As state secretary of the party, he masterminded election campaigns for Peter Beattie, Anna Bligh and Kevin Rudd, before establishing his lobbying firm and 'bagging' Adani as a client. He came to work with Palaszczuk under an agreement that enabled him to keep his day job with his lobbying firm. It was a surprising appointment to say the least, given the decades of scandals in Queensland about the power wielded by the mining lobby and the lack of transparency in government. The premier breezily dismissed concerns about conflict of interest. Anti-Adani groups were outraged. Ben Pennings from the direct action protest group Galilee Blockade gatecrashed a press conference held by Jackie Trad where he 'yelled questions about Mr Milner'. He was eventually removed. A spokesperson from GetUp! complained that the Milner appointment was 'a massive conflict of interest', especially during an election campaign.[50]

In the lead-up to the Queensland election, Adani suffered a further blow to its reputation when ABC *Four Corners* aired Stephen

Long's investigation of Adani's environmental reputation in India. It was yet another powerful indictment of the company's record of destruction and non-compliance. But Long had a parallel story to tell as well – Adani's role as a corporate bully in its own country. While gathering information about Adani's operations, the *Four Corners* team had their cameras shut down and their footage deleted, and were detained and questioned for hours by police. The team were 'left in no doubt that their investigations into the Indian company triggered the police action'.[51] In environmental circles, the program created 'a massive amount of internet and social media traffic'.[52]

On 9 November, the #StopAdani movement launched its Queensland election campaign in Brisbane and Mackay 'to kick off an even more targeted effort in the coming weeks right up until election day'. The aim was to ensure that 'all candidates reject Adani's dirty mine'.[53] Ellen Roberts, lead organiser in Queensland for GetUp!, explained that its members 'are primed and ready to take it to Adani this election. Our members will be holding phone banking parties, with the goal of making over 100 000 calls to the voters who will determine the future of Adani's billion-dollar bail-out. We'll also be on the ground talking to people and going hard online with digital ads'.

Millie Anthony, Queensland campaigner for the Australian Youth Climate Coalition, said, 'AYCC will be focussed on trailing candidates to highlight the Stop Adani message, doorknocking in Clayfield, talking to voters on their way to and from work and covering Brisbane with posters. Our mobile billboard will follow leaders on the campaign trail during the last two weeks of the election'.

The critical issue for the #StopAdani campaign was whether, if sufficient pressure was applied, Palaszczuk's hand could be forced to oppose the NAIF loan. Her government's signature was required to authorise the expenditure of the funds.

Once the election was underway, Labor's prevaricating stance on the mine became a liability as #StopAdani's months of work in the state paid dividends. 'Labor found that they couldn't cut through on any other issue', recalls Paul Oosting. By the end of the first week the premier was forced to concede that she would block any NAIF loan. As Alex McKinnon observed in the *Saturday Paper*, the huge swing to the Greens in opinion polls in a swathe of inner-city Brisbane electorates was confirmation that 'anti-Adani sentiment was hurting them [the government] enough to force a response'. Described later as the 'Adani veto bombshell', it was seen as 'the turning point in the election'.[54] Henceforth, it became the Adani election.

This was a clear victory for the #StopAdani movement. Yet there's no doubting the influential role GetUp! played in the campaign. Not only were they the largest activist organisation in the Queensland election, they rivalled the major parties with their on-ground resources, deploying 749 volunteers who together made 130 000 calls to electors in 10 targeted seats and who dispatched 65 000 pieces of direct mail.[55] After Palaszczuk was forced to renounce her support for the NAIF loan, the focus of GetUp!'s campaign was directed at the Liberal Party, which continued to support the loan.[56] But in reality, grassroots campaigners kept up a focus on both parties during the campaign. Neither Opposition leader Tim Nicholls nor Palaszczuk could appear anywhere in the state 'without confronting a cohort of anti-Adani diehards waving signs for the cameras'.[57]

And Palaszczuk wasn't about to get any help from federal Labor. Federal Opposition leader Bill Shorten decided to keep a low profile in the election, largely, it was believed, to avoid awkward questions on where he stood on the mine. 'Shorten tied himself in knots', one journalist recalled, 'trying to articulate his various positions on the mine earlier this year, sometimes changing his mind mid sentence'.[58]

Much like Shorten, Palaszczuk had a contradictory stance on the mine. She wanted to have a bet each way on Labor's policy. Well-known as a cautious political operator, she was ultimately driven by the politics of the issue. An overwhelming number of Queenslanders did not support a government hand-out to Adani, which meant that she was forced to announce the veto on the loan. It worked in her government's favour. As Sarah Elks, who covered the election for the *Australian,* later wrote of the premier's victory:

> Operatives, strategists and senior players from both sides of the political divide have told the *Weekend Australian* that the Adani veto was political gold ... It diverted the attention of the green activists who had dogged the Premier's first campaign week, and encouraged the powerful GetUp! ... to barrack for the ALP.[59]

Ruling out a loan for Adani through the NAIF doesn't necessarily mean that the railway line to Abbot Point won't be built. Immediately after the election the Palaszczuk government was asked whether or not it would support an application to the NAIF from Aurizon for the railway.[60] But in February 2018, Aurizon withdrew its application for a loan to build the railway, leaving Adani further isolated.[61]

Chinese banks pull out

Once all the Australian banks had walked away from Adani, and the NAIF had been taken out of play, Adani had little option but to try to secure finance from China.

Since it announced its plans for the Carmichael mine in 2011, Adani has failed to meet a succession of deadlines it announced to begin work on the Carmichael site. These failures alone confirm that the company has struggled to convince banks and financial institutions to back its plans. As mentioned, established banks, including the biggest coal-funding banks in the world, dropped out early as potential funders over environmental concerns about the project. And, as already discussed, the cosy deal with the State Bank of India had quickly unravelled under charges of cronyism. China became the only viable option for Adani.

On the surface, China appeared an unlikely starter for the project. Funding massive new coal projects by China's state-controlled banks seems contrary to President Xi Jinping's commitments, in the wake of the Paris climate talks, to reduce its carbon emissions by cleaning up its coal sector and by a massive investment in renewable energy. Yet, like many of the world's carbon-intensive countries, there is a difference between China's domestic and international commitments on climate change. As environmental journalist Beth Walker has pointed out, while China cuts coal at home, its state-owned companies and banks continue to drive new coal expansion overseas. China's efforts to cut emissions are being 'undercut by Chinese backed coal power plants planned and under construction from Indonesia to Pakistan, Turkey to the Balkans – as well as in Africa and Latin America'. These plants 'could boost global emissions and lock developing countries into fossil fuel intensive energy systems for decades'.[62]

China's banks are global players. According to S&P Global Intelligence, of the 23 biggest banks in the world, six are Chinese. At the end of the day, any one of these big Chinese banks could fund the project if they wanted to. But, as state-owned banks, any finance, especially on a project as large as Carmichael, would most likely require approval by the Chinese Communist government.

The Turnbull government appreciated the need for such protocol. Through the Department of Foreign Affairs and Trade (DFAT), it wrote to the Chinese government's National Development and Reform Commission assuring them that the project had secured all necessary environmental approvals. The action only came to light in late October 2017 in a Senate estimates committee hearing during which Francis Adamson, the secretary of the department, revealed the information under questioning. Of course, this was not the first time that diplomatic action was leveraged to support the Australian coal industry. However, the media, together with Senate crossbenchers, worried about the Australian government spruiking a foreign corporation to a foreign country. Yet both Attorney-General George Brandis and Adamson expressed ignorance about who had generated the letter.[63]

Adamson said that the letter had not been written by anyone in her department but her 'interpretation' of its genesis lay with a request to government from Adani, who wanted to confirm government support for the project. For his part, Brandis didn't know whether Adani had requested the letter but defended its purpose, 'to dispel the misinformation campaign from the radical left'. Adamson only deepened the mystery surrounding the depth of the government's role in supporting Adani when she acknowledged that DFAT had 'several hundred pages' of information relating to formal representations that it had made to potential financiers of the project. This sat at odds with her comment that it wasn't 'DFAT's role to seek finance for the project'.[64]

In fact, Trade Minister Steve Ciabo and Resources and Northern Development Minister Matt Canavan later met with the deputy head of the Chinese National Development and Reform Commission in Cairns to discuss investment co-operation in northern Australia.[65] Given the previous letter the government sent to the commission, it's most likely that Adani was high on their agenda for discussion.

Only months later was the role of the Turnbull government in helping Adani seek finance for the mine revealed. Documents obtained under a Freedom of Information request by Tom Swann from The Australia Institute clearly show that Adani asked the Australian government to help secure funding from the Chinese and that DFAT acted upon this request. One email was sent from Canberra to China and Indian embassy staff with the subject line: 'China: Adani's Carmichael coal project – update on project financing request'.[66]

Before any of this information came to light, Adani had publicly confirmed long-held speculation that it was in talks with Chinese backers. 'Adani seeks finance from China', blared the headline in the *Australian* on 31 October 2017. Adani Mining's chief executive in Australia, Jeyakumar Janakaraj, told Reuters that the company was in 'advanced discussions' with Chinese export credit agencies.[67] How far advanced such discussions really were and whether any attempt had been made to secure the requisite approval from the Chinese government is hard to determine. However, the letter Adani had obtained from the Australian government had already been sent to Beijing and Adani no doubt believed that this would strengthen the company's hand with authorities. In addition, the ABC reported in early November that the Chinese state-owned enterprise, China Machinery Engineering Corporation, was in negotiations with Adani for financial backing.[68]

Announcing that it was in 'advanced discussions' proved a tactical error for Adani. It prompted swift counter-measures from influential figures. Geoff Cousins made representations to the Chinese embassy in Canberra, along with prominent investment banker Mark Burrows, to try to head off any official approval in China for a loan to Adani. Cousins and Burrows put a case to the embassy officials that China's international reputation, built up over recent years, in strengthening its financial governance and developing renewable energy would be put at risk if it backed the Carmichael mine. The pair also provided evidence that the Australian people did not support the mine. They received confirmation that any investment from a Chinese corporation would require the approval of the Chinese government. No such proposal had been put to the Chinese. Cousins and Burrows were also given a commitment that the issues they had raised would be passed onto Beijing.[69]

Chinese authorities were also under pressure from another source. Former Labor foreign minister Bob Carr, whose involvements since retiring from politics in 2013 included a position as director of the Australia-China Relations Institute at the University of Technology Sydney, also became involved in lobbying China to drop any funding of the Carmichael mine. Cousins had rung Carr, prior to his visit to the Chinese embassy in Canberra, seeking advice on protocol for the visit. When Cousins informed him of the nature of the visit, Carr realised the opportunity to make a bigger impact on the Chinese. On the same day that Cousins had planned his trip to talk with senior officials at the Chinese embassy, Carr was due to have lunch with the Chinese Ambassador in Sydney. Carr told Cousins: 'If I get a really good brief from you I'll draw him to one side and I will say the same things to him that you will be relaying to officials in Canberra'.

Carr's involvement continued. For several weeks during October, he was involved in countering 'the attempt by the Turnbull government to secure the project with Chinese funding'. After direct discussions with political and financial leaders in China, he revealed that he had been told by 'a senior government official' that no Chinese financial institution would fund the mine.[70] Cousins also received confirmation that 'Beijing has listened to your concerns'.

By early December 2017, two of China's biggest banks, the Industrial & Commercial Bank of China and the China Construction Bank, had issued statements that they would not be providing funding to the Carmichael mine. Equally significant was confirmation from the Chinese Embassy that the Chinese Machinery Engineering Corps had terminated their negotiations with Adani.[71] These declarations, while leaving open the possibility that one of the other big Chinese banks might come to Adani's rescue, was nonetheless seen as another nail in the coffin. All up it looked like the Chinese government was sending a message that they wanted nothing to do with the Carmichael mine.

Federal politics and support for Adani

The continuous campaigning against Adani has taken a toll on the pro-coal sentiment among both the major parties in federal parliament. Not only have they witnessed on-the-ground campaigns against the banks and against the Palaszczuk government, they are receiving regular anti-Adani traffic through their inboxes and social media accounts. Since the beginning of 2017, federal Liberal MPs around the country have been feeling the pressure of the campaign: '[They] are being put on the spot by either GetUp! or local #StopAdani groups who are asking them point-blank whether they support the mine or not'.[72]

The pressure is also on federal Labor to oppose the mine. As this book has shown, Labor has long tried to maintain a dual position of supporting renewable energy together with expanding the export coal industry. The fallacies and contradictions in this position are now causing divisions in the party. Under Shorten's leadership, Labor has been trying to hold together rival constituencies: its inner-city vote, which has been under increasing threat from the Greens, and its 'coal belt' seats in North Queensland. These tensions played out in the Queensland state election.

From his previous position of backing the Adani mine, Shorten attempted to soften Labor's stance. His journey though the minefield of Adani politics is revealing in several ways, but especially the tortured position Labor now finds itself in on the issue.

According to Geoff Cousins, Shorten rang him just before Christmas 2017 seeking help on how Labor could change its position on Adani without incurring sovereign risk through cancelling the approval granted for the mine. Shorten asked Cousins to accompany him on a trip to North Queensland to work through the options, but to do so out of the glare of publicity. Cousins, accompanied by ACF's CEO, Kelly O'Shanassy, offered him confidentiality for the duration of the trip, but couldn't guarantee he could keep their discussions out of the media longer than that.

An escorted trip by a political leader deep into iconic environmental areas is a rare event in Australia. Bob Brown complained that he extended the offer many times for leaders from both major political parties to join him on a tour into Tasmania's South West Wilderness. Only Graham Richardson, who had been environment minister under Bob Hawke, and later Mark Latham, Labor Opposition leader during John Howard's prime ministership, took up the offer. Richardson was so affected by his trip that he worked to protect the very wilderness area that Brown had been advocating for, but Latham, although offering to protect 200 000 hectares of Tasmanian forest, was also under pressure to be seen to protect timber workers' jobs.[73]

Shorten was taking a political risk when he reached out to Cousins for a guided tour; would he respond more like Richardson or Latham? However, he appeared to have been deeply affected by the experience. As Cousins later explained:

> We had him [Shorten] many kilometres out to sea off Port Douglas, snorkelling, which was interesting to see – a leader of the opposition snorkelling around a very remote place. We had with us Professor Terry Hughes, one of the world's leading experts on reef science, and he had laminated photographs of that exact spot over the last many years so Shorten could see, whilst he was snorkelling above, what that exact area looked like 10 years ago, five years ago, and so on. He was visibly affected by that, he was in the water a good long while. It was quite a dramatic thing to see a senior politician actually prepared to look deeply into that.[74]

Cousins said they then flew over the Adani mine site and Shorten was able to see the absence of activity on that site or around it.

> We then landed nearby and we had a distinguished groundwater scientist with us who was able to show him some remarkable natural springs, which have plants in them which don't exist anywhere else on Earth, and discuss with him the

impacts on groundwater and the artesian basin. He had to walk a long way and spend a lot of time with people, and he did that extremely well. At the end of it all, Shorten said to me this was compelling material to see and hear.[75]

Cousins gave Shorten legal advice that the ACF had obtained which maintained that revoking the approval for the mine would not trigger a sovereign risk issue, or leave the government exposed to a compensation claim from the company, because the power in Section 145 of the EPBC Act to revoke an approval 'is clear and unambiguous, and is essential for the minister to protect the environment from significant impacts not assessed prior to an approval being granted'.[76]

At the end of the trip, Shorten and Cousins sat down, and, according to Cousins, Shorten said 'How do we crystallise this in essence?' Cousins replied:

> I told him you've got to get to the point where you have a
> clear policy with action, and appropriate action in this case
> relates to a revoking of the licence. Anything less than that is
> nice statements. What you need to say is the following: 'When
> we are in government, if the evidence is as compelling as we
> presently believe it to be regarding the approval of the Adani
> mine, we will revoke the licence as allowed in the act.' Shorten
> said to me 'I get it, I understand.' He said 'I'm going to lead
> on that, I'm going to go forward, there comes a time when you
> need to lead and this is it.'

Yet Shorten later called Cousins to inform him of delays in announcing the new policy because he was having difficulties in bringing all his colleagues around to the new position.

The approach of the March 2018 federal by-election for the inner-city Melbourne federal seat of Batman revealed the difficulty

Shorten was still having changing Labor's policy on the Carmichael mine. The #StopAdani campaign had succeeded in making the mine among the most prominent issues in the campaign, and Labor was in a two-way contest with the Greens, uncertain of its hold on the seat. As veteran political reporter Jim Middleton explained, Adani is 'a generic metaphor for: do you want to save the environment? Are you in support of real measures to prevent climate change? So it really plays'.[77]

Shorten opted for a heavily qualified position for Labor on the Carmichael mine. In February 2018, he stood in front of a 'Stop Adani' sign in Melbourne and declared to reporters that he was 'increasingly sceptical' of the project, a signal that Labor was moving to the position he had indicated to Geoff Cousins.[78]

However, after his appearance in Melbourne for the Batman by-election, Shorten was in Townsville, where he declared that there was a role for coal in Australia and that the Carmichael mine was 'just another project'. Behind the scenes the pressure had been piling up on Shorten from the national branch of the Construction, Forestry, Mining and Energy Union (CFMEU) and its members in North Queensland. As Tony Maher, the national president of the CFMEU, explained to the press, any move by Labor to block the mine 'would expose Labor politically in Queensland, and open a divisive debate within the ALP about the future of coal mines in Australia'.[79]

Finally, Cousins rang Shorten and told him that he could no longer publicly hold back on the details of their trip; there was pressure to call out Labor's lack of a definitive position on the mine. A strategy meeting of relevant environment groups was subsequently held 'and it was agreed that we would now go on the attack'.[80]

Cousins' motive in going public proved controversial; had the hard operator of the environment movement over-reached, forcing Shorten to retreat? For Cousins the motive was straightforward and had its intended impact. After his interview on *7.30* detailing the trip to the reef and his intention to change party policy, Shorten told the media that he was personally opposed to the mine. As Cousins explained: 'Even though he [Shorten] subsequently danced around this commitment, if you were a potential funder of the mine you would have to weigh up the risk that, as a potential prime minister, Shorten might find a way to knock this thing over'. In other words, the intention to release the details of Shorten's trip was a continuation of the strategy of targeting the financial sector.

As the publicity over Shorten's trip to the Great Barrier Reef confirmed, the major political parties are reluctant to shed their pro-coal positions and adjust to the reality that the battle for public opinion on Adani has been won by the progressive forces opposed to it. ReachTEL undertook a public opinion poll on 25 January 2018, commissioned by the #StopAdani Alliance. It found 65.1 per cent of Australians opposed or strongly opposed the Carmichael mine, up from 52 per cent in March 2017. Significantly, 75 per cent of Labor voters and 43 per cent of Liberal voters opposed the mine.[81]

Based on these figures, it will be politically risky for either of the major parties to actively campaign on a pro-Adani policy going into the next federal election (due in the second half of 2019). And this is not just because the public opposes the Carmichael mine. From the seven years he has spent fighting Australia's export coal industry, Paul Oosting can detect a growing sophistication in the public's understanding of the wider implications arising from the fight against the Carmichael mine. When he began working on Get-Up!'s environmental campaigns in 2011, 'it was difficult to explain the connection between Australia's export coal industry and global warming and the threat to the Great Barrier Reef. That debate has come a long way and the Adani campaign has been a key focus for the public to understand those links'.[82] Of course, this effort has reflected the work of a wide range of environmental groups, scientists, business groups dependent on the reef, and the Greens.

The significance of the opposition to Adani which has been built up over the past seven years is hard to overstate. The power of the fossil fuel network has suffered a severe blow. The public has seen through its relentless pro-coal evangelism. And the bipartisan tradition of endorsing the exploitation of Australia's natural resources as essential for jobs and export income is no longer the shibboleth it used to be. After a string of defeats for environmentally harmful projects in the past decade, including the end of exploiting old-growth forests, the curbs placed on coal seam gas and the defeat of the proposal to industrialise the Kimberly Coast, it is clear that Australians no longer give development projects the open-ended support of previous years. Neither of the major parties have fully embraced this reality.

The last line of defence

Few individuals have fought the Adani mine as relentlessly as Adrian Burragubba and the Wangan and Jagalingou peoples. He and his supporters have used the court system to expose the weaknesses of the native title system to provide self-determination for Aboriginal people. He's helped stimulate a renewed dialogue about the *Native Title Act 1993* and helped stall commencement on the mine.

I sat down with Adrian and his political advisor, Anthony Esposito, at a café on Brisbane's South Bank in January 2018. I was apprehensive. What would he make of my understanding of his cause? Aboriginal leaders are understandably wary of white researchers and commentators. I had a page of questions I was interested in asking him, unsure which would resonate. Having studied his campaign, I was clear about one thing: the native title system in Australia is broken if it could, on the one hand, grant a lease for a mine that would devastate his people's traditional country while, simultaneously, finding that his people's rights as traditional owners would not be infringed. As I explained my position, we relaxed into an open, friendly and informative conversation.

I have studied and written about Aboriginal and environmental activists in several projects. Invariably such people are charismatic, with a capacity to inspire others and a fearlessness about confronting power structures. However, the toll on their personal lives is high. And so it is with Burragubba. The fight to revive the spirit of Eddie Mabo has come at a personal cost; it consumes his every waking moment, disrupts his family life and has put on hold his previous professional life. He survives on donations.

By the time we met, the Wangan and Jagalingou had suffered a string of defeats in the courts – two adverse decisions in the National Native Title Tribunal (NNTT), as previously discussed. They fared no better in the Federal Court or in the Queensland Court of Appeal, each of which invoked 'black letter' law to uphold a narrow interpretation of the *Native Title Act*. Even the lies that Adani told about the number of jobs that would be generated by the project were not sufficient grounds for courts to reconsider the legality of the approval process.

However, nothing symbolised the intersecting power of mining interests and government more than the so-called McGlade decision of the Federal Court which came down in early February 2017. Instigated by the Noongar people of south-west Western Australia, the court found that Indigenous Land Use Agreements (ILUA) were null and void if they weren't signed by all native title applicants. In effect, all such ILUAs were placed in limbo. The Wangand & Jagalingow moved quickly to have their agreement with Adani struck out. But the Turnbull government moved at double speed to have the problem rectified. In what was widely acknowledged as 'a fix for Adani', the government quickly had legislation before parliament that restored the previous arrangement whereby ILUAs could be granted with a majority of applicants.[83] As Murrawah Johnson explained, the lobbying by the Queensland government, the mining lobby and the Queensland Resources Council, and the federal Attorney-General, was dedicated to 'undo[ing] the McGlade decision, and they're hoping that this [would] keep the Adani ILUA alive'.[84] To Adrian Burragubba it was a reminder of how the system is geared towards powerful interests.

However, at the time of writing (March 2018) the Wangan and Jagalingou have not exhausted their legal options to stop the mine. They are awaiting an appeal in the Federal Court which challenges the 'fake' ILUA with a hearing set for March. By now, Burragubba knows what he's up against – a set of interlocking interests that work together; hostile coverage in the Murdoch press; criticism from some Aboriginal spokespeople; and a conservative legal system that sees little consequence in the Aboriginal culture that is set to be destroyed no matter how unreliable the data produced about jobs and economic benefits.

'We are not done yet', explains Burragubba. The Wangan and Jagalingou intend to exhaust all the legal avenues including a possible appeal to the High Court. As Burragubba says, 'Adani cannot move on the critical infrastructure for the mine until they get us out of the way'.[85]

As we concluded our interview, it was hard not to be struck by the tenacity of Burragubba's vision of self-determination for his people and his capacity to explain the importance of spiritual connection to the land that remains the source of the Wangan and Jagalingou's identity.

Adani – a house of cards?

Gautam Adani should be a worried man. By the end of 2017 he had faced a string of reversals in Australia at the hands of the environmental movement which called into question the overall health of his company. An international credit ratings agency recently listed Adani in a group of highly indebted and over-leveraged Indian companies that it called 'House of Debt' companies: Adani's gross borrowings were approximately A$2.5 billion with a mounting debt to earnings ratio.

Adani has intensified its attempts to stifle critics of its operations. As mentioned in Chapter 2, Adani has tried to limit the ability of critics to mount court actions on environmental grounds; more recently it has attempted to bully its few critics in the Indian media. In recent years India has struggled, and largely failed, to uphold the standards of a robust free press. In 2017, India was ranked 136 out of 180 for press freedom according to the World Press Freedom Index.[86] Those concerned about the freedom of the press in India report 'an extraordinary level of submissiveness displayed by the media'.[87] Recently, intimidation against journalists doing investigative stories has been waged through the technique known as Strategic Lawsuits against Public Participation (SLAPPs). The technique amounts to vexatious litigation by wealthy corporations which issue defamation suits against critics in an attempt to silence them, knowing the likelihood of winning is remote and secondary to their motivations. Rare in the Australian judicial system, the most egregious SLAPP suit here was the so-called Gunns20 case issued by Gunns Ltd against critics of the its proposed pulp mill in the Tamar Valley.[88]

In India, corporate attacks on the media are backed up by the Modi government. According to his critics, Modi is seen as dedicated to 'muzzling liberal voices who are still struggling to survive in India's media landscape. Hindu nationalist Modi loves to hate liberal-leaning media'.[89]

In such a climate it is not surprising to find Adani at the forefront of mounting SLAPP suits against the media. In July 2017, the editor of the *Economic & Political Weekly*, Paranjoy Guha Thakurta:

> became the first top-level editorial casualty of corporate India's increasing tendency to file multi-crore defamation cases as a means of countering critical reporting, resigning after the directors of the trust which runs the storied journal ordered him to take down an article on the Adani group.[90]

The articles had raised questions about the company's finances and tax arrangements, which Adani claimed were defamatory to its reputation.

Adani also had in its sights the *Wire*, a small and relatively new multimedia news platform that has sought to build credibility through its fearless approach to investigative reporting and 'speaking the truth'.[91]

Adani had already issued half a dozen SLAPP suits against the *Wire* when, in November 2017, it decided to publish a series of five articles on Adani's Australian operations written by Kabir Agarwal, an Indian freelance journalist. Aware that the Indian public had been ill-informed about the controversy surrounding the company in Australia and the mounting civil campaign against it, Agarwal had travelled to Australia in an effort to 'bring to the Indian reader, the entire Adani story in Australia'. Before being accepted by the *Wire*, Agarwal had been rebuffed by other media outlets with his series on Adani out of concern 'that Adani will sue them'.[92]

After the first of his articles was published in the *Wire*, Agarwal was approached by a representative from Adani expressing the company's displeasure over his work and then issued a direct threat: 'You must remember that we have a history of filing law suits against the *Wire*'. Agarwal heard from Adani after the second article – dealing with the impact of the Carmichael on global warming – had appeared. Angry with the information from experts that Agarwal had cited, the company requested the opportunity to offer their own information on the issue. Given 24 hours to respond, the company never got back to Agarwal. Following publication of all five articles, Adani issued its defamation writ. It claimed that its global reputation was damaged by the Australian financial experts Agarwal quoted saying that the mine did not stand up financially.

Concerned about the writ, Agarwal phoned a contact that he had in Adani's Indian headquarters and inquired why the company had targeted the *Wire* 'when you know we're not going to stop writing about Adani and you are not going to win this law suit'. The answer was blunt: 'You [the *Wire*] might not be afraid but other outlets, they might be afraid. Our idea is to scare these others ... to build a perception that Adani should not be touched'.[93]

In all likelihood, a court will eventually throw out the defamation suit against Agarwal's articles, but in the meantime, they bear the burden of its impacts: 'Instead of spending time doing actual journalism, we have to spend it with the lawyers'.

Adani's reputation in India as a corporate bully continues to sit side by side with its image as a rogue corporation. According to Agarwal, Adani has an unsavoury image as a corporation among Indians who know its track record and closeness to Modi.[94]

However, in keeping with his restless entrepreneurial spirit Adani has, over recent years, moved into new fields of investment: the manufacture of solar power; jet fighters and drones; and fertilisers and smelting among others.[95] Some commentators think that the company has expanded too quickly in too many directions and relied too heavily on borrowing to finance its diverse operations.[96] It is at risk of overreach and critics of the company have raised doubts about its ability to repay its debts in a timely manner.

Adani's power plants in Mundra suffered a 'jaw dropping' decline of 418 per cent between 2016 and 2017. Such losses have forced Adani to announce that it would step away from using expensive imported coal. This confirms the assessment of financial experts that the Carmichael mine is unviable under Adani's business plan.[97] Unable to sell the plant, Adani's best hope is a government bailout.[98] The *Financial Times* reported that one senior investment banker in Mumbai claimed that most banks in India 'will already be nearing their regulated lending limits to the Adani Group'.[99] And, although Adani's relationship with Modi remains strong, it can no longer rely on the same undivided attention it once received: 'Modi has other corporate houses to take care of, so that Adani is one among many now'.[100]

Adani's Australian operations have become a drag on the overall performance of the company. The Abbot Point Coal Terminal – the crux of Adani's so-called 'pit to plug' strategy – is running the risk of becoming a stranded asset if the Carmichael mine doesn't proceed. The port is running at half its capacity and refinancing it will prove tricky. According to financial analyst Tim Buckley, the value of the port has been tied to the success of the mine.[101] But, as Buckley adds, if Adani were to write off its Australian assets – the port and the lease on the mine – 'that would remove US$1.5 billion from the company's value book, leaving it with debt worth more than the value of the company'.[102]

And there's little to doubt about the long-term projections for the declining demand for thermal coal. The road to renewables has been a bumpy one and India has bucked recent trends by maintaining its high usage of coal. However, in November 2017, the new Indian Energy Minister RK Singh committed to significantly lift the country's renewable energy targets. Most experts see a faster than expected drop in the price of renewables and the consequent danger for the export thermal coal sector.[103]

While Adani decides on his next move, there is no let-up in the campaign against his company. The Batman by-election generated near-saturated media coverage of the issue and, behind the scenes, the Australian Centre for Corporate Responsibility (ACCR) shifted its campaign against the MCA from BHP to Rio Tinto in preparation for its annual general meeting in April 2018. As it did with BHP, ACCR is seeking to move a motion, from a group of shareholders, for Rio to review its membership of the MCA. Executive Director Brynn O'Brien explained that ACCR had been engaging with Rio in the early months of 2018 on the issue of its membership: 'Rio's investors have similar concerns to BHP's, about the risks to shareholder value that flows from misaligned ... [by MCA] on climate and energy policy issues.[104]

By mid-March 2018, the pressure exerted on the MCA by its

two biggest funders appears to have had an effect. When the powerful lobby group released an updated energy and climate change policy, it was hard to ignore how obviously coal had been downgraded, mentioned only once in the document. This was a far cry from its previous policy document issued in 2015, which championed the role of coal, claiming that technology gains were dramatically cutting the carbon footprint of coal-fired power, and emphasised the role coal had played and would continue to play in meeting the energy needs of developing nations.[105] The new document promoted the role of the mining industry in creating the new low emissions technologies. Is the turnaround just another attempt at 'greenwash'? Even if the new policy is as much about spin as substance, it represents a substantial retreat in the MCA's willingness to promote coal.

Australia's 'big four' banks, the international banks, the NAIF and the MCA have all been brought to heel by the campaign against Adani. The campaign has had its ups and downs, including most recently in the Batman by-election, but the trend has been heading in the one direction: Adani has been backed into a corner.

Conclusion

Ideological fervour, propaganda, lies and institutional corruption have been the quartet of forces orchestrated by the fossil fuel power network that created and sustained the proposal to build the Carmichael mine. Employment has been the fig leaf of justification for the project. Large chunks of the case for the economic benefits have evaporated under legal challenge and when exposed by financial experts and investigative journalism. Australian governments have willingly embraced a rogue corporation; one depicted as such by Indian as well as Australian commentators.

Some have argued that the struggle surrounding Adani is a potent example of Australia's broken system of government. But 'broken' for whom? The system works very effectively for the oligarchy it has come increasingly to serve. Perhaps more aptly, the quick approval of the mine, the expansion at Abbot Point and the 'slush fund' created to fund the rail line from the Galilee Basin to Abbot Point, together with the attempts to quash dissent from environment groups and the cuts to their funding, confirm how skewed our democracy has become in serving corporate interests. Yet, if government exists to serve the national interest and to be accountable to people, the conflict over Adani raises disturbing questions about the health of our democracy.

The political support given to the mine offers a compelling insight into the realities of power in Australia. The combined influence of mining barons, their peak lobby groups, the lobbyists employed by the mining corporations along with News Corporation, the Institute of Public Affairs and the 'big four' banks has resulted in the consolidation of an oligarchic model of power in Australia, especially around fossil fuels. Together these interconnected interests captured the mainstream political parties and imposed a massive expansion of the coal industry on a public increasingly worried about climate change and the fate of the Great Barrier Reef.

Activist Anthony Esposito has spent years closely observing this dynamic:

> They [governments and the mining industry and lobbyists] are all in the same game. The system is geared to override human rights, first nation rights and democratic rights. It's geared towards … powerful interests and they govern the system. And they don't think its corrupt because it's normalised; everybody knows the rules of the game.[1]

And economist Tim Buckley has come to similar conclusions:

> I've studied every industry in Australia and I've never seen collusion between governments and industry in the way I've seen in coal mining. It's the revolving door of government and mining in Australia. They are just way too in bed with each other.[2]

Adani, of course, with his background in crony politics in India, believed he could stitch up the Australian approval system when he bought into the Galilee Basin. He surrounded himself with Australian political insiders who not only thought the same way but, presumably, told him what he wanted to hear. After all, why would he spend billions of dollars at Abbot Point and at the Carmichael site before he had even secured a land use agreement, finance or a railway to the port?

Of course, the fossil fuel power network promoting coal and the Carmichael mine engaged in relentless propaganda and lies about the economic benefits of the project and its environmental impact. This campaign is one of the most egregious examples of the infiltration of post-truth politics in Australia.[3] That the mine was 'good for humanity' was, perhaps, the starkest example of the alternative reality constructed to promote the mine. Not far behind were the claims about the health of the Great Barrier Reef made by the likes of then Queensland Premier Campbell Newman and current Foreign Minister Julie Bishop.

The cronyism and the propaganda that drove the proponents of the mine serve as another reminder of the institutional corruption at the heart of Australian democracy. Mining is especially prone to such corruption as the 2018 report from Transparency International, titled *Corruption Risks: Mining Approvals in Australia*, made clear. There is:

> A high potential for industry influence and state and policy capture in the awarding of approvals for large mining infrastructure projects in Western Australia and Queensland – State Agreements and coordinated projects. The research noted that the inadequate regulation of political donations and lobbyists, the movement of staff between government and industry, and the culture of mateship are significant factors that could enable influence to occur in the approval [process].[4]

These findings merely add to repeated warnings that Australia's international reputation for the integrity of its democracy has been in slow decline over recent years. The lack of a concerted national response to the issue of corruption confirms just how cosy the system has become in servicing corporate interests, of which the fossil fuel industry is among the most powerful. Political donations, the proliferation of lobbyists and lack of adequate regulation for them, and lucrative post-political careers in the corporate world grease the system. Neither of the major political parties has a comprehensive plan for democratic reform. Why would they? The system suits them.

The transformation of the political system has been dramatic. The political ties developed over several decades between the fossil fuel power network and the Liberal/National parties has meant the rise of anti-environmentalism as a mainstream feature of Australian political debate, along with the sidelining of science in the debate over policy. As a consequence, Australia is lagging behind international action on climate change in its quest to further support for the export coal industry. Along with the United States, our politics has been infused with a right-wing inspired, clownish debate on climate science which has masked the impact of Australia's role as a major exporter of climate change and in the growing global rate of premature death from air pollution. The fact that these issues rarely feature in the mainstream media or are taken up by the major parties highlights the anti-environmentalism that has been shaped by the fossil fuel power network. Labor has not been immune from its influence – reinforced by its trade union ties – as it has pursued the same fallacy as the Liberal/Nationals parties: that the export coal industry can grow without having a destructive impact.

The fight over Adani has exposed several deficiencies in Australia's environmental legal framework – the *Environment Conservation and Biodiversity Act 1999* – that is supposed to ensure that mega developments are in the national interest. These deficiencies include relying on companies' own environmental impact statements; the absence of any provision to take account of the impact of global warming; and the lack of any provision to take account of a proponent's environmental track record. Australia needs a revised legislative framework to protect the country's environment in an age of climate change. The fact that Australia already has record levels of species loss adds to the urgency of rethinking the protection of our unique environment.

However, there is no sugar-coating one of the greatest environmental challenges facing the nation. The further demise of the Great Barrier Reef – forecast by no less a figure than Sir David Attenborough[5] – is tragically symbolic of the creeping influence of anti-environmentalism into mainstream politics. None of the major parties has been prepared to unequivocally put the reef's long-term health before the interests of the fossil fuel industry. Over the next few decades the export coal industry in Australia is very likely to be in structural decline. However, as Kelly O'Shanassy, director of the Australian Conservation Foundation, correctly observes: 'The death of so much of our reef was not an accident. It was conscious choice. The government and coal companies knew this was coming yet for years they chose to undermine action on global warming. They laughed as they threw coal around Parliament'.[6]

Saving the remainder of the reef demands that the world transition out of coal and, as has been pointed out in this book, Australia must take a lead in this shift. Yet the Turnbull government continues to ignore this reality. In April 2018 it announced – to predictable fanfare – another package for the Great Barrier Reef. The addition of $500 million of funding doubles down on existing threats to the reef from water pollution and the crown-of-thorns starfish. In announcing the package, the government's hyperbole went into overdrive; the package was a 'game changer' and the reef would be protected for future generations.

Yet critics continue to remind the government that the major threat to the reef increasingly comes from climate change. And, as has been the pattern, the government appeared to time its announcement in the lead-up to the UNESCO World Heritage Committee meeting, scheduled for 24 June to 4 July.[7] Here was yet another smokescreen to cover up the government's support for the coal industry and its plans for the Galilee Basin.

The deficiencies in the National Native Title Tribunal process that have emerged in the fight against Adani mean it is time to reconsider this fundamentally flawed system. Aboriginal people still lack sovereignty, a fact highlighted by their inability to veto projects. Native title holders who choose to oppose development to protect their culture are powerless.

So, outside the narrow criterion of 'creating jobs', the very institutions of democracy failed in the Adani case to defend the national interest.

Yet the battle over Adani also reveals the robust side of Australian democracy. At the time of writing the network of power behind the plans to open up the Galilee Basin has suffered a series of severe blows. In time, it could well go down in history as one of the greatest environmental victories in Australia, if not the greatest.

The environmental and activist movements in Australia have been strengthened and invigorated by fighting Adani. Trends that have been fermenting over previous years have intensified, including harnessing social media to recruit mass memberships and to mount campaigns that target corporate interests effectively. Moreover, the links forged between national and international environmental organisations have given additional power to these groups which was lacking even a few years ago. The campaign against Adani is rated as the biggest environment campaign ever run in Australia[8] and it has united the environment and climate change movements. A deeply interconnected progressive political space has been created around #StopAdani. It is surely a portent of the future. As mentioned several times in this book, a number of corporate leaders have watched developments in this area with a growing awareness that they no longer have things quite their own way due to their vulnerability to social media campaigns.

Supporters of the Carmichael mine have begun to grasp that a victory for the environmental movement over Adani could well become reality. The *Australian* newspaper's veteran journalist Paul Kelly, who declared his support for the 'moral' case for the mine long advocated by the mining industry and its conservative supporters, can see the significance of any victory. 'Killing off Adani', he wrote:

> will bring progressive and green momentum to a zenith. On
> display will be its moral power, its ability to smash through
> government and court approvals, its capture of the financial
> sector and its delivery of a decisive blow to the once-strong
> pro-development, pro-coal ethos.[9]

Is it possible to speak of victory over the Carmichael mine? Judg-
ments on this matter differ. If Adani were a conventional corporation it would almost certainly be the case that options for funding
the mine have run out and that political support has dwindled in the
face of overwhelming public opinion. Logic says the mine is dead in
the water and that the environmental and activist movements have
secured possibly their greatest victory. Yet, as was the case with the
Gunns proposed woodchip mill in Tasmania, the formal death of
large corporate development projects can take a long time to settle.
In the case of Adani, the company's creditors and auditors will likely
force the issue by declaring the Carmichael mine and possibly even
Abbot Point stranded assets. That could be many months away if,
indeed, it does eventuate.

Yet a conventional ending for the Carmichael mine is not,
as matters stand, guaranteed. As discussed throughout this book,
Adani is a rogue corporation and it may continue to explore unconventional ways to raise funds to build the mine and explore markets
other than India. If nothing else, Gautum Adani has been dogged in
his pursuit of opening up the Galilee Basin. Thus, some in the environmental movement fear a loss of focus as pressure rises to move
scarce resources elsewhere. As Geoff Cousins is apt to remind his
fellow environmental activists: environmental battles 'are relentless
long-term marathons'.

But there is also a broader point about the current state of play
over the Carmichael mine. When, and if, the project is declared

stillborn, it represents just one battle in the ongoing war over coal. This will likely prove to be much tougher.

As Bob Brown and Tim Flannery warned more than a decade ago, Australia needs to transition away from coal. Just about every serious commentator on the future of energy now agrees. Yet there is no sign that this is even on the horizon of the major political parties. It is not clear whether the environmental and activist movements can together sustain their current effort for this larger challenge. Demand for thermal coal, at least in the short term, continues to defy predictions about its inevitable, long-term structural decline. From mid-2016, all of the Australian-listed thermal coal miners experienced rises in their share prices, reflecting continuing strong demand in Asian markets which Australia has helped develop. The coal barons and their lobbyists remain powerful and cashed up. Clive Palmer has a proposal before the federal government to mine the Galilee Basin.

Predictions on the future of thermal coal have been fluctuating wildly in the face of rapidly changing markets, new technology and the active role China has been playing in constructing new coal-fired power plants in the developing world. Nonetheless, the writing is on the wall for the future of coal. As the *Financial Times* noted in September 2017, 'the promise of eternally rising world demand for coal, which was the consensus expectation just a few years ago, can no longer be taken for granted'.[10] The prospect of pouring a billion dollars of public money into opening up the Galilee Basin seems more reckless than ever.

One useful starting point in refocusing on this larger challenge of ending coal would be to try to change the geopolitics of the fossil-fuel industry at the international level. Why is it that large fossil fuel-exporting nations, like Australia, incur no penalty for the climate change they export, often to less developed nations? Political leaders in Australia can get away with contributing modest targets for emissions reduction while being a major source of the global climate change problem. Minister for Northern Australia Matt Canavan shamelessly offered this deficiency as one of the justifications for the Carmichael mine.

Pressuring corporations that fund and benefit from coal mining is likely to be a continuing source of action to reduce greenhouse gas emissions. As the *Sydney Morning Herald* reported at the beginning of 2018:

> When it comes to corporate Australia and climate change, 2018 is shaping up as a perfect storm. Investors, regulators and litigation lawyers are all circling. Ramping up their scrutiny of how companies are planning for climate change, how they are tackling it, and what information they are releasing about the risks it poses to their operations.[11]

In this regard, the campaign waged against Australia's 'big four' banks, pressuring them into releasing stronger commitments on climate change and backing away from funding Adani, shows a path towards continued action on climate change. And, as mentioned above, there is growing pressure on corporations to declare the risk of climate change to their shareholders.

The lessons from Adani are clear. As messy as democratic politics often is, the collective actions of ordinary people are needed to hold vested interests to account. Whether collective action will save the world from catastrophic climate change is a difficult question to answer. Ahead of the November 2017 UN climate talks in Bonn, climate negotiators warned 3°C of warming by 2100 was an increasing possibility. The world map of human suffering would be redrawn and Australia cannot escape its contribution. The Adani project would simply exacerbate Australia's role as an exporter of climate change and a laggard in taking action. Most Australians do not support this outcome, but the oligarchs keep pushing it. It is surely time this power was curtailed.

Notes

Introduction
1   Hamilton, 2017
2   The *Sydney Morning Herald*, 30 April 2016
3   The *Guardian*, 13 February 2017
4   The *Canberra Times*, 14 February 2017
5   Kohler, 2017a
6   Kohler, 2017b
7   Kohler, 2017a
8   Greenpeace, 2016a
9   Mogus, 2017

The great coal rush
1   Shearer et al., 2017
2   Pearse, McKnight and Burton, 2012
3   *Business Standard*, 25 January 2013
4   Paul, 2013
5   Turner, 2017
6   The *Australian*, 12 September 2015
7   Priestly, 2010
8   The *Independent*, 2 December 2012
9   The *Financial Times*, 6 June 2011
10 The *Times of India*, 14 September 2009
11 Pearlman, 2012
12 McKnight and Burton, 2013
13 Cited in ABC *AM*, 10 February 2010
14 Cited in Campbell, 2014, p. 2
15 State Government of Queensland, 2010
16 The *Sydney Morning Herald*, 6 June 2011

17 ABC *News*, 3 January 2012
18 ABC *AM*, 20 February 2010
19 Barrett, 2014
20 Barrett, 2014
21 *Australian Financial Review*, 28 June 2014
22 Hooper, 2014
23 Walker, 2012
24 West, 2012
25 West, 2012
26 Rundle, 2014
27 Cited in Cadzow, 2012
28 Readfearn, 2011b
29 The *Sydney Morning Herald*, 6 October 2013
30 The *Courier Mail*, 18 September 2011
31 Lee, 2015
32 Ferguson, 2012
33 The *Sydney Morning Herald*, 4 February 2012
34 Bryant, 2012b
35 *Australian Financial Review*, 29 June 2017
36 Ferguson, 2012
37 Ferguson, 2012
38 Finnegan, 2013
39 Bryant, 2012
40 The *Independent*, 10 June 2010
41 Hume, 2012
42 Samiha Shafy, 2013
43 The *Sydney Morning Herald*, 14 November 2014
44 Ferguson, 2012

45 The *Guardian*, 18 September, 2013
46 *Business Spectator*, 7 March 2015
47 Lee, 2015
48 *New Matilda*, 29 September, 2011
49 *New Matilda*, 29 September, 2011
50 Adams, 2007
51 Union of Concerned Scientists, nd
52 Skeptical Science, blog, 9 June 2011
53 Manning, 2010
54 The *Australian*, 9 May 2009
55 Cadzow, 2012
56 Paul, 2013
57 Economic Times, 18 September 2011
58 Paul, 2013
59 Paul, 2013
60 Joseph, 2015

India's coal baron
1 Bahree, 2014a
2 *Reuters Money News*, 4 May 2014
3 *Times of India*, 10 April, 2014
4 Crabtree, 2013
5 Singaravel, 2013
6 Crabtree, 2013
7 The *Australian*, 20 August 2011
8 Crabtree, 16 June 2013
9 *Economic Times*, 22 June, 2002
10 Crabtree, 2013
11 *India Today*, 28 November 2008
12 *India Today*, 20 August 2011
13 Arora and Puranik, 2004
14 Arora and Puranik, 2004
15 Deb, 2016
16 Sastry, 2014
17 RenuKumar, 2015
18 Varadarajan, 2014
19 Cited in Yardley and Bajaj, 2011
20 Cited in Nayar, Arindam and Arora, 2014
21 The *Economist*, 4 May 2014
22 Titus, 2007
23 *Washington Post*, 17 December 2010
24 Roy, 2015
25 Livemint, 2 March 2018
26 Jose, 2012
27 Jose, 2012
28 Price, 2012
29 Fernandes, 2003
30 *Times of India*, 10 April 2014
31 Rajshekhar, 2013
32 Jaffrelot, 2015; Mehta, 2010; Deb, 2016
33 McKenna, 2016
34 Price, 2016
35 Yardley and Bajaj, 2011
36 Rajeshekhar, 2013
37 Yardley and Bajaj, 2011
38 Nayar, et al., 2014
39 *Reuters Business News*, 11 April 2014
40 Megha Bahree, 2014b
41 *Reuters Business News*, 11 April 2014
42 The *Economist*, 4 May 2014
43 Villatt, 2004
44 Villatt, 2004
45 *Forbes Business*, 17 July 2014
46 Yardley and Bajaj, 2011; Bahree, 2014b
47 Mahaprashasta, 2013
48 Nayar, et al., 2014
49 Cited in Antholis, 2014
50 Down to Earth Fortnightly on Politics of Development, Environment and Health, 31 October 2010
51 Down to Earth Fortnightly on Politics of Development, Environment and Health, 9 May 2012
52 The *Economic Times*, 9 May 2012
53 Ministry of Environment and Forestry, 2013
54 Ministry of Environment and Forestry, 2013
55 Bahree, 2014b
56 *Hindustan Times,* 25 July 2011
57 Karnatake Lokayukta, 2011
58 Perspective Document, 2014
59 Betigeri, 2015
60 For a summary of the issue see Betigeri, 2015
61 *Daily News and Analysis*, 13 June 2013
62 National Green Tribunal, 2016
63 The *Times of India*, 2012

64 Global Research, 9 December 2016
65 Satish, 2012
66 *Business Standard*, 27 February 2012
67 National Green Tribunal, 2016
68 Down to Earth Fortnightly
    on Politics of Development,
    Environment and Health, 5 August
    2013
69 Koutsoukis and Flitton, 2014
70 Koutsoukis and Flitton, 2014
71 Greenpeace, 'Palm Oil Giant Wilmar
    Caught in Palm Oil Scandal', press
    release, 22 October 2013
72 Ruchi Soya Industries Limited,
    25 May 2016
73 Environmental Justice Australia,
    2015
74 *Daily Nation (Zambia)*, 3 April 2015
75 *Daily News and Analysis*, 3 September
    2013
76 Ministry of Finance, 2012
77 *Economic and Political Weekly*,
    December 2016
78 *Economic and Political Weekly*, April
    2016
79 Long, 2015
80 The *Wire*, 14 January 2014
81 *Times of India*, 26 July 2014
82 *Reuters Business News*, 11 April 2014
83 Dreze, 2014
84 Jaffrelot, 2015
85 Appa, 2014
86 Price, 2016
87 Gopalakrishnan, 2014
88 *India Samvad*, 16 February 2017
89 Mohan, 2015

The coal wars begin

1 Pearse, 2009; Hamilton, 2007, 2010,
   2014; Pearse, McKnight and Burton,
   2013; Baer and Burgman, 2012
2 Kelly, 1994
3 Kelly, 1994
4 The *Australian*, 15 October 1997
5 Hosking, 2016
6 Mooney, 2014
7 Media release, Anthony Albanese,

   6 July 2006
8 Abjorensen, 2015
9 Howard, 2010
10 The *Age*, 26 April 2008
11 Beresford, 2015
12 Cited in Pincock, 2007
13 Rundle, *Crikey*, 12 October 2017
14 Burton, 2014
15 The *Age*, 30 July 2015
16 The *Age*, 17 May 2005
17 Cited in Source Watch, 'Robin
    Batterham'
18 ABC *PM*, 2004
19 Connolly and Orsmond, 2011
20 Pincock, 2007
21 Baker, 2005
22 Baker, 2005
23 The *Sydney Morning Herald*,
    16 January 2007
24 *New Matilda*, 4 April 2007
25 Interview, Bob Brown, November
    2017
26 Quiggin, 2015
27 The *Courier Mail*, 22 July 2014
28 Cited in Hudson, 2017b
29 Pearse, 2009; Pearse, McKnight and
    Burton, 2013
30 *Green Left Weekly*, 22 February 2006
31 Garnaut and Counsel, 2002
32 Hamilton, 2007
33 Garnaut and Counsel, 2002
34 Pearse, 2009
35 Pearse, 2009
36 Readfearn, 2011a
37 *Australian Business Review*, 1 May
    2013
38 *RenewEconomy*, 25 September 2017
39 Grundoff, 2013
40 CFMEU Mining and Energy
    Division, Submission Select
    Committee on Fuel and Energy,
    August 2008
41 The *Sydney Morning Herald*,
    4 February 2017
42 Kelly, 2016
43 Hamilton, 2007 and Hamilton, 2017
44 Oreskes and Conway, 2010

45   Manne, 2012
46   Hamilton, 2007, 2010; McKewon,
      2012; Taylor, 2014
47   McKewon, 2012
48   AntiNuclear.net, 2013; the *Age*,
      8 June 2005
49   The *Sydney Morning Herald*,
      25 August 2013
50   The *Sydney Morning Herald*,
      6 November 2013
51   Cowie, 2012
52   Marriott, 2011
53   Taylor, 2014
54   Hamilton, 2014
55   Manne, 2011
56   McKnight, 2010
57   McKnight, 2013
58   The *Age*, 23 October 2006
59   The *Advertiser*, 17 January 2007
60   The *Age*, 28 October 2006
61   The *Sydney Morning Herald*,
      27 January 2007
62   ABC *Lateline*, 2007
63   ABC *Lateline*, 2007
64   *Crikey*, 15 February 2007
65   *Daily Telegraph*, 15 February 2007
66   *Sunday Mail*, 18 February 2007
67   *Crikey*, 15 February 2007
68   The *Australian*, 9 February 2007
69   The *Australian*, 9 February 2007
70   *Crikey*, 9 February 2009
71   Interview, Bob Brown, November
      2017
72   Interview, Bob Brown, November
      2017
73   Hills, 2012
74   Knott, 2011
75   Interview, Bob Brown, November
      2017
76   The *Guardian*, 5 September 2002
77   The *Australian*, 12 February 2007
78   The *Australian*, 12 February 2007
79   Interview, Bob Brown, November
      2017
80   Interview, Bob Brown, November
      2017
81   Bregman, 2017

82   The *Sydney Morning Herald*, 5 March
      2007

Coal nation

1   The *Age*, 21 December 2016
2   The *Australian*, 23 August 2014
3   *Inside Waste*, 23 June 2011
4   Hannan, 2015
5   Media release, the Greens,
      25 February 2006
6   The *Age*, 26 February 2007
7   Taylor, 2012
8   Project SafeComm, 'Coal Industry
      Chiefs Overheat Kevin's Climate', nd
9   The *Sydney Morning Herald*, 21 April
      2008
10   The *Age*, 10 May 2008
11   Taylor, 2012; see also Burgmann and
      Baer, 2012
12   *Green Left Weekly*, 13 September
      2009
13   *Green Left Weekly*, 13 September
      2009
14   *Crikey*, 7 September 2009
15   Flannery, 2010
16   ABC *AM*, 16 December 2009
17   Cited in Harrison, 2011
18   Climate Institute, 29 July 2009
19   The *Courier Mail*, 29 May 2009
20   Wilkinson, Cubby and Duxfield,
      2009
21   *New Matilda*, 11 March 2009
22   Kelly, 2014
23   The *Australian*, 11 June 2014
24   Chubb, 2014
25   ABC *News*, 1 December 2009
26   Cited in Seccombe, 2017
27   The *Age*, 11 June 2014
28   McKenzie-Murray, 2016
29   ABC *Lateline*, 12 August 2012
30   ABC *Four Corners*, 2009
31   *Australian Financial Review*, 16 July
      2017
32   The *Sydney Morning Herald*, 5 May
      2010
33   McKnight and Hobbs, 2013;
      Mitchell, 2012

34 Aulby, 2017
35 The *Sydney Morning Herald*, 27 May 2010
36 The *Sydney Morning Herald*, 8 February 2010
37 The *Sydney Morning Herald*, 2 February 2011
38 Gittins, 2013
39 Baird, 2014
40 Baird, 2014
41 The *Sydney Morning Herald*, 16 April 2011
42 Cited in *The AIM Network*, 26 February 2016

Coal before coral
1   The *Sydney Morning Herald*, 4 April 2010
2   The *Guardian*, 4 April 2010
3   ABC *News*, 6 April 2010
4   Grech and McCook, 2015
5   Burton, 2013
6   ABC *News*, 15 June 2009
7   The *Sydney Morning Herald*, 19 December 2010
8   Cited in *New Matilda*, 1 December 2011
9   Connolly and Henley, 2010
10 McKenzie-Murray, 2016
11 McKenzie-Murray, 2016
12 Market Forces, 2012
13 Cited in Market Forces, 2013
14 Chang, 2017
15 Polgate Griffin and Miller Associates, 2012
16 Davis, 2006
17 Cited in Lloyd, 2012
18 Lloyd, 2012
19 O'Callaghan, 2014
20 The *Sydney Morning Herald*, 1 February 2013
21 The *Sydney Morning Herald*, 1 February 2013
22 Interview, Bob Brown, November 2017
23 The *Guardian*, 9 May 2014
24 The *Guardian*, 26 April 2013

25 ABC *News*, 10 October 2012; Cooley, C, nd
26 The *Guardian*, 26 April 2013
27 The *Guardian*, 26 April 2013
28 The *Guardian*, 20 August 2014
29 The *Sydney Morning Herald*, 23 July 2014
30 Great Artesian Basin Protection Group, Homepage
31 North Queensland Conservation Council, 10 October 2012
32 Milman, 2014
33 *Dredging Today*, 5 March 2013
34 The *Sydney Morning Herald*, 1 February 2013
35 Stephens, 2012
36 Australian Institute of Marine Science, media release, 2 October 2010
37 McPhail, 2014
38 Meskell, 2013
39 The *Guardian*, 16 June 2013
40 UNESCO World Heritage Committee, 2012
41 Keane, 2012
42 Lewis and Wood, 2012
43 AAP, 30 August 2013
44 Fight for Our Reef, media release, 19 June 2013
45 Greenpeace, 2011
46 *Australian Financial Review*, 8 March 2012
47 The *Australian*, 10 March 2012
48 The *Australian*, 10 March 2012
49 *Australian Financial Review*, 3 March 2012
50 ABC *News*, 11 June 2012
51 The *Australian*, 16 April 2013
52 *Crikey*, 5 April 2013
53 *Crikey*, 14 April 2015
54 *Crikey*, 5 April 2013
55 The *Guardian*, 12 June 2013
56 *Independent Australia*, 6 April 2013
57 *Eco news*, 23 July 2013
58 The Australia Institute, 2014
59 The *Guardian*, 24 October 2013
60 ABC *Four Corners*, 2014

61   Senate Environment and
      Communications References
      Committee, 2014
62   ABC *Four Corners*, 2014
63   Hughes, 2014
64   Senate Environment and
      Communications References
      Committee, 2014, p. 89
65   Senate Environment and
      Communications References
      Committee, 2014, p. 77
66   Senate Environment and
      Communications References
      Committee, 2014, p. 121
67   The *Guardian*, 15 August 2015
68   The *Guardian*, 10 December 2013
69   The *Sydney Morning Herald*,
      25 September 2014
70   Robson, 2017
71   Robson, 2017
72   ABC *News*, 29 January 2014
73   Senate Environment and
      Communications References
      Committee, 2014, p. 131
74   McPhail, 2014
75   Dr Reichelt, personal communication
76   The *Guardian*, 2 March 2014
77   Great Barrier Reef Marine Park
      Authority, 2013
78   ABC *7.30*, 16 April 2014
79   The *Courier Mail*, 7 May 2014
80   ABC *Four Corners*, 2014
81   Senate Environment and
      Communications References
      Committee, 2014, p. 127
82   The *Sydney Morning Herald*,
      18 September 2015
83   Dr Reichelt, personal communication
84   ABC *News*, 7 October 2014
85   Interview Bob Brown, November
      2017
86   The *Guardian*, 13 November 2014
87   ABC *News*, 7 October 2014
88   Senate Environment and
      Communications References
      Committee, 2014, p. 77

In the shadow of Joh
1   The *Sydney Morning Herald*, 30 June
      2015
2   Kampmark, 2016
3   IESC
4   ABC *News*, 8 July 2014
5   ABC *News*, 17 November 2014
6   The *Australian*, 19 November 2014
7   ABC *News*, 17 November 2014
8   Cox, 2015
9   Willacy, 2015
10   The *Brisbane Times*, 2 March 2017
11   Seccombe, 2014
12   ABC *News*, 10 November 2014
13   ABC *News*, 1 July 2015
14   ABC *News*, 1 July 2015
15   Patience, 1985
16   Jackman, 2012
17   Bahnisch, 2015
18   Hurst, 2015
19   The *Brisbane Times*, 21 January 2015
20   Scott, 2015
21   Scott and Scott, 2014
22   Bryant, 2012
23   Orr, 2011
24   Bryant, 2012
25   Cited in Jackman, 2012
26   Jackman, 2012
27   Jackman, 2012
28   The *Courier Mail*, 17 January 2014
29   Fitzgerald, 2015
30   The *Brisbane Times*, 28 February
      2012
31   Lowe, 2012
32   The Wilderness Society, 9 August
      2016
33   The *Brisbane Times*, 8 June 2012
34   Mackay Conservation Group, 2014
35   Keim and McKean, 2014
36   ABC *News*, 29 July 2016
37   The *Courier Mail*, 28 November
      2014
38   The *Sydney Morning Herald*, 3 June
      2012
39   The *Sydney Morning Herald*, 3 June
      2012
40   Christine Jackman, 2012

41 The *Sydney Morning Herald*, 7 February 2015
42 Keim, 2014
43 Aulby and Ogge, 2016
44 Keim, 2014
45 The *Brisbane Times*, 8 November 2014
46 Senate Select Committee, 2014a
47 ABC *News*, 6 February 2012
48 Thomas, 2014
49 The *Australian*, 9 August 2014
50 The *Australian*, 30 May 2012
51 The *Courier Mail*, 21 August 2012
52 Wadrill, 2013
53 Paul, 2013
54 The *Sydney Morning Herald*, 11 May 2012
55 Birmingham, 2013
56 *Eco News*, 26 September 2012
57 *Times of India*, 19 June 2013
58 *Australian Financial Review*, 16 September 2014
59 *Times of India*, 19 June 2013
60 Manning, 2014
61 *Queensland Country Life*, 5 July 2017
62 Cited in Readfearn, 2015
63 Readfearn, 2015; Aulby and Ogge, 2016
64 Aulby and Ogge, 2016
65 Beresford, 2008
66 Beresford, 2015
67 McClymont and Besser, 2014
68 Readfearn, 2015
69 Readfearn, 2015
70 Maharaj, 2017
71 White, 2016
72 The *Guardian*, 15 January 2015
73 Burton, 2014
74 Seccombe, 2015
75 Burton, 2014
76 Campbell, 2014
77 Campbell, 2014
78 Peel, Campbell and Denniss, 2014
79 Campbell, 2015a
80 Campbell, 2015b
81 Readfearn, 2015
82 The *Queensland Times*, 23 May 2013
83 The *Brisbane Times*, 21 August 2015
84 De'ath et al., 2012
85 MySunshineCoast website, 13 May 2014
86 ABC *News*, 2 August 2017
87 Aulby and Ogge, 2016
88 The *Courier Mail*, 3 August 2013
89 The *Courier Mail*, 3 August 2013
90 The *Queensland Times*, 28 November 2012
91 Readfearn, 2015
92 Aulby and Ogge, 2016
93 Readfearn, 2015
94 Cox, 2015
95 Krien, 2017
96 Cox, 2015
97 Tham, 2010
98 Keane, 2015
99 *Australian Financial Review*, 1 February 2013
100 Aulby and Ogge, 2015
101 ABC *News*, 5 May 2014
102 Remeikis, 2014
103 The *Courier Mail*, 29 June 2014
104 ABC *News*, 21 May 2014
105 Fitzgerald, 2015b
106 ABC *News*, 1 December 2017

The Abbott government and 'standing up for coal'

1   Seccombe, 2014
2   Seccombe, 2014
3   Seccombe, 2014
4   *AAP*, 14 April 2014
5   The *Guardian*, 13 June 2014
6   The *Guardian*, 16 June 2014
7   The *Australian*, 14 January 2010
8   The *Australian*, 14 January 2010
9   Bob Santamaria interview, Australian Biography Project, 1997
10 Manne, 2011
11 Leiberman, 2012
12 Pell, 2011
13 *Crikey*, 28 October 2011
14 Cowie, 2012
15 Marr, 2012
16 Duffy, 2009

17   Fernyhough, 2015
18   Fernyhough, 2015
19   The *Sydney Morning Herald*, 25 May 2015
20   The *Sydney Morning Herald*, 1 April 2014
21   Cited in *Independent Australia*, 29 May 2013
22   Cited in *Independent Australia*, 29 May 2013
23   *Renew Economy*, 19 August 2015
24   ABC *News*, 5 March 2014
25   Public Radio International, 16 April 2014
26   *Australian Financial Review*, 24 January 2015
27   The *Sydney Morning Herald*, 2 June 2014
28   *MPN News,* 8 April 2014
29   Sparrow, 2015
30   Climate Council, 8 May 2015
31   The *Guardian*, 14 August 2014
32   Holmes, 2015
33   The *Sydney Morning Herald*, 13 October 2014
34   *RenewEconomy*, 29 May 2014
35   *Australian Financial Review*, 21 August 2015
36   Cited in the *Conversation*, 19 August 2014
37   The *Guardian*, 3 February 2017
38   Seccombe, 2015
39   ABC *PM*, 17 July 2013
40   Bradshaw, 2015
41   Sarma, 2015
42   *Nation*, 1 April 2015; *Financial Times*, 17 November 2015
43   *Livemint*, 13 December 2017
44   The *New York Times*, 17 November 2014
45   The *Sydney Morning Herald*, 19 December 2013
46   ABC *News,* 2 May 2014
47   ABC *News,* 10 June 2015
48   *RenewEconomy*, 28 November 2016
49   Parkinson, 2015
50   The *Guardian*, 23 July 2015

51   Cited in McKenzie-Murray, 2015
52   The *Guardian*, 14 May 2015
53   Milne, 2017
54   The *Guardian*, 30 October 2013
55   Great Barrier Reef Marine Park Authority, 2014
56   The *Sydney Morning Herald*, 15 November 2014
57   ABC *News*, 21 November 2014
58   The *Guardian*, 21 November 2014
59   The *Guardian*, 25 November 2014
60   The *Guardian*, 23 November 2014
61   The *Chronicle*, 14 June 2014
62   Cited in *RenewEconomy*, 17 November 2014
63   The *Sydney Morning Herald*, 17 November 2014
64   The Australian, 18 November 2014
65   *VANews*, 5 September 2014
66   *Financial Times*, 26 November 2014
67   *Financial Times*, 26 November 2014
68   *Livemint*, 6 November 2017
69   *Times of India*, 20 November 2014
70   Department of Foreign Affairs FOI Request Ref. No. 15/23911. Note: the $7 billion figure quoted by the SBI is under the $16 billion cost widely cited by other sources.
71   The *Australian Financial Review*, 24 June 2014
72   Long, 2017
73   Buschan and Ramanathan, 2015
74   ABC *AM*, 3 April 2017
75   Institute of Public Affairs, Media Release, 8 February 2013
76   The Coalition 2030 Vision for Developing Northern Australia, 2013
77   The *Sydney Morning Herald*, 21 June 2013
78   Australian Government, 2015
79   The *Sydney Morning Herald*, 21 June 2013
80   Cited in Canavan, 2014
81   Staples, 2014
82   Staples, 2014
83   Canavan, 2014
84   Minerals Council of Australia, 2014

85 Burdon, 2014
86 The Australia Institute, 2015
87 The *Sydney Morning Herald*,
    25 September 2015
88 GBRMPA, 2014
89 GBRMPA, 2014
90 The *Guardian*, 21 March 2015
91 The *Independent*, 23 March 2015
92 Callick, 2013
93 Wallace, 2015
94 The *Guardian*, 12 December 2014
    and 26 February 2015
95 The *Courier Mail*, 8 December 2014
96 The *Conversation*, 5 February 2015
97 The *Guardian*, 27 October 2014
98 The *Guardian*, 21 March 2015
99 The *Guardian*, 16 June 2014
100 The *Sydney Morning Herald*,
    9 December 2014
101 The *Sydney Morning Herald*,
    9 December 2014
102 Climate Change Network, 2014
103 The *Guardian*, 4 August 2017

Malcolm Turnbull
1   The *Australian*, 20 October 2015
2   The *Australian*, 14 September 2015
3   ABC *News*, 15 September 2015
4   The *Daily Telegraph*, 15 September
    2015
5   The *Guardian*, 21 June 2017
6   Turnbull, 2009
7   Manne, 2016
8   ABC *News*, 22 July 2011
9   Cited in Lyons, 2014
10 Manning, 2016
11 The *Sydney Morning Herald*,
    29 August 2009
12 Manning, 2015
13 Vice.com, 30 June 2016
14 Manne, 2012
15 Manne, 2016
16 Manne, 2012a
17 Beresford, 2015
18 *New Matilda*, 19 September 2015
19 *New Matilda*, 19 September 2015
20 Manne, 2016

21 The *Saturday Paper*, 21–27 February
    2015
22 The *Sydney Morning Herald*,
    9 February 2017
23 The *Sydney Morning Herald*,
    6 October 2015
24 The *Guardian*, 18 September 2015
25 Cited in the *Guardian*, 5 April 2017
26 The *Guardian*, 27 October 2015
27 The *Gladstone Observer*, 1 July 2016
28 The *Guardian*, 21 June 2017
29 Hudson, 2016
30 The *Guardian*, 19 February 2017
31 ABC *News*, 19 June 2017
32 The *Sydney Morning Herald*,
    27 October 2015
33 The *Sydney Morning Herald*,
    27 October 2015
34 The *Australian*, 28 October 2015
35 *RenewEconomy*, 8 October 2015
36 *RenewEconomy*, 8 October 2015
37 Seccombe, 2016
38 SBS *News*, 8 December 2015
39 2Celsius Network, 30 November
    2015
40 *RenewEconomy*, 1 December 2015
41 The *Guardian*, 2 December 2015
42 *New Matilda*, 12 December 2015
43 Mackenzie, 2015
44 The *Guardian*, 27 May 2016
45 The *Guardian*, 27 May 2016
46 ABC Triple J, 30 May 2016
47 Interview, anonymous
48 Interview, anonymous
49 The *Guardian*, 13 December 2017
50 The *Guardian*, 2 February 2018
51 International Energy Agency, 2015
52 The *Economist*, 10 October 2015
53 Cited in Climate Change News,
    2 December 2015
54 *Business Standard*, 2 October 2015
55 *Climate Change News*, 30 November
    2015
56 Johnson, 2015
57 Johnson, 2015
58 Johnson, 2015
59 Hewson, 2017

60 The *Queensland Times*, 8 June 2017
61 Market Forces Submission, Senate Economics References Committee, 2017, Submission No. 69
62 The *Australian*, 29 July 2017
63 Australia Senate Economics References Committee, 2017, Submission No. 111
64 The Australia Institute, 2017
65 Senate Economics References Committee, 2017, Submission No. 85
66 Australian Conservation Foundation, 2017
67 Greenpeace, 2016b
68 ABC *News*, 1 June 2016
69 The *Guardian*, 13 May 2017
70 Ker, 2017
71 The *Cairns Post*, 8 March 2017
72 The *Sydney Morning Herald*, 2 November 2017
73 The *Guardian*, 28 June 2017
74 SBS, 21 June 2016
75 *Independent Australia*, 23 June 2016
76 Matthew Canavan, web page 2 December 2015
77 The *Australian*, 5 January 2017
78 *Australian Financial Review*, 2 February 2017
79 ABC *News*, 1 February 2017
80 The *Sydney Morning Herald*, 28 February 2017
81 Greenpeace, 2016c
82 *New Matilda*, 27 June 2016
83 *Border Mail*, 12 August 2016
84 *Australian Financial Review*, 5 July 2017
85 ABC *News*, 5 December 2017
86 The *Guardian*, 10 March 2017
87 Hamilton and Karoly, 2017
88 The *Guardian*, 1 February 2017
89 The *Guardian*, 20 January 2017
90 ABC *News*, 2 February 2017
91 *Australian Financial Review*, 22 September 2017
92 *Australian Financial Review*, 22 September 2017
93 The *Guardian*, 23 March 2017

'This huge black hole'

1 Wangan and Jagalingou Family Council, 26 March 2015
2 The *Guardian*, 15 May 2015
3 Interview, Adrian Burragubba, January 2018
4 Wangan and Jagalingou Family Council, 'Our Fight' website
5 Interview, Adrian Burragubba, January 2018
6 Wangan and Jagalingou Submission, 2015
7 Interview, Adrian Burragubba, January 2018
8 Interview, Adrian Burragubba, January 2018
9 Ministry of Tribal Affairs, 2014
10 Interview, Adrian Burragubba, January 2018
11 Cited in Wangan and Jagalingou Submission, 2015
12 Wangan and Jagalingou Submission, 2015
13 Interview, Anthony Esposito, January 2018
14 Wangan and Jagalingou Submission, 2015
15 Briggs, Quiggin and Lyons, 2017
16 Quicke, Dockery and Hoath, 2017
17 Wangan and Jagalingou Submission, 2015
18 Wangan and Jagalingou Submission, 2015
19 Wangan and Jagalingou Family Council, 2017a
20 Arnautovic, 2017
21 Cited in Arnautovic, 2017
22 Wagan and Jagalingou Family Council, 2017a
23 Geritz and Harvey, 2013
24 Wagan and Jagalingou Family Council, 2017a
25 The *Australian*, 3 December 2015
26 Wangan and Jagalingou Family Council, 2016
27 Lyons, Brigg and Quiggin, 2017

28 Wangan and Jagalingou Family Council, 2015
29 Sydney Criminal Lawyers Association, nd
30 The *Australian*, 12 March 2016
31 *Australian Financial Review*, 20 May 2015
32 The *Australian*, 22 October 2016 and the *Indian Express*, 22 October 2016
33 Cited in the *Guardian*, 24 October 2016
34 Cited in the *Guardian*, 24 October 2016
35 Wangan and Jagalingou Family Council, 2015
36 *Adani Mining v. Adrian Burragubba & Others*, 2015
37 Wangan and Jagalingou Family Council, 2015
38 *Adani Mining v. Adrian Burragubba & Others*, 2015
39 The *Brisbane Times*, 14 April 2015
40 *Queensland Country Life*, 3 March 2015
41 Wangan and Jagalingou Family Council media release, 29 May 2015
42 Indigenous Environment Network, nd
43 World Resources Institute, 15 July 2015
44 Lewis, 2014
45 Indigenous Environmental Network, nd
46 Indigenous Environmental Network, nd
47 *Edmonton Journal*, 3 June 2015
48 Wangan and Jagalingou Family Council, 2015
49 West, 2015
50 West, 2015
51 The *Guardian*, 26 March 2015
52 Wangan and Jagalingou Family Council, 2015
53 Wangan and Jagalingou Family Council, 2015
54 Wangan and Jagalingou Family Council, 2015

55 Wangan and Jagalingou Family Council, 2015
56 ABC *News*, 23 November 2015
57 The *Guardian*, 8 December 2015
58 The *Australian*, 23 December 2015
59 The *Australian*, 7 March 2018

The legal challenge from 'greenies'
1 The *Sydney Morning Herald*, 20 August 2015
2 The *Sydney Morning Herald*, 15 December 2017
3 Whelan, 2015
4 *Daily Mercury*, 8 August 2015
5 *MCG Annual Report 2014–2015*
6 *MCG Annual Report 2014–2015*
7 *MCG Annual Report 2014–2015*
8 Hepburn, 2015
9 Hepburn, 2015
10 Hepburn, 2015
11 Peel, 2008
12 Sahukar, 2016
13 *Ballina Shire Advocate*, 18 December 2013
14 Lowe, 2010
15 *Australian Financial Review*, 7 August 2015
16 *Australian Financial Review*, 7 August 2015
17 The *Courier Mail*, 17 March 2015
18 The *Australian*, 5 August 2015
19 The *Australian*, 7 August 2015
20 The *Sydney Morning Herald*, 7 August 2015
21 Attorney-General of Australia website, 18 August 2015
22 The *Sydney Morning Herald*, 15 December 2017
23 ABC *News*, 10 November 2016
24 *BuzzFeed* News, 2 November 2016
25 *New Matilda*, 21 June 2016
26 The *Guardian*, 29 August 2016
27 *Australian Financial Review*, 24 August 2015
28 Clark, 2015
29 Milman and Evershed, 2015
30 *Daily Mercury*, 6 August 2015

31 The *Guardian*, 6 August 2015
32 The *Daily Telegraph*, 29 October 2016
33 *Australian Financial Review*, 7 August 2015
34 ABC *News*, 7 August 2015
35 The *Courier Mail*, 8 May 2016
36 The *Courier Mail*, 1 October 2016
37 Friends of the Earth Australia, nd
38 Friends of the Earth Brisbane, nd
39 The *Sydney Morning Herald*, 5 November 2011
40 Friends of the Earth Brisbane, 2012
41 *New Matilda*, 30 March 2015
42 The *Courier Mail*, 27 April 2016
43 *Economic Times*, 29 August 2016
44 Land Court of Queensland, 2015
45 Land Court of Queensland, 2015
46 Land Court of Queensland, 2015
47 Land Court of Queensland, 2015
48 Land Court of Queensland, 2015
49 Manning, 2014
50 Land Court of Queensland, 2015
51 *Green Left Weekly*, 16 June 2016
52 The *Sydney Morning Herald*, 28 April 2015
53 The *Sydney Morning Herald*, 28 April 2015
54 The *Guardian*, 1 May 2015
55 Cited in *BuzzFeed News*, 12 April 2017
56 EDO Qld Case Summary: 'Adani Carmichael Land Court Objection'
57 *BuzzFeed News*, 12 April 2017
58 EDO Qld Case Summary: 'Adani Carmichael Land Court Objection'
59 Land Court of Queensland, 2015
60 The *Guardian*, 27 April 2015
61 The *Saturday Paper*, 27 February 2016
62 ABC *News*, 16 December 2015
63 Australian Conservation Foundation, 'The Story of Us'
64 Bell-James, 2016
65 Environmental Justice Australia, 2015
66 McKinnon, 2016
67 Hepburn, 2015b
68 McKinnon, 2016
69 Environment Law Australia, nd
70 The *Guardian*, 6 May 2016
71 McKinnon, 2016
72 Peel, 2008
73 Australian Human Rights Commission, 2009
74 *Business Spectator*, 6 August 2015
75 The *Guardian*, 29 August 2016
76 The *Guardian*, 29 August 2016
77 ABC *News*, 14 July 2017
78 The *Sydney Morning Herald*, 2 April 2016

The banks under attack

1 The *Sydney Morning Herald*, 25 May 2014
2 The *Guardian*, 28 July 2013
3 Kemp, 2016
4 McKibben, 2016
5 Alexander, Nicholson and Wiseman, 2014
6 *RenewEconomy*, 10 October 2014
7 The *Sydney Morning Herald*, 25 May 2015
8 Greenpeace Australia, 2010
9 Greenpeace press release, 21 October 2010
10 Grunwald, 2015
11 Greenpeace Australia, 2010
12 *Crikey*, 16 November 2010
13 The *Australian*, 15 August 2015
14 The *Guardian*, 27 October 2014
15 The *Sydney Morning Herald*, 2 May 2014
16 ABC *News*, 7 August 2015
17 The *Guardian*, 25 November 2014
18 Adams, 2015
19 The *Sydney Morning Herald*, 23 February 2014
20 Butler, 2014
21 Louvel et al., 2016
22 Beresford, 2015
23 The groups were: Greenpeace, GetUp!, the Australian Conservation Foundation, 350.org, Australian

Marine Conservation Society, Australian Youth Climate Coalition, Friends of the Earth, SumOfUs, Lock the Gate, Bank Track and the Mackay Conservation Group.

24 The *Australian*, 1 November 2016
25 *Australian Financial Review*, 15 January 2013
26 Coombs, 2016a
27 Coombs, 2016b
28 Funnell, 2017
29 Rodan and Mummery, 2017
30 *Australian Financial Review*, 15 January 2013
31 *Australian Financial Review*, 15 January 2013
32 Bragg, 2017
33 Bragg, 2017
34 Vromen, 2016
35 Quit Coal, 2014
36 *AdNews*, 4 November 2014
37 Front Line Action on Coal, 20 May 2015
38 *New Matilda*, 21 May 2015
39 *New Matilda*, 10 June 2015
40 *Green Left Weekly*, 14 November 2014
41 *AYCC Annual Report*, 2014
42 Flannery, 2016
43 Nagel, 2017
44 *Australian Financial Review*, 1 May 2017
45 The *Sydney Morning Herald*, 6 March 2015
46 The *Sydney Morning Herald*, 22 November 2016
47 The *Age*, 3 May 2014
48 ABC *News*, 21 May 2015
49 Market Forces, nd
50 The *Australian*, 11 April 2017
51 The *Australian*, 11 April 2017
52 Roskam, 2017
53 Regan, 2014
54 *New Matilda*, 6 August 2015
55 The *Sydney Morning Herald*, 5 August 2015
56 The *Sydney Morning Herald*,

57 5 September 2015
57 The *Guardian*, 3 September 2015
58 The *Sydney Morning Herald*, 3 September 2015
59 *New Matilda*, 2 September 2015
60 *New Matilda*, 2 September 2015
61 The *Australian*, 14 December 2015
62 Cited in Phys.org, 19 September 2015
63 ABC *Rural News*, 29 June 2015
64 The *Sydney Morning Herald*, 7 September 2015
65 ABC *News*, 9 September 2015
66 News.com, 8 September 2015
67 *Newcastle Herald*, 15 July 2015
68 *Business Insider Australia*, 7 September 2015
69 *Australian Financial Review*, 5 October 2015
70 The *Guardian*, 6 October 2015
71 *Australian Financial Review*, 10 April 2015
72 Oosting, 2017
73 Beresford, 2015
74 Cited in Glaetzer, 2016
75 Glaetzer, 2016
76 Interview, Oosting, January 2018
77 Interview, Oosting, January 2018
78 Mogus and Liacas, 2016
79 Interview, Oosting, January 2018
80 Interviews, Bob Brown, November 2017; Geoff Cousins, November 2017

The end game?

1 Interview, Paul Oosting, January 2018
2 Interview, Geoff Cousins, November 2017
3 The *Australian*, 23 September 2006
4 Mayne, 2006
5 Interview, Geoff Cousins, November 2017
6 Interview, Geoff Cousins, November 2017
7 The *Guardian*, 17 March 2017
8 *Daily Mercury*, 16 March 2017

9   The *Sydney Morning Herald*,
    16 March 2017
10 *North Queensland Register*, 17 April
    2017
11 Interview, Geoff Cousins, November
    2018
12 Interview, Geoff Cousins, November
    2017
13 Interview, Geoff Cousins, November
    2017
14 The *Guardian*, 22 March 2017
15 Interview, Geoff Cousins, November
    2017
16 Agarwal, 2017
17 The *Guardian,* 14 January 2017
18 Interview, Geoff Cousins, November
    2017
19 The *Australian*, 7 June 2017
20 The *Australian*, 29 May 2017
21 The *Australian*, 14 June 2017
22 The *Courier Mail*, 11 July 2017
23 The *Brisbane Times*, 12 November
    2017
24 The *Australian*, 7 June 2017
25 The *Age*, 15 February 2017
26 The *Age*, 15 February 2017
27 Interview, Geoff Cousins, November
    2017
28 The *Age*, 10 April 2017
29 Bones, 2017
30 *Australian Financial Review*, 10 July
    2017
31 ABC *News*, 8 August 2017
32 The *Guardian*, 17 January 2018
33 Swan et al., 2017
34 Interview, Geoff Cousins, November
    2017
35 Interview, Geoff Cousins, November
    2017
36 The *Guardian*, 15 July 2017
37 The *Sydney Morning Herald*,
    6 December 2017
38 *Australian Financial Review*,
    26 September 2017
39 *Australian Financial Review*,
    26 September 2017
40 The *Australian*, 4 October 2017

41 *Australian Financial Review,*
    22 September 2017
42 *Newcastle Herald*, 20 December
    2017
43 The *Courier Mail*, 1 February 2015
44 The *Sydney Morning Herald*,
    7 January 2015
45 ABC *News,* 21 January 2015
46 The *Guardian*, 4 November 2017
47 Cited in the *Conversation*,
    7 November 2017
48 Elks, 2017
49 Elks, 2017
50 The *Australian*, 30 August 2017
51 The *Australian*, 30 August 2017
52 ABC *Four Corners*, 'Digging into
    Adani', 5 October 2017
53 Interview, Geoff Cousins, November
    2017
54 #StopAdani media release,
    9 November 2017
55 The *Weekend Australian*,
    9–10 December 2017
56 GetUp!, 2018
57 Interview, Paul Oosting, January
    2018
58 McKinnon, 2017
59 The *Saturday Paper*, 2 December
    2017
60 Elks, 2017b
61 The *Australian*, 19 January 2018
62 The *Courier Mail*, 8 February 2018
63 Walker, 2016
64 The *Guardian*, 26 October 2017
65 The *Guardian*, 26 October 2017
66 The *Age*, 23 November 2017
67 The *Guardian*, 1 March 2018
68 ABC *News*, 23 November 2017
69 ABC *News*, 23 November 2017
70 Interview Geoff Cousins, November
    2017
71 The *Australian*, 6 December
    2017
72 *Australian Financial Review*,
    5 December 2017
73 Daniles, 2017
74 Beresford, 2015; interview, Bob

Brown, November 2017
75 Murphy, 2018
76 Murphy, 2018
77 Murphy, 2018
78 Cited in the *Guardian*, 3 February 2018
79 The *Guardian*, 3 February 2018
80 The *Guardian*, 19 February 2018
81 Interview, Geoff Cousins, November 2017
82 The *Sydney Morning Herald*, 2 February 2018
83 Interview, Paul Oosting, January 2018
84 Brigg, Quiggin and Lyons, 2017
85 Gregoire, 2017
86 Wagan and Jagalingou Family Council
87 Mannathukkaren, 2017
88 Mannathukkaren, 2017
89 Beresford, 2015
90 Swain, 2017
91 The *Wire*, 18 July 2017
92 Interview, Kabir Agarwal, March 2018
93 Interview, Kabir Agarwal, March 2018
94 Interview, Kabir Agarwal, March 2018
95 Interview, Kabir Agarwal, March 2018
96 Buckley and Nicholas, 2017
97 The *Guardian*, 7 May 2018
98 Buckley and Nicholas, 2017
99 *Financial Times*, 11 November 2017
100 *Financial Times*, 11 November 2017
101 Interview, Kabir Agarwal, March 2018
102 News Click, 2 December 2017
103 The *Guardian*, 15 November 2017
104 Buckley and Nicholas, 2017b
105 *Australian Financial Review*, 29 January 2018
106 The *Sydney Morning Herald*, 14 March 2014

Conclusion

1 Interview, Anthony Esposito, January 2018
2 *Newcastle Herald*, 28 January 2017
3 Brevini, Woronov and Mortimer, 2017
4 Transparency International, 2018
5 The *Sydney Morning Herald*, 10 December 2017
6 The *Green Journal AU*, 14 June 2017
7 ABC *News* 29 April 2018
8 Statement by Geoff Cousins in the *Weekend Australian*, 3 March 2018
9 Kelly, 2018
10 Crooks and Kao, 2017
11 The *Sydney Morning Herald*, 20–21 January 2018

Bibliography

Books

Bahnisch, M (2015), *Queensland: Everything You Ever Wanted to Know But Were Afraid to Ask*, NewSouth, Sydney

Beresford, Q (2008), *The Godfather: The Life of Brian Burke*, Allen and Unwin, Sydney

Beresford, Q (2015), *The Rise and Fall of Gunns Ltd*, NewSouth, Sydney

Bregman, R (2017), *Utopia for Realists and How We Can Get There*, Bloomsbury, London

Burgmann, V and Baer, H (2012), *Climate Change Politics and the Climate Movement in Australia*, Melbourne University Press, Melbourne

Ferguson, A (2012), *Gina Rinehart*, Macmillan, Sydney

Fernendes, V (2014), *Modi: Leadership, Governance and Performance*, Orient Paperbacks, New Delhi

Flannery, T (2016), *Atmosphere of Hope: Searching for Solutions for the Climate Crisis*, Text Publishing, Melbourne

Hamilton, C (2007), *Scorcher: The Dirty Politics of Climate Change*, Black Inc, Melbourne

Kelly, P (1994), *The End of Certainty: Power, Politics and Business in Australia*, Allen and Unwin, Sydney

McClymont, K and Besser, L (2014), *He Who Must Be Obeid: The Untold Story*, Vintage Books, Sydney

Manne, R (2011), *Essays Against the New Australian Complacency*, Black Inc, Melbourne

Manning, P (2015), *Born to Rule: The Unauthorised Biography of Malcolm Turnbull*, Melbourne University Press, Melbourne

Milne, C (2017), *Christine Milne: An Activist Life*, UQP, Brisbane

Oreskes, N and Conway, E (2010), *Merchants of Doubt: How a Handful of Scientists Obscured the Truth on Issues from Tobacco to Global Warming*, Bloomsbury Press, London

Patience, A (ed.) (1985), *The Bjelke-Petersen Premiership 1968–1983: Issues in Public Policy*, Longman Cheshire, Melbourne

Patrick, A (2016), *Credlin & Co: How the Abbott Government Destroyed Itself*, Black Inc, Melbourne

Pearse, G, McKnight, D and Burton, B (2013), *Big Coal: Australia's Dirtiest Habit*, NewSouth, Sydney

Price, L (2016), *The Modi Effect: Inside Narendra Modi's Campaign to Transform India*, London, Hodder

Rodan, D and Mummery, J (2017), *Activism and Digital Culture in Australia*, Rowman & Littlefield, London

Taylor, M (2014), *Global Warming and Climate Change: What Australia Knew and Buried*, ANU Press, Canberra

Turner, C (2017), *The Patch: The People, Pipelines and Politics of the Oil Sands*, Simon and Schuster, Toronto

White, A (2016), *Shadow State: Inside the Secret Companies That Run Britain*, Oneworld Publishers, London

Journal articles

Antholis, W (2014), 'India's climate change politics in a Modi government', Brookings Institute, 30 July 2014

Arora, B and Puranik, R (2004), 'A review of corporate social responsibility in India', *Development*, vol. 47, no. 3

Brevini, B, Woronov, T and Mortimer, A (2017), 'Truthiness and the Adani Carmichael mine', Sydney Environment Institute, 16 October 2017

Bridges, K (2015), 'King Coal in the land down under', *Penn Stability Review*, vol. 1, no. 6

Coombs, A (2016b), 'The limits of "new power"', *Griffith Review*, 51, January 2016

De'ath, G et al. (2012), 'The 27-year decline of coral cover on the Great Barrier Reef and its causes', Proceedings of the National Academy of Sciences, vol. 109, no. 44

Downer, L (2015), 'Political leadership in contemporary Queensland', Research Report no. 25, TJ Ryan Foundation

Ferguson, P (2009), 'Anti-environment and the Australian culture war', *Journal of Australian Studies*, vol. 33, no. 3

Hamilton, C (2017), 'Love in a hot climate: The horrible mess of climate change politics', *Meanjin*, 13 November

Jaffrelot, C (2015), 'What "Gujarat model"? – Growth without development and with socio-political polarisation', *South Asia: Journal of South Asian Studies*, vol. 38, no. 4

McCright, A and Dunlop, R (2011), 'Cool dudes: The denial of climate change among conservative white males in the United States', *Global Environmental Change*, vol. 21, no. 4

McKewon, E (2012), 'Talking Points Ammo: The use of neoliberal think tank fantasy themes to delegitimise scientific knowledge of climate change in Australian newspapers', *Journalism Studies*, vol. 13, no. 2

McKnight, D (2010), 'A change in the climate? The journalism of opinion at News Corporation', *Journalism*, vol. 11, no. 6

McKnight, D and Hobbs, M (2013), 'Public contest through the popular media: The mining industry's advertising war against the Australian Labor Party', *Australian Journal of Politics*, vol. 48, no. 3

Manne, R (2011), 'Bad news: Murdoch's *Australian* and the shaping of the nation', *Quarterly Essay*, no. 43

Marr, D (2012), 'Political animal: The making of Tony Abbott', *Quarterly Essay*, no. 47

Mehta, N (2010), 'Ashis Nandy vs the state of Gujarat: Authoritiarian developmentalism, democracy and the politics of Narendra Modi', *South Asian History and Culture*, vol. 1 no. 4

Bibliography

Meskell, L (2013), 'UNESCO's World Heritage Convention at 40: Challenging the economic and political order of international heritage conservation', *Current Anthropology*, vol. 54, no. 4

Mitchell, A (2012), 'Lobbying for the dark side', *Meanjin Quarterly*, vol. 71, no. 2

Peel, J (2008), 'Climate Change Law: The Emergence of a New Discipline', *Melbourne University Law Review*, vol. 32, no. 3

Pearse, G (2009), 'Quarry vision: Coal, climate change and the end of the resources boom', *Quarterly Essay*, no. 33

Priestley, M (2010), 'Australia, China, India and the global financial crisis', Parliament of Australia

Rundle, G (2014), 'Clivosaurus: The politics of Clive Palmer', *Quarterly Essay*, no. 56

Titus, D (2007), 'Corporate lobbying and corruption-manipulating capital', *Indian Law Journal*, vol. 4, no. 3

Sastry, T (2014), 'Civil society, Indian elections and democracy today', *Working Paper 564*, Indian Institute of Management, Bangalore

Scott, A and Scott, R (2014), 'Parliament under Campbell Newman 2012–2013', *Research Report No. 1*, TJ Ryan Foundation

Scott, R (2015), 'Parliament under Campbell Newman 2014', *Research Report No. 13*, TJ Ryan Foundation

Reports/official documents

Alexander, S, Nicholson K and Wiseman, J (2014), *Fossil free: The development and significance of the fossil free divestment movement*, Melbourne Sustainable Society Institute, University of Melbourne

Aulby, H (2017), *The tip of the iceberg: Political donations from the mining industry*, The Australia Institute

Aulby, H and Ogge, M (2016), *Greasing the wheels: The systemic weaknesses that allow undue influence by mining companies on government: a QLD case study*, The Australia Institute/Australian Conservation Foundation

Australian Conservation Foundation (2017), *Dirty deeds done for dirt cheap*, Australian Conservation Foundation

Australian Government (2015), *Our north our future: White paper on developing northern Australia*, Australian Government

Australian Human Rights Commission (2009), *Independent review of the Environment Protection and Biodiversity Conservation Act (1999)*, Australian Human Rights Commission

Australian Youth Climate Coalition (2014), *AYCC annual report, 2014*, Australian Youth Climate Coalition

Bradshaw, S (2015), *Powering up against poverty: Why renewable energy is the future*, Oxfam

Buckley, T and Nicholas, S (2017), *Adani: Remote prospects Carmichael status update 2017*, Institute for Energy Economics and Financial Analysis

Campbell, R (2014), *The mouse that roars: Coal in the Queensland economy*, The Australia Institute

Campbell, R (2105a), *Outclassed: How Queensland's schools and social services are affected by mining industry assistance and lobbying*, The Australia Institute

Campbell, R (2015b), 'Subsidisation of Abbot Point coal port expansion', Briefing Note, 16 January, The Australia Institute

Canavan, M (2016) Submission No 493, House of Representatives Standing Committee on the Environment, Inquiry into Register of Environmental Organisations

Climate Change Network (2014), Climate Change Performance Index 2014

Connolly, E and Orsmond, D (2011), 'The mining industry: From bust to boom', Reserve Bank Australia

Geritz, M and Harvey, P (2013), 'Lack of evidence of the impact of native title rights key for decision to grant mining lease', Clayton Utz

GetUp! (2018), 'GetUp's election campaign 2017 Queensland', GetUp!

Great Barrier Reef Marine Park Authority (2013), 'Abbot Point, Terminal 0, Terminal 2 and Terminal 3 capital dredging', Great Barrier Reef Marine Park Authority

Great Barrier Reef Marine Park Authority (2014), Great Barrier Reef Outlook Report 2014, Great Barrier Reef Marine Park Authority

Greenpeace (2016a), *Less value, more harm: A reality check on coal*, Greenpeace

Greenpeace, (2016b), *Off track: Why NAIF can't approve the Carmichael rail project*, Greenpeace

Greenpeace, (2016c), *Exporting climate change, killing the reef: Australia's post-Paris contribution*, Greenpeace

Greenpeace Australia (2010), *Pillars of pollution: How Australia's big four banks are propping up pollution*, Greenpeace Australia

Grundoff, M (2013), *Pouring more fuel on the fire*, The Australia Institute

Karnatake Lokayukta (2011), *Report on the reference made by the Government of Karnatake under Section 7 (2-A) of the Karnataka Lokayukta Act, 1984*, Karnatake Lokayukta

Land Court of Queensland (2015), *Adani Mining Pty Ltd v Land Services of Coast and Country Inc & Ors [2015] QLC 48*, Land Court of Queensland

Langey, H (2018), *Corruption risks: Mining approvals in Australia*, Transparency International Australia

Independent Expert Scientific Committee (2103), 'Carmichael Coal Mine and Rail Project Queensland', Independent Expert Scientific Committee

International Energy Agency (2015), *India Energy Outlook,* International Energy Agency

Lyons, K, Brigg, M and Quiggin, J (2017), 'Unfinished Business: Adani, the state and the Indigenous rights struggle of the Wangan and Jagalingou traditional owners' council', The University of Queensland

Mackay Conservation Group (2014), *Submission to the Select Committee into Certain Aspects of Queensland Government Administration*, Submission 73

Mackenzie, K (2015), 'Australia's financial system and other climate risks', The Climate Institute

Mogus, J and Liacas, T (2016), 'How progressive campaigns are won in the 21st Century', NetChange Consulting

Minerals Council of Australia (2014), *Submission No. 479 House of Representatives Standing Committee on the Environment, Inquiry into Register of Environmental Organisations,* Minerals Council of Australias

Minerals Council of Australia (2015), *MCG Annual Report 2014–2015*, Minerals Council of Australia

Ministry of Finance, India (2012), *White Paper on Black Money,* Ministry of Finance

Ministry of Environment and Forests (2013), *Report of the Committee for Inspection of M/s*

Bibliography

Adani Port & SEZ ltd. Mundra, Gujarat, Ministry of Environment and Forests
National Green Tribunal (2016), 'Appeal no. 79 of 2013', National Green Tribunal
National Green Tribunal (2016), 'Penalty of INR 1000 Crores on the Delta Group', National Green Tribunal
National Native Title Tribunal (2015), 'Adani Mining v. Adrian Burragubba, Patrick Malone and Irene White on behalf of the Wangan and Jagalingou People', National Native Title Tribunal
Peel, M, Campbell, R and Denniss, R (2014), *Mining: The age of entitlement,* The Australia Institute
Polglaze Griffin and Miller Associates, *2012 Great Barrier Reef shipping: Review of environmental implications,* Abbot Point Working Group
Priestley, M (2010), 'Australia, China, India and the Global Financial Crisis', Parliament of Australia
Queensland Audit Office (2104), *Environmental regulation of the resources and waste industries,* Queensland Audit Office
Quicke, S, Dockery, A and Hoath, A (2017), *Aboriginal assets? The impact of major agreements associated with native title in Western Australia,* University of Western Australia and Curtin University
Readfearn, G (2015), *Too close for comfort: How the coal and gas industries get their way in Queensland,* The Australia Institute
Schucking, H (2013), *Banking on coal,* BankTrack
Senate (Australia), Environment and Communications References Committee (2015), *Australia's environment,* Parliament House
Senate (2014a), *Select Committee on Certain Main Aspects of Queensland Government Administration,* Parliament House
Senate Environment and Communications References Committee (2014), *Management of the Great Barrier Reef,* Parliament House
Shearer, C, Chio, N, Myllyvirta, L, Yu, A and Nace, T (2017), 'Boom and bust 2017: Tracking the global coal plant pipeline', Coal Swarm/Sierra Club/Greenpeace
The Australia Institute (2015), *Powers of deduction: Tax deductions, environmental organisations and the mining industry,* The Australia Institute
The Australia Institute (2017), 'Freedom of Information Requests on Adani and the Northern Australia Infrastructure Facility', 18 February
Transparency International (2018), *Corruption risks: Mining approvals in Australia,* Transparency International
Schucking, H (2013), *Banking on coal,* BankTrack
Swan, T, Campbell, R and Browne, B (2017), *Mainly coal advocacy: What does the MCA stand for?,* The Australia Institute
World Heritage Committee (2012), 'Mission Report Great Barrier Reef', UNESCO
Yang, A and Cui, Y (2012), Global Coal Risk Assessment Data Analysis and Market Research, World Resources Institute, Working Paper
Youvel, Y (2016), *Still coughing up for coal: Big banks after the Paris Agreement,* BankTrack

Theses

Arnautovic, K (2017), 'Resources, race and rights: A case study of native title and the Adani Carmichael coal mine', Honours thesis, Edith Cowan University

Newspaper/magazine/radio/television feature articles

ABC *Counterpoint* (2004), 'Tony Abbott warrior thinker', 13 December

ABC *Four Corners* (2014), 'Battle for the reef', 18 August

ABC *Four Corners* (2015), 'Malcolm and the malcontents', 9 November

ABC *Lateline* (2007), 'Tony Jones speaks with Tim Flannery', 7 February

ABC *PM* (2004), 'Leaked documents reveal fossil fuel influence in White Paper', 7 September

Abjorensen, N (2015), 'The Liberal Party's faction problem', *Inside Story*, 6 July

Adams, C (2015), 'Bank exposure to coal projects drowning in greenwash', the *Conversation,* 1 September

Adams, T (2007), 'Monckton saves the day', the *Guardian,* 6 May

Agarwal, K (2017), 'Adani Australia's story: What's all the fuss about?', the *Wire*, 17 October

Appa, G (2014), 'Gujarat's troubling environmental record', LSE blogs, South Asia, 4 April

Arindam, M and Arora, S (2014), 'All along the waterfront', *Outlook India*, 10 March

Bahree, M (2014), 'Doing big business in Modi's Gujarat', *Forbes Asia*, 12 March

Bahree, M (2014b), 'Indian billionaire Gautam Adani finds a savior in the Modi govt', *Forbes Asia*, 17 July

Baker, R (2005), 'How big energy won the climate battle', the *Age*, 30 July

Baird, J (2014), 'A carbon tax's ignoble end', the *New York Times*, 24 July

Barrett, J (2014), 'The mythology behind Clive Palmer's Mineralogy', *Australian Financial Review*, 14 June

Bell-James, J (2016), 'From insider lobbying to grassroots campaigns; the Australian Conservation Foundation's strategy shift is paying off', the *Conversation*, 14 June

Betigeri, A (2015), 'Adani faces questions over conduct at home', the *Sydney Morning Herald*, 3 October

Bragg, A (2017), 'What business needs to do to beat GetUp and activists on social media', the *Australian Financial Review*, 25 October

Briggs, M, Quiggin, J and Lyons, K (2017), 'The last line of defence: Indigenous rights and Adani's land deal', the *Conversation*, 19 June

Brown, B (2014), '"I am a conservationist" – is Abbott the only person who believes that?', the *Guardian,* 16 June

Bryant, N (2012), 'Can do? Campbell Newman's bid for Queensland', the *Monthly*, December 2011–January 2012.

Bryant, N (2012a), 'Gina Rinehart's quest for respect and gratitude', the *Monthly*, May

Bryant, N (2012b), 'Gina Rinehart: The world's richest woman', *BBC Magazine*, 9 June

Buckley, T and Nicholas, S (2017b), 'The further unravelling of Adani's Carmichael coal project', *RenewEconomy*, 19 December

Burdon, P (2014), 'Government inquiry takes aim at green groups that get political', the *Conversation*, 16 April

Burton, B (2014), 'Big Coal flexes its $100 million PR muscle on soft sell', *Canberra Times,* 7 May

Butler, S (2014), 'Westpac the world's most sustainable firm? That's a bad joke', *Green Left Weekly*, 9 February

Cadzow, J (2012), 'The iron lady', *Good Weekend* magazine, the *Sydney Morning Herald*, 21 January

Chang, C (2017), 'How Australia is being screwed over its gas', news.com.au, 17 March

Chubb, P (2014), 'The day the Rudd government lost its way on climate change', the *Age*, 10 May

Clarke, C (2015), 'The government versus the environment: lawfare in Australia', the *Conversation*, 18 August

Clarick, R (2013), 'Julie Bishop: All the right moves', the *Australian*, 28 September

Connolly, E and Henley, J (2010), 'The Great Barrier Reef scandal', the *Guardian*, 6 April

Coombs, A (2016a), 'Turning clicktivists into real-world activists', *Australian Financial Review*, 4 February 2016

Cowie, T (2012), 'The Power Index: Australia's most influential thinkers', *Crikey*, 20 January

Cox, L (2015), 'Adani's Carmichael mine is unbankable, says Queensland Treasury', the *Sydney Morning Herald*, 30 June

Cox, L (2015b), 'Indian miner Adani hires Labor and Liberal staffers to make its case', the *Sydney Morning Herald*, 4 July

Crabtree, J (2013), 'Gautam Adani, founder, Adani Group', the *Financial Times*, 16 June

Crooks, E and Kao, J (2017), 'The future of coal in seven charts', the *Financial Times*, 19 September

Daniles, P (2017), 'Local GetUp! initiative gives thumbs down to Adani coal mine', *Port Macquarie News*, 26 May

Davis, M (2006), 'The fine art of persuasion', the *Sydney Morning Herald*, 30 December

Deb, S (2016), 'Unmasking Modi: The violence, insecurity, and rage behind the man who has replaced Ghandi as the face of India', *New Republic*, 3 May

Dreze, J (2014), 'The Gujarat Muddle', the *Hindu*, 11 April

Duffy, M (2009) ,'The missing element of self-doubt', the *Sydney Morning Herald*, 5 December

Elks, S (2017), 'Mr Fix-It back on the job', the *Australian*, 13 June

Elks, S (2017b), 'How Adani veto turned tide for ALP', the *Weekend Australian*, 9–10 December

Eltham, B (2017), 'Adani coal mine is a symptom of the crisis in Australian politics', *New Matilda*, 10 October

Farrelly, E (2016), 'The great tragedy of Malcolm Turnbull', the *Sydney Morning Herald*, 18 June

Fennell, A (2017), 'From slacktivism to "feel good" protests, activism is broken: Here's how to fix it', *ABC Future Tense*, 25 October

Fensom, A (2015), 'India to the rescue as Australia eyes coal's crown', the *Diplomat*, 5 April

Fernyhough, J (2015), 'Fossil fuels industry's wet dream', the *New Daily*, 12 June

Finnegan, W (2013), 'The miner's daughter', the *New Yorker*, 25 March

Fitzgerald, T (2015), 'Queensland political ethics: A perfect oxymoron', the *Drum*, 23 January

Fitzgerald, T (2015b), 'Queensland must put a stop to the political rot', the *Drum*, 29 January

Flanagan, R (2012), 'Australia's problem? We never talked about Kevin Rudd', the *Guardian*, 28 February

Flannery, T (2010), 'Rudd's ETS backflip', the *Monthly*, June

Gallop, G (2012), 'Gina Rinehart, Fairfax and the "war" politics of the Australian right', the *Conversation*, 19 June

Garnaut, J and Counsel, J (2002), 'Different shades of Hugh', the *Sydney Morning Herald*, 17 August

Gerathy, S (2016), 'Eddie Obeid: the rise, reign and recession of NSW's most notorious powerbroker', ABC *News*, 15 December

Gittins, R (2013), 'Mining tax message: No bipartisanship, no reform', the *Sydney Morning Herald*, 18 February

Glaetzer, S (2016), 'All eyes on Paul Oosting's next move', the *Mercury*, 13 August

Gopalakrishnan, A (2014), 'The limits of charisma', *Indian Express*, 13 February

Grech, A and McCook, L (2015), 'Shipping in the Great Barrier Reef: the miners' highway', the *Conversation*, 24 May

Gregoire, P (2017), 'Keep Adani Out: An interview with Wagan and Jagalingou Council's Murrawah Johnson', Sydney Criminal Lawyers, 20 March

Grunwald, M (2015), 'Inside the war on coal', *Politico*, 26 May

Hepburn, S (2015a), 'Court challenge will test coal mining's culpability', the *Conversation*, 15 January

Hepburn, S (2015b), 'Adani court case leaves the climate question unanswered', Deakin Law School Newsroom, 6 August 2015

Hills, B (2012), 'The Devil's Advocate', *Good Weekend* magazine, the *Sydney Morning Herald*, 30 June

Hamilton, C (2008), 'Clive Hamilton v. Paul Kelly: climate death match', *Crikey*, 11 December

Hamilton, C (2010), 'Think tanks, oil money and black ops', ABC *News*, 29 September

Hamilton, C (2014), 'The Dirty Dozen: Australia's biggest climate foes, part 1', *Crikey*, 15 April

Hamilton, C (2017), 'That lump of coal', the *Conversation*, 15 February

Hamilton, C and Karoly, D (2016), 'The Climate Change Authority Report: A dissenting view', ABC *News*, 5 September

Harrison, P (2011), 'Hearts and minds: how industry campaigns work', the *Conversation* 16 August

Hewson, J (2017), 'The Queensland election outcome is a death knell for Adani's coal mine', the *Conversation*, 7 December

Holmes, D (2015), 'The Bjorn supremacy – is Australia getting the climate advice it deserves?', the *Conversation,* 23 April 2015

Hooper, C (2014), 'Lives of the magnates: Inside the worlds of Clive Palmer, Gina Rinehart, Andrew Forrest and Nathan Tinkler', the *Monthly,* February

Hosking, S (2016), 'How John Howard made it possible for the Liberal Party to govern', the *Conversation*, 22 April

Hudson, M (2016), 'Another prime minister, another endorsement for coal, but why?', the *Conversation*, 26 October

Hudson, M (2017b), 'Is BHP really about to split from the Minerals Council's hive mind?', the *Conversation*, 22 September

Hughes, T (2104), 'Mounting evidence shows dredge spoil threat to the Great Barrier Reef', the *Conversation*, 8 August

Hume, T (2012), 'The iron ore lady: Why the world's richest woman is mired in controversy', the *Independent*, 15 June

Hurst, D (2015), 'Crash-through Campbell Newman may have said sorry for the last time', the *Guardian*, 29 January

Ingaravel, K (2013), 'The rise of Gautam Adani', *Wealth Matters*, 5 September

Jackman, C (2012), 'Carrying the can', the *Australian*, 12 August

Johnson, K (2015), 'Modi's coal conundrum', *Foreign Policy*, 11 December

Joseph, T (2015), 'Adani's $10 billion gamble', *Business Today*, 18 January

Jose, V (2012), 'The emperor uncrowned: The rise of Narenda Modi', the *Caravan Magazine*, 1 March

Kampmark, B (2016), 'Fossil fuel corruption and the environment: The problem with Australia's Adani mining', *Global Research*, 9 December

Keane, B (2015), 'Hundreds of donors hidden by Newman's donation laws', *Crikey*, 22 January

Keene, B (2102), 'The rise and rise of mining company donations', *Crikey*, 21 February

Kelly, D (2016), 'With friends like these: just how close are the IPA and the Liberal Party?', the *Conversation*, 7 June

Kelly, P (2018), 'Shorten shown up as an opportunist too smart by half', the *Weekend Australian*, 3–4 March

Kemp, L (2016), 'The fossil fuel divestment game is getting bigger thanks to the smaller players', the *Conversation*, 12 September

Ker, P (2017), 'Eyes on Adani Carmichael mine as Malcolm Turnbull meets with Narendra Modi', the *Australian Financial Review*, 10 April

Keim, S (2014), 'Clive Palmer, Jeff Seeney and Campbell Newman's Straddie donation', *Independent Australia*, 10 June

Keim, S and Mckean, A (2014), 'Clouds over the Sunshine state', the *Australian*, 25 September

Kiren, A (2017), 'Revealed: Gautam Adani's coal play in the state facing global-warming hell', the *Sydney Morning Herald*, 9 June 2017

Knott, M (2011), 'The man who killed Rudd's mining tax', *Business Spectator*, 29 November

Kohler, A (2017a), 'Speech – the great coal hoax', the *Constant Investor*, 16 June

Kohler, A (2017b), 'The great coal hoax', the *Australian*, 13 February

Koutsoukis, and Flitton, D (2014), 'Concerns at Barrier Reef contractors humanitarian, environmental record', the *Sydney Morning Herald*, 5 September

Leiberman, B (2012), 'The Catholic church and climate change', *Yale Climate Connections*, 14 February

Lewis, R (2014), 'Canada tar sands linked to cancer in native communities', *Al Jazeera*, 8 July

Lewis, P and Woods, J (2012), 'Australians seeing through the feel-good mining ads', the *Drum*, 24 April

Long, S (2015), 'Adani's Galilee Basin complex corporate web extends to tax havens', ABC *News*, 21 December

Long, S (2017), 'Clean coal explained: Why emissions reduction from coal remains a pipe dream', ABC *News*, 2 February

Lowe, I (2010), 'Public interest environmental law: Challenges and opportunities over the next 50 years', *Impact*, Issue 89

Lucas, T (2015), 'How online activist groups are raising millions to keep corporations in line', Mashable Australia

Ludlow, M (2014), 'Need for coal fires Galilee', the *Australian Financial Review*, 9 August

Lyons, J (2014), 'Raging Turnbull', *Good Weekend* magazine, the *Sydney Morning Herald*, 16 September 2014

Lloyd, G (2012), 'Tony Burke: Man in the hot seat', the *Australian*, 4 February

McKibben, B (2016), 'Australia leads way in fossil fuel divestment', the *Saturday Paper*, 17–23 December

McKinnon, A (2017), 'The future of the Adani mine', the *Saturday Paper*, 2 December

McKenna (2016), 'Gautam Adani's dream to light India's darkened nights', the *Australian*, 4 June

McKenzie-Murray, M (2016), 'The real story on the Great Barrier Reef', the *Conversation*, 4–10 June

McKnight, D (2013), 'Murdoch and his influence on Australian political life', the *Conversation*, 7 August

Maharaj, B (2017), 'South Africa, a mafia shadow state?', *Daily Maverick*, 15 August

Manne, R (2012), 'How vested interest defeated climate science: A dark victory', the *Monthly*, August

Manne, R (2012a), 'One morning with Malcolm Turnbull', the *Monthly*, April

Manne, R (2012b), 'Lord Monckton and the future of the Australian media', the *Monthly*, 2 August 2012

Manne, R (2016), 'Malcolm Turnbull: A brief lament', the *Monthly*, December

Manning, P (2010), 'A resourceful climate sceptic', the *Age*, 22 August

Manning, P (2014), 'While superpowers act on climate, Australia and India double down on coal', *Crikey*, 13 November

Manning, P (2014), 'The bust is already here: can Rinehart make Galilee coal profitable?', *Crikey*, 7 August

Mayne, S (2006), 'The colourful past of Geoffrey Cousins', *Crikey*, 25 September

Murphy, K (2018), 'Geoff Cousins reveals how Bill Shorten wavered on the Adani mine', the *Guardian*, 28 February

Milman, O (2014), 'Criticism over Great Barrier Reef Deals for Gina Rinehart Mining Company', the *Guardian*, 19 August

Milman, O (2015), 'ANZ "will not finance" dirty coal plants and pledges $10bn for clean energy', the *Guardian*, 6 Ocotber.

Milman, O and Evershed, N (2015), 'Australia has denied environmental approval to just 18 projects since 2000', the *Guardian*, 12 August

Mitchell, T (2015), 'The trial and tribulations of Adani mining: Four of their shakiest claims', *New Matilda*, 10 May

Mogus, J (2017), 'A theory of change that made the impossible possible', NetChange Consulting

Mohan, R (2015), 'Narendra Modi's war on the environment', *Al Jazeera America*, 10 April

Mahaprashasta, A (2013), 'The great land grab', *Frontline*, 17 May

Mooney, C (2014), 'When did the Republicans start hating the environment?', *Mother Jones*, 12 August

Nayar, L, Arinda, M and Aroro, S (2014), 'All along the waterfront', *Outlook India*, 10 March

O'Callaghan, K (2014), 'David versus Goliath – Maules Creek versus Big Coal', the *AIM Network*, 6 May

Oosting, P (2017), 'Come down from the clouds, you elite politicians', the *Guardian*, 7 July

Orr, G (2011), 'Over the top with Campbell Newman', *Inside Story*, 28 March

Parkinson, G (2015), '10 things we learnt about Tony Abbott's war on renewables', *RenewEconomy*, 12 June

Paul, C (2013), 'GVK's big Australian bet', *Forbes Asia*, 15 January

Pearlman, J (2012), 'Gina Rinehart: the Australian mining magnate at the top of the rich list', the *Telegraph*, 31 August

Pearse, G (2011), 'The climate movement: Australia's patrons of climate change activism', the *Monthly*, September

Pell, G (2011), 'One Christian perspective on climate change: 2011 Global Warming Policy Foundation Annual Lecture', Westminster Cathedral Hall, London

Pincock, S (2007), 'Climate politics: Showdown in a sunburnt country', *Nature*, 14 November

Priestly, M (2010), 'Australia, China, India and the Global Financial Crisis', Parliament of Australia

Quiggin, J (2014), 'Climate change and the intellectual decline of the right', the *Conversation*, 18 August

Rajshekhar, M (2013), 'Gautam Adani: Meet the man who built Rs 47000 crore infrastructure empire', the *Economic Times*, 5 September

Readfearn, G (2011a), 'Australia's place in the global web of climate denialism', ABC *News*, 29 June

Readfearn, G (2011b), 'Wielding power the Rinehart way', *Crikey*, 19 August

Readfearn, G (2017), 'Ten years ago Turnbull called out Peter Garrett on climate. What went wrong?', the *Guardian*, 21 June

Regan, J (2014), 'King Coal in Australia faces rising investment backlash', Reuters, 24 June

Remeikis, A (2014), 'LNP fundraising club QForum shrouded in secrecy', *Brisbane Times*, 27 November

Ritter, D (2013), 'Thermal coal exports killing our future', the *Australian*, 16 April

Roskam, J (2017), 'Why the Liberals will never GetUp!', the *Australian Financial Review*, 23 June

Rowley, N (2014), 'How John Howard could help Tony Abbott around on climate change', the *Conversation*, 24 November 2014

Sahukar, N (2016), 'Australia's environment: breaking the one-stop-shop deadlock', *Impact*, Issue 97

Saram, E (2015), 'Coal is not the answer to India's energy poverty, no matter what Tony Abbott says', the *Guardian*, 7 August

Satish, J (2012), 'Adani group in makeover to blur their troubled past', the *Economic Times*, 23 February

Seccombe, M (2014), 'Greg Hunt's hostile attack on the environment', the *Saturday Paper*, 6 December

Seccombe, M (2015), 'How the Minerals Council of Australia has govt's ear on coal', the *Saturday Paper*, 24 October

Seccombe, M (2015b), 'Newman government courts Adani on Galilee Basin coal deal', the *Saturday Paper*, 22 November

Seccombe, M (2017), 'How the religious right stall climate action', the *Saturday Paper*,
  26 August
Slezak, M (2017), 'Australia's greenhouse gas emissions soar in latest figures', the
  Guardian, 4 August
Sparrow, J (2015), 'Maurice Newman versus the United Nations: the logic behind crazy',
  ABC, the *Drum*, 11 May
Staples, J (2014), 'Attacks on NGOs are a threat to our democracy', *Civil Society and
  Democracy*, 25 July
Stephens, T (2012), 'The Great Barrier Reef at the crossroads', the *Conversation*, 4 June
Stevens, M (2015), 'Adani, the new coal Tar Baby', the *Australian Financial Review*,
  10 April
Taylor, L (2012), 'Coal hard light of day for dud scheme', the *Sydney Morning Herald*,
  17 June
Thakurta, P (2017), 'The incredible rise and rise of Gautam Adani: Part one', the *Citizen*,
  31 January
Thomas, H (2014), 'Clive Palmer "tried to corrupt" Queensland deputy premier Jeff
  Seeney', the *Australian*, 9 August
Turnbull, M (2009), 'Abbott's climate change is policy bullshit', the *Sydney Morning
  Herald*, 7 December
Villatt, N (2004), 'Gujarat model of land grab', *Tehelka Magazine*, vol. 12, no. 27
Vromen, A (2016), 'New style lobbying: How GetUp! channels Australians' voices', *the
  Conversation*, 14 June
Walker, B (2016), 'China stokes global coal growth', *China Dialogue*, 23 September
Walker, J (2012), 'Clive Palmer – having it all', the *Australian*, 18 August
Wallace, C (2015), 'Bishop's gambit', the *Monthly*, April
Waterford, J (2014), 'Joh Bjelke-Petersen, Clive Palmer play politics by different rules',
  the *Sydney Morning Herald*, 3 October
West, J (2012), 'Mining magnate, property tycoon, politician – just who is Clive
  Palmer?', the *Conversation*, 29 April
West, M (2015), 'Adani shown the door by traditional owners', the *Sydney Morning
  Herald*, 4 July
Whitbourn, M (2016), 'Liberal donations scandal highlights ICAC's important work',
  the *Sydney Morning Herald*, 24 March
Whitbourn, M (2017), 'Former NSW Labor minister Ian Macdonald found guilty of
  misconduct in public office', the *Sydney Morning Herald*, 30 March
Wilkinson, M, Cubby, B and Duxfield, F (2009), 'Ad campaign aims to crush emissions
  trading plan', the *Sydney Morning Herald*, 17 November
Willacy, M (2015), 'Adani Mining: Senior Queensland bureaucrats frozen out of
  government's Galilee Basin deal', ABC *News*, 1 July
Yardly, J and Bajaj, V (2011), 'Billionaire's rise aids India, and the return is favoured', the
  New York Times, 26 July

Websites
AntiNuclear.net (2013), 'Mike Nahan from Institute of Public Affairs', 5 March,
  <antinuclear.net/2013/05/03/mike-nahan-from-institute-of-public-affairs-western-
  australias-minister-against-renewables/>

Bones, M (2017), 'Why Westpac cared on Adani, and what we
    need to do next', 28 April, <myfuturessuper.com.au/blog/
    why-westpac-cared-on-adani-and-what-we-need-to-do-next>

Buckingham, J (2015), 'Revolving Doors Queensland', 27 March,
Climate Analytics (2016), 'Paris Agreement has put a date on the end
    of coal-fired power', 4 November, <climateanalytics.org/latest/
    paris-agreement-has-put-a-date-on-the-end-of-coal-fired-power>

Canavan, M (2015), 'Climate change is uncertain', 2 December 2015,
    <www.mattcanavan.com.au/climate_change_science_is_uncertain>

Environment Law Australia (nd), 'Carmichael coal cases in the Federal Court',
    Environmental Law Australia website, <envlaw.com.au/carmichael-coal-mine-case/>

Environmental Justice Australia (2015), 'Explained: How gutting EPBC protections
    will let governments break their own law', <www.envirojustice.org.au/projects/
    explained-how-gutting-epbc-protections-will-let-governments-break-their-own-
    laws/>

Friends of the Earth Australia (nd), 'Our History', <www.foe.org.au/history>

Friends of the Earth Brisbane (2012), 'Environmental Protest Given Green Light
    in Queensland' 9 January, <www.brisbane.foe.org.au/news-and-media/
    environmental-protest-given-green-light-in-queensland>

Landconflictwatch.org (2014), 'Perspective document on coal mining in Hasdeo Arand
    region', <www.landconflictwatch.org/sites/default/files/Implications-of-Mining-in-
    Hasdeo-Arand-coloured.pdf>

Indigenous Environment Network (nd), 'Tar Sands', <www.ienearth.org/what-we-do/
    tar-sands/>

Lee, K (2014), 'Gina's Bollycoal Adventure', the *AIM Network*, 5 January, <theaimn.com/
    ginas-bollycoal-adventure/>

McKinnon, E (2016), 'ACF versus the environment minister – our Adani court case
    explained', <www.acf.org.au/acf_vs_environment_minister>

Market Forces (nd), 'The Adani List: Companies that could make or break the
    Carmichael Coal Project', <www.marketforces.org.au/info/key-issues/theadanilist/>

Market Forces (2012), 'Financing reef destruction: How banks are using our money to
    destroy a national icon', <www.marketforces.org.au/wp-content/uploads/2013/10/
    MF_Financing_Reef_Destruction.pdf>

Mitchell, T (2016), 'Climate change: Almost half of Australia is still ignorant or confused,
    new poll reveals', The Insider: The Official New Matilda Blog, 7 June
Nagel, J (2017), 'How ignoring your customers leads to big
    profits', Linked In, 24 February, <www.linkedin.com/pulse/
    how-ignoring-your-customers-leads-big-profits-jeremy-nagel>

Quit Coal (2014), 'ANZ, quit coal and the climate warriors', 21 November,
    <www.quitcoal.org.au/anz-quit-coal-climate-warriors>

Readfearn, G (2012), 'What the world's richest woman Gina Rinehart
    thinks about climate change', 27 June, <www.desmogblog.com/
    what-world-s-richest-woman-gina-rinehart-thinks-about-climate-change>

Readfearn, G (2016), 'Why thinking Australians will not be fooled by Murdoch's latest
    hypocritical attack on green groups', 25 October, <desmogblog.com>

RenuKumar, N (2015), 'Friends with benefits: India's crony capitalism
and conflict of interest regions', globalatlanticcorruptionblog.
com, <globalanticorruptionblog.com/2015/10/19/
friends-with-benefits-indias-crony-capitalism-and-conflict-of-interest-regulations/>

Robson, F (2017), 'By George! The controversies of an Australian
government MP', <www.sbs.com.au/topics/life/feature/
george-controversies-australian-government-mp>

Roy, S (2015), 'Adani's roadblock in Australia is about his record in India', 7 August
<www.firstpost.com/world/adanis-roadblock-in-australia-is-about-his-record-in-
india-2381438.html>

Shafy, S (2013), 'Coal boom could destroy Great Barrier Reef', *Spiegel* online, 21 May,
<www.spiegel.de/international/world/australia-debates-how-to-protect-the-great-barrier-
reef-a-900911.html>

Samarendra, D and Rose, M (2014), 'Copper colonialism: British miner Vedanta
KCM and the copper loot of Zambia', <www.foilvedanta.org/articles/
copper-colonialism-foil-vedanta-zambia-report-launched/>

Union of Concerned Scientists (nd), 'Global Warming Skeptic Organisations',
<www.ucsusa.org/global-warming/solutions/fight-misinformation/global-warming-
skeptic.html#.WubJKDVSpjA>

Varadarajan, S (2014), 'The cult of cronyism', *YaleGlobal Online*, 2 April

Wardill, S (2013), 'Rejected railway bid the reason Clive Palmer turned against
Newman Government', 1 November, <www.news.com.au/national/queensland/
rejected-railway-bid-the-reason-clive-palmer-turned-against-newman-government/
news-story/a949eb67c5ddf3e049bb52fac0bec680?from=publicrss>

Wangan and Jagalingou Family Council (2015), 'Submission to the Special Rapporteur
on Indigenous Peoples by the Wangan and Jagingou Family Council', Wangan and
Jagalingou Family Council,

Wangan and Jagalingou Family Council (2016), 'Adani court decision: Traditional owners
say fight to stop Qld's Carmichael continues', Wangan and Jagalingou Family
Council,

Wangan and Jagalingou Family Council (2017a), 'Update on the situation of the Wangan
and Jagalingou People's opposition to the proposed Carmichael coal mine', Wangan
and Jagalingou Family Council,

Watching the Deniers (2011), 'The paranoid style of the IPA,
Part 2', <watchingthedeniers.wordpress.com/2010/05/09/
the-paranoid-style-of-the-ipa-part-2-examining-the-claims-of-john-roskams-letter/>

Whelan, J (2015), 'Community organising graduate profile: Ellen
Roberts', The Change Agency.org, <www.thechangeagency.org/
community-organising-graduate-profile-ellen-roberts/>

Acknowledgments

Many people have helped bring this book to fruition. First among these is Phillipa McGuinness, Executive Publisher at NewSouth Publishing, whose enthusiasm, wise counsel and constructive feedback helped shape all stages of the manuscript. Alongside her is the team at NewSouth who have my gratitude for their professionalism, efficiency and friendliness. They are simply a wonderful group of people to work with. I would particularly like to thank Rosina Dimarzo and Sophia Oravecz for all their efforts and Jocelyn Hungerford for her editorial expertise on the final draft.

Several people offered themselves for extended interviews and I would like to thank Dr Bob Brown, Geoff Cousins, Paul Oosting, Adrian Burragubba, Anthony Esposito and Kabir Agarwal. Dr David McKnight provided a number of constructive suggestions that improved the manuscript. Dr Russell Reichelt provided written communication on the Great Barrier Reef Marine Park Authority. Angela Bowne SC performed the valuable service of providing legal advice, for which I thank her enormously. I would also like to thank Howard Pedersen for feedback on Chapter 9. I had the good fortune to supervise Kate Arnautovic for her Honours thesis (First Class) on native title and the Carmichael mine. Our discussions about her research added many helpful insights.

A large part of the book was written in Budapest over the summer of 2017 and I would like to thank our friends in that wonderful city for making our stay such an enjoyable one.

I would like to thank my colleagues at Edith Cowan University for their support and to my friends and my children and their partners who always have a lively interest in my writing projects.

Finally, the greatest debt is to my wife Marilyn who, as she has done previously, gave generously of her time to discuss the project and to read and comment on every draft, an effort which has left an indelible imprint on the book. Her love and support and her interest in my writing projects have my deepest gratitude.

Naturally, the author takes full responsibility for the contents of the book.

Index

Index